STUDIES IN
EARLY
CHRISTIANITY

STUDIES IN EARLY CHRISTIANITY

François Bovon

Baker Academic

Grand Rapids, Michigan

© 2003 by J. C. B. Mohr (Paul Siebeck)

Published by Baker Academic
a division of Baker Publishing Group
P.O. Box 6287, Grand Rapids, MI 49516-6287
www.bakeracademic.com

Printed in the United States of America

First cloth edition published 2003 by J. C. B. Mohr (Paul Siebeck), P.O. Box 2040, D72010 Tübingen, Germany.

First paperback edition published 2005 by Baker Academic.

For the paperback edition, chapters 3, 8, and 9 have been translated from the German, and corresponding adjustments have been made to the table of contents and indexes. Translations © 2005 by Baker Book House Company.

Library of Congress Cataloging-in-Publication Data is on file at the Library of Congress, Washington, D.C.

ISBN 0-8010-2935-X

Preface

Circumstances and inclination have driven me to write and publish articles. The papers that are collected and reprinted here are the result of academic lectures, contributions to symposia, Festschriften and special investigations. With the exception of a few bibliographical modifications, they are published here as they appeared the first time.

At the suggestion of Dr. Siebeck, the numerous French papers have been translated, and I would like to thank all those who turned them into English or helped me polish my own writing in that language: Laura Beth Bugg, Jane Haapiseva-Hunter, Ken McKinney, Laura Nasrallah, Charles Frederic Stone, and David Warren.

Dr. Hengel advised me to open the book with an unedited paper, general enough to introduce the collection but specific enough to indicate my fields of interest: Luke-Acts, non-canonical or so-called apocryphal literature, and early Christian theology. The first article fulfils this request. This paper, "The Apostolic Memories in Ancient Christianity," was delivered at the International Meeting of the Society of Biblical Literature at Lausanne (Switzerland) in July 1997. I am grateful to Dr. Ann Graham Brock who improved my English and helped me sharpen my argument. The paper was also presented to the New Testament Dissertation Seminar at the Harvard Divinity School the following year.

I did not realize how much work is needed in order to create a collection of essays, to harmonize them, and to make everything ready for publication. I express my gratitude to Ms. Linda Grant, a former Master of Divinity student at the Harvard Divinity School, who did not spare her skill and energy to prepare with me the manuscript for publication and read the proofs. My gratitude is also great to Dr. Eugene McGarrie who established the indices of ancient and modern authors. I am responsible for the index of subjects.

Mohr Siebeck published my dissertation more than thirty years ago. I was then in contact with Dr. Hans-Georg Siebeck. Today his son, Dr. Georg Siebeck, showed me the same hospitality and the same generosity. I am grateful to be, in a modest way, part of this venerable scholarly tradition. I would also like to thank Dr. Siebeck's collaborators, particularly Dr. Henning Ziebritzki and Ms. Ilse König.

Last but not least, I wish to express my gratitude to Prof. Dr. Martin Hengel and his colleagues, who expressed their interest in this collection and accepted the volume as part of the "Wissenschaftliche Untersuchungen zum Neuen Testament."

Cambridge, MA   F.B.
May 2003

Contents

Part Three: Apocryphal and Patristic Literature

The Apostolic Memories in Ancient Christianity

In this paper[1] I would like to ask several related questions about the memories of the apostles in ancient Christianity: were the Christians of the first centuries interested in the history of their religious movement? What memories of their apostles did they keep and develop? How did the first Christians choose from among their traditions? What parts of the past did they feel free to develop extensively? Do we not meet surprising cases of forgetfulness?

There are no straight and unanimous answers to such questions, because for a significant period of time early Christianity was not a homogeneous movement. What, therefore, explains the colorful range of opinions on these questions? Answers are often indirect or implicit. Therefore new questions arise in the mind of the interpreter: who were the keepers of the memories, and who was most willing to forget? What were the reasons for accepting or rejecting the protective shadow of the holy history[2] and what were the social forces behind these opinions? Jesus himself was not always remembered: when the apostle Paul deals with ethical problems he makes reference to Jesus' teaching, but he does not always refer specifically to either his Lord or to the origin of the wisdom traditions he utilizes (see Rom 12:14; 1 Thess 5:2)[3]; why? A whole generation of apologists in the second century is very discreet in using the names of both Jesus and his followers (see the *Supplicatio* of the Athenian Athenagoras, for example).

It is my hypothesis that there was a natural and distinct tendency to memorialize the first Christian generation, the generation of the apostles and witnesses, both men and women, and this for several reasons. The first was to create an ethical model based on examples drawn from the Hebrew scriptures, Jesus' life, the lives of the apostles, and the more recent destiny of the martyrs. The second reason was to follow the command of love and develop the Christian notion of communion: to love is to remember. The third reason articulates the defense of the

---

[1] This paper was presented at the international meeting of the Society of Biblical Literature, Lausanne, July 1997.

[2] On the notion of beginnings of Christianity, see Harold W. Attridge and Gohei Hata, "Introduction," in *Eusebius, Christianity, and Judaism* (ed. Harold W. Attridge and Gohei Hata; Detroit: Wayne State University Press, 1992) 27–49; Ron Cameron, "The *Gospel of Thomas* and Christian Origins," in *The Future of Early Christianity: Essays in Honor of Helmut Koester* (ed. Birger A. Pearson; Minneapolis: Fortress, 1991) 381–92.

[3] See Helmut Koester, *Ancient Christian Gospels: Their History and Development* (Philadelphia: Trinity Press International, 1990) 52–62.

truth and the preservation of a holy doctrine in reaction to opponent groups. A fourth reason, related to the third, concerns the authority of Christian ministry, the apostolic origin of the most important episcopal seats. All of these reasons explain not only the collection and preservation of memories but also their transformation and, finally, the constitution of newly created ad hoc memories. But to these historical reasons I would like to add a theological one, perhaps an all-encompassing one: as long as the Christians of antiquity tried to preserve the historicity of the revelation and the very real incarnation of their Lord, they could not avoid emphasizing the historical and human face of the communication of the gospel, that is to say, the actual value of the apostles themselves, including both their voices and their role as intermediaries.

I will also attempt to explain why the early Christians sometimes avoided the names of Peter and Paul, the roles of Mary Magdalene and Johanna, the fates of John and James, and the teachings of Thomas and Luke. One reason is the early Christian focus on Christology: Jesus' teaching and the Lord's redemption, rather than the occasional fate of his first disciples, was of seminal importance to those Christians. The second reason has to do with the priority of the "message" over its messengers, because the Christian message is a gospel proclaimed and not a material legacy handed down. A third explanation considers the passage of time and the evolution of doctrine, because in time the words, attitudes, and reactions of the first Christian generation became archaic and were no longer bearable to the generations that followed, which were probably better educated and less ready to suffer persecution, or less inclined to defend radical opinions. A fourth reason, which is related to the evolution of church order, can also be offered: the present situation of the Christian communities and their interrelations with one another were of definitive importance. The titling of a bishop, the precedence of the patriarch of a venerable see, and the ascribed destiny of a holy figure became as relevant as the memory of apostles such as James and Andrew.

The Memory

Let us start with a kind of *terminus a quo*: the work of Eusebius of Caesarea. As a historian, Eusebius knows how to distinguish his sources; as a theologian, he knows how to ponder them. He cherishes the scriptures in which he seems to have complete confidence; then he calculates from case to case the value of ancient venerated stories,[4] such as that of Thaddaeus, ἱστορίαν ἐλθοῦσαν εἰς ἡμᾶς ("an account which has come down to us," *Hist. eccl.* 1.12.3). Eusebius adheres to the canonical Gospels when he presents the selection of the Twelve out of a larger group of disciples and mentions the special favor they received (*Hist. eccl.* 1.10.7). He then relies on the book of Acts and on the Epistle to the Galatians for other

---

[4] See, for example, Eusebius, *Hist. eccl.* 1.1.8.

stories: the names of the apostles, the appearances of the Resurrected One, the choice of Matthias as an apostle, and the martyrdom of Stephen (*Hist. eccl.* 1.12.1–5; 2.1–3). Eusebius has a clear interest in these figures and he gathers as much material about them as his critical conscience will permit. Book 2 of his *Historia ecclesiastica* is devoted to the period of time following the ascension of Christ and preceding the death of the apostles. He demonstrates an interest in the apostolic seats and their authentic successions: he explains, for example, how Peter, James, and John did not dispute the episcopal seat of Jerusalem but decided together to confer it on James the Just, the brother of the Lord (*Hist. eccl.* 2.1.3). Oddly, he is not very clear about the location of the apostles during the church's earliest years; on one occasion, however, he observes that God was patient with Israel and waited forty years before punishing Jerusalem, and that during this time of forbearance the presence of the apostles in the city was like a protective wall (*Hist. eccl.* 3.7.8). But on another occasion (*Hist. eccl.* 3.5.2), speaking of the persecution of Stephen, he refers to the subsequent flight of the disciples as coinciding with the beginning of the world mission, the collective realization of Christ's command (Matt 28:19).

It would be wrong to believe that Eusebius's interest in the first generation of Christians is peculiar to him. A similar interest, both historical and theological, is found even earlier in the texts of Christian authors such as Tertullian and Irenaeus. In his *De praescriptione haereticorum*, the African theologian makes polemical use of the apostolic heritage by basing the authenticity of the truth on the reliable sequence of bishops, beginning with the apostles. He supports his argument with the examples of Polycarp of Smyrna, who was installed by the apostle John, and of Clement of Rome, who was ordained by Peter (*Praescr.* 32.1–3). A little later in the same treatise, in a similar argument, Tertullian states that the best places to identify the authentic epistles of the apostles are in the churches with an apostolic seat. He adds that in such churches one finds not only authentic writings but also authentic memories (*Praescr.* 36.1–3), which for him – writing in the late second to early third centuries – means that both the person of the apostle and his writings receive equal credence. With respect to the church in Rome, Tertullian chronicles several apostolic stories that are absent from the canonical writings but nevertheless highly valuable in his eyes: these include the martyrdom of Peter, which is similar to Christ's; the beheading of Paul, which is similar to the fate of John the Baptist; and the ordeal of John, who is dipped into boiling oil (*Praescr.* 36.1–3).

This catholic interest in both succession and tradition was certainly polemical and built a defense against similar claims by the Gnostics. We know, for instance, that this type of argument had been advanced by Ptolemaios in his *Letter to Flora*.[5] Elsewhere we encounter the examples of Basilides claiming a connection

---

[5] Preserved by Epiphanius of Salamis, *Pan.* 33.7.9.

to Peter through Glaukias[6]; of Valentine arguing a relation to Paul via Theodas[7]; of the disciples of Carpocrates affirming an affiliation with Salome, while others claim an affiliation with Mary Magdalene or Martha[8]; and of the Naasenes, who said that they received their teaching from Mary Magdalene through James, the brother of the Lord.[9] Truly, the notions of tradition and succession were nothing new in antiquity. Philosophical schools had used them for centuries,[10] but what was new in the Christian church since Irenaeus (the way having been prepared by Hegesippus, see Eusebius, *Hist. eccl.* 4.22.1–6) was a link established between doctrinal transmission and the succession of bishops: the value of a tradition could no longer be sufficiently established by claims to apostolic origin but depended as well on the apostolic succession of bishops.

Even Aristides of Athens, one of the Christian apologists who – it was said – was not particularly interested in the fate of the apostles, acknowledges the role of the first generation in the proclamation of the gospel. In his *Apologia*, which was probably written during the reign of Antoninus Pius (138 to 146 C.E.),[11] Aristides mentions the twelve disciples within the context of the salvific economy. He refers to the crucifixion, resurrection, and ascension of Jesus Christ, then adds the mission of the twelve disciples and their teaching in the several provinces of the inhabited earth.[12]

I am arguing here against the opinion of a strong exegetical school of scholars, ranging from Franz Overbeck to Martin Dibelius to Rudolf Bultmann's disciples (like Günther Bornkamm), which holds that in the first Christian generations there was no religious interest in the fate of the apostles; that is, that there was no *Sitz im Leben*, no setting for such memories, because the kerygma was focused exclusively on Jesus Christ. Because of several specific statements in the Pauline epistles and the existence of archaic traditions that are preserved in the book of Acts, I would say – on the contrary – that conditions were favorable for the formation of traditions concerning the apostles and their first communities.[13]

---

[6] Clement of Alexandria, *Strom.* 7.106.4. According to *Elench.* 20.7.1, traditionally attributed to Hippolytus of Rome, Basilides had been the disciple of Matthias.

[7] Clement of Alexandria, *Strom.* 7.106.4.

[8] Origen, *Cels.* 5.62. Origen speaks of disciples of Harpocrates, but he must have confused Harpocrates with Carpocrates.

[9] *Elench.* 5.7.1.

[10] See Hans von Campenhausen, *Kirchliches Amt und geistliche Vollmacht in den ersten drei Jahrhunderten* (2d ed.; BHT 14; Tübingen: Mohr/Siebeck, 1963) 172–76.

[11] See David Harold Warren, "The Text of the Apostle in the Second Century: A Contribution to the History of Its Reception" (Ph. D. diss., Harvard University, 2001) 124–29.

[12] Aristides, *Apol.* 15.2. The text of Aristides must be established from a Syriac version and a Greek adaptation found in the *Life of Barlaam and Ioasaph,* traditionally assigned to John of Damascus. This text is therefore far from certain. Both versions, however, mention the mission of the twelve disciples after Easter. See the edition of Edgar J. Goodspeed, *Die ältesten Apologeten. Texte mit kurzen Einleitungen* (1914) (Göttingen: Vandenhoeck & Ruprecht, 1984) 19–20.

[13] Jacob Jervell, "Zur Frage der Traditionsgrundlage der Apostelgeschichte," *ST* 16 (1962)

The teachings of the apostles were used in the formulation of new sermons; apostolic examples were chosen for catechetical purposes; prayers, particularly eulogies, recalled the memory of the first Christian witnesses. Each community tried to remember the story of its origin. The christological speeches of Acts preserved archaic material[14]; *1 Clement*, after enumerating examples drawn from the Bible and from the life of Jesus, refers to models of "our generation" that include the martyrdoms of Peter and Paul and the tortures of holy women.[15] One of the oldest Christian prayers, quoted in the book of Acts, emphasizes not only the work of Christ but also the ethical responsibility of the first Christian generation.[16] Additionally, one of the traditions behind the conversion of Cornelius in the canonical book of Acts probably reflects the story of the founding of the church in Caesarea (Acts 10:1–11,18). Similarly, the name of Lydia is connected with the origin of the church at Philippi (Acts 16:14, 40). Even the earliest forms of the creed do not neglect the presence of the disciples at the resurrection of Jesus and their subsequent apostolic witness. A good portion of the short hymn found in 1 Tim 3:16 is devoted to this early time period in the church's life: after the words "he was manifested in the flesh, justified by the Spirit and contemplated by the angels," the text continues that "he was proclaimed among the nations and believed in the world."

It seems as if the entire Christian construction is based not on Christ alone, but on the fulfillment of the holy scriptures through Jesus Christ as preached and accepted by the apostolic church. Paul himself recognizes these two poles when he makes a distinction between the *work* of reconciliation accomplished by Christ and the *logos* of reconciliation proclaimed by the apostles (2 Cor 5:19–20). The prologues to the Gospel of Luke and the Epistle to the Hebrews both articulate the time of the salvation of Jesus and the time of the proclamation through his chosen witnesses (see Luke 1:1–4 and Heb 2:3–4).[17] The canonical Acts of the Apostles are not a completely new genre nor are they an unexpected creation. We know that apostolic successes were narrated, because at the end of the first century Luke writes that at the Jerusalem conference "there was silence among the whole gathering, and every one listened to Barnabas and Paul explaining (ἐξηγοῦμαι) all the work that God had accomplished through them and how he opened the door of the faith to the pagans."[18]

25–41; ET in *Luke and the People of God: A New Look at Luke-Acts* (Minneapolis: Augsburg, 1972) 19–49; François Bovon, "L'origine des récits concernant les apôtres," *RTP* 3/17 (1967) 345–50; reprinted in idem, *L'œuvre de Luc: Études d'exégèse et de théologie* (LD 130; Paris: Cerf, 1987) 155–62.

[14] See, for example, Acts 10:34–43.

[15] *1 Clem.* 5.1–6.3.

[16] See Acts 4:24–30.

[17] See François Bovon, "La structure canonique de l'Évangile et de l'Apôtre," *CrSt* 15 (1994) 559–76; English translation, see pp. 163–77.

[18] Acts 15:12; see also Acts 14:27; 15:3, and Luke 10:17.

This interest in both the first mission and the well-being of the first communities of believers was probably remembered in liturgical celebrations. The communication of news was not a profane activity but just as much a part of early Christian worship as thanking God and asking for help. The letters of Ignatius of Antioch confirm this effort to remember: community delegations as well as letters exchanged evince an effort to preserve memories that time and geographical distance might otherwise have eliminated. Ignatius rejoices when favorable news reaches him, this time not about Jesus Christ but about the recovery of peace in his own church at Antioch (*Phld.* 10.1–2).[19] Not only the canonical and apocryphal acts of the apostles but also the first acts of the martyrs testify to this decisive momentum of the *communio sanctorum*. The author of the *Passion of Marianus and James* writes:

> The very noble witnesses of God conferred also upon us this mission to proclaim (*praedicare*) his [God's] glory ... . When they began under the inspiration of the heavenly Spirit a sublime fight against the persecutions of a wild world and the attacks of the pagans, they [Marianus and Iacobus] commissioned us to bring to the knowledge of our brothers and sisters the story of their struggle ... in the thought that tribulations of those who had gone before could strengthen as examples of faith the multitude and particularly the people of God.[20]

It must be immediately added that these memories of the apostles were partisan and marked by ideological biases. The early centuries of Christianity can be described as a long struggle among different communities to establish authentic, legitimated memories, so that one could say, "Tell me who your apostle is and I will tell you who you are." The distinction between early Christian groups was largely made by their affiliation to a particular apostle and their characterization of this foundational figure. Note, for example, the very different treatment the authors of the Pastoral Epistles and Luke-Acts give to Paul: the former venerates Paul as virtually the sole apostolic intermediary, and the latter merely respects him as a beloved witness alongside the group of the Twelve. The churches of Asia Minor, according to Polycrates of Ephesus, proudly to rely on John and Philip (see Eusebius, *Hist. eccl.* 3.31.2–3). The early Syrian churches, who show an intense interest in the apostles,[21] try to preserve their own memories of the apostles,

---

[19] See also Ignatius, *Smyrn.* 11.1–3.

[20] *Passion of Marianus and James* 2–3. See Gustav Krüger and Gerhard Ruhbach, eds., *Ausgewählte Märtyrerakten* (SAQ 2/3; Tübingen: Mohr/Siebeck, 1965) 67; Paul Monceaux, *La vraie légende dorée. Relations de martyre* (Paris: Payot, 1928) 202–3; Herbert Musurillo, *The Acts of the Christian Martyrs: Introduction, Texts and Translations* (Oxford: Clarendon, 1972) 194–97; see also the "Passion of Montanus and Lucius," in Krüger and Ruhbach, *Ausgewählte Märtyrerakten*, 75–82.

[21] Geo Widengren insisted on the intense interest in the apostles on the part of the Syrian Christians; see Geo Widengren, *Muhammad, the Apostle of God, and His Ascension* (Uppsala: Lundequistska bokhandeln, 1955) 65–72; mentioned by Walter Schmithals, *Das kirchliche Apostelamt: Eine historische Untersuchung* (FRLANT 79; Göttingen: Vandenhoeck & Ruprecht, 1961) 171 n. 370.

choosing to remember Thomas and Thaddaeus on one side and Jesus' family, particularly James, the brother of the Lord, on the other.[22] Among the few remains of Judaeo-Christianity, the teaching of Elkasai (according to patristic witnesses) and the *Life of Mani* attest to the divisions and tensions that existed among the several groups mentioned by Epiphanius over the true relationship between Christian origins and the authentic understanding of the selected apostles.[23] What is true for Syria is also true for other regions, whether it be Africa or Greece, and for other cities, whether it be Rome or Alexandria. The fact remains and cannot be ignored: for many groups, the mediation of the apostles was extremely important.

What I can confidently say, then, is that the very existence of stories in the gospels confirms an interest in apostolic memories; and that not only twelve men but also several women and other men serve as agents of the evangelical communication. The tendency to select certain apostles as the guarantors of a particular community is already perceptible in the earliest Christian documents and can explain several omissions and marginalizations. Clearly, the presence of human mediation is central from the earliest times.

Further confirmation of this relevance of memory can be found in three related phenomena that occurred within early Christian tradition-building: first, in the intellectual decision that the apostles were not numerous individuals but members of a constituted group, a board of religious leaders; second, in the slow merging of two originally distinct categories, the Twelve called by the historical Jesus and the apostles sent by the resurrected Lord; and third, in the additional dimension of locating Paul in either category. These three steps were connected by a special understanding of Jesus' disciples, which considered them less as missionaries and more as founders of the church. Despite Günter Klein,[24] Luke was neither the first nor the only one to speak of the twelve apostles in this way.

Let me mention a few texts here. As a constituted *group* the apostles are mentioned in the canonical Epistle to the Ephesians (Eph 2:20: ἐποικοδομηθέντες ἐπὶ τῷ θεμελίῳ τῶν ἀποστόλων καὶ προφητῶν ...; see further Eph 3:5; 4:11). They are also mentioned by Clement of Rome in his *First Epistle* (chapter 42), where the vision of Christ's resurrection is constitutive for the group of the apostles, yet Paul is also called an apostle (*1 Clem.* 47.1–4; 5.3–7); and in *2 Clem.* 14.2 the church relies on the books of the prophets and on the apostles.[25] We also find the apostles

---

[22] Marie-Joseph Pierre, intr. and trans., *Aphraate le Sage persan, Les exposés* (2 vols.; SC 349, 359; Paris: Cerf, 1988–89) 1. 79–83.

[23] See Luigi Cirillo, "Livre de la révélation d'Elkasaï," in *Écrits apocryphes chrétiens* I (ed. François Bovon and Pierre Geoltrain; Bibliothèque de la Pléiade 442; Paris: Gallimard, 1997) 1.827–72; Albert Henrichs and Ludwig Koenen, "Der Kölner Mani-Kodex (P. Colon. inv. nr. 4780) ΠΕΡΙ ΤΗΣ ΓΕΝΝΗΣ ΤΟΥ ΣΩΜΑΤΟΣ ΑΥΤΟΥ," *ZPE* 19 (1975) 1–85; 32 (1978) 87–199; 44 (1981) 201–318; 48 (1982) 1–59.

[24] See Günter Klein, *Die zwölf Apostel: Ursprung und Gehalt einer Idee* (FRLANT 77; Göttingen: Vandenhoeck & Ruprecht, 1961).

[25] Not yet on the books of the apostles!

mentioned as a group in the letters of Ignatius of Antioch: in his letter to the Philadelphians, the apostles constitute the "presbytery of the church" (*Phld.* 5.1) and Jesus Christ is the door to the Father through which the patriarchs, the prophets, and the apostles enter (*Phld.* 9.1); elsewhere, the Lord does nothing without the Father or without the apostles (*Magn.* 7.1; 13.1; *Trall.* 7.1; *Eph.* 11.2). Again, in the canonical Epistle written by Jude (v. 17) we find "Remember the words pronounced by the apostles of our Lord."[26] And in 2 Pet 3:2, we find a curious reworking of the wording in Jude 17, from "the apostles" to "your apostles," which was probably done to avoid their confiscation by other Christian groups. A little earlier, in 2 Pet 1:16, Peter and the others have been ἐπόπται ("eyewitnesses") of Christ's magnitude at the transfiguration.

There are other texts as well. The *Epistle of Barnabas* (5.9) speaks of the selection of the apostles by Jesus Christ for the purpose of proclaiming the gospel; these men were sinners, but they were saved by the Lord. In *Shepherd* of Hermas 13.1 (Vis. III 5.1) the white stones of the vision, fitted together, are the apostles, the bishops, the teachers, and the deacons; in 92.4 (Sim. IX 16.4) the stones of the construction are ten for the first human generation, twenty-five for the following, thirty-five for the prophets and servants, and forty for the apostles[27]; in 93.5 (Sim. IX 16.5) the forty apostles preached the gospel to the dead and gave them the seal; in 94.1 (Sim. IX 17.1) the twelve apostles preached the Son of God to the twelve tribes of Israel; and in 102.2 (Sim. IX 25.2) the believers of the eight mountains are the apostles who taught the whole world and who never went wrong because the Spirit led them (therefore their place is with the angels). Finally, in the *Epistle of Polycarp* the apostles brought the gospel (6.3) and Paul and the other apostles are examples of perseverance (9.1).

The conception of the twelve apostles as a church-founding group occurs in several writings at the end of the first century and the first half of the second. Instead of attributing the influence to Luke, I consider this theological construction to be an element of the institutionalization of the early church. Several Christian groups were in search of a holy origin and firm ground. Luke-Acts clearly limits the number of apostles to the Twelve, under the leadership of Peter.[28] The book of Revelation, which mentions the apostles three times (Rev 2:2; 18:20; 21:14), notes precisely that the protective walls of the new Jerusalem possess twelve foundations and that on them one can read the names of the apostles (probably one on each foundation, but how can they be visible? Rev 21:14). Written around 130 C.E., *Barn.* 5.3 mentions the twelve apostles, but this verse has been suspected of being

---

[26] See Eric Fuchs and Pierre Reymond, *La deuxième épître de saint Pierre: L'épître de saint Jude* (2d ed.; CNT 2/13; Geneva: Labor et Fides, 1988) 180: "On pourrait dire que toute l'œuvre de Jude tient dans cette intention de faire mémoire, de rappeler ce sur quoi la foi chrétienne est fondée."

[27] Why forty?

[28] I date the composition of Luke-Acts between 80 and 90 C.E.

an interpolation; 5.9, however, which I mention above, brings together the calling of the Twelve according to the canonical Gospels and the title "apostle." A few years later, between 140 and 150 C.E., we find in Hermas 94.1 (Sim. IX 17.1), also mentioned above, that the twelve mountains represent the twelve tribes to which "the Son of God was preached by the apostles," which probably presupposes one apostle for each tribe (see the canonical logion of Q on the twelve thrones, Matt 19:28//Luke 22:30). The Christian *Ascension of Isaiah* 3.2, probably dated early second century C.E., mentions explicitly "the prophecy of the twelve apostles" (3.21; see also 4.3)[29]; the same is true of a fragment of the *Kerygma Petrou*,[30] also dated early second century C.E.: "I choose you, twelve disciples, considering you worthy of me, following the will of the Lord. Seeing in you faithful apostles, I am sending you into the world in order to preach the gospel to the inhabitants of the earth." The twelve apostles share their authority with Paul in the the *Apocalypse of Paul*[31] (Nag Hammadi Codex V,2), probably dated the second or third century C.E. Here Paul receives from the little child who represents the Savior the following command: "Now it is to the twelve apostles that you shall go, for these are the elect spirits, and they will greet you." Later in the text, Paul must ascend to the fourth heaven and from there he considers the earth, seeing the twelve apostles placed at his left and at his right; he himself occupies the central position. The twelve apostles will accompany the Apostle in his ascension to the subsequent heavens, in his spiritual discovery of the esoteric meaning of visible reality.

From the middle of the second century the expression "the twelve apostles" became very common. This is confirmed by the two secondary titles (titles later than the text itself) of the *Didache*, namely, the *Doctrine of the Twelve Apostles* and the *Doctrine of the Lord to the Nations through the Twelve Apostles*.[32] We also find confirmation in the title of another work, a lost gospel mentioned by Origen, namely, the *Gospel of the Twelve Apostles*[33]; and in still another title, the *Acts of Peter and the Twelve Apostles*, from Nag Hammadi (NHC VI,1).

---

[29] The Greek text has "prophecy," the Ethiopic has "teaching"; see Paolo Bettiolo et al., *Ascensio Isaiae*, vol. 1: *Textus* (CChr.SA 7; Turnhout: Brepols, 1995) 62–63, 142–43; see also Enrico Norelli, *Ascensio Isaiae*, vol. 2: *Commentarius* (CChr.SA 8; Turnhout: Brepols, 1995) 192–95, 212–14. In "Ascension d'Isaïe" (in *Écrits apocryphes chrétiens*, 1.505), Enrico Norelli dates the text to the beginning of the second century C.E.

[30] Quoted by Clement of Alexandria, *Strom.* 6.6.48; see Michel Cambe, "Prédication de Pierre," in *Écrits apocryphes chrétiens*, 1.19. In his introduction to *Écrits apocryphes chrétiens*, 1: 6, Cambe dates the text between 110 and 120.

[31] See George W. MacRae and William R. Murdoch, introduction to the *Apocalypse of Paul* in *The Nag Hammadi Library* (ed. James M. Robinson; rev. ed.; New York: HarperSanFrancisco, 1990) 257: "Nothing in *Apoc. Paul* demands any later date than the second century for its composition."

[32] Willy Rordorf and André Tuillier, eds. and trans., *La Doctrine des Douze Apôtres (Didachè)* (SC 248; Paris: Cerf, 1978) 11–17. The number twelve does not appear in the indirect tradition, see pp. 108 nn. 2–4 and 109 n. 1.

[33] See Origen, *Hom. Luc.* 1. 2.

Actually, the statement "Tell me who your apostle is and I will tell you who you are" is only partially applicable to my argument and needs a qualification, namely: "How do you see your apostle?" Adversaries could venerate the same apostle, and yet emphasize different aspects of his or her personality, or of his or her ministry. Peter was claimed not only by the early catholic churches but also by gnostic groups who viewed him as a mystic missionary or a spiritual leader.[34] The several portraits of Paul also serve as a warning: church leader in the Pastoral Epistles, theologian of the universal church as the Body of Christ in the Epistle to the Ephesians, martyr for righteousness in *1 Clement*, and esoteric mystic in the *Apocalypse of Paul* from Nag Hammadi (NHC V,2). Even the figure of James the Just, the brother of the Lord who was the possession of the Judaeo-Christian churches, could be reversed and reinterpreted. We see this in the numerous Nag Hammadi treatises related to James: the *Apocryphon of James* (NHC I,2); the *Apocalypses of James* (NHC V,3 and V,4); and the *Gospel of Thomas*, with its veneration of James.

Even Marcion, who was totally devoted to Paul (he was the apostle *par excellence*), did not reject completely the Galilean disciples of Jesus but gave to them a new interpretation. According to Marcion, Jesus chose the Twelve but during his lifetime he could not convince them that he was the Son of the unknown God rather than the Son of the negative divinity of the Hebrew Bible. Nevertheless, at some moments – at the confession of Peter, at the transfiguration, at the disciples' request that Jesus teach them how to pray – the first disciples understood Jesus' divine mission. Later, the resurrection helped them receive a correct understanding of the revelation, but – and this is Marcion's construction – they fell back into a legalistic interpretation of Jesus' words.[35]

The apostles who were neglected by the main streams of early Christianity, that is, by the church in Jerusalem or the church of the Hellenists in the capital and then in Antioch, would be taken up by other groups. One has only to remember the lively existence of Mary Magdalene in Gnostic and ascetic circles (see the *Gospel of Mary*, the *Pistis Sophia*, and the *Acts of Philip*), the argument of the Montanists and their appeal to Philip's prophetess daughters,[36] and the traditions about Philip, Thomas, and John that are imbedded in the Nag Hammadi Library.[37] Fi-

---

[34] NHC VI,1, mentioned above (*Acts of Peter and the Twelve Apostles*); see also NHC VII,3 (*Apocalypse of Peter*).

[35] Adolf von Harnack (*Marcion: das Evangelium vom fremden Gott* [2d ed.; Leipzig: Hinrichs, 1924; Darmstadt: Wissenschaftliche Buchgesellschaft, 1996] 39) writes: "Die Urapostel waren nicht dezidierte Irrlehrer, aber sie sind in einer schweren Konfusion stecken geblieben, ..."

[36] See Eusebius, *Hist. eccl.* 5.17.3, and Origen, *1 Corinthians Fragment (14:36)*; see Pierre de Labriolle, ed., *Les sources de l'histoire du montanisme* (Fribourg [Switzerland]: Librairie de l'Université, 1913) 55.

[37] See the *Gospel of Philip* (NHC II,3), the *Letter of Peter to Philip* (NHC VIII,2), the *Gospel of Thomas* (NHC II,2), and the *Book of Thomas the Contender* (NHC II,7).

nally, we can mention the philosophical and ascetic *Acts of Andrew* and the strange revelations enclosed within the *Questions of Bartholomew.*

Such are a few examples of memories about the group of the apostles, the twelve apostles themselves, and individual characters such as Peter, Paul, and John.

The Oblivion

The plea for the preservation of apostolic memories should not conceal a strange phenomenon: the frequent silence in the Christian tradition about the life and death of these major Christian heroes. Even Luke, who is so interested in the beginnings of Christianity, fails to communicate any information about Peter's destiny once the apostle had achieved a kind of exemplary missionary travel (Acts 9:32–11:18), escaped from prison (Acts 12:3–10), and played his role as head and speaker of the apostolic council (Acts 15:7–11). Concerning Paul, Luke is not ready to collect any information dealing with the result of his call on Caesar and the end of his life (Acts 28:30–31). And what was the destiny of the others? All that Luke is willing to communicate is scanty and concerns Judas's tragic suicide (Acts 1:15–20) and the martyrdom of James the son of Zebedee (Acts 12:1–2). What about John, who stands in the shadow of Peter in two or three stories (Acts 3:1–11; 4:13–19; 8:14), Andrew, Philip (the apostle distinct from Philip the evangelist), Thomas, Bartholomew, Matthew, James the son of Alphaeos, Simon the Zealot, Judas the son of James (Luke 6:14–16; Acts 1:13–14) and Matthias, the one chosen to be an apostle by lot (Acts 1:21–26)? What about the group of women who followed Jesus from Galilee: Mary Magdalene, Johanna the wife of Chouza, Suzan, and the many others (Luke 8:1–3)? What about Jesus' family, especially Mary, whose name Luke has preserved at the beginning of his gospel (Luke 1:26–2:52) and at the beginning of Acts (Acts 1:14)? The literary genre of Luke-Acts is not sufficient to explain such disrespectful treatment, and Luke is the author most familiar with apostolic legends.

The other canonical gospels chronicle the period after Easter, but this is only to establish a historical basis for the kerygma and for a Christian interpretation of Jesus' teaching; there is no concern for the fate of the Twelve. One could mention Matthew's Easter story, the commissioning of the disciples to go to the ends of the earth, but no fulfillment of this promise is narrated by the Evangelist (Matt 28:16–20). Or, we could mention the last layer of the Gospel of John (chapter 21), which briefly speaks of Peter's future ministry and prophesies enigmatically about his martyrdom, along with the beloved disciple's final sojourn on earth during Jesus' absence (John 21:18–23).

The numerous early Christian letters, the apocalyptic writings, the first collections of legal material, the first wisdom documents, the most ancient sermons – none provides any clue about the fate of Jesus' disciples, the Twelve, the apostles, or the first Christians. We recognize that some communities remain silent about women, Mary Magdalene in particular, retreating probably into a misogynistic attitude[38]; but why do we not meet in the first two centuries the hagiographic vein that will blossom in the fourth century? Why do the first panegyrics of Paul, Peter, and John originate in the time of John Chrysostom[39] and not in the time of Polycrates or Serapion?

The first explanation that comes to mind, which is the one advanced by Martin Dibelius and Günther Bornkamm,[40] is a christological one. As long as Jesus Christ is the central figure of the salvific drama, the content of the revelation and the mediator of the divine reconciliation, his disciples can only be cumbersome and should remain marginal to his role. As we know, the argument of numerical age was decisive during that time period, so it was possible to say that even if Jesus were a latecomer, his divine nature, the Logos, was older than Moses and prior to Homer or Socrates[41]; the same could not be said about Jesus' disciples.

The second explanation, which is related to the first, is inherent in the definition of the Christian faith. If the essential matter of faith is the kerygma, then the responsibility of the apostles is to imitate the role of John the Baptist in the Fourth Gospel, to be a voice without personality (see John 1:23), to be only preachers and not actors of the salvific drama. Their fates, even their tribulations and heroic deaths, do not attract the attention of Christian teachers and ministers. Their lives are eclipsed by the bright evidence of their message.[42]

A third explanation is related to the real passing of time. Some intellectual categories, the sections of the creed and the spiritual sensibilities that were part of the very beginnings of Christianity, were no longer bearable one century later. Christians of Hellenic origin could no longer understand and transmit conceptions connected with the Semitic roots of Christianity; ideas concerning the end of time and the material nature of God's spiritual gifts, for instance, became obsolete. Therefore some apostolic memories faded or were neglected, just as you might find on your own bookshelves volumes of your parents' books that you have no interest in reading. Much apostolic literature, as well as much early patristic lit-

---

[38] On the roles of women in the early church, see Elisabeth Schüssler Fiorenza, *In Memory of Her: A Feminist Theological Reconstruction of Christian Origins* (Tenth Anniversary Edition; Crossroad: New York, 1994).

[39] See, for example, John Chrysostom, *Panégyriques de saint Paul: Introduction* (ed. and trans. A. Piédagnel; SC 300; Paris: Cerf, 1982).

[40] Martin Dibelius, "Stilkritisches zur Apostelgeschichte, 1923," in *Aufsätze zur Apostelgeschichte* (ed. Heinrich Greeven; 4th ed.; FRLANT 60; Göttingen: Vandenhoeck & Ruprecht, 1961) 9–28, esp. 11–12; see also Günther Bornkamm, *Bibel: Das Neue Testament* (ThTh 9; Stuttgart/Berlin: Kreuz, 1971) 81–85.

[41] See Justin, *1 Apol.* 23.1; 44.8; 60.10; Charles Munier, *L'Apologie de saint Justin: Philosophe et martyr* (Par. 38; Fribourg [Switzerland]: Éditions Universitaires, 1994) 60–65.

[42] See Jacques Dupont, "L'apôtre comme intermédiaire du salut dans les Actes des Apôtres," *RTP* 112 (1980) 342–58; reprinted in idem, *Nouvelles Études sur les Actes des Apôtres* (LD 118; Paris: Cerf, 1984) 112–32.

erature, was lost not so much because of rigid or official censorship, but because of a growing lack of interest.[43]

A fourth explanation has to do with conflicting ecclesiologies. As soon as a Christian church decided to follow the steps of one apostle or a group of apostles, that community tended to embrace that decision at the expense of the other apostolic figures. Of course some of these churches, like the early Catholic movement, chose to establish themselves on the foundation of the twelve apostles and in the legacy of Peter and Paul,[44] but we know of others who were proud to be the faithful disciples of, singularly, John the beloved disciple,[45] or Thomas,[46] or Bartholomew,[47] or Mary Magdalene.[48] It is interesting to note that if some Judaeo-Christian communities considered Paul their enemy, other churches simply ignored him. Not only does Justin Martyr not mention him, but later Aphrahat the wise Persian mentions only Peter in his *Speeches*: in 1.41 [1.17] Simon is called the true stone, the one who tried to walk on the water; in 1.336 [7.15] Simon Peter is an example of conversion after denial; and in 1.453 [10.4] Jesus is the good Shepherd who cared for the flock, followed by Peter, while now it is the responsibility of the Christian ministers to look after the sheep.[49]

Conclusion: Apostleship, Mariology, and Christology

Let me summarize my point: on the one hand Christian literature of the first centuries tells stories about the apostles. In this stock of shared knowledge, the reader finds the following: Jesus chose the Twelve who received the title of apostles, a title that was also given to Paul. Jesus also had women among his followers, one of whom was even the first to discover the empty tomb and receive a revelation of the Resurrected One.[50] A list of women disciples has been preserved,[51] and the

---

[43] Martin Dibelius, *Studies in the Acts of the Apostles* (trans. M. Ling; London: SCM Press, 1956) 103; Ernest Haenchen, *Die Apostelgeschichte: Neu übersetzt und erklärt* (10th ed.; KEK 3; Göttingen: Vandenhoeck & Ruprecht, 1956) 87.

[44] See the two witnesses of Gaius and Dionysius of Corinth that are preserved by Eusebius (*Hist. eccl.* 2.25.6–8).

[45] See Raymond E. Brown, "Chart One: The History of the Johannine Community," in idem, *The Community of the Beloved Disciple* (Ramsey, N.J.: Paulist Press, 1979) 166–67.

[46] On the Thomas community, see Gregory Riley, *Resurrection Reconsidered: Thomas and John in Controversy* (Minneapolis: Fortress, 1995).

[47] Even though hesitates to speak of a community associated with Bartholomew, see Jean-Daniel Kaestli, "Questions de Barthélemy," in *L'évangile de Barthélemy d'après deux écrits apocryphes* (ed. Jean-Daniel Kaestli and Pierre Cherix; Apocryphes 1; Turnhout: Brepols, 1993) 1–95.

[48] Origen, *Cels.* 5.62; see François Bovon, "Le privilège pascal de Marie-Madeleine," *NTS* 30 (1984) 50–62; ET in *New Testament Traditions and Apocryphal Narratives* (trans. Jane Haapiseva-Hunter; PTMS 36; Allison Park, Pa.: Pickwick Publications, 1995) 147–57, 228–37.

[49] Pierre, *Aphraate le Sage persan*, 1.231–32, 425–26, 501–02.

[50] See note 48 and Antti Marjanen, *The Woman Jesus Loved: Mary Magdalene in the Nag Hammadi Library and Related Documents* (Leiden: Brill, 1996).

title "apostle" has been given to some of them.[52] We know also of partnered apostles.[53]

The apostles may be called pillars of the church, or better, her foundation. Chosen companions, they became witnesses of the resurrection and from time to time they performed miracles as confirmation of the divine power of their message. First located in Jerusalem, they later went into the mission fields of the world. We have lists of their names,[54] and they had their own disciples, some of whose names are also known to us. Several were married, others not.[55] Most of them died as martyrs.

On the other hand, during the same time period there is a great ignorance of – and an evident lack of interest in – the apostles' education, personal idiosyncrasies, and the details of their lives. The numerous inconsistencies I mentioned at the beginning of this essay can be summarized here by a simple question: why this double treatment, these two opposite attitudes, of remembrance and forgetfulness, toward Jesus' first disciples and witnesses?

In conclusion, I will propose an answer based not on sociological but on theological grounds. As we know, the first two Christian centuries were also hesitant about Christology, vacillating between incarnation theology and docetism. There is, for example, a strange but evocative description of Jesus' origin by the Valentinians. To avoid too crude a conception of Jesus' birth and to protect the divine essence of Christ, they stipulated that Jesus was born of Mary "as through a pipe."[56] This strange expression allowed them to censor central elements of the Christian tradition and maintain their own docetic Christology. As long as Mary was only a pipe, or an innocent channel, the divinity of the Savior was not threatened, therefore the emphasis given to the Virgin Mary in the first centuries was tightly interwoven with Christology.[57] In a church where the divine aspect of Christ was underlined, Mary remained a marginal figure and her role constrained and ancillary. But in a church where incarnation was decisive, the person of Mary became

---

[51] See Luke 8:1–3; François Bovon, *Das Evangelium nach Lukas, Lk 1,1–9,50* (EKKNT 3.1; Zürich: Benzinger; Neukirchen-Vluyn: Neukirchener Verlag, 1989) 396–401.

[52] On female apostleship, see Schüssler Fiorenza, *In Memory of Her*, 43–48, 168–75, 285–333.

[53] See, for example, Aquila and Priscilla (or Prisca) in Acts 18:18, 26; Rom 16:3; 1 Cor 16:19; 2 Tim 4:19; also Andronicus and Junia in Rom 16:7; probably Peter and his wife in 1 Cor 9:5.

[54] See Mark 3:16–19, Matt 10:2–4, Luke 6:13–16, and Acts 1:13–14.

[55] Clement of Alexandria, *Strom.* 3.52.4; 3.53.1; 7.63.3; mentioned in Eusebius, *Hist. eccl.* 3.30.1.

[56] Quoted by Irenaeus, *Haer.* 1.7.2 and 3.11.3. The original Greek text of the first passage is preserved by Epiphanius of Salamis, *Pan.* 31.22.1. The sentence is often mentioned in heresiological literature of antiquity; see Michel Tardieu, "'Comme à travers un tuyau': Quelques remarques sur le mythe valentinien de la chair céleste du Christ," in *Colloque international sur les textes de Nag Hammadi (Québec, 22–25 August 1978)* (ed. Bernard Barc; BCNH.E; Québec: Presses Universitaires de Laval; Louvain: Peeters, 1981) 151–77.

[57] See Jaroslav Pelikan, *Mary Through the Centuries: Her Place in History and Culture* (New Haven: Yale University Press, 1996) 30, 39–65.

an indispensable intermediary, and a vivid interest in her person, her fate, and her origin arose. In other words, if one believes that *Dieu a besoin des hommes* – that is, that God needs human mediation to reveal himself and to be the Savior – then, logically, human intermediaries cease to be gray shadows and receive blood, bones, and flesh. What is true for the figure of Mary is equally true for the person of the apostles.

As long as the Christian message is an immediate revelation or an intellectual proclamation, it needs only human voices and the apostles remain tools without individuality, witnesses disappearing behind their message. But as soon as the Christian kerygma becomes ethical and proposes a way of life in which imitation is an integral part, then the apostles become indispensable; they become real persons. Their fate, their personality, and their decisions become part of the Christian manifesto.

Bibliography

Agnew, F. "The Origin of the New Testament Apostle-Concept: A Review Research." *Journal of Biblical Literature* 105 (1986): 75–86.

Betz, Hans Dieter. "Apostle." *Anchor Bible Dictionary.* 6 vols. New York: Doubleday, 1992. 1: 309–11.

Bienert, Wolfgang A. "The Picture of the Apostle in Early Christian Tradition." *New Testament Apocrypha.* Edited by Wilhelm Schneemelcher. Translated by Robert McL. Wilson. Revised Edition of the Collection Initiated by Edgar Hennecke. 2 vols. Louisville, Ky: Westminster/John Knox Press, 1991/92. 2: 5–27.

Bovon, François. *Luc le théologien: Vingt-cinq ans de recherches (1950–1970).* Second edition. Geneva: Labor et Fides, 1988.

idem. "La structure canonique de l'Évangile et de l'Apôtre." *Cristianesimo nella storia* 15 (1994): 559–76; English translation here pp. 163–77.

Brock, Ann Graham. *Mary Magdalene, the First Apostle: The Struggle for Authority.* Harvard Theological Studies 51. Cambridge, Mass.: Harvard University Press, 2003.

Campenhausen, Hans von. *Kirchliches Amt und geistliche Vollmacht in den ersten drei Jahrhunderten.* Second edition. Beiträge zur historischen Theologie 15. Tübingen: Mohr Siebeck, 1963.

Ehrhardt, A. *The Apostolic Succession in the First Two Centuries of the Church.* London: Lutterworth Press, 1953.

Goodspeed, Edgar Johnson. *The Twelve: The Story of Christ's Apostles.* Philadelphia: J.C. Winston Co., 1957.

Klein, Günter. *Die zwölf Apostel: Ursprung und Gehalt einer Idee.* Forschungen zur Religion und Literatur des Alten und Neuen Testaments 77. Göttingen: Vandenhoeck & Ruprecht, 1961.

Krik, J.A. "Apostleship since Rengstorf." *New Testament Studies* 21 (1974/75): 249–64.

Molland, E. "Le développement de l'idée de succession apostolique." *Revue d'histoire et de philosophie religieuses* 34 (1954): 1–29.

Nagel, W. "Der Begriff des Apostolischen in der christlichen Frühzeit bis zur Kanonsbildung." Habilitationsschrift, Leipzig, 1958.

Schmithals, Walter. *Das kirchliche Apostelamt. Eine historische Untersuchung.* Forschungen zur Religion und Literatur des Alten und Neuen Testaments 79. Göttingen: Vandenhoeck & Ruprecht, 1961.

Schneemelcher, Wilhelm. "Introduction to Writings Relating to the Apostles." *New Testament Apocrypha*. Edited by Wilhelm Schneemelcher. Translated by Robert McL. Wilson. Revised Edition of the Collection Initiated by Edgar Hennecke. 2 vols. Louisville, Ky.: Westminster/John Knox Press, 1991–92.

Wagenmann, J. *Die Stellung des Apostels Paulus neben den Zwölf in den ersten zwei Jahrhunderten*. Beihefte zur Zeitschrift für die neutestamentliche Wissenschaft 3. Berlin: de Gruyter, 1926.

Widengren, Geo. *Muḥammad, the Apostle of God, and his Ascension*. Uppsala: Lundequistska bokhandeln, 1955.

Wikenhauser, A. "Apostel." *Reallexikon für Antike und Christentum*. 18 vols. to date. Stuttgart: Anton Hiersemann, 1950. 1: 553–55.

I. Luke-Acts

Studies in Luke-Acts: Retrospect and Prospect*

Introduction

Let me begin with a personal note. Three experiences in my work on Luke-Acts will explain both the selection of the topics I shall discuss in this article and my view of the present situation in the study of Luke-Acts.

(1) After ten years of reading the recent studies of Luke-Acts[1] and then working on the text itself,[2] I made the observation that the general understanding of the theology of the Gospel of Luke on the basis of its redactional elements was rarely helpful in my efforts to write a commentary on this Gospel. Just as contributors to the more recent volumes of the *Theological Dictionary to the New Testament*[3] no longer propose interpretations generally applicable to all three synoptic Gospels, the exegete working with a particular pericope can no longer be satisfied with generalizations about Lukan theology. Indeed, such general assumptions may actually be impediments rather than useful tools for understanding a particular text. This is not universally recognized because the attention of scholars has been held by another problem, namely, the substitution of a diachronic redactional interpretation of the gospels by a synchronic literary interpretation.[4] The underlying dilemma is, of course, the old question of the connection between ex-

---

  * An earlier version of this paper was presented to the Luke-Acts Seminar of the Society of Biblical Literature on 25 November 1991 in Kansas City. I would like to thank Professors David Moessner and David L. Tiede for the invitation. I also want to thank my former assistants, Isabelle Juillard and Eva Tobler, who helped me during the preperation of this article, as well as Jane Haapiseva-Hunter, who corrected and improved the English of my text.

[1] François Bovon, *Luke the Theologian: Thirty-Three Years of Research (1950–1983)* (PTMS 12; Allison Park, Pa: Pickwick, 1987) esp. 418.

[2] François Bovon, *L' Évangile selon saint Luc (1,1–9.50)* (CNT 3a; Geneva: Labor et Fides, 1991).

[3] See, for example, Eduard Schweizer, "υἱὸς κτλ.," *TDNT* 8 (1972) 363–92

[4] For examples of this approach see Charles H. Talbert, *Reading Luke: A Literary and Theological Commentary on the Third Gospel* (New York: Crossroad, 1982); Robert C. Tannehill, *The Narrative Unity of Luke-Acts: A Literary Interpretation* (2 vols.; FF; Philadelphia: Fortress, 1986); Roland Meynet, *Quelle est donc cette Parole? Lecture "rhétorique" de l'Évangile de Luc (1–9, 22–24)* (2 vols.; LD 99; Paris: Cerf, 1979); idem, *L 'Évangile selon saint Luc. Analyse rhétorique* (2 vols.; Paris: Cerf, 1988); idem, *Avez-vous lu saint Luc? Guide pour la rencontre* (Lire la Bible 88; Paris: Cerf, 1990); and Jean-Noël Aletti, *L'art de raconter Jésus-Christ. L'écriture narrative de l' évangile de Luc* (Parole de Dieu; Paris: Seuil, 1989).

egesis and biblical theology. A promising solution might be to immerse oneself in a single relevant text, as Odette Mainville has done in her recent dissertation on Acts 2:33,[5] and to obtain universality through the understanding of particularity – in other words, to follow Kierkegaard rather than Hegel.

(2) A growing acquaintance with Christian apocryphal literature[6] convinced me that prior to their canonization the gospels shared both the fortune and the misfortune of the apocryphal literature, namely, a free and rapid reception but an unstable textual transmission. For centuries this remained the fate of the apocryphal materials. An understanding of the life and fate of the gospels during the second century is decisive for a better knowledge not only of the patristic period but also of the texts of the gospels themselves. Textual critics of the New Testament can no longer work in isolation from historians of the canon. Everything from codicology to hermeneutics and from historical exegesis to theological interpretation belongs together. Distinctions such as the one between "Primitive Christianity" (*Urgemeinde*) and "Ancient Church" should be banished, and we should speak of "early Christian literature" as a whole rather than of a specific New Testament literature. Richard Pervo[7] is correct in reprimanding those who make a firm distinction between the canonical and apocryphal acts, as if the former were designed to build up the Christian community and the latter to delight the general public. From a New Testament point of view, the quarrel between Marcion and Tertullian over the Gospel of Luke[8] is extremely relevant. My own picture of the Gospels may be shaken like the second-year undergraduate's image of Christ in a critical course on the Bible. The "historical gospel," like the "historical Jesus," is a vulnerable, this-wordly, conditioned, and enigmatic reality. It is advisable to admit this not only for the sake of our scientific reputation but also for the sake of our theological position.

(3) Twenty-five years ago, I read with great enthusiasm the diary of Claude Lévi-Strauss, *Tristes tropiques*,[9] and planned to publish a study on existential analysis – with which I was quite familiar – and structural analysis, of which I had just become aware.[10] Since then, I have had many conversations with friends from

    [5] Odette Mainville, *L'Esprit dans l'œuvre de Luc* (Héritage et Projet 45; Québec: Fides, 1991). An exhaustive analysis of a single verse, Acts 2:33, opens the door to a general understanding of the Holy Spirit in Luke-Acts; in turn, this understanding displays the connections with such vital issues as the Hebrew scriptures, christology, and ecclesiology.

    [6] Helmut Koester and François Bovon, *Genèse de l'écriture chrétienne* (Mémoires premières; Turnhout: Brepols, 1991).

    [7] Richard Pervo, *Profit with Delight: The Literary Genre of the Acts of the Apostles* (Philadelphia: Fortress, 1987).

    [8] Tertullian *Marc.* 4.

    [9] Claude Lévi-Strauss, *Tristes tropiques* (Le monde en 10 × 18, 12–13; Paris: Union Générale d'éditions, 1962).

    [10] Roland Barthes, François Bovon, Franz J. Leenhardt, Robert Martin-Archard, and Jean Starobinski, *Structural Analysis and Biblical Exegesis: Interpretational Essays* (PTMS 3; Pittsburgh: Pickwick, 1974).

Lyons (at CADIR: Centre d'Analyse du Discourse Religieux)[11] and from Paris (at CANAL: Centre d'Analyse pour l'histoire du judaïsme hellénistique et des origines chrétiennes de l'École pratique des hautes études, section des Sciences religieuses), as well as with colleagues in the Studiorum Novi Testamenti Societas, where I led a seminar on linguistics and exegesis together with other scholars.[12] Although I was convinced that a synchronic view was necessary and that structural analysis could bring to light the coherence of a biblical pericope or book, I was also disturbed by the technocracy of several semiotic procedures, by the methodological dichotomy imposed between genetic and structural explanation of a text, and by the refusal of many semioticians to engage in a resulting discussion of the meaning of the text. Fortunately, these positions, while more pronounced in France, were less prominent in America, where interest in the growth of the text and in hermeneutical issues remained alive.[13] Structure and genesis, synchrony and diachrony are complementary and should be held together. This was in fact the methodological ideal of the theoreticians of the historical method in its golden age and is expressed particularly in the works of Hermann Gunkel.[14]

The Traditions and Sources Behind Luke-Acts

During the last two decades, the leading position of the two-source hypothesis has been challenged in several quarters. That the Gospel of Matthew was Luke's source has been vigorously affirmed not only by modern students of Griesbach,[15] but also by such scholars as Michael D. Goulder.[16] In his bitter polemic against what he labels "the old paradigm," Goulder develops a new model consisting of eight hypotheses. The following quotation characterizes the model:

---

[11] See the periodical of CADIR, *Sémiotique et Bible*, as well as one of their publications, Groupe d'Entrevernes, *Signs and Parables: Semiotics and Gospels Texts* (PTMS 23; Pittsburgh: Pickwick, 1978).

[12] François Bovon, "Le dépassement de l'esprit historique," in *Le Christianisme est-il une religion du livre? Actes du colloque organisé par la Faculté de théologie protestante de l'Université des sciences humaines de Strasbourg du 20 au 23 mai 1981* (Études et travaux 5; Strasbourg: Association des publications de la Faculté de théologie protestante et Association de la civilisation romaine, 1984) 111–24.

[13] Edgar V. McKnight, *Meaning in Texts: The Historical Shaping of a Narrative Hermeneutics* (Philadelphia: Fortress, 1978).

[14] François Bovon, "Hermann Gunkel, Historian and Exegete of Literary Forms," in idem and Grégoire Rouiller, eds., *Exegesis: Problems of Method and Exercises in Reading (Genesis 22 and Luke 15)* (PTMS 21; Pittsburgh: Pickwick, 1978) 124–42.

[15] William R. Farmer, *The Synoptic Problem: A Critical Analysis* (2d ed.; Dillsboro, N.C.: Western North Carolina Press, 1976).

[16] Michael D. Goulder, *Luke: A New Paradigm* (2 vols.; JSNTSup 20; Sheffield: Sheffield Academic Press, 1989).

Luke wrote his Gospel about 90 for a more Gentile church, combining Matthew and Mark. He re-wrote Matthew's birth narrative with the aid of the Old Testament, and he added new material of his own creation, largely parables, where his genius lay. The new material can almost always be understood as a Lukan development of matter in Matthew. There was hardly any L *(Sondergut)*.[17]

"Dispensing" with Q (his fourth hypothesis is that "Q is a total error"[18]) as well as with L, Luke's special source, Goulder is obliged to assign to Luke a degree of freedom and creativity that is incompatible with the respect for tradition that Luke claims for himself. His last remaining defense to save the evangelist from arbitrary imagination is the Lukan as well as Matthew respect for liturgy and calendar.

My own attempts to change the old paradigm according to the hypothesis put forth by this British scholar were unsuccessful. In the case of one pericope I tried in my commentary to build the argument on the Griesbach hypothesis. The attempt, however, to imagine how Luke could have modified Matthew – with regard to order as well as style – led to a cul-de-sac. The liveliness of the gospel tradition had to give way to the assumption that a narrow–minded author was laboriously copying another's work. Only fancy in the style of Goulder brought some atmosphere of warmth to my laborious, useless attempt.[19] The history of the origins of Christianity cannot be illuminated by such a paradigm. The weight of the ongoing oral tradition on one hand the ideological force (from the kerygma as well as from wisdom theology) of the reinterpretation of the Christian message on the other hand, together suggest a different approach to understanding Luke, who stands at the crossroads of the synoptic tradition and the Pauline mission.

French criticism has proposed two extreme solutions to the synoptic problem. The most complex is that of Marie-Émile Boismard,[20] who constructs many intermediate steps, while that of Philippe Rolland[21] is quite simple. Rolland's efforts are commendable insofar as he attempts to integrate the main first-century Christian churches – Jerusalem, Antioch, Caesara, and Rome – into the history of the synoptic tradition. He further believes that the traditional elements – the creeds and gospels of the several churches – were definitely maintained in the further developments. According to his theory, the tradition began with the primitive (oral) gospel of the Twelve in Jerusalem. The gospel experienced a double reception: in

---

17 Ibid., 1.22–23.

18 Ibid., 1.22.

19 I was not entirely convinced by C.M. Tuckett, ed., *Synoptic Studies: The Ampleforth Conferences of 1982 and 1983* (JSNTSup 7; Sheffield: JSOT Press, 1984); not particularly by H. Benedict Green ("The Credibility of Luke's Transformation of Matthew") in that same volume (pp. 131–55).

20 Marie-Émile Boismard, Arnaud Lamouille, and P. Sandevoir, *Synopse des quatre Évangiles en français,* vol. 2: *Commentaire* (Paris: Cerf, 1972).

21 Philippe Rolland, *Les premiers évangiles. Un nouveau regard sur le problème synoptique* (LD 116; Paris: Cerf, 1984).

Antioch in a pre-Matthean form as the gospel of the Hellenists, and in Ephesus or Philippi – that is, in the Pauline school – in a pre-Lukan form. While Matthew then developed, using additional ingredients, the Hellenist form of the Gospel, Luke received and amplified the Pauline form, also adding new elements. Some of these new elements are common to both (two forms of Q, which he believed to be the gospel of those "Fearing God"), while others are proper to each of the two evangelists *(Sondergut)*. Matthew and Luke, then, are not dependent upon Mark's Gospel, which is seen as a conflation of the two preliminary forms, the pre-Matthean and the pre-Lukan Gospel. Mark is a witness of the church in Rome, Matthew of the church in Antioch, and Luke belongs to the missionary team of Paul.

I remain attached, perhaps stubbornly, to the two-source hypothesis. But I also agree with Helmut Koester,[22] who emphasizes the vital corollary of an oral tradition that was thoroughly reformulated in view of changing congregational interests. This implies my rejection of the thesis of Birger Gerhardsson,[23] who understands the gospel tradition in terms of a strict rabbinic-type transmission. My study of the unpredictable and unstable life of apocryphal traditions made me aware of the flexible trajectories to which synoptic stories and speeches were subject. The discovery of the *Gospel of Thomas* as well as the elegant solution of the problem of the "minor agreements," by reference to an ongoing oral tradition that existed alongside documents that were already written (compare Sigmund Mowinckel's explanation for the existence of the Elohist in the Hebrew Bible[24]), confirms this opinion.[25]

Q and L, the synoptic sayings source and the source of the Lukan special materials, are no longer just possible, but rather fruitful and productive hypotheses. The lively interest in Q, understood as both sapiential and apocalyptic, is fascinating. If the first volume of my commentary owes much to the older works on Q by Dieter Lührmann, Paul Hoffmann, and Heinz Schürmann,[26] the second volume is heavily indebted to the dozen books written on Q during the last ten years, particularly that of John Kloppenborg and the volume from the Journées Bibliques

---

[22] Helmut Koester, *Ancient Christian Gospels: Their History and Development* (Philadelphia: Trinity, 1990) 334–36; François Bovon, *L'Évangile selon saint Luc*, 27–29.

[23] Birger Gerhardsson, *Memory and Manuscript: Oral Tradition and Written Transmission in Rabbinic Judaism and Early Christianity* (ASNU 22; Lund: Gleerup, 1961).

[24] Sigmund Mowinckel, *Erwägungen zur Pentateuchquellenfrage* (Oslo: Universitetsforlaget, 1964).

[25] See Koester, *Ancient Christian Gospels,* 75–128; Timothy A. Friedrichsen, "The Matthew-Luke Agreements Against Mark," in Frans Neirynck, ed., *L'Évangile de Luc: The Gospel of Luke* (2d ed.; BETL 32; Leuven: Leuven University Press and Peeters, 1989) 335–92.

[26] Dieter Lührmann, *Die Redaktion der Logienquelle. Anhang: Zur weiteren Überlieferung der Logienquelle* (WMANT 33; Neukirchen-Vluyn: Neukirchener Verlag, 1969); Paul Hoffmann, *Studien zur Theologie der Logienquelle* (3d ed.; NTAbh n.s. 8; Münster: Aschendorff, 1982); Heinz Schürmann, *Traditionsgeschichtliche Untersuchungen zu den synoptischen Evangelien. Beiträge* (KBANT; Düsseldorf: Patmos, 1968).

entitled *Logia*,[27] not to mention the recent commentary on the special materials (L) of Luke by Gerd Petzke.[28] In a closing chapter, following the commentary on L itself, Petzke presents an original and instructive summary of the primary emphases (*Schwerpunkt*) of L: the artistic method of good storytelling, present in L as well as in Luke; the function of the parables, which invite the readers to identify themselves centaining the world of the narrative; and the portrait of a half-historical and half-mythological Jesus.[29] The book concludes with a discussion of Jesus' interest in the individual, as well as an exposition of several topics of Lukan theology.

The Text of Luke-Acts

With great modesty – his name does not appear on the title page – executive editor J.K. Elliott has produced two volumes containing the text of the Gospel entitled *The Gospel According to Luke*.[30] It is important to specify that these two volumes, which are the fruit of an old project of the American and British Committee of the International Greek New Testament Project, are not a new critical edition of the Greek text. Rather, the printed text is nothing other than the old Textus Receptus, but it has received a full critical apparatus. For each verse one will find, following the Textus Receptus, a list of the defective manuscripts, a list of citations of the verse by the Fathers (a unique and formidable source of information), and a full apparatus of the Greek, Latin, and Syriac New Testament manuscripts. The information is presented in an easily readable format, and many valuable observations can be made. For example, for Luke 11:2 (the beginning of the Lord's Prayer) the famous reading "Your Spirit come upon us and purify us" (minuscule 700 and Gregory of Nyssa, *Homiliae in orationem dominicam* 3.737–38) is presented well. Unfortunately, the source for of this strange reading by Maximus the Confessor (not Maximus of Turin, as Bruce M. Metzger[31] wrongly assumes) is not mentioned.

---

[27] John S. Kloppenborg, *The Formation of Q: Trajectories in Ancient Wisdom Collections* (SAC; Philadelphia; Fortress, 1987); Ronald A. Piper, *Wisdom in the Q-tradition: The Aphoristic Teaching of Jesus* (SNSTMS 61; Cambridge: Cambridge University Press, 1989); Migaku Sato, *Q und Prophetie, Studien zur Gattungs- und Traditionsgeschichte der Quelle Q* (WUNT 2, Reihe 29; Tübingen: Mohr, 1988); Dieter Zeller, *Kommentar zur Logienquelle* (SKKNT 21; Stuttgart: Katholisches Bibelwerk, 1984); Joël Delobel, ed., *Logia, Les paroles de Jésus – The Sayings of Jesus. Mémorial J. Coppens* (BETL 49; Leuven: Leuven University Press, 1982).

[28] Gerd Petzke, *Das Sondergut des Evangeliums nach Lukas* (Zürcher Werkkommentare zur Bibel; Zürich: Theologischer Verlag, 1990).

[29] Ibid., 235–41; Petzke explains well how one should deal with myths in a scientific century through *Entmythologisierung* and *Remythisierung*, in dialogue with Rudolf Bultmann on one side and Eugen Drewermann on the other.

[30] *The Gospel According to St. Luke* (ed. American and British Committees of the International Greek New Testament Project; 2 vols.; The New Testament in Greek 3; Oxford: Clarendon, 1984–1987).

[31] Bruce M. Metzger, *A Textual Commentary on the Greek New Testament* (London/New York: United Bible Societies, 1971) 155.

Why not? Presumably because this church father lived after the chronological deadline (500 C.E.). Another feature of this edition is that the apparatus, for all practical purposes, is a permanent source of mistakes for both the author and the reader. In spite of these limitations, the two volumes are a welcome tool, providing a handy and comprehensive view of the manuscript evidence for the Gospel of Luke.

In recent years, sympathy for the Western text of Luke and Acts has been growing in France. In the new edition of the introduction to textual criticism by Léon Vaganay, Christian-Bernard Amphoux has made a good case for this form of the Lukan text.[32] At the same time, Marie-Émile Boismard and Arnaud Lamouille on the one side,[33] and the late Edouard Delebecque on the other,[34] came to the conviction that the two recensions of the Acts of the Apostles are equally venerable and equally Lukan. These French scholars are convinced that the so-called western readings of Acts bear marks of genuine Lukan style. But the discovery of Papyrus Bodmer XIV–XV ($\mathfrak{P}^{75}$), the oldest witness for the Gospel of Luke, has established the great age and value of the Egyptian text.[35] Therefore, only two solutions remain for supporters of the Western text: either the two texts are both witnesses of a lost original (the theory of Boismard and Lamouille) or Luke himself produced two editions of Luke-Acts (the strange hypothesis of Delebecque). This latter theory is not new; it was already proposed by Friedrich Blass.[36] In contrast to Blass, however, Delebecque believes that the Western text is an amplification by Luke himself (!) of the text preserved in the Egyptian tradition.

In his defense of the Western text, Christian-Bernard Amphoux goes even further and places it in the primary position:

On the basis of this hypothesis, those who, following von Soden's exceptional insights, have upheld the primitive character of the "Western" text have, by their persistence in the face of opposition and technical difficulties, been the pioneers of what could be, in the not too distant future, a radical new conception of first-century Christianity.[37]

I remain rather skeptical with respect to such hypotheses. I still prefer the shorter Egyptian text and cannot believe in a double edition of Luke-Acts written by

---

[32] Léon Vaganay and Christian-Bernard Amphoux, *Initiation à la critique textuelle du Nouveau Testament* (2d ed.; Paris, Cerf, 1986); ET: *An Introduction to New Testament Textual Criticism* (trans. Jenny Heimerdinger; Cambridge: Cambridge University Press, 1991).

[33] Marie-Émile Boismard and Arnaud Lamouille, *Le texte occidental des Actes. Reconstitution et réhabilitation* (2 vols. Synthèse 17; Paris: Éditions Recherche sur les Civilisations, 1984). Since 1984 these authors have published a large commentary on the Book of Acts: idem, *Les Actes des deux apôtres* (3 vols.; ÉtBib n.s. 12–14; Paris: Gabalda, 1990).

[34] Edouard Delebecque, *Les deux Actes des apôtres* (ÉtBib n.s. 6; Paris: Gabalda, 1990).

[35] Victor Martin and Rodolphe Kasser, *Papyrus Bodmer XIV–XV, Évangiles de Luc et de Jean*, $\mathfrak{P}^{75}$ (2 vols.; Cologny/Geneva: Bibliotheca Bodmeriana, 1961).

[36] Friedrich Blass, *Acta apostolorum, sive Lucae ad Theophilum liber alter, editio philologica* (Göttingen: Vandenhoeck & Ruprecht, 1895).

[37] Vaganay and Amphoux, *Introduction*, 171.

Luke himself. However, I admire the originality of Amphoux's research. Using Luke 5 as a test case, he attempts to reconstruct the history of the text from the first to the second century. He believes that Papia's knowledge of the Gospel tradition and the responsibility assigned to Polycarp by Ignatius favor a first edition of the four Gospels in the first quarter of the second century. The text of this edition would be similar to the longer Western text. Only later, after the disillusionment of the Bar Kokhba rebellion, did the church's theological schools – first in Rome and then in Alexandria – prepare a second edition of the New Testament. According to Amphoux, the successful text of this revised edition is the Egyptian text of about 175 C.E.[38]

The Structure of Luke's Gospel

A new kind of Lukan study, encompassing rhetorical, structural, and literary interpretations, has emerged as a result of two complementary causes. The first cause is the gradual increase of skepticism facing the historical-critical method, particularly the two-source hypothesis and the excesses of redaction criticism. The second cause is the growing interest in literary interpretation in the fields of English and French literature. In this new approach, each gospel is not primarily the result of the composition of traditional materials, actualized by a historical author confronting a particular ecclesiastical or existential situation; rather, it is "an intricately designed religious universe, with plot and character development, retrospective and prospective devices, linear and concentric patterning, and a continuous line of thematic cross-reference and narrative interlockings."[39]

I know of five new commentaries and interpretations along these lines, two in English and three in French. Charles H. Talbert[40] combines a literary view with a socio-cultural approach: the literary structure and function of the twofold work of Luke are dependent on the historical situation of Christianity at the end of the first century. In his view, such a narrative in two parts – one devoted to the founder of a new religious movement, the other devoted to his successors – had a legitimizing function in antiquity: "This narrative of Jesus and the early Church is a legitimation document: its story is told with a persuasiveness intended to give certainty."[41] Three elements support this purpose of the work: (1) the story of the martyrdom of the hero; (2) the stories of his great works, namely, his miracles;

---

[38] Christian-Bernard Amphoux, "Les premières éditions de Luc, I, Le texte de Luc 5." *EThL* 67 (1991) 312–27; idem, "Les premières éditions de Luc, II, L'historie du texte au IIᵉ siècle," *EThL* 68 (1992) 38–48.

[39] Werner Kelber, "Redaction Criticism: On the Nature and Exposition of the Gospels," *PRSt* 6 (1979) 14, quoted in Talbert, *Reading Luke*, 2.

[40] Talbert, *Reading Luke*.

[41] Ibid., 5.

(3) the memory of the prophecies and oracles, which are now fulfilled in the life of the founder of the religious and philosophical movement. It is not always easy, however, to see the connection between these propositions[42] and the shape of the literary interpretation. Talbert no longer divides Luke's gospel into three parts, as Hans Conzelmann does,[43] but into four: "Prophecies of future greatness" (1:5–4:15); "Anointed with the Holy Spirit" (4:16–9:50); "Guidance on the Way" (9:51–19:44); "Martyrdom and vindication" (19:45–24:53).

The exegetical sensitivity of Robert C. Tannehill[44] is well known. From his new perspective, theological insights are no longer gained through synoptic comparison and genetic explanation (redaction versus tradition) but, in his own words, by detecting "disclosures" that Luke "has carefully provided," "disclosures of the over-arching purpose which unifies the narrative." The "literary clues show the importance of these disclosures."[45] "On the borderline between character and plot,"[46] Tannehill reads a story emerging "as a dialogue between God and a recalcitrant humanity."[47] Lukan literary devices are parallelisms, internal connections, progressive sequences, and repetitions. French scholars such as Roland Meynet, Charles L'Eplattenier, and Jean-Noël Aletti are driven by the same forces that drove Tannehill and Talbert. Searching for a similar general coherence, they use the tools of ancient rhetoric (Meynet) and narratology (Aletti).

As a student of Georges Mounin, Meynet received a good education in linguistics.[48] He contrasts Hebraic and Greek rhetoric and elaborates the Jewish rules of story-writing: what corresponds to the Greek *dispositio* is a coherent appeal to special figures, parallelisms, chiasms, repetitions, inclusions, and so on. What has been wrongly labeled the episodic style of Luke is actually a series of sequences constituting an organic literary composition of these very figures. Like Talbert, he sees in the Gospel a story in four stages: the coming of Jesus, prepared by John (1:5–4:13); the call of the disciples in Galilee (4:14–9:50); the progression of Jesus and his disciples to Jerusalem (9:51–21:38, note this late break); and what he calls the Passover of Jesus the Christ (22:1–24:53).[49] In his latest work,[50] Meynet, after dividing the four stages mentioned above into a total of twenty-eight sequences, places two sequences at the heart of the Gospel: the last sequence of stage two

---

[42] One of these propositions has been criticized; it does not seem that a genre existed with (1) the life of the founder, and (2) the story of his successors. See David L. Balch, "The Genre of Luke-Acts: Individual Biography, Adventure Novel, or Political History?" *SWJT* 33 (1990) 5–6.

[43] Hans Conzelmann, *Die Mitte der Zeit, Studien zur Theologie des Lukas* (2d ed.; BHTh 17; Tübingen: Mohr Siebeck, 1962).

[44] Tannehill, *The Narrative Unity of Luke-Acts.*

[45] Ibid., 1.1.

[46] Ibid.

[47] Ibid., 1.2.

[48] See Meynet's first work, *Quelle est donc cette Parole?* 1.11–19.

[49] Meynet, *L'Évangile selon saint Luc.*

[50] Meynet, *Avez-vous lu saint Luc?*

(9:1–50: the disciples called to do what Jesus does), and the first sequence of stage three (9:51–10:42: the departure to the passion). Even if Meynet remains cautious, he has the unfortunate tendency to see concentric structures everywhere – the triumph of the chiasm in the Hebrew narrative structure.

My two objections to these works concern their structural divisions and the paraphrastic character of their interpretation. For example, if one compares Meynet and Talbert on the beginning of the travel narrative (9:51ff.), one discovers two completely different divisions of the text, although both presuppose the presence of a chiasm at this point. For Talbert,[51] 9:51–10:24 forms a concentric unity: 9:51–56 = A; 10:1–24 = A¹; and 9:57–62 = B. A and A¹ point to the Lukan theology of the word (mission and missionary behavior), A to the future Christian mission in Samaria and A¹ to the mission to the Gentiles; B points to the costs of discipleship. For Meynet,[52] there is a much larger chiasm: 9:51–56 corresponds to 10:38–42 and is determined by the notion of departure; 9:57–10:11 is determined by the announcement of the kingdom of God and human free will in the light of this announcement. An example of paraphrastic interpretation appears in Tannehill's comments on the story of the feeding of the five thousand: (a) the Twelve have a prominent role in the story, (b) the narrative "focusses on the interaction between Jesus and the twelve," (c) the excess of food "suggests that the apostles are abundantly supplied for their future mission."[53]

A positive aspect of the work of literary interpreters, in spite of their reluctance to use source criticism, is the fact that they are quite open to the exploration of intertextuality. This is true particularly with respect to the relationship of the Gospels to parallels and to analogous stories in Hebrew scripture, as, for example, in the case of the relationship of the feeding of the five thousand to the cycle of the stories of Elijah (1 Kings 17) and Elisha (2 Kgs 4:42–44).[54]

Luke and Judaism

I was surprised by the recent lively debate stemming from the discussion between Jacob Jervell and the exegetical consensus. For most exegetes, Luke is a Gentile trying to legitimate a gentile Christianity that is free from the law, yet related to scripture. For Jervell, however, the theological perspective of Luke-Acts is rooted not in the failure of the Christian mission to the Jews, but in its success.[55]

---

[51] Talbert, *Reading Luke*, 114–19.
[52] Meynet, *Avez-vous lu saint Luc?* 32–37.
[53] Tannehill, *Narrative Unity of Luke-Acts*, 216–17.
[54] See the allusion to Jean-Noël Aletti's Work above (p. 27).
[55] Jacob Jervell, *Luke and the People of God: A New Look at Luke-Acts* (Minneapolis: Augsburg, 1984). For my own opinion on this position, see Bovon, *Luke the Theologian*, 334–39.

In the 1980s, attention focused quite unexpectedly on the way in which Luke shows positive appreciation for the Jewish people, the Jewish law, and the Jewish temple. Two phenomena may help to explain this sparking of interest: first, the more general debate about the relationship of Judaism and Christianity after the Holocaust; and second, the introduction of sociological methods into the field of New Testament scholarship. The first phenomenon raises theological reflection on the question of the law. Is the Jewish law still relevant for Luke? If so, in what sense? The second phenomenon requires some thought about the social situation of Luke and his audience. As a consequence, many interpreters today think that Luke himself was a Jew and that his main interest was Israel rather than the gentile mission. Is this assumption correct?

While theology served as the starting point in the 1960s,[56] it now appears to be only an implication of a particular socio-cultural reading. To use Jean-Paul Sartre's definition of freedom, Luke is determined by his personal social background and is not free to reject these determinants ("The main point is not what has been done to the human being, but what he does about what has been done to him"[57]). I have chosen several divergent positions to illustrate the recent discussion.

Robert L. Brawley,[58] for instance, tries to break the conventional pattern. For him, Luke 4:16–30 is not an example showing that the gospel was rejected by the Jews and therefore passed on to the Gentiles. Rather, it is a piece of literature that was meant to designate the identity of Jesus. Similarly, the second half of Acts is not a long description of a Christian church that has cut the lines by which it was anchored in Judaism, but simply a description of the Pauline mission:

Therefore, the standard paradigm for understanding Luke's view of the relation between Christianity and Judaism should pivot 180 degrees. That is, rather than setting Gentile Christianity free, Luke ties it to Judaism. And rather than rejecting the Jews, Luke appeals to them.[59]

Luke does not reject the non-Christian Jews but offers reconciliation with them.

As is well known, the position of Jack T. Sanders[60] is completely different. He refuses to delete the anti-Jewish traits of Luke-Acts:

In my own contribution to the debate, I examined the way in which the author of Luke-Acts presented the Jewish leaders, Jerusalem, the Jewish people, the Pharisees, and what I chose to call the periphery, Samaritans, proselytes, and God-fearers. I concluded, among

---

[56] Bovon, *Luke the Theologian*, 323–39.

[57] "Jean-Paul Sartre répond," *L'Arc* 30 (1966) 95.

[58] Robert L. Brawley, *Luke-Acts and the Jews: Conflict, Apology, and Conciliation* (SBLMS 33; Atlanta: Scholars Press, 1987).

[59] Ibid., 159.

[60] Jack T. Sanders, *The Jews in Luke-Acts* (London: SCM, 1987); idem, "The Jewish People in Luke-Acts," in *Luke-Acts and the Jewish People: Eight Critical Perspectives* (ed. Joseph B. Tyson; Minneapolis: Augsburg, 1988) 51–75; idem, "Who Is a Jew and Who Is a Gentile in the Book of Acts?" *NTS* 37 (1991) 434–55.

other things, that Haenchen was essentially correct, that the author of Luke-Acts does view the Jewish people generally as opposed to the purposes of God, as unable to understand their own scriptures, and as both foreordained to reject and wilfully rejecting their own salvation.[61]

Sander's main goal is to investigate the reason for this theological attitude. In his opinion, it is not Jewish persecution that motivated the negative judgment on the part of Luke, but intellectual and practical Jewish opposition to the Christian message. Having established this understanding of Luke – which is correct, in my view – Sanders continues to condemn Luke, accusing him of an anti-Judaim as stark as that in the Gospel of John.

The doctoral dissertation of Matthias Klinghardt[62] is a very insightful work, but difficult to read. He begins with questions about Luke's understanding of the content and function of the Mosaic law. With regard to the content, he arrives at a fine and subtle solution. Luke's reading of the law underlines rules of purity and the renunciation of wealth (see Luke 16). The Apostolic Decree (Acts 15:28–29) states that the Gentiles must also follow several rules of purity, and the Gospel of Luke shows that a wealthy Jewish Christian is subject to the moral law of poverty. Henceforth, voluntary poverty becomes a necessary legal condition for obtaining salvation (the polemic against the Pharisees is so bitter because they impose only external purity requirements but no internal moral conditions). In contradistinction to Paul, Luke is not replacing salvation through works with salvation through faith, but rather salvation through ritual works with salvation through Christ and moral works. The required obedience has not only a soteriological function but also an ecclesiological component: it brings the convert into the company of the real people of God. According to Klinghardt, the gentile Christians are the poor in the Lukan congregation while the Jewish Christians are the rich. Luke tries to convince these rich Jewish Christians to accept the poor gentile converts as brothers and sisters.

In an analysis of Acts 13:38–39 and 15:10–11, Klinghardt demonstrates that Luke is arguing on an ecclesiological as well as on a soteriological level. One of the important functions of the law is to determine who belongs to the true Israel. This implies that the law has not been abolished. These verses should not be understood, as they usually are, against the background of Pauline theology. The Lukan community is mixed and includes a strong Jewish-Christian element. In this community, obedience to the law and union with Christ belong together, just as the Decalogue and the commandment of love (Luke 10:25–37) form a unity.

---

[61] Sanders, "Who Is a Jew," 436.

[62] Matthias Klinghardt, *Das lukanische Verständnis des Gesetzes nach Herkunft, Funktion und seinem Ort in der Geschichte der Urchristentums* (WUNT 2/32; Tübingen: Mohr Siebeck, 1988).

The works of Kalervo Salo[63] and Philip F. Esler[64] also deserve attention. Salo finds that Luke's interest in the law is practical rather than theological. The Jewish Christians are invited to maintain a formal obedience to the law, while the gentile Christians are liberated from its burden. For the former, one can speak of a covenant in the law (νόμος), but for the latter only of a covenant. Esler's approach is determined more by a socio-cultural than by a theological perspective. What motivates Luke is both his community's critical discussion with Judaism and its strong crisis of identity. Three factors are pertinent: the converts' former religious affiliations (ranging from pagan idolatry to Jewish conservatism); their economic situation (including the highest as well as the lowest strata of the economic spectrum); their political positions (ranging from submission to Rome to a determination to fight for independence). Luke freely reshapes the gospel tradition for a practical response to the needs of his fellow Christians. Luke-Acts may thus be described as an exercise in legitimating a sectarian movement.

To conclude this section, I would add some personal comments. First, among the books of the New Testament Luke-Acts is the text that is both the most open to universalism and the most favorable to Israel. Luke describes the Jewish roots of the church and the universal geographical expansion of the gospel with equal affection. Second, it is unfortunate that in the heat of the present discussion and its polemic there is a tendency to forget the previous discussion. The names of Frank Stagg, Philippe Menoud, Jacques Dupont, J.C. O'Neill, Joachim Gnilka, Augustin George, Stephen G. Wilson, and Paul Zingg, scholars who wrote in the 1960s and 1970s, rarely appear.[65]

Third, to a greater degree than many recent writers, I would emphasize the discontinuity between Israel and the church. The ideological defense of the universalism that is visible throughout the Gospel of Luke and the Acts of the Apostles[66] appears to me to be the religious counterpart of Roman imperial ambitions. Luke's description of the Christian communities in their confrontation with the Judaic world is, from the sociological point of view and in the terminology of Ernst Troeltsch, a testimony of a sectarian identity. The situation of Christianity in the time of Luke is not yet that of early catholicism. Summing up his entire work in Acts 28:26–27, Luke quotes Isa 6:9–10. One cannot be blind with respect to the function of this last quotation, especially in the light of its introduction and interpretation (Acts 28:25, 28). The introduction underlines the consensus be-

---

[63] Kalervo Salo, *Luke's Treatment of the Law: A Redaction-Critical Investigation* (AASF, Dissertationes humanarum litterarum 57; Helsinki: Suomalainen Tiedeakatemia, 1991).

[64] Philip F. Esler, *Community and Gospel in Luke-Acts: The Social and Political Motivations of Lucan Theology* (SNTSMS 57; Cambridge: Cambridge University Press, 1987).

[65] The studies of all these scholars, as well as those of Hans Conzelmann, Ernst Haenchen, and Jacob Jervell are discussed in Bovon, *Luke the Theologian*, 323–43.

[66] François Bovon, "Israel, die Kirche und die Völker im lukanischen Doppelwerk," *ThLZ* 108 (1983) 403–14.

tween the Hebrew prophet Isaiah and the Christian preacher Paul, both inspired by the Spirit of God and both contrasted with the Jewish leaders, whose discord Luke mentions explicitly (Acts 28:25: "they disagreed with each other"). The interpretation of the quotation from Isaiah asserts: "Let it be known to you then that this salvation of God has been sent to the Gentiles; they will listen" (Acts 28:28). There remains only one uncertainty: is there a slight hope for the salvation of Israel expressed in the last phrase of the quotation, if one can read it in the future tense, "and I shall heal them"? I would answer this question positively. Luke is then, indeed, a pupil, albeit an indirect pupil, of Paul (compare Rom 11:25–36).[67]

Finally, salvation is offered by God, who showed a continuing love during the entire life and ministry of Jesus. Jesus' words (see Luke 6:47) are the actual revelation of the will of God and the eschatological and Spirit-empowered interpretation of the law. Like the prophetic scriptures, the law maintains the dual function of testifying to the future of the divine economy of salvation and of preparing the expression of the new obedience (see the twofold commandment of love). However, conversion is more important than obedience, because it is the way to God for human beings; the way of God to human salvation is found throughout the entire life of Jesus and in his resurrection.[68]

The Theology of Luke

Luke is a good storyteller, pleasant to read and easy to understand. It is more difficult to grasp what he believes and why he writes. As a theologian, he is an enigmatic figure. This explains the great variety of keys used to understand his theology.

In the 1950s, Philipp Vielhauer and Hans Conzelmann presented Luke as a creative mind and a theologian of history who was able to rethink eschatology in terms of the history of salvation.[69] Twenty years later, due to the intellectual force of the works of such Roman Catholic theologians as Heinz Schürmann, Joseph Ernst, Gerhard Schneider, Augustin George, and Joseph Fitzmyer, the Third

---

[67] François Bovon, "'Schön hat der heilige Geist durch den Propheten Jesaja zu euren Vätern gesprochen' (Act 28,25)," *ZNW* 75 (1984) 345–50; English translation here pp. 113–19.

[68] On the topic of Luke and Judaism see also Lawrence M. Wills, "The Depiction of the Jews in Acts," *JBL* 110 (1991) 631–54; and David A. Neale, *None but the Sinners: Religious Categories in Gospel of Luke* (JSNTSup 58; Sheffield: Sheffield Academic Press, 1991). That Jesus is for the sinners and against the Pharisees is, according to Neale, not a historical memory but an ideological interpretation. On Luke's view of the temple, see Bovon, *L'Évangile selon saint Luc*, 139 n. 28 (with bibliography).

[69] Philipp Vielhauer, "Zum 'Paulinismus' der Apostelgeschichte," *EvTh* 10 (1950–1951) 1–15, reprinted idem, *Aufsätze zum Neuen Testament* (ThBü 31; Munich: Kaiser, 1965) 9–27; Conzelmann, *Die Mitte der Zeit.*

Evangelist developed a much more pastoral character.[70] The main theological weight was no longer placed on the view of the end of the time, but on the time of the church – a time that was not so separated from the time of Christ's life. In the numerous books and articles published by Jacques Dupont,[71] the Lukan Christ occupies center stage. Not merely the cross or the teaching or the resurrection, but the whole course of his life from the birth to the ascension is the focus of attention.[72] I am quite comfortable with this christological understanding of Luke's work, and I am tring to connect it with the Lukan theology of the word of God and its necessary human and historical mediation. Of course, Lukan théology does not emphasize knowing Christ per se, his nature and his metaphysical identity, but – to use Philipp Melanchthon's definition – "his benefactions." Several scholars, such as Robert F. O'Toole and Robert J. Karris,[73] have insisted upon this soteriological accent to Luke's theology.

No general agreement has been reached concerning Luke's theology during the last decade, but a number of specific tendencies can be identified:

(1) Constantly recurring is the emphasis on Luke's ethics (many state that Luke is a pragmatic thinker), particularly on the ethics of money (Luise Schottroff and Wolfgang Stegemann[74]), or, more recently, on the ethics of loving one's enemies (Josephine Massyngbaerde Ford[75]).

(2) More original is the theological consideration of the Lukan stories, which are no longer read as holy scripture but as mythopoeic art. Eugen Drewermann[76] presents a Jungian type of psychoanalytic understanding of the birth stories. From a post-Bultmannian perspective, Gerd Petzke[77] reads Luke and his special

---

[70] Heinz Schürmann, *Das Lukasevangelium I* (HThKNT 3; Freiburg; Herder, 1969); Joseph Ernst, *Das Evangelium nach Lukas übersetzt und erklärt* (RNT; Regensburg: Pustet, 1977); Augustin George, *Études sur l'œuvre de Luc* (SB; Paris: Gabalda, 1978); Gerhard Schneider, *Das Evangelium nach Lukas* (2 vols.; 2d ed.; ÖTKNT 3.1–2; Gütersloh: Gütersloh Verlagshaus and Würzburg: Echter Verlag, 1984); Joseph A. Fitzmyer, *The Gospel According to Luke* (2 vols.; AB 28–28A: New York: Doubleday, 1981–1985).

[71] A bibliography of Dupont's works can be found in *À cause de l'Évangile: Études sur les Synoptiques et les Actes offertes au P. Jacques Dupont O.S.B à l'occasion de son 70e anniversaire* (LD 123; Paris: Cerf; Bruges: Saint-André, 1985) 809–26.

[72] Emmeram Kränkl, *Jesus, der Knecht Gottes: Die heilsgeschichtliche Stellung Jesu in den Reden der Apostelgeschichte* (Biblische Untersuchungen 8; Regensburg: Pustet, 1972); Gerhard Lohfink, *Die Himmelfahrt Jesu: Untersuchungen zu den Himmelfahrts- und Erhöhungstexten bei Lukas* (SANT 26; Munich: Kösel, 1971).

[73] Robert F. O'Toole, *The Unity of Luke's Theology: An Analysis of Luke-Acts* (GNS 9; Wilmington, Del.; Glazier, 1984); Robert J. Karris, *Luke: Artist and Theologian: Luke's Passion Account as Literature* (Theological Inquiries; New York: Paulist, 1985).

[74] Luise Schottroff and Wolfgang Stegemann, *Jesus von Nazareth: Hoffnung der Armen* (2d ed.; Urban Taschenbücher 639; Stuttgart: Kohlhammer, 1981).

[75] Josephine Massyngbaerde Ford, *My Enemy is My Guest: Jesus and Violence in Luke* (New York: Crossroad, 1984).

[76] Eugen Drewermann, *Dein Name ist wie der Geschmack des Lebens: Tiefenpsychologische Deutung der Kindheitsgeschichte nach dem Lukasevangelium* (Freiburg: Herder, 1986).

[77] See above n. 28.

materials in a dialectic of demythologizing mythological statements and mythologizing historical events; this is presented in a polemical dialogue with an over-scientific modern conception of reality.

(3) It is strange that during the years of heated debate over Lukan salvation history there was no consideration of Luke's theology in the narrower sense, that is, as a doctrine about God. Following Jacques Dupont's complaint about this omission, Karl Erlemann[78] investigated the Lukan description of God through an analysis of the metaphors, parables, and references to the Hebrew scriptures. According to Erlemann's investigation, Luke's God is more the Lord than the Judge. It is in God's function as the Lord that God will rescue and save. While respecting the freedom of human beings, God rejoices when his people accept the offer of salvation. As Mammon is the negative counterpart of God, it is logical that the renunciation of possessions becomes the corollary of faith in Christ the Lord. The image of God also has an integrative force in its ecclesiological function.

(4) What could be called a typological reading of Luke, or an understanding of his work in light of the Hebrew Bible, follows the line of patristic interpretation. David P. Moessner, in his important book, analyzes the Lukan travel narrative and arrives at the conclusion that Luke saw this decisive step in the career of Jesus as a counterpart and antitype of the founding event of Israel, namely, as the exodus of the people from Egypt to the Promised Land. According to this perspective, Jesus is seen as the last prophet, indeed as a prophet like Moses (Deut 18:15, 18), that is, the rejected messenger of God from the Deuteronomistic tradition. As a consequence, Israel is seen as a "stiff-necked people": "Luke's central section is the story of the journeying salvation of the new Exodus prophesied by Moses to the people of the Horeb covenant as the fulfillment of the promises to Abraham and his descendants."[79]

The First Reception of the Gospel of Luke

The history of interpretation is a relatively young discipline. Historians found the historical investigations of the exegetes too theological; exegetes were disappointed by the results of the historians because of the lack of theological relevance. In the guild of New Testament scholars, the history of intepretation is often perceived as an interesting cultural addition, but not an indispensible tool. In my view, the earliest reception of a New Testament book, although there may be only a few witnesses for this reception, is of capital importance. I have suggested to a doctoral student the idea of writing a dissertation about the Gospel of Luke in the

---

[78] Karl Erlemann, *Das Bild Gottes in den synoptischen Gleichnissen* (BWANT 126; Stuttgart: Kohlhammer, 1988).

[79] David P. Moessner, *Lord of the Banquet: The Literary and Theological Significance of the Lukan Travel Narrative* (Minneapolis: Fortress, 1989) 290.

second century: extending the Lukan trajectory into this period and asking who was interested in Luke. Why did the Gnostics use an allegorical method of interpretation for a document that seems to us to be historically rather than metaphorically oriented? What form of the text did Marcion have at his disposal? Did he also use some of the same written sources Luke used, as, for example, the source of Luke's special material or an earlier form of the Gospel (Proto-Luke)? Was Marcion the only one who corrected Luke's text? Marcion accused the catholics of doing as much, and Tertullian does not refute this criticism. What kind of influence did the Gospel of Luke have on apocryphal texts such as the *Protevangelium of James*, the *Infancy Gospel of Thomas,* the *Apocalypse of Peter*, and the *Gospel of Thomas*? What can be said about the most ancient witnesses to the direct textual transmission: that is, the title, the presentation, and the text of the oldest extant copies on papyrus, especially $\mathfrak{P}^{75}$ (Papyrus Bodmer XIV-XV)? At the date of the writing of this papyrus (ca. 225 C.E.), the Gospel of Luke was already detached from the Acts of the Apostles, and the latter was transmitted separately. Luke is no longer an "author": he has become one of the evangelists. His work is no longer a piece of historical literature written and distributed for private profit; it has become sacred scripture for ecclesiastical edification.

The oldest extant notices about the evangelist are also noteworthy, regardless of their historical value. The Muratorian Canon gives the name "Luke" to the author – a name that never occurs in the text of the work itself – and describes him as a fellow worker of the apostle Paul. Unfortunately, we do not possess the testimony of Bishop Papias of Hierapolis; but we do have the witness of Irenaeus, as well as the so-called *Antimarcionite Prologue*, the first part of which may have been written at the end of the second century.[80]

Not much more can be said at this stage, because most of the preceding questions have not yet been sufficiently investigated. Such an investigation is vital, however, because the enigmatic second-century life of the texts that later became incorporated into the New Testament is relevant for understanding the texts themselves in their historical matrix. Historical method has taught us to look for themes that existed prior to the writing of the Gospel and that may have exerted a literary influence. Other scholars, working exclusively with the preserved text, have been dismantling and rebuilding its structure and ideological economy. It is also necessary, however, to appreciate this Gospel as it was read in the second century and to allow this understanding to illuminate what the text could have been in its original state.

---

[80] Koester, *Ancient Christian Gospels*, 334–36; Bovon, *L'Évangile selon saint Luc*, 27–29.

Conclusion

First of all, it seems a relatively easy task to enumerate the fields of research and to circumscribe the relevant duties of each discipline. I am in good company when I advocate a multiplicity of approaches. In view of the diversity of the methods of inquiry, however, it is more difficult to take the next necessary step: to find the intellectual strength to coordinate the several fields of inquiry.

The following example may serve to illustrate my hopes for the direction of future research. *The Birth of the Codex*, written by two librarians, Colin H. Roberts and T. C. Skeat, is in my opinion a theological work.[81] Through firsthand information about the origin of the codex and through codicological insights, it brings to light the social world and the beliefs of the Alexandrian Christians at the turn of the third century. Such an endeavor truly provides a fresh understanding and marks a notable advance in the field of theology.

It is necessary to overcome exclusivistic methods. Interest in the structure of Luke-Acts and in rules of literary composition are not incompatible with the historical perspective. Indeed, literary devices that try to uncover the overall structure of an ancient work must be situated at a specific time and in a particular society. There may be universally valid laws for the telling of a story, but it is still necessary to know the local habits of Greeks and Jews in the period of late antiquity. An analogous request can be made of historians and philologists. Because of the nature of biblical texts, historical and philological work that is done in hermetic isolation from religion and theology will result in a misunderstanding of the Gospel and its message.

My second comment is a request that I address to myself as well as to teachers and scholars whom I know. The level of philological sophistication, as far as I can judge, is usually excellent in the interpretation of the Hebrew Bible, but there are too many commentators of the New Testament who fall short of this same level of philological expertise. Some may be interested only in the study of sources, others give attention only to literary structure; if one adds to this the general decline of learning in the disciplines of the classical humanities, one can well understand the reasons for the existing deficiencies in philology.

Discussions with my friend Bertrand Bouvier, the professor of modern Greek in the University of Geneva, have given me a new sensitivity for the biblical language of the New Testament. If one devotes close and sensitive attention to each word, the word becomes alive and shines brightly. In Luke 5:6, for example, συγκλείω must not be read with disregard for the preposition σύν: the composite verb describes a circular movement by which fish are imprisoned together. In the following verse, κατένευσαν should not be translated "they called" to those in an-

---

[81] Colin H. Roberts and T. C. Skeat, *The Birth of the Codex* (The British Academy; London/ New York: Oxford University Press, 1983).

other boat to help, as in some commentaries. Philological accuracy requires the translation of κατανεύω as "to make signs." These observations lead to the conclusion that the Lukan text describes a traditional way of fishing in the ancient world.[82]

Interest in the small details is not dictated by the belief that small is beautiful, but by the conviction that through concrete and specific cultural and social realities one can learn about the general and universal structures of human life. Is it not said in the biblical tradition that spiritual life is bound to historical events, and that universal salvation comes through the election of particular people – Israel, Christ Jesus, and Christian fellowship?

My third and last comment concerns the theological orientation of Luke. In my opinion, the evangelist's vital preoccupation is to give shape to the memory of Jesus and to capture and confirm in words the remembrance of his deeds and sayings. However aesthetically pleasing the result of the work of his pen may be, his artistic shaping of the tradition corresponds to a necessity of his faith, namely, to give written support to the oral teaching and preaching. Otherwise the message would raise hopes without assuring confidence and continuity, and the gospel message might be caused to stumble in the face of Jewish and pagan opposition that sought to disfigure Jesus' intentions and actions. Luke is certain that the ministry of Jesus is nothing less than the final word of God, the fulfillment of prophecies and the anticipation of the last events. He is fully convinced that the coming of Jesus is the decisive and final step in the history of God with his people. The words of Jesus the Lord are for Luke the source of life; Jesus' fate, death, resurrection, and ascension are the prelude to the last days. Beginning with those events, the recapitulation of the course of Jesus' ministry, the proclamation of the word, the manifestation of the Spirit, and the practice of the double commandment to love are the great things that must be told. This is exactly what Luke endeavors to tell in the book of Acts, while remembering that this movement into the future is not yet triumphant.

---

[82] Bovon, *L'Évangile selon saint Luc*, 226–27.

Meteorology in the Synoptics (Luke 12:54–56 par.)[*]

I. The South Wind and the West Wind

a) Meteorology

Biblical scholars are usually more interested in archaeology than in meteorology. The drawback of this preference is obvious. They do not experience something that has not changed since the time of Jesus: the climate of Palestine and the Mediterranean region. They prefer to focus on the destruction and excavation of civilizations. Yet even present-day knowledge of the winds can help us better understand the ancient texts. It is understandable that agrarian peoples, such as lived in the Palestine of that time, or seafaring peoples, as in ancient Greece, have left behind many documents that speak, literally or metaphorically, of the winds.[1]

Israel was concerned especially with the east wind,[2] which brings drought from the desert. This wind harms plants and grains. We are told as much in the dream of Pharaoh that is reported in Hebrew and in a Palestinian perspective: "Then he fell asleep and dreamed a second time; seven ears of grain, plump and good, were growing on one stalk. Then seven ears, thin and blighted by the east wind, sprouted after them. The thin ears swallowed up the seven plump and full ears. Pharaoh awoke, and it was a dream" (Gen 41:5–7). This east wind yielded so many proverbs that the prophets used it metaphorically in heralding the divine judgment; for example, Ezek 17:10: "When it [the vine] is transplanted, will it thrive? When the east wind strikes it, will it not utterly wither, wither on the bed where it grew?"

From the west, that is, from the sea, come the winter rains and the summer dew. The west wind brings the clouds.[3] How can we forget the hope of the king and

---

[*] Lecture delivered at the Kirchliche Hochschule in Berlin on November 8, 1992. I thank Cilliers Breytenbach and Eckhard Plümacher of the Institut zur Erforschung des Urchristentums in der Spätantike for the invitation and Anita Thomas and Christoph Freymond for generously undertaking the translation into German. English translation by Matthew J. O'Connell. Copyright © Baker Book House Company, 2005.

[1] Oddly enough, I have found few publications on the subject. On Luke 12:54–56 see C. P. März, "Lk 12, 54b–56 par. Mt 16, 2b.3 und die Akoluthie der Redequelle" in SNTSU (11 Linz: A. Fuchs, 1986), 83–96.

[2] Hebrew qādîm; see Gen 41:6.

[3] Hebrew: rûaḥ yām; see Exod 10:19.

the people during the endless droughts and tragic famines? Who could change the weather? Who could make the wind blow from the west and no longer from the east? "Elijah said to Ahab, 'Go up, eat and drink; for there is a sound of rushing rain.' So Ahab went up to eat and drink. Elijah went to the top of Carmel; there he bowed himself down upon the earth and put his face between his knees. He said to his servant, 'Go up now, look toward the sea.' He went up and looked, and said, 'There is nothing.' Then he said, 'Go again seven times.' At the seventh time he said, 'Look, a little cloud no bigger than a man's hand is rising out of the sea'" (1 Kgs 18:41–44).

There are other winds, too, which could be identified with the four quarters of heaven. Knowledge of the winds went with knowledge of the land; meteorology became geography and even cosmology. The material effects of the winds yielded an intellectual structure and, finally, theological metaphors. The "four winds" became a way of speaking of the entire earth; thus the expression "from the four winds" meant "from everywhere" (Jer 49:36; Matt 24:31), while the vision of Zechariah, starting from the four winds, developed a cosmological vision that leads to a universal judgment (Zech 6:1–8).

This knowledge, which was both true-to-life and theoretical, was part of Israel's wisdom tradition. At a later period, we find the same interest expressed in the *Ethiopic Apocalypse of Enoch* (*1 En.* 18, 1; 33–36) and especially in the astronomical section (*1 En.* 76). Knowledge of the winds has meanwhile expanded: the entire universe is now divided into twelve winds (three from each quarter of heaven). Eight of these (two from each quarter) are winds of judgment, and four (one from each quarter) are heralds of life and prosperity.[4] In some manuscripts of *3 Enoch*, we no longer have a "bunch of winds," as in *Ethiopic Enoch*, but a list of all the winds; these no longer reflect meteorological reality but rather the text of the Bible (the list is a kind of concordance under the term "Wind").[5]

In addition to a practical and theoretical approach to the winds, the Israelite sapiential tradition also had a religious and theological view of them. Thus some texts give expression to the belief that God is the creator and master of the winds, just as God is the creator and master of the sea or the mountains (Jer 10:13; Amos 4:23; 1QH IX, 9–13). To judge by one ancient image, Israel believed that the winds, like the waters, were kept in containers that God could open or close as he wished (see Rev 7:1). The mobility of the winds made possible the belief that God used them as messengers or as carriages for

---

[4] On this passage see Siegbert Uhlig, *Das äthiopische Henochbuch* (JSHRZ 5.6; Gütersloh: Gütersloher Verlagshaus, 1984) 653–56.

[5] See P. Alexander, "3 (Hebrew Apocalypse of) Enoch (Fifth-Sixth Century A.D.)," *OTP* 1:307–8.

his journeys. The winds were also connected with the cherubim (Ps 104:3–4; Greek *Vit. Ad.* 38.3).

Farmers had to keep an eye on the heavens and note the direction of the wind; later on, wise men did the same.[6] Their wisdom conceived of a God who was not only radically active in creation but who also used weather and history to manifest himself in the life of his people.

b) The Connection with Geography

First, a clarification: when people travel from Lake Geneva to Rome or Berlin, they take it for granted that the climate changes and that the winds and their names are different. We can imagine how such changes caused headaches for translators in the ancient world. Take, for example, the Jewish translators of the Hebrew Bible who had to translate a Palestinian text while living in Alexandria. In Egypt and in Greece the blazing hot, destructive wind blows not from the east, as in Palestine, but from the south. What, then, were they to do with the text: let it stand or change it? Either they said nothing about the direction from which the wind blew or they adapted the text to fit their own geographical place. This interpretive decision is of special interest to us here because the Greek word for the destructive wind is νότος. Although this word originally meant "wet winter wind," it was also used for the dry summer wind of the Sahara. In any case, it always referred to a south wind. In the eighth plague of the Exodus story, it is the wind that brings the locusts: in Hebrew, qādîm, the east wind. In the Septuagint this word is translated as νότος, the south wind (Exod 10:13, twice). Elsewhere, too, in the Old Testament, qādîm is often translated as νότος (Exod 14:21; Job 38:24; Ps 77[78]:26; Ezek 27:26; 40:44; 42:20).[7] This is the very word that Luke uses in our pericope (Luke 12:54–56).

To sum up: In Palestine the rain usually comes from the west, as it does in Egypt and Greece. But in Egypt and Greece the drought winds and hot weather come from the south and not from the east, as in Palestine.

c) Meteorology and Geography in Luke 12:54–56

If we now turn to our passage in Luke we find a meteorological situation that reflects climatic conditions in Egypt or, better, in Greece rather than those in Palestine. Climatic conditions in the Aegean area are these: In the summer the dry wind comes from the Sahara or the south, as I noted above. This wind is the

---

[6] See Hans Wilhelm Hetzberg, "Wind," *BHH* 3:2175.

[7] See Gerd Theissen, *The Gospels in Context: Social and Political History in the Synoptic Tradition* (trans. Linda M. Maloney; Minneapolis: Fortress, 1991), 253.

"noxious wind from Africa" (*pestilens Africus*), called νότος.[8] This is reflected in Luke 12:55: "When you see the south wind (νότος) blowing, you say, 'There will be scorching heat'; and it happens." In contrast, bad weather and rain come from the west, as Luke says in the preceding verse: "When you see a cloud rising in the west, you immediately say, 'It is going to rain'; and so it happens" (Luke 12:54). A few years ago I was in Athens at the end of August, when the south wind was blowing so strongly from the Sahara that the temperature was unbearable. People talked not of a hot but of a burning wind. And I observed that the Modern Greek word for the weather thus brought by the south wind was the very word Luke uses in our passage: ὁ καύσων (or in everyday language ἡ κάψη).[9]

II. The Source, Q 12:54–56

a) State of the Question

European scholars today often differ from their American counterparts on the sociological and theological locus of Source Q, the collection of sayings attributed to Jesus and contained in the canonical gospels. Another document, the apocryphal *Gospel of Thomas*, also contains some of these sayings. The Q section of the Society for Biblical Literature, led by James M. Robinson, believes that the earliest layer of Q consisted of wisdom sayings.[10] The somewhat older works of Dieter Lührmann and Paul Hoffmann, as well as the recent study by Japanese scholar Migaku Sato, claim, however, that Q was prophetic rather than sapiential in nature.[11] Behind this academic debate lies an important problem that is decisive for grasping the nature of the message of Jesus and of the first Christians: can we still claim that the sayings of Jesus in Q are apocalyptic and that eschatology is constitutive for Christianity? I hope to interpret our pres-

---

[8] R. Böker, "Νότος," *Der Kleine Pauly: Lexikon der Antike* (ed. Konrat Ziegler and Walter Sontheimer; 5 vols.; Munich: Deutscher Taschenbuch Verlag, 1979) 4:168.

[9] I recall the conversation I had at that time with my friend, Christos Yannaras. It was on the day of the burial of Nikos Nissiotis, former director of the Ecumenical Institute of Bossey. Since then I have discussed the philological aspect of the matter with another friend, Bertrand Bouvier, professor of modern Greek literature.

[10] See James M. Robinson, "The Q Trajectory: Between John and Matthew via Jesus," in *The Future of Early Christianity* (ed. Birger A. Pearson; Minneapolis: Fortress, 1991), 173–94; J. S. Kloppenborg, *The Formation of Q: Trajectories in Ancient Wisdom Collections* (SAC; Philadelphia: Fortress, 1987).

[11] See Dieter Lührmann, *Die Redaktion der Logienquelle* (WMANT 33; Neukirchen-Vluyn: Neukirchener, 1969); Paul Hoffmann, *Studien zur Theologie der Logienquelle* (NTAbh NF 8; Münster: Aschendorff, 1972); Migaku Sato, *Q und Prophetie. Studien zur Gattungs- und Traditionsgeschichte der Quelle Q* (WUNT 2/29; Tübingen: Mohr, 1988).

ent passage of the Bible in such a way that I can offer a possible, partial answer to this problem.

b) The Reconstruction of Q 12:54–56

We must first of all compare the version in Luke's gospel with those of the other gospels, that is, the gospel of Matthew (16:2–3) and the *Gospel of Thomas*. In the first part of the passage, Luke and Matthew differ notably in their meteorological statements. Matthew contrasts evening and morning, one red sky with another, and in so doing distinguishes between good weather and bad.[12] Luke is different: he refers not to the red sky or the time of day, and therefore not to two dangers, but to the rain and the heat. Some exegetes have questioned whether Matthew and Luke used the same tradition and the same Q source.[13] In my view, the differences between the two gospels become understandable if we take into account the redactional freedom of each evangelist, as well as the different countries in which they lived, and their meteorological situation. Matthew seems to reflect the meteorological conditions of Palestine or Syria but Luke the climate of the Aegean region, as I said earlier.

The part played by the country in which an author or copyist lives is confirmed by some ancient manuscripts of Matthew that omit the meteorological situation (Matt 16:2b–3). These copyists were Egyptians (Sinaiticus, B, X, Γ, etc.). They preferred perhaps to omit a description that did not seem to fit the landscape in which they lived.[14]

Saying 91 of the *Gospel of Thomas* begins with a christological reference: "They said to him: Tell us who you are, that we may believe in you." Secondly, the saying as given presupposes a short version, one that omits information about the weather. Thirdly, the prophetic statement resembles that of Luke, if we ignore the christological insertion in the middle: "You test the face of the sky and of the earth, and him who is before you you have not known, and you do not know (how) to test this moment (καιρός)" (*Gos. Thom.* 91).[15]

If we try to reconstruct the Q formulation used in the utterance of Jesus, we can omit Luke's address, "You hypocrites!" since it is a typical expansion. We can also prefer Luke's expression, "the appearance of earth and sky" (Matthew speaks only of the "sky"). Finally, we can decide in Luke's favor once again when

---

[12] For the text-critical problem, see n. 14.

[13] See Ulrich Luz, *Matthew 8–20: A Commentary on the Gospel of Matthew* (trans. James E. Crouch; Hermeneia; Minneapolis: Fortress, 2001), 347.

[14] Luz, ibid., cautiously chooses the short text.

[15] Translation of *Gos. Thom.* 91 from Wilhelm Schneemelcher, ed., *New Testament Apocrypha* (trans. R. McL. Wilson; Louisville: Westminster/John Knox, 1991) 1:128.

he writes: "Why do you not know how to interpret (δοκιμάζειν) the present time (τὸν καιρὸν δὲ τοῦτον)?" Matthew reads: "But you cannot interpret the signs of the times (τὰ δὲ σημεῖα τῶν καιρῶν)."[16]

It can be said, in conclusion, that:

a) The main emphasis in this passage comes at the end, where Jesus draws the theological conclusions. This part is constant in the text tradition and is transmitted in all three texts.

b) The first part has to do with local conditions, and each transmitter of the saying seems to have been free to use it as he wished. Luke, for his part, adapts the statement about the meteorological situation to his own country, namely, Greece. He speaks of the south wind (νότος) and of burning heat (καύσων).

III. The Meaning of Verse 56

a) ὁ καιρὸς οὗτος *in Q and on the Lips of Jesus*

Many exegetes act too hastily in their interpretation of this statement of Jesus: "You know how to interpret the appearance of earth and sky, but why do you not know to interpret the present time?" They connect "the present time" with all sorts of things; for example, the commission of Jesus; the presence of the Christ; the unfolding of salvation history; or the postponement of the Parousia.[17] But we should avoid reading our own thoughts into the text and should rather respect the enigmatic character of the saying of Jesus. In Jewish and early Christian literature, "the present time," like "the present age," is usually contrasted with the time or age or world that is still to come. Here, however, the Lukan Jesus does not contrast "the present time" with the future, the eschatological time, but rather

---

[16] The reader must assume the presence of the infinitive διακρίνειν in the second half of the saying. For this meaning of the verb διακρίνω see W. F. Arndt and F. Wilbur Gingrich, *A Greek-English Lexicon of the New Testament* (Chicago: University of Chicago Press, 1957), s.v. διακρίνω.

[17] For Josef Ernst the reference is to Israel in a particular phase of its history (*Das Evangelium nach Lukas* [RNT 3; Regensburg: Friedrich Pustet, 1977], 416). For I. H. Marshall it refers to events connected with the activity of Jesus (*The Gospel of Luke* [NIGTC; Exeter: Paternoster, 1978] 550). For Jean-Daniel Kaestli it is the decisive character of the present time and not an apocalyptic reading of the signs of the immanent end (*L'eschatologie dans l'œuvre de Luc: Ses caractéristiques et sa place dans le développement du Christianisme primitif* [Nouvelle série théologique 22; Geneva: Labor et Fides, 1969], 21–22). For A. George "the present time" is the time of the mission of Jesus ("'Interpréter ce temps' (Luc 12, 54–56)," *Bible et vie chrétienne* 64 [1965]: 20). For G. Klein "the present time" is neither that of the coming of Jesus nor of the messianic gift, but the history of this world after the coming of Jesus ("Die Prüfung der Zeit [Lukas 12, 54–56]," *ZTK* 61 [1964]:377–78).

establishes an opposition between "the present time" and the weather, between the historical situation and natural circumstances.[18]

At this point we are in touch not only with the convictions of the Q community but also perhaps with the view of Jesus himself. He is not speaking here directly of God and his plans, but on the contrary is urging his hearers to examine their own time, their history, and their humanity. There is no evasion here of the *condition humaine*, the universal human limitation, no theology cut off from anthropology and history.

As a prudent farmer or skilled sailor can foresee the weather, so we must learn not only to consider the present, that is, our time, but also to discover the future that is latent in the present. We need to do both: to read human history in our own reality and, more importantly, to decipher God's plan present in it. When Matthew speaks of "the signs of the times" in interpreting the saying, he gives a suitable interpretation of the words of Jesus.

If we open our eyes, as Jesus expects of us, by paying such careful attention to the present time, just as we pay careful attention to the weather, what do we see? It is worth noting that Jesus does not make his question more specific nor does he give an answer. He follows his usual practice of teaching in such a way that he himself does not give the answer but brings his hearers to the point at which they themselves are compelled to seek the answer. In his teaching, Jesus uses neither a simple informative language nor a figurative or symbolic language to express the desired reality. No, Jesus is neither a journalist who informs nor an expert who says what one must do nor a poet who gives hints. He employs kinds of language that most of the time are insufficiently used: dialogical and performative discourse.[19] He neither imposes himself on his hearers nor overwhelms them, nor does he limit himself to giving only partial information. He speaks in such a way that his hearers can develop a relationship with him. Through his language, which is open yet mysterious, clear yet allusive, he urges us to accept a possible new task: he urges us to interpret our time as a time in which divine promises are being fulfilled. It is impressive to see how a criticism ("why do you not know . . .") can turn into a promise, with all the elements that linguists have discovered in this complicated form of discourse.[20] But Jesus also issues an invitation. He invites his hearers to fulfill for themselves the promises that have been given. This is a prophetic

---

[18] See James Barr, *Biblical Words for Time* (2d ed.; SBT 33; London: SCM, 1969), 50–85; Henry J. Cadbury, "Some Lukan Expressions of Time," *JBL* 82 (1963):272–78, says little about καιρός.

[19] On the language of Jesus see Jacques Dupont, *Pourquoi des paraboles? La méthode parabolique de Jésus* (Lire la Bible 46; Paris: Cerf, 1977); Wolfgang Harnisch, *Die Gleichniserzählungen Jesu* (Uni-Taschenbücher 1343; Göttingen: Vandenhoeck und Ruprecht, 1985).

[20] See John R. Searle, *Speech Acts: An Essay in the Philosophy of Language* (Cambridge: Cambridge University Press, 1969), 57–61.

interpretation of a present time that has already been enriched with the divine future. Jesus thus combines the prophetic and the sapiential traditions.

b) The Evangelists

The editors of Q and later on the composers of the gospels were ready, so to speak, to enter into a dialogue with Jesus. This is why they introduced into the words of Jesus some of their own interpretations of the meaning of "the present time." They understood themselves to be invited to do so, and even to have been guilty had they not done so. Matthew is saying: "In the present time are present the signs of the time, that is, the promises of the last days." Thomas thinks: "In the present time Christ has visited us as the transcendent presence of the divine world."[21] But what does Luke discover when he opens his eyes and his believing mind in order to interpret "the present time"?

IV. Luke and ὁ καιρὸς οὗτος

a) The Context

It is important to understand Luke's text on its own terms. Luke 12:49–59 stands between a parable on the government of the Church (the good and the wicked servant, Luke 12:41–48) and a dialogue on conversion (the tower of Siloam, Luke 13:1–9). The verses immediately preceding our passage (vv. 49–53) are still addressed to the disciples, but in our passage the crowd is mentioned as listening (vv. 54–59). The initial verses (vv. 49–53: the apocalyptic disagreement on the coming of Jesus) ground the life of the church in Christology; the final verses (vv. 54–59: our passage and the short parable on reconciliation while on the way to the judge) begin with the presence of the historical Jesus in order to give expression to the return to God. The change of audience in verse 54 serves to link the christological "I" of the preceding verses with the human or ecclesiological "You" who need to understand "the present time." The rhetorical question at the end of our three verses (v. 56) is repeated in a significant way by Luke himself in the next verse (57), which is redactional: "And why do you not judge for yourself what is right?" This redundant question not only repeats the preceding question (v. 56) but is also an introduction to the well-known exhortation to be reconciled with the adversary on the way to the judge (vv. 58–59).

---

[21] See Michael Fieger, *Das Thomasevangelium: Einleitung, Kommentar und Systematik* (NTAbh NF 22; Münster: Aschendorf, 1991), 237–38.

b) The Text

What disturbs Luke in his following of Christ is the illogical attitude of the audience and (we sense) of his own generation. These people know how to predict the weather but are incapable of understanding "the present time." In his view this inconsistency deserves the name "hypocrisy." He therefore adds this cry to the Sayings Source Q: "You hypocrites! You know how . . ." (v. 56). "Hypocrite" does not signify what it does in Molière's *Tartuffe*, that is, a person who claims to be something he is not; as in the biblical tradition, it means a person who is blind when it comes to himself or herself, and who has not come to grips with his or her own historical existence in "the present time."

But in Luke "the present time" means:

a) Our time is not simply a period of time but a time that is contrasted with another time: the time of God, which is yet to come.

b) Consequently, the present time is a time of sin but also a time of waiting, a time of the presence of Jesus, a time of decision, a time of disagreement; it is a time of involvement and the opposite of a spectacle. "The present time" proves to have a double content: on the one hand, the reality of our blindness, our hypocrisy, and, on the other, the voice of Jesus Christ, the manifestation of God's plan, the accomplishment of his work.[22]

c) καιρός in Greek

In Greek the word καιρός has a wide range of meanings.[23] First of all, it signifies the decisive point, then the place or more often the time at which the favorable opportunity occurs. Depending on the philosophical or theological convictions of the writer, this favorable opportunity, this καιρός, may have an existential, ethical, liturgical, theological, or eschatological reference. In the Septuagint the word can translate a broad range of concepts: môʿēd (time), ʾaḥarōn (the ensuing time), qēṣ (end). As the book of Daniel shows, the concept is used, for the most part, in an apocalyptic context.[24]

d) καιρός in Luke

Two sentences in Luke's gospel shed light on his understanding of καιρὸς οὗτος. The first is Luke 18:29b–30: "There is no one who has left house or wife or brothers or parents or children, for the sake of the kingdom of God, who will not get back very much more in this age [or: this present time], and in the age to come

---

[22] See above, n. 17.

[23] See Gerhard Delling, "καιρός κτλ.," *TDNT* 3:455–64, esp. 457.

[24] See Dan (LXX) 7:12; 9:27; 11:35; 12:4, 7.

eternal life." We see here a Jewish division of time, but the two times refer, first and foremost, to the two Christian levels of "the present time" with their suffering and, even now, the anticipation of the blessings of the end.

The second text, Luke 19:44, occurs in the lament of Jesus over Jerusalem: "They will not leave within you one stone upon another, because you did not recognize the time of your visitation." The meaning here is that the time of the divine visitation, our time, is not yet the time to come; therefore no one may interpret Luke's eschatology as a "present eschatology." That means that "this time," our time, has a connection to the coming time. Otherwise, Jesus, and Luke after him, would be directing our gaze only to the coming time and not first of all to our time, as in fact he does in Luke 12:56. Is it not in Luke's gospel that Jesus says, "the kingdom of God is among you" (17:21)? Luke sees the present time, when the life, activity, death, and resurrection of Jesus are taking place, as embedded in the future, which means the kingdom of God, justice, and eternal life. Our time is, on the one hand, a period of apocalyptic waiting and, on the other, a period of eschatological fulfillment. It is a time in which eschatological events are taking place. It is a time of fulfillment, a καιρός. But it is also a time of tribulation (Acts 14:22); that is, it is still ὁ καιρὸς οὗτος. Because of this twofold understanding of "this time" Luke is a theologian of both salvation history and its opposite.[25]

e) Practical Aspect

Luke is trying to speak both to Christian communities and, at the same time, to a broader audience: he wants to be understood by pagans no less than by Jews. Pagans will remember the Tower of the Winds, erected in the agora of Athens in the first century BCE. It has not only four but eight directional markings and points to the eight corresponding winds, which are represented by flying human figures. Opposite Boreas, the north wind, is νότος, the wind that blows from the south.[26] They will also remember Hesiod, who regarded both the north wind and the south wind as divinities, the sons of Aurora and Astraius (*Theog.* 378–80). They will remember, too, that Καιρός was a Greek god; according to Pausanias

---

[25] See François Bovon, *Luke the Theologian: Thirty-three Years of Research (1950–1983)* (trans. Ken McKinney; Princeton Theological Monograph Series; Allison Park, Penn.: Pickwick, 1987), 9–77 and 419–27.

[26] On the Tower, νότος was understood to be a wind that brings rain, and was symbolized by a beardless man who is emptying a vessel. See Robert Boulanger, *Grèce* (Les Guides Bleus; Paris: Hachette, 1974), 221–22. On the depiction of the winds see Roland Hampe, *Kult der Winde in Athen und Kreta* (Sitzungsberichte der Heidelberger Akademie der Wissenschaften, Philosophisch-Historische Klasse 1; Heidelberg: Winter, 1967); Kora Neuser, *Anemoi: Studien zur Darstellung der Winde und Windgottheiten in der Antike* (Archaeologica 19; Rome: Giorgio Bretschneider, 1982).

(5.14.9), there was an altar dedicated to this god[27] at the entrance into the stadium at Olympia.

Luke wanted to speak to his contemporaries, but he did not share their sacralization of nature; he sees nature as reduced to a lower level, just one part of the divine creation. He expected, then, that his readers would indeed be aware of the weather but that they would also have an eye on their present time. He did not speculate about the eschatological presence of God in our historical time. What he does by means of his work is to narrate the history of "the present time" and urge every reader to pass judgment on "the present time," that is, on both Luke's time and the reader's time too. His wisdom is part of his convictions as a prophet.

V. The First Commentators

Once the synoptic tradition had been put in writing and had become sacred Scripture, the "dialogue" with Jesus and his exhortation took new and different forms. It became a commentary that was separate from the complete text. This was the case in Tertullian's dispute with Marcion, in which we find the first surviving exegesis of our passage: "In this narrative he [Jesus] calls them 'hypocrites,' 'because they know how to interpret the appearance of the earth and the sky, but not how to discern the present time,' even though they should really have recognized him, because he fulfilled everything foretold of him and taught it to them."[28]

It is worth noting that Tertullian's interpretation of ὁ καιρὸς οὗτος follows a christological line, which is in keeping with saying 91 of the *Gospel of Thomas*. This christological exegesis is continued in the ninety-fifth homily of Cyril of Alexandria on the Gospel of Luke, where it is expanded to form an almost baroque structure. The patriarch begins with the literal meaning: ". . . for people focus their attention on such things and, through lengthy observation and practice, acquire the ability to predict when the rain will fall or when powerful winds will come; we see sailors to be very expert in this area."[29] Instead of proceeding on to the next verse on "the present time," Cyril first offers an allegorical interpretation of rain and wind. Only then does he advance to verse 56: "They must not miss the time of salvation by failing to be aware of it: the time, that is, in which our rescuer came, in which an accurate knowledge of the truth reached the human race, and in which grace made its radiance known."

---

[27] See Delling, "καιρός," 458.
[28] Tertullian, *Marc.* 4.29.15.
[29] Cyril of Alexandria, *Sermones in Lucam* 95.

VI. Results

In my opinion, the biblical writings are still relevant to our generation. Our interpretation has endeavored, on the one hand, to be "objective," in the sense of expressing detached scholarship. On the other hand, we ought also take pains to be in continuity with the interpretations of the evangelists and the early Christian writers. We today ought to become part of the procession of exegetes leading from the evangelists to the doctors of the church. Those theologians did not simply adapt the text to their own meteorological situation in order to be understood and taken seriously. They also accepted the exhortation of Jesus to pass judgment on their own time, their own lives, their Church, and their society.

Some years ago, I was asked to lead a Bible study for the annual meeting of pastors and priests working in the hospitals and nursing homes of France and other French-speaking countries.[30] I had a sense that this biblical passage was addressed to them. Like the farmers and seamen of antiquity, these men and women had a good knowledge of their practical and professional tasks. But did they know, do we know, how to experience and pass judgment on "the present time"? How can we be open to God in our everyday lives? How can we discover what is out of tune?

In order to prepare for this Bible study I went to a place where a biblical scholar is not usually found: for the first time in my life I approached the international meteorological organization in Geneva. I was welcomed with surprise and delight. They gave me some information on meteorology, and I left the place with a poster containing thirty-eight photographs of the sky. I learned the names of the clouds, how high in the heavens they are, and the winds connected with them, and I learned something about the weather which these clouds herald.[31]

The first exercise at the meeting was to connect seven sentences, such as "Tomorrow I will set my plants" or "Tomorrow I will not go on an outing," with seven of the pictures of clouds on the poster. To the great surprise of all the participants their attempts were fruitless. Nowadays, people no longer know how to read the sky. In this area our practical knowledge is much less developed than the knowledge possessed by Jesus' audience.

We see the sky and the clouds, but we have lost much of our practical knowledge because our weather forecasts come no longer from the sky but from the television screen.

---

[30] I am referring to the XVIIIèmes Journées des aumôneries protestantes, held in Geneva, April 14–17, 1991. The theme of the meeting was: "Former, se former" ("Educating others and ourselves").

[31] The reference is to the World Meteorological Organization, Avenue de la Paix 7 bis, CH 1202, Geneva, Switzerland.

The disillusionment of the participants in the meeting did, however, lead them to reflect on their own καιρός, its connection with the final reality, with God's plan, with their existential decision and the role of Christ in our time, or, as the New English Bible puts it, with God's "fateful moment." In my opinion, the words of Jesus that we hear in the gospels cannot be reduced to an unvarying definition of wisdom or of apocalyptic. As our passage shows, Jesus and, after him, those who passed on the Synoptic tradition, moved on from wisdom to prophecy. Their voice is personal, flexible, independent, and authoritative. I hope that we are able to hear it, enter into a dialogue with it, and take a position of personal responsibility toward it.

Apocalyptic Traditions in the Lukan Special Material:
Reading Luke 18:1–8

Contemporary New Testament scholarship gives evidence of two trends. Some scholars, particularly those interested in the historical Jesus or the source of the logia (Q), are going backward, trying to reach Christian origins and still influenced by the romantic dream of the pure beginning.[1] Others are pressing forward, tracing the development of early Christian traditions, both in the canonical and non-canonical texts (particularly the Nag Hammadi Codices), in an attempt to follow the several streams of Christianity. These scholars continue to be influenced by the philosophical construction of organic evolution.[2]

In his long and creative career, Helmut Koester took into consideration both approaches. He has argued that no quest for the historical Jesus can succeed without due consideration of the motives of the early church,[3] and that no trajectory from the earliest sayings to Justin Martyr and Valentinus can be reconstructed unless it originates with Jesus the victim.[4] At the risk of speaking extravagantly, I would say that our colleague has always been like one of the angels of John 1:51: "ascending and descending upon the Son of Man" (ἀναβαίνοντας καὶ καταβαίνοντας ἐπὶ τὸν υἱὸν τοῦ ἀνθρώπου). In this paper I shall try to walk in his footsteps and apply his methodology. Accordingly, I seek to trace the trajectory backward from Luke to the historical Jesus, while still respecting the influence of the original events upon the later developments..

I shall work on a passage from Luke's special material (*Sondergut*), because recent scholarship has for the most part neglected this source. A rapid glance at the many new studies on Jesus shows that the Lukan special material in general, and Luke 18:1–8 (the parable of the unjust judge and the insistent widow) in particular, do not play any significant role. The same regretable neglect appears to extend

---

[1] The influence of the Enlightenment is still perceptible, and the work of Johann Gottfried Herder merits reinvestigation.

[2] It is well known that Charles Darwin's and Georg Wilhelm Friedrich Hegel's works have had a formidable impact upon theologians and scholars, such as Ferdinand Christian Baur and Johann Adam Möhler in the nineteenth century, and many New Testament exegetes of the twentieth.

[3] See his dissertation, *Synoptische Überlieferung bei den apostolischen Vätern* (TU 65; Berlin: Akademie, 1957).

[4] See Helmut Koester, "Jesus the Victim," *JBL* 111 (1992) 3–15.

also to the study of the early Christian communities and the reception of Jesus' teaching in the first centuries.

My task is not an easy one, because the distinction of layers, the separation of redaction and tradition, is problematic with respect to this passage. As modern scholars have drawn them, the diverging reconstructions of the evolution of the short parable from its earliest oral stage to its final written version by Luke are proof and witness of the difficulty of this task.[5] A genetic analysis of the passage becomes more difficult because the story is simple only at a superficial level. Even the Greek presents difficulties: what is the meaning of εἰς τέλος in v. 5: "till the end" or "finally"? Also in verse 5, should the rare verb ὑπωπιάζω be taken literally ("to strike under the eye," "to give him a black eye") or metaphorically ("to bruise," "to mortify")? Does the present tense λέγει ("he says") in verse 6 refer to the following or preceding sentences? In verse 7b, what is the meaning of μακροθυμῶ: "to be patient" or "to be late"? And why the present tense after the future perspective of verse 7a ("And will not God grant justice to his chosen ones")? Finally, in verse 8a, does ἐν τάχει mean "soon" or "quickly"?

Despite these philological difficulties the inquiry into the development of this pericope is worth undertaking, because the text impinges on such major issues as the early Christian eschatological expectation in a time of apparent divine silence. Study of this pericope may also shed light on a neglected early Christian community, the community that authored the Lukan Special material.

In this paper, therefore, I shall try to disentangle the several layers of the text. Furthermore, I begin with the assumption that the text as it stands is the result of several successive reinterpretations, which now exist in tension and, at the same time, relate to one another in a manner analgous to a cybernetic system. I shall work backward from the Lukan redaction to the redaction of the special material, and then to the traditions lying behind these two successive rewritings. In attempting to understand the several versions of the story, I have a further objective: to uncover and isolate the early Christian community behind the Lukan special material.

The Lukan Redaction

As usual, the exegete finds the Lukan redactional activity in the framework of the parable and its placement within the larger literary context of the Third Gospel.

---

[5] The reader can judge this from the general overview presented some years ago by Heinrich Zimmermann, "Das Gleichnis vom Richter und der Witwe (Lk 18, 1–8)," in Rudolf Schnackenburg, Josef Ernst, and Joachim Wanke, eds., *Die Kirche des Anfangs. Festschrift für Heinz Schürmann* (Freiburg: Herder, 1978) 79–95; more recently, Charles W. Hedrick, *Parables as Poetic Fictions: The Creative Voice of Jesus* (Peabody, Mass.: Hendrickson, 1994) 187–207; Darrell L. Bock, *Luke*, vol. 2: *9:51–24:53* (Baker Exegetical Commentary on the New Testament; Grand Rapids: Baker Books, 1996) 1444–56.

Several scholars, such as Walter Grundmann and Joseph Fitzmyer,[6] rightly connect the parable with the apocalyptic speech in Luke 17.[7] Others, such as Roland Meynet[8], underscore several parallels between this parable and the succeeding parable of the Pharisee and the tax collector (Luke 18:9–14).[9]

Within this particular passage, the Lukan rewriting is most evident at the beginning and end of the pericope. Luke 18:1 is full of redactional expressions: "to be necessary" (δεῖν), "to pray" (προσεύχεσθαι).[10] The same is true of verse 8b, where the particle for restriction "and yet" (πλήν), and the expression "on earth" (ἐπὶ τῆς γῆς) are typical of Luke.[11]

Verses 1 and 8b contain a number of literary motifs that are characteristic of Luke's pastoral focus. Their manifest concern over the delay of the Parousia, the theological relationship between faith and prayer, the existential bond between God and the individual believer, and the mediation of the Son of Man consistently reflect Lukan concerns.[12]

It is probable that Luke also corrected verses 7–8a, the explanation of the parable, by inserting a gloss (Luke 18:7b), explicating the delay of the Parousia.[13] The Lukan reinterpretation is: Certainly God will vindicate his elect, but for the time being he will be slow, or "late."[14]

---

[6] See Walter Grundmann, *Das Evangelium nach Lukas* (2d ed.; ThHKNT 3; Berlin: Evangelische Verlagsanstalt, 1969) 346; Joseph A. Fitzmyer, *The Gospel According to Luke* (2 vols.; Garden City: Doubleday, 1981–85) 2. 1175–76.

[7] Luke 17:8b ("And yet, when the Son of Man comes, will he find faith on earth?") reveals a connection with 17:37 ("Where the corpse is, there the eagles will gather") and 17:19 ("Your faith has made you well"). See Eduard Schweizer, *Das Evangelium nach Lukas übersetzt und erklärt* (NTD 3; Göttingen: Vandenhoeck & Ruprecht, 1982) 184.

[8] Roland Meynet, *L'Évangile selon saint Luc. Analyse rhétorique* (2 vols.; Paris: Cerf, 1988) 1. 171–75; 2. 176–77; idem, *Avez-vous lu saint Luc? Guide pour la rencontre* (Lire la Bible 88; Paris: Cerf, 1990) 211–13.

[9] Both texts use of the term παραβολή (vv. 1 and 9), and an interpretation follows each parable (vv. 6–8, and 14). In both texts the verb "to say" is important, and the topic is the prayer.

[10] "To get tired" (ἐγκακεῖν) is known in the Pauline and deutero-Pauline epistles and thus is also appropriate for Luke.

[11] The last expression is also known by Matthew and Mark (see Matt. 9:6 and Mark 2:10, for example).

[12] See Gerhard Schneider, *Parusiegleichnisse im Lukas-Evangelium* (SBS 74; Stuttgart: KBW Verlag, 1975) 71–78; idem, *Das Evangelium nach Lukas Kapitel 11–24* (2d ed.; ÖTKNT 3/2; Gütersloh: Gütersloher Verlagshaus Gerd Mohn, 1984) 360; Jean-Daniel Kaestli, *L'eschatologie dans l'œuvre de Luc. Ses caractéristiques et sa place dans le développement du christianisme primitif* (Nouvelle série théologique 22; Geneva: Labor et Fides, 1969) 37. Luke's interpretation of the parable seems to be influenced by Sir 35:15–19; see Hedrick, *Parables as Poetic Fictions*, 188 n. 3.

[13] I do not take the phrase καὶ μακροθυμεῖ ἐπ᾽ αὐτούς to be a question. In declining to do so, I am diverging from the NRSV.

[14] For this interpretation of μακροθυμῶ, see Harald Riesenfeld, "Zu μακροθυμεῖν (Lk 18,7)," in *Neutestamentliche Aufsätze. Festschrift Josef Schmid* (ed. Josef Blinzler et al; Regensburg: Pustet, 1963) 214–17.

The Redaction of the Lukan Special Material

Stories such as the good Samaritan, Martha and Mary, Zachaeus, and the journey to Emmaus, have universally been loved by Sunday school children and admired by professional exegetes.[15] The parable under discussion shares the same high literary quality. Scholars usually grant Luke the victory crown for literary excellence. In my opinion, however, the crown and the praise belong to the author of Luke's special source (*Sondergut*),[16] an author greater than Luke.

An expression like "who neither feared God, nor had respect for people" in verse 2 echoes the language of the prodigal son, who confesses having sinned "against heaven and before you" (Luke 15:18, 21). Internal dialogues and monologues are a literary device that this author employs with considerable skill. Compare this form (vv. 4–5) with that of the rich man (Luke 12:17–19), or its content with another very similar parable of the Lukan special material, the parable of the friend disturbed during the night (Luke 11:7–8).

The author's artistry, his attention to psychological reactions, his articulation of the tension between a good action and a bad intention, all indicate a high level of education and, indeed, some level of philosophical training.[17] For this writer as for Luke, the main character of the parable is the oppressed woman, the neglected widow. She earns this focal attention because she is unfortunate and because she tries to remedy her bad fortune. Her courage and perserverance are of paramount concern to this author, who is responsible for a rewriting of the parable, and especially for the lesson drawn in verse 8a, introduced by the marker words, "I tell you" (λέγω ὑμῖν): "I tell you that he [God] will soon grant justice." This lesson is an expression of hope for the community, which identifies itself with the widow. The widow's insistent request is a parabolic expression of the ongoing prayer of the believers. This interpretation of the parable departs from the Lukan one on two points. First, the author of the special material insists on the prayers of the chosen ones, of the community, whereas Luke underscores the prayer, faith, and commitment of the individual believer. Second, the author of the special material (despite a Greek education) evinces a strong apocalyptic expectation. For this author, God's vindication is scheduled to take place "soon" (ἐν τάχει, v. 8a); for Luke, the present time is characterized by the delay of the Parousia.[18]

---

[15] Luke 10:30–36, 38–42; 19:1–10; 24:13–32. The results of a poll of school children in Germany revealed that the best known stories of the Bible are practically all from what scholars have determined to be Luke's special material.

[16] Under the category of Lukan special material, I consider only material that appears in the sections proper to Luke, which can be found in Luke 3–24. The documents used by the evangelist in the birth and infancy narratives are from another origin.

[17] See particularly Gerd Petzke, *Das Sondergut des Evangeliums nach Lukas* (Zürcher Werkkommentare zur Bibel; Zürich: Theologischer Verlag, 1990).

[18] See François Bovon, *Luc le théologien. Vingt-cinq ans de recherches (1950–1975)* (2d. ed.; Monde de la Bible; Geneva: Labor et Fides, 1988) 11–84.

The Tradition of the Special Material

In an effort to go behind the composition of Luke's source, one might consider verse 7a: "And will not God grant justice to his chosen ones who cry to him day and night?"[19] Here, at the parable's center, one finds not only the human side (the widow of the parable, or the chosen ones of the interpretation) but especially the divine side (the judge of the parable, and God in the interpretation). This sentence reflects an older interpretation of the parable, an interpretation that I would attribute to the oral layer of the special material. According to this interpretation, God, the supreme judge, will come soon to vindicate his people. The widow has become here a metaphor for the remnant of Israel. The decisive expression "his chosen ones," "his elect," confirms this understanding of the widow. Moreover, the prayers of this community are a collective, liturgical, and ethical activity. This group of faithful and patient believers are, says the text, "crying ... day and night." The verb βοῶ ("to cry") is an evocative way of alluding to the torments of this early Christian group, isolated and marginalized, separated from its Lord and fervently awaiting the Parousia.

This community neither received nor transmitted Jesus' parable without interpretation, without biblical connections and an awareness of biblical intertextuality. The voice of its prophets invite the community to connect the pair "judge/widow" to the relationship between God and Israel, as it appears in the Hebrew Scriptures.[20] The judge's laziness corresponds to God's silence and Jesus' absence. The beseeching widow, like the "chosen ones," the "elect," of this early Christian community, searches for a positive self-definition. As a collective entity, the widow (who represents the "chosen ones"), although separated from her husband, hopes nonetheless for a reunion with God (as the expression "coming to him" in verse 3 makes clear).

I should note at this point that parables can draw their rhetorical strength either from their ability to evoke everyday life or from the exceptional character of the episode they relate. German scholars use the term *Gleichnis* for the first type and *Parabel* for the second.[21] Luke 18:1–8 evidently belongs to the second type of parable. The unexpected corruption of the judge is an integral part of the story, a story that functions through an argument *a minori ad maius*: If such a judge finally gives an anwer, how much more will God ultimately respond to our supplications. Despite the negative portrayal of the judge, for the early Christian interpreters the story could still serve as an analogy for God. For these first inter-

---

[19] Verse 7b has been registered as a Lukan addition in harmony with verse 8b.

[20] On God as a judge, see Gen 16:5; 18:25; 31:53; and Ps 7:11. For Israel as a widow, see Isa 54:4. God's care for widows appears in Deut 10:18 and Ps 68:5. For God and Israel as a married couple, see Isa 54:5–8; Jer 2:2; 3:8–9; Ezek 16:6–14; and Hos 2–3.

[21] See Eta Linnemann, *Gleichnisse Jesu. Einführung und Auslegung* (6th ed.; Göttingen: Vandenhoeck und Ruprecht, 1975) 13–14.

preters of the parable, who were probably prophets of that early Christian community, the parable had a single and unambiguous meaning: "Yes," they say to the people of God, "you are like the widow, but God is like the judge and even better than the judge. He will come soon and vindicate you, his elect. Do not be afraid, do not be upset."

Going further back to verse 6, one encounters perhaps the oldest interpretation given by the early Christian prophets.[22] The formal introduction: εἶπεν δὲ ὁ κύριος ("And the Lord said") is a marker of development, of retelling the story, of first interpretation. In contrast to the later reading, here the focus lies entirely on the judge (subject of the verb λέγει, "he says"), and this first commentary approaches the original meaning of the parable. Actually, verse 6 is not even an interpretation, but an interpellation, a command to listen, similar to the saying "let anyone with ears to hear listen!"[23] The prophet, repeating Jesus' parable after Easter, is in effect saying: "Listen, fellow Christians, to what the judge says." Instead of using the past, "the judge said" (εἶπεν), he prefers to underscore the duration of that voice with "the judge says" (λέγει).

The Oldest Story

The judge's words and deeds constitute an ironic story,[24] related to the freedom of God[25] but existing originally without any other explanation than the one offered by the context in which the communication occurs.[26] If in verse 6 there echoes the archaic voice of an early prophet, it is also probable that in verses 2–5 there resounds the ironic and original voice of the historical Jesus, transmitted by a prophet and transcribed by the author of the special material.[27] As they now stand, these verses undoubtedly bear the mark of the author of the special nar-

---

[22] That is, unless this sentence is just the beginning of the interpretation of verse 7a.

[23] See, for example, Mark 4:9 or Luke 14:35.

[24] See Wolfgang Harnisch, "Die Ironie als Stilmittel in Gleichnissen Jesu," *EvTh* 32 (1972) 421–36, esp 430–36; Hedrick, *Parables as Poetic Fictions*, 187, 201–7.

[25] See Hans Weder, *Die Gleichnisse Jesu als Metapher. Traditions- und redaktionsgeschichtliche Analysen und Interpretationen* (FRLANT 120; Göttingen: Vandenhoeck & Ruprecht, 1978) 267–73, esp. 270–71.

[26] Schweizer (*Evangelium nach Lukas*, 184) is of the opinion that without verses 7 and 8a, the parable would have been incomprehensible unless Jesus had spoken it in a situation that clarified its meaning.

[27] It was not the focus of this paper to compare Luke 18:1–8 with the parable of the friend disturbed during the night (Luke 11:5–8); see Ceslas Spicq, "La parabole de la veuve obstinée et du juge inerte, aux décisions impromptues (Lc 18:1–8)," *RB* 68 (1961) 68–90, esp. 86–87. Some further points of contact should be mentioned between Luke 18:1–8 and Luke 21. In chapter 21, one also finds a widow (vv. 1–4), the Christian community in the pronoun "you" (see, for example, vv. 12–19), a reflexion over the end of time (vv. 5–36), the notion of vindication (ἐκδίκησις, v. 22), the suffering of the community (vv. 12–24), the necessity of patience (v. 19), and the role of prayer (v. 36).

rative and probably also of Luke himself; but the plot of the story, the choice of the characters, and the abrasive nature of the incident may reveal the teaching of the historical Jesus.

Conclusion

At this point, let me summarize the conclusions of this study. First, Luke 18:1–8 is a good example of the development of Jesus' sayings and parables in the life of the early church. A terse, rather shocking parable (vv. 2–5) is preserved by Jesus' followers. Their memory is not motivated by love for anecdotes or historical evidence. It is a highly partisan, selective memory that interprets the story before elaborating on it. In verse 6, then in verse 7a, then in verse 8a, and then finally in verse 8b (and probably also in verse 7b), several successive interpretations emerge. These reinterpretations, like the trajectory of a rocket cruise missile, constitute a series of reorientations and corrections.

Second, along this trajectory, one meets a Christian community with a strong self-identity, united in an intense apocalyptic expectation: the "chosen ones," the "elect" are "crying" intensely "day and night." Their leaders (probably prophets) promise them imminent vindication, an eschatological reversal that should occur in the immediate future as an apocalyptic and cosmic event. In some Christian communities at an early stage, therefore, Jesus' teaching was understood in apocalyptic categories.[28]

Third, this community was Greek-speaking but it had Jewish roots; it strongly identified itself with the true Israel, the "chosen ones."[29] Its prophets exhorted the community during a time of suffering and isolation. Just as the creation and the Christians are "groaning" in Rom 8:19–23, here the community is "crying," inasmuch as full redemption remains only a fervent hope. Accordingly, the community is likened to God's spouse, separated from Him but waiting prayerfully during the present time of tribulation.[30]

Is it possible to say something more precise concerning this community? Luke himself comes out of the church of the Hellenists, and Stephen (also a Hellenist) is the only member of the early Christian communities depicted in Luke-Acts as using the title "Son of Man" to refer to Jesus.[31] I would suggest that the topography of the Lukan special material coincides, broadly speaking, with the exten-

---

[28] This point has to be emphasized at a time when many historians of early Christianity insist on the wisdom character of both Jesus' teaching and early Christian thought.

[29] This community is similar to the one at Qumran; see Lawrence H. Schiffman, *Reclaiming the Dead Sea Scrolls: The History of Judaism, the Background of Christianity, the Lost Library of Qumran* (Philadelphia: The Jewish Publication Society, 1994) 329–39.

[30] Compare the similar relation between the "bride" and the "Lamb" in Rev 18:23, 21:9, and 22:17.

[31] See Acts 7:56; also Luke 17:22; 21:36.

sion of the Hellenists from Jerusalem to Syria, through Samaria and Galilee (Acts 6:1–8:40; 11:19–30). Jesus' travel narrative in Luke 9–19 could be the prototype and the antitype of the expansion of these communities. If this hypothesis is correct,[32] then the "chosen ones" of Luke's special material would be at home in Jerusalem,[33] in Judaea (Bethphage, Bethsaida, and the Mount of Olives [Luke 19:22]), in Jericho (Luke 18:35; 19:1), and in Samaria and Galilee.[34]

Luke's gospel provides a fascinating door to the history of early Christianity and to Jesus' fate. By discerning and analyzing the several layers of its composition, modern interpreters gain insight into the evolutionary process of transmission regarding the sayings attributable to Jesus. Step by step they can try to go back to the original teaching of the historical Jesus, but step by step also they can follow the first decades of the early churches: ἀναβαίνοντας καὶ καταβαίνοντας ἐπὶ τὸν υἱὸν τοῦ ἀνθρώπου.

---

[32] I am not aware of any alternative hypothesis that seeks to place the Lukan special material within a particular early Christian group.

[33] Compare Luke 9:51; 13:22 and 19:28.

[34] Luke 9:51–52. The reader will find a full bibliography of this Lukan pericope in vol. 3 of my commentary, *L Évangile selon saint Luc* (CNT 3c; Geneva: Labor et Fides, 2001) 163–75. At present, the reader may consult Fitzmyer, *Gospel According to Luke*, 2.1181–82; or Frans van Segbroeck, *The Gospel of Luke: A Cumulative Bibliography 1973–1988* (BETL 88; Leuven: Leuven University Press, 1989) nos. 158, 159a, 311, 531, 854, 925, 1845, 2553, and 2738.

The Law in Luke-Acts[*]

1. Some Explanations

Values exist above norms, which themselves are above laws, the category to which the commandments belong.[1] In Luke, peace and eternal life, the ultimate values, are rooted in the God who established union with God's people. Righteousness and justice are the norms around which the law and its ordinances are oriented.

What do I mean when I use the word "law" and speak of "Luke?" The term νόμος ("law" or "prescription") springs twenty-seven times from the pen of the Evangelist, nine times in the Gospel and eighteen times in Acts. The word ἐντολή ("commandment") is used four times; and δικαίωμα ("prescription") appears once in the plural. The word ἔθος ("custom" or "practice") is used ten times, in the singular in the Gospel and in the plural in Acts. Several times "Moses" is al luded to as a "legislator" and reference is even made to "the law of Moses." Throughout Luke's work, the law in question is the one that God gave to Moses, that is, the "living oracles" (Acts 7:38). It is not one law among others, dictated through human wisdom, but the expression of the will and plan of God, mediated through both the person of Moses and human writing. Thus there exists a connection between the "it is necessary" (δεῖ) of salvation history (Luke 2:49, 9:22; Acts 19:21) and the imperatives contained in the law. Luke speaks of this law in an absolute manner, as in Acts 6:13 for example: κατὰ τοῦ τόπου τοῦ ἁγίου καὶ τοῦ νόμου ("against the holy place and the law"); but he does this without specifying how this law might be connected with other laws of the world, which, though he knows of the existence of Roman law and is familiar with the rules of *aequitas romana*, he nonetheless ignores.[2]

The antiquity of the law

Clearly, this law did not originate with the Christians. Like most of the authors of his time, Luke is proud to assert the antiquity of the institutions to which he is

---

[*] I thank Laura Beth Bugg for the translation of this paper.

[1] I have borrowed this model from my colleague Gabriel Widmer, theologian and philosopher of religion.

[2] See Jacques Dupont, "*Aequitas Romana*. Notes sur Actes 25, 16," *RSR* 49 (1961) 354–85; reprinted in idem, *Études sur les Actes des apôtres* (LD 45; Paris: Cerf, 1967) 527–52.

connected (Acts 7:2–38). Philo, for instance, in his *De legatione ad Gaium* writes: "All men, Emperor, have implanted in them a fierce love for their country and a high esteem for their proper laws . . ."[3] The people of Israel possess the distinction of ancient practices that go hand in hand with the law of Luke's Lord (ἐν τῷ νόμῳ κυρίου, "in the Law of the Lord," Luke 2:24), which is also that of Moses, the eminent human lawmaker (κατὰ τὸν νόμον Μωϋσέως, "according to the law of Moses," Luke 2:22). Luke, like Philo and Josephus, does not hesitate to cite this law in Greek. During a time when it was fashionable to attack blood sacrifices and allegorize myths, the Evangelist was also heir to a liberal interpretation that insists on spiritualization.

The novelty of Jesus

Because both the law of Moses and the history of the Israelites are assumed knowledge, they are neither introduced nor explained by Luke. As a storyteller, Luke weaves together the thread of his narrative with the new meaning he proposes, both the life of Jesus as prophet and messiah as well as the communication of his message. And it is precisely here where the novelty of his gospel lies. Part of my purpose in this paper will be to define the ties that Luke establishes between the ancient law of Moses and the new axioms of Jesus, while not forgetting the Christian ordinances, such as the Apostolic Decree (Acts 15:23–29), that were inspired by the Holy Spirit and added by the church.

Luke the evangelist

When I speak of Luke, I am referring to the anonymous author of the Gospel and of Acts, the author who desires to "write" (γράψαι, Luke 1:3), and who is the follower of the first witnesses and hearers of the Word (Luke 1:2).[4] It is important to keep this in mind and to provide some explanation for it, because modern translations do not rely directly on the manuscripts themselves but on various editions that – while they result from good intentions – are nonetheless subject to modern limitations. The oldest manuscripts are the indirect bearers of a lost original. Since a document as important as the Apostolic Decree exists in at least two forms (of which one demands moral obedience and the other ritual obligation) this disconcerting situation has direct bearing on our subject.[5]

---

[3] Philo, *Legat.* 277.
[4] See François Bovon, "Évangile de Luc et Actes des Apôtres," in *Évangiles synoptiques et Actes des Apôtres* (ed. Joseph Auneau et al.; Petite bibliothèque des sciences bibliques. Nouveau Testament 4; Paris: Desclée, 1981) 267–69.
[5] See Gerhard Schneider, *Die Apostelgeschichte* (2 vols.; HTKNT 5; Feiburg: Herder, 1982) 2. 168–92.

The distinction between moral law and ritual commandments

Though he himself is a supporter of the law's spiritual emphasis, Luke does not ignore its ritual component. The infancy narratives, as well as some of Jesus' injunctions, call for literal observance of the law. Mary, Jesus' mother, observes the Mosaic commands regarding purification and offers a pair of turtledoves and two young pigeons (Luke 2:24) as is proper for a ritual sacrifice. Later, Luke surprises his readers by citing a Jesus who, though he favorably views the spiritualization of observances as they are summarized in the double commandment of love (see Luke 10:25–28) and the ten commandments (Luke 18:18–23), nevertheless demands both obedience to precise ritual obligations, such as those concerning the tithe of mint, rue, and herbs, as well as proper respect for the great ordinances regarding judgment and the love of God (Luke 11:42). Luke, who, like Jesus and Paul, clearly extols the essential moral and spiritual nature of the law, probably upholds these ritual precepts only for Christians of Jewish origin, the hearers of Jesus, and the first Jewish-Christians.

The ecclesial function of the law

Like any legal *corpus* in antiquity, the law of Moses is not concerned with prescription alone, even if it is interpreted more in the moral than the ritual sense. The law cannot be separated from the people who draw their identity from it (the same is true for the law and the temple). As Jacob Jervell has noted, there is an ecclesial component to the law.[6] Through their connection to the law, people affirm their belonging to Israel, the people of God. But just as there are both ritual and moral commandments, Luke asserts that it is helpful to make distinctions with regard to the people of God. Actually, Luke follows Paul and the Christian Hellenists in giving a new definition to the people of God that modifies the ethnico-ecclesial dimension of the law of Moses.

The prophetic and christological function of the law

Luke has stories he must tell and he knows that God "moves," "lives," and "transforms." His religion is therefore not fixed in the letter of a law that offers flexibility only through interpretation. For him, the law of Moses is also prophecy (see Deut 18:15, 18, cited in Acts 7:37). Actually, it is scripture, particularly the writings of the prophets and the Psalms, that gives the author of Luke-Acts the arsenal of christological prophecies he needs to confirm both the messianic nature

---

[6] See Jacob Jervell, *Luke and the People of God: A New Look at Luke-Acts* (Minneapolis: Augsburg, 1972) 133–51, esp. 141.

and the providential and scriptural character of the passion and resurrection of Jesus.[7]

2. The Main Problems

These explanations thus lead to some major problems for the critical reader.[8] What, for instance, is the relationship between the law of Moses, the precepts of Jesus, and the ordinances of the apostles? And if salvation is accepted as the common point of reference, then how must we relate the human efforts that are imposed by the law and proposed by Jesus to the salvific work of God and his agent the Messiah?

By the same token, how do we connect the ethical behavior of believers to their faith and repentance? And if there is agreement regarding the type of obedience defined by the law and laid out by Jesus, then how can we explain the ethos of the first Christians and their ethical behavior as it is lived out in the Acts of the Apostles? A close reading of the Gospel of Luke and the book of Acts gives rise to questions that clearly reveal the tensions between the ideal prescriptions of the Gospel and the lived reality in Acts. For example, have the upper-class women who invite the apostles to stay at their homes (Acts 16:15) forgotten Jesus' command that each one should abandon all of his or her possessions (Luke 12:33; 14:33)?

And is there in Luke, as there is in Paul, a critique of the law and the notion of surpassing in Christ the legal system inherited from Moses? Clearly, Luke is a storyteller, but his faith is sufficiently structured so that we can detect the theology that forms the background of his writing. The question is whether or not this theology contains a critique of the law.

It is evident that evangelical commands are joined to the law; but if they often confirm the law, do they also at times correct it? For example, do they impose greater moral purity than ritual purity? Do they require a more rigorously radical commitment in matters of love for a neighbor that becomes love of enemies? Do they urge greater internal freedom from material possessions and familial ties?[9]

Finally, if the gospel proclaims first and foremost the coming of the kingdom of God and its power and justice, how do we account for the impact of this eschatological dimension on the present reality of the law?

---

[7] See François Bovon, *Luc le théologien. Vingt-cinq ans de recherche (1950–1975)* (2d. ed.; Le Monde de la Bible; Geneva: Labor et Fides, 1988) 85–117.

[8] Another explanation of the problems can be found in Kalervo Salo, *Luke's Treatment of the Law: A Redaction-Critical Investigation* (AASF 57; Helsinki: Suomalainen Tiedeakatemia, 1991) 13–23.

[9] On the relationship between the demands of the law and those of the gospel, see Matthias Klinghardt, *Gesetz und Volk Gottes. Das lukanische Verständnis des Gesetzes nach Herkunft, Funktion und seinem Ort in der Geschichte des Urchristentums* (WUNT 2/32; Tübingen: Mohr Siebeck, 1988).

3. The Major Lukan Texts Relating to the Law

Obedience to the law

First, there are biblical passages where obedience to the law suggests an understanding that this adherence is proper. In these cases, Jesus stands beside Moses the lawmaker and reminds the reader that Moses was the defender of righteousness and justice. These occurrences are numerous throughout the Gospel and Acts, and they reveal the value of both moral and ritual precepts. Zechariah and Elizabeth are "righteous" and "live blamelessly according to all the commandments and regulations of the Lord" (Luke 1:6). Jesus says to the ten healed lepers, "Go and show yourselves to the priests" (Luke 17:14), thus submitting himself to an injunction from the book of Leviticus (Lev 13:49; 14:2–32). The Lukan Paul, for his part, circumcises Timothy because the latter is the son of a Christian mother of Jewish origin (Acts 16:1–3). To the jurist with whom he discusses eternal life, the Lukan Jesus asks, "What is written in the law?" (Luke 10:26) before saying to him, "Do this and you will live" (Luke 10:28). To the rich man, Jesus quotes the ten commandments (Luke 18:20).

From obedience to righteousness and from righteousness to eternal life

In some of these passages, and others as well, we see that the "doing" of ethics, the obedience to the law, leads to salvation and eternal life. This is sound Jewish theology. The rich man, by keeping all the commandments, has seemingly done well. He simply lacks one final task for complete obedience (Luke 18:18–23).

From the necessity of forgiveness to salvation, through faith

There is another way of thinking that again corresponds to Jewish theology. According to this perspective, persons cry out for help from the depths of their misery – whether spiritual or social – receive pardon and show proof of a childlike trust, but they do not perform other works that certain beggars (as Martin Luther uses the term) perform: these would be the tax collector in the parable, the centurion at Capernaum, the shepherds of the Christmas story, the prodigal son. Zacchaeus and Cornelius turn toward God and God's son in a way that shows evidence of an evangelized spirit, a spirit that is not calculating.[10] Luke likes to apply a stereotypical formula to the stories of these characters: "Your faith has saved you" (see, for example, Luke 7:50; 8:48; 17:19; 18:42). It is in this same way that Luke, as both a historian and a theologian, places on the lips of the apostle Paul an understanding of justification by faith that is not so far removed from the under-

---

[10] See Luke 2:8–20; 7:1–10; 15:11–32; 18:9–14; 19:1–10; see also Acts 10:1–11, 18.

standing that Paul expresses in his authentic epistles:[11] "Let it be known to you therefore, my brothers, that through this man forgiveness of sins is proclaimed to you, by this Jesus everyone who believes is set free from all those sins from which you could not be freed by the law of Moses."[12]

Silence concerning the law

Closely related to the above-mentioned passages are texts that speak of God, salvation, and Christian behavior without reference to the law of Moses. The proper attitude during persecutions, ethical considerations pertaining to money, and eucharistic communion are all advocated through the words of Jesus, the parables, and stories in Acts, which ignore all mention of the Mosaic commandments. The sermon on the plain, the farewell dialogue, and the closing statements in Acts should also be mentioned here.[13]

Criticism of the law

Passages in Luke that relativize or criticize the law are rare and possess neither the shocking character nor the intensity of their Pauline parallels. Luke 16:16 ("The law and the prophets were in effect until John ..."), for example, reveals one stage of salvation history without denigrating prescriptions that came before it. The only explicitly critical passage, which is found in Acts 15:10, concerns circumcision: "Therefore, why are you provoking God by placing on the neck of the disciples a yoke that neither our ancestors nor we ourselves have been able to bear?"

4. The Bibliography on the Subject

If I may offer my services as a guide, I would like to propose the following: in *Luc le théologien*,[14] under the entry entitled "law" in the index (p. 476) and in the chapter concerning Israel and the church (chapter 7, pp. 342–61), the reader will find a summary of the positions of Hans Conzelmann, Ernst Haenchen, Augustin George, John Cochrane O'Neill, Jacob Jervell, Joachim Gnilka, and Jacques Dupont. In my article "Études lucaniennes: rétrospective et prospective," the interested reader will find the echoes of an intense debate concerning Luke's attitude

---

[11] For another opinion see Philipp Vielhauer, "Zum Paulinismus der Apostelgeschichte," *EvT* 10 (1959–51) 1–15; reprinted in idem, *Aufsätze zum Neuen Testament* (TB 31; Munich: Kaiser, 1965) 9–27.

[12] See Acts 13:38–39 (trans. NRSV).

[13] See Luke 6:20–49; 12:11–33; 14:16–24, 33; 22:14–38; see also Acts 2:42–47; 4:32–35; 5:1–16.

[14] See above, p. 62 n. 7.

toward the Jewish people, which has taken place during the last decade or so.[15] This debate has recently been undertaken by another generation of exegetes who have appeared on the scene: Robert Lawson Brawley, Jack T. Sanders, Matthias Klinghardt, Kaleryo Salo, and Philipp Francis Esler.[16]

A magnificent bibliography on Luke, published in 1989 and compiled by Frans van Segbroeck, spans the years 1973 to 1988.[17] Under the heading "Law" (p. 226), the Belgian scholar refers to over twenty titles of articles, monographs and theses. Finally, the following are authors whom I have not previously mentioned: Ulrich B. Müller, Stephen G. Wilson, François Vouga, Craig L. Blomberg, and F. Gerald Downing.[18]

I have examined *New Testament Abstracts* for the more recent years, between 1989 and 1998, and the debate over Luke and Judaism appears to have receded since 1991. I was able to find only a few relevant articles, particularly one by Joseph Augustine Fitzmyer and another by Helmut Merkel.[19]

5. The Attainment of Salvation according to Acts

In his Gospel, Luke has already shown that he is not content simply to recall the law; instead, he makes reference to the newness and innovation of the historical Jesus and his message. In the book of Acts, Luke emphasizes the missionary efforts of the apostles, who are the human expression of the word of God that provides salvation for all people. The road that leads to salvation does not go through the law. Instead, it is routed through the acceptance of the good news that, in spite of Luke's attempt to respect various situations, remains constant.

---

[15] François Bovon, "Études lucaniennes: rétrospective et prospective," *RTP* 125 (1993) 113–35, esp. 125–29: English translation, see above pp. 28–32.

[16] Robert Lawson Brawley, *Luke-Acts and the Jews: Conflict, Apology, and Conciliation* (SBLMS 33; Atlanta: Scholars Press, 1987); Jack T. Sanders, *The Jews in Luke-Acts* (London: SCM, 1987); Matthias Klinghardt, *Gesetz und Volk Gottes* (see n. 9 above); Kaleryo Salo, *Luke's Treatment of the Law* (see n. 8 above); and Philip Francis Esler, *Community and Gospel in Luke-Acts: The Social and Political Motivations of Lukan Theology* (SNTSMS 57; Cambridge: Cambridge University Press, 1987).

[17] Frans van Segbroeck, *The Gospel of Luke: A Cumulative Bibliography 1973–1988* (BETL 88; Leuven: Leuven University Press/Peeters, 1989).

[18] Ulrich B. Müller, "Zur Rezeption gesetzeskritischer Jesusüberlieferung im frühen Christentum," *NTS* 27 (1980–81) 155–85; Stephen G. Wilson, *Luke and the Law* (SNTSMS 50; Cambridge: Cambridge University Press, 1984); François Vouga, *Jésus et la Loi selon la tradition synoptique* (Le Monde de la Bible; Geneva: Labor et Fides, 1988); Craig L. Blomberg, "The Law in Luke-Acts," *JSNT* 22 (1984) 53–80; F. Gerald Downing, "Freedom from the Law in Luke-Acts," *JSNT* 26 (1986) 49–52.

[19] Joseph Augustine Fitzmyer, *Luke the Theologian: Aspects of his Teaching* (New York: Paulist; London: Chapman, 1989) 175–202; Helmut Merkel, "Israel im lukanischen Werk," *NTS* 40 (1994) 371–98.

God

God, the benevolent creator who orchestrates universal salvation at the end of time, is both the beginning and the end of this road. God's clarion call of victory sounds the reveille of the resurrection: from among the dead God awakens his Son, the powerful (Luke 4:36) and suffering (Acts 26:23) Messiah sent to Israel (Acts 10:36). It is no longer the name of Moses, the representative of the law, or the name of Abraham, the symbol of the promise, but the name of Jesus Christ that opens the door of salvation to human beings (Acts 4:12). This piece of news is *good* news, and as such it must be made known. The verb εὐαγγελίζομαι is used frequently by Luke and it carries this specific meaning.[20]

At the beginning of the last days there is the divine εὐδοκία (Luke 10:21), a symbol of the generosity God exhibits during the course of history. Humans have already witnessed this sign of benevolence in creation (Acts 14:15–18; 17:23–29). And from the time that God appeared to Abraham (Acts 7:2), spoke to Moses (Acts 7:30–39), and crowned David (Acts 13:22), the people of Israel should never have stiffened their necks, as they have constantly been doing (Acts 7:51–53).

The word of salvation

For the time being, this divine salvation is given to the Christians in the form of a message that recalls the newly-happened foundational events and reveals the meaning that is assigned to them: ὁ λόγος τῆς σωτηρίας ταύτης ("the word of this salvation") is, therefore, that which keeps alive the magnificent works of God as memory while at the same time anticipating its tangible realization as prolepsis.[21] To benefit from this word and to rejoice in the fulfillment of its promises is to know how to listen.

Listening

The responsibility of all people, whether Jew or Gentile, is to listen, and this in the dual meaning that the verb ἀκούω possesses: both to pay attention and to adhere to the meaning of the words; both to understand and to act. The imperative αὐτοῦ ἀκούετε ("Listen to him") at the end of the transfiguration narrative signifies at the same time both "Lend him your ears" and "obey him." (Luke 9:35).[22]

---

[20] See Luke 1:19; 2:10; 3:18; 4:18, 33; 7:22; 8:1; 9:6; 16:16; 20:1; also Acts 5:42; 8:4, 12, 35, 40; 10:36; 11:20; 13:22; 14:7, 15, 21; 15:35; 16:10; 17:18.

[21] See Gerhard Lohfink, *Gottes Taten gehen weiter: Geschichtstheologie als Grundvollzug neutestamentlicher Gemeinden* (Freiburg: Herder, 1985).

[22] See François Bovon, *L'Évangile selon saint Luc (1, 1–9, 50)* (CNT 3a; Geneva: Labor et Fides, 1991) 489.

πίστις and μετάνοια

Luke uses two complementary terms for this human response in all its intensity, this firing movement of the entire being – spirit, soul and body. The first term is πίστις, which implies both the confidence given to a person (not the respect accorded to a law text) and the desire for the verity of a word whose truth, historical accuracy, and promise of eschatological fulfillment cannot for the moment be proven.[23] The second term is μετάνοια, which presents faith in terms of transformation and movement. The human returns to God and turns away from self. Where once a person was bent in his or her sins, he or she is now straightened and turned toward the light of Christ.[24]

Spontaneity and calculation

This human posture is not calculated; nor is it the result of an egoistic plan. It does not prevent a person from being thoughtful, however, as is evident in the twin parables of the farmer who measures the cost and the king who counts his troops (Luke 14:28–33). This movement, at the same time reflective and spontaneous, is one of an undivided spirit and of a heart that conceives of no other sentiment than the love of God.

We must remember from where this being who is transformed through the hearing of the good news originates: it is through Christ and his word of pardon that the believer is removed from the vicious circle of the world of sin. An imposed typology, formerly valid for the ancestors of Israel, is still valid in our day for the descendants of Abraham; but they were unwilling to obey him, they rebuked him, and turned their hearts back to Egypt (Acts 7:39). The interaction of Jesus, who cures through his word and signs, with the characters in Luke's gospel who are eager to join him, illustrate and manifest what the vocabulary of faith, conversion, and proclamation expresses in the book of Acts. The old man Simeon, the centurion of Capernaum, the prodigal son, and Zacchaeus are the first Christians, and this through their attitude of listening, loving adherence, repentance, conversion, and faith.[25]

The role of the Holy Spirit

What remains implicit in the Gospel of Luke and is made explicit in the Acts of the Apostles is the manifestation of the Spirit, the fulfillment that takes place at the time of Pentecost, following the Risen One's promise to his disciples (Luke 24:29; Acts 1:8). Clearly, Luke more readily associates the work of the Holy Spirit with

---

[23] See van Segbroeck, *Gospel of Luke*, 225 (the entry entitled "faith" in the thematic index).
[24] See Bovon, *Luc le théologien*, 285–307.
[25] See Luke 2:25–35; 7:1–10; 15:11–32 and 19:1–10.

the act of the apostolic word, but the Spirit also passes from preachers to listeners and transforms their hearts (what Luke in his words calls the "purification of hearts," Acts 15:9).[26]

The gift of the law

It was with this same intention of salvation and determination to bestow life that the law was given to Israel. According to Luke, God did not change: the divine commandments were living oracles, the λόγια ζῶντα (Acts 7:38) that Moses received from God to give to the Israelites. Rather, it is humans who have poorly understood them and, in the end, disobeyed. If God has to start all over again, in two successive covenants, it is not that God corrects Godself nor that God is corrected: it is human beings who are corrected and who are chastened by this final offer, one that is again a gift and not an imposed rule. As the law was given to human beings, so also Christ gives μετάνοινα (repentance and conversion), which also stands as a gift from God.[27]

6. So What about the Law in the Gospel of Luke?

The beginning of the Christian life

Luke thus outlines in Acts the spread of the word of God due to the preaching of the apostles and witnesses, the formation of the Christian communities, and the opening of the church first to god-fearers then to Gentiles. In this way, the Evangelist places great importance on the life of the first Christians through time. For example, the ongoing life he describes in the summaries found in Acts 2:42–47, 4:32–35 and 5:12–16, and in the story of the Jerusalem conference (Acts 15) goes hand in hand with signs of obedience and expects ethical proof of sharing and perseverance. Luke does not, however, brutally reinsert the law of Moses into the new economy. Indeed, the law is curiously absent from the book of Acts. If rules are necessary, then they are issued with new effort by the church and the apostolic college with the aid of the Holy Spirit. They make up ἡ διδαχὴ τῶν ἀποστόλων ("the teaching of the apostles," Acts 2:42).

The continuation and progression of the Christian life

The unfolding course of the Christian life is described more abundantly in Luke's Gospel than in Acts. In his Gospel, Luke ponders the future of Christianity and

---

[26] See Bovon, *Luc le théologien*, 211–54.
[27] See Acts 11:18: ἄρα καὶ τοῖς ἔθνεσιν ὁ θεὸς τὴν μετάνοιαν εἰς ζωὴν ἔδωκεν ("Then God has given even to the Gentiles the repentance that leads to life").

the constancy of faith: "the Son of Man, when he comes, will he find faith on earth?" (Luke 18:8). Very often, he redirects the meaning of certain parables toward this continuity. Parables initially dealing with decision become parables of perseverance under Luke's pen.[28] For example, Luke adds ἐν ὑπομονῇ ("with endurance") to the parable of the sower (Luke 8:15).[29]

How does one stay connected to the Savior? How does one go from short-term hearing to lasting listening? How does one go from the verb ἀκούω ("to hear") to the verb ποιῶ ("to do"), from ἀκούω ("to hear") to φυλάσσω ("to keep") (Luke 11:28)? The response is twofold: it is necessary to live in faith, and in order to live in faith it is necessary to practice a certain ethic. Curiously, as we have seen in Acts and have found in the Gospel, the law of Moses and its prescriptions are not introduced in an authoritarian manner, for such legalism would run the risk of furthering new transgressions.

The reinterpretation of the law

In keeping with the Jewish Hellenistic heritage that the God-fearers followed before their adherence to Christianity, and faithful also to the type of Christianity he joined – namely, the Hellenist movement and the Pauline mission – Luke believes that it is necessary to give a radical, new interpretation of the law when confronted by Pharisaic Judaism (Luke 11:37–54). For the Evangelist, it is Jesus who chooses and begins this hermeneutical effort:

a) Jesus resolutely places the gift before the demand, divine grace before human obedience.

b) According to Jesus, the law does not consists in the addition of innumerable obstacles that the greatest of observers may boast of having easily surmounted it. The law, according to Jesus, is a series of generous warnings addressed to pilgrims who are ill-suited for life.

c) Directed toward God, the law yields to grace and, turned toward humans, it grants priority to the embrace of loving enthusiasm. To the question asked by Jesus, "What is written in the law?" (Luke 10:26), the lawyer responds by citing the two-pronged commandment on love: "You will love the Lord your God with all your heart and all your soul and all your strength and all your mind ..." (Luke 10:27). Jesus describes this response as excellent: ὀρθῶς ἀπεκρίθης ("you have answered correctly," Luke 10:28). In this instance, to obey means "to love," and the imperative nature of the command becomes a promise when transposed into

---

[28] See Gerhard Schneider, *Parusiegleichnisse im Lukas-Evangelium* (SBS 74; Stuttgart: KBW Verlag, 1975).

[29] See Lucien Cerfaux, "Fructifiez en supportant (l'épreuve). A propos de Luc VIII, 15," *RB* 64 (1957) 481–91; reprinted in idem, *Recueil. Études d'exégèse et d'histoire religieuse* 3, Supplément (Gembloux: Duculot, 1962) 111–12.

the future. Moreover, enthusiastic love is emphasized by the importance placed on the response of the whole person.

The hierarchy of values

Thus Luke bears witness to a decisive hermeneutical reorientation: the Jesus whom he evokes has given up imposing submission to an impersonal law and advocates free adherence to a personal God. In this way he has modified not only the human attitude toward the law, but also the very nature of the law itself; the law is not a string of equivalent prescriptions, but a pyramid in which a hierarchy is to be honored. Luke believes that the two-part love commandment and the ten commandments, those aspects of the law that demand complete fidelity, constitute the top of the pyramid. Such a hierarchy of values is consistent with the attitude that Christ expects of his disciples. The Pharisees, as he sees them, are wrong because they exhaust themselves by calculating the priority of the tithe and the least amount of herbs and vegetables, all the while ignoring the command regarding love for God (Luke 11:42). But when we begin by responding in faith and accompany it with love and fairness, then all the rest follows.

Jewish ritual

Exactly what, then, is meant by "all the rest"? According to Luke 11:42, to which I now turn, it is the detail of the Mosaic law, even in its most formal and ritualistic aspects. Though he has become a Christian, Paul shows great respect in Acts for the temple, for circumcision, for the taking of vows, and for the calendar of Jewish festivals.[30] But, it is as a justified and righteous Christian that Paul practices these observances. It is only because he is a Jew that he conforms to them; such obedience is not demanded of Christians who are of pagan origin.

The spiritual law of Christians

Thus the virtues Luke admires in Cornelius are moral virtues, and these are the same virtues that the Lukan Peter expects from every person: "God shows no partiality, but in every nation anyone who fears him and does what is right is acceptable to him" (Acts 10:34–35). The key to the Lukan ethic is found in this phrase, an ethic that takes on the law in a spiritual manner.

In his own unique way, then, Luke adopts the Pauline categories. Without being a direct disciple of Paul, he understands his message: that the image of God, the role of Christ, the importance of faith, the enforced perseverance, and the spiritual rereading of the law are essential. If he firmly grasps these great ca-

---

[30] See Acts 16:1–3; 18:18; 20:16; 24:14; 25:8; 26:22; and 28:17.

tegories, it is because his Jewish-Hellenistic background has prepared him to do so. Whether it is because Luke does not understand or because he does not care to include the most personal aspects of Paul's conception, he does not take up Paul's reflection on the risks of strict obedience, that is, the idea that the law is capable of producing disastrous effects.

Christian asceticism

Surprisingly, Luke respects certain unexpected aspects of Jesus' message. He follows closely the line of Matthew and certain Jewish-Christians. He is delighted that Jesus has joined certain commandments to a law that is already rich with commands, and that these prescriptions constitute a straightening of observance. These additions concern areas in which Judaism escapes excess. The Lukan Jesus asks, for example, that one renounce money (Luke 12:33; 14:33), leave one's family to follow him (Luke 14:26), and, in short, that one renounce the benefits of creation.

Through these demands, Luke does not intend to reintroduce justification through works, but to emphasize that love for God impacts all other preoccupations; this is especially evident in the statement made with regard to the two missionaries, Barnabus and Paul: these two men "have risked their lives [literally, 'their souls'] for the sake of our Savior Jesus Christ" (Acts 15:26). Luke 16:13 has already stated this truth in other terms: "No slave can serve two masters at the same time ..." Nor is the apostle Paul, in fact, averse to such an extreme demand. He affirms that one cannot please both his spouse and his God at the same time (1 Cor. 7:32–35). These convergent messages in the gospels and the epistles are not being led by a legalism that considers itself inspired by the Torah, but by the beginning of an asceticism inspired by Christ's rigorism.

The first ecclesiastical canons

These additions express, in a colorful way, the absolute personal fidelity that each Christian owes to Christ. Other regulations resolve new problems that present themselves to the churches that are called to "go the distance" – from the ascension to the parousia – on earth. Above all, these rules are primarily related to the community and they set the churches apart from pagans and Jews. They form the first expression of ecclesiastical law, for it is important that structure be given to the offering of prayers, the sharing of bread, and so on.

7. Conclusion

A reasonable and universal Christianity

At the Jerusalem conference Luke has the apostolic authorities speak these words: "It has seemed good to the Holy Spirit and to us to impose on you no further burden than these that are necessary" (Acts 15:28). These words are in response to a demand made by Christians of pharisaic background (Acts 15:5), who wanted to impose circumcision on all believers. Such an action would, however, "provoke God by placing on the neck of the disciples a yoke that neither our ancestors nor we have been able to bear" (Acts 15:10). Within the context of this chapter in Acts, the debates at the Jerusalem conference appear rather Greek in their longing. There is a necessary minimum, but it must not turn into a required maximum: μηδὲν ἄγαν ("nothing in excess!"). The proper position is situated between the "nothing" of the pagan-Christians, who stand a good chance of offending the Jewish-Christians, and the "all" of the Jewish-Christians, who risk the loss of the pagan-Christians. By placing the Jerusalem conference and the apostolic decree in such a strategic position in the book of Acts, Luke creates a picture of Christianity that is both reasonable and universal, capable of being accepted by both the Jews on one hand and the Greeks and Romans on the other. We must remember that the ancients declared a religion that made unreasonable prescriptions to be super-stition.[31] The minimum imposed on pagan-Christians is deemed indispensable. Why? Luke does not explain further. The answer probably has to do with the necessary unity and cohesion of the community during eucharistic meals, values that Luke must preserve at all costs. Nothing more is required of pagan-Chris-tians, for if circumcision were demanded of all then the Christian church would again become a Jewish sect, and the mission to the pagans would lose its justification.

The rejection of circumcision (here Luke follows Paul, his theological mentor) goes hand in hand with the spiritualization of the requirement, the role of faith as the criterion for membership, and the name of Jesus Christ as the sole stipulation for salvation. Because of this doctrinal position, Luke thus presents Christianity as the reasonable and universal version of the past law of Israel, which in the eyes of the Christian apologete is bound up in rigid exclusivism. Christianity makes certain demands and compels one to go through a narrow door, but the door is one of faith and not of law. The image of the yoke disappears, for it is not a yoke that Christians wear reluctantly; rather it is the name of Jesus to which they cling freely. If they have something to "wear," (the same verb, βαστάζω) by donning this name, then it will not be the rule of the law, but the painful effects of the apos-tolic witness (Acts 9:15: "He [that is, Saul, alias Paul] is an instrument whom I

---

[31] See Downing, "Freedom from the Law."

have chosen to bring my name before Gentiles and kings and before the people of Israel."

Even if there is one God, creator and redeemer, there are for Luke two great stages of salvation history: the ancient system of the law and the prophets, and the new system of the kingdom of God and its evangelist, Jesus (Luke 16:16).

The role of the law in the new economy

The Evangelist does not develop a conception of the law as if he were a systematic theologian. In actuality, he relates interdependent and successive stories. All the same, he displays a solid theological position in the face of the Jewish theology of the law; but such a position means that he has been considered conservative by some[32] and liberal by others.[33]

In any case, Luke is not antinomian. He admires the antiquity and value of the law. He recognizes its usefulness for Jewish-Christians, and he outlines its spiritual meaning for pagan-Christians; more generally, he defines its universal value for all reasonable beings. But he realizes that certain aspects of the law are connected to what he sees as a past and outdated history of the people of Israel. His hero, Jesus, utilized the law well by valorizing its essential commandments, limiting the authority of other prescriptions, and adding precepts that proclaim the imminence of the kingdom.

Above all, the gift of the invitation to life precedes the sense of obligation. Forgiveness leads to freedom, and complete attachment to God pushes to the background that which never should have been placed in the foreground. This intense love for the gospel leads believers toward an ascetic life that is ultimately more rigorous than the demands of the law. Such a live is, however, no longer a matter of contractual obedience, but of impassioned listening.[34]

---

[32] See, for example, Hans Conzelmann, *Die Mitte der Zeit. Studien zur Theologie des Lukas* (5th ed.; BHTh 17; Tübingen: Mohr Siebeck, 1964); Jervell, *Luke and the People of God.*

[33] See Wilson, *Luke and the Law*; Blomberg, "Law in Luke-Acts."

[34] This article was already in the final stages when I discovered the title of a recent article on the same subject; see Helmut Merkel, "Das Gesetz im lukanischen Doppelwerk," in *Schrift und Tradition (Festschrift Josef Ernst)* (ed. K. Backhous and F.G. Untergassmair; Paderborn: Schöning, 1996) 119–33.

The Lukan Story of the Passion of Jesus (Luke 22–23)*

Dedicated to the memory of Dom Louis Leloir

This essay,[1] which is divided into two parts, will focus on Luke's story of Jesus' passion (Luke 22–23) from two perspectives. In the first part, I will focus on the story from a synchronic and narrative perspective, without daring or wishing to adopt a particular terminology.[2] In the second part, I will examine the question of Luke's sources, following a diachronic progression.

I. Synchronic Approach: Luke's Literary Accomplishment

From a literary perspective, a careful reading of Luke 22–23 suggests that attention ought to be paid to a number of diverse realities. First, we must consider the movement of this text from the standpoint of a story that is simultaneously fixed within its letter, or composition, and also mobile through the invitation to the voyage it presents to the reader. Second, we need to uncover the spatial and temporal coordinates that establish both the limits of and the possibilities for this story. Third, there is a need to analyze the interplay of the characters – so particular to the story of the passion – with the continuity of the one main character,

---

* I express my thanks to Dr. Charles Frederic Stone, who offered to translate this article.

[1] An earlier form of this paper was presented at the 1992 seminar of the Journées Bibliques de Louvain. At their arrival, the seminar participants learned with sadness the news of the recent death of Dom Louis Leloir on 15 August 1992, who otherwise would have been among them. A longtime professor at the University of Louvain, this specialist in Oriental Christian literature was also a Bible scholar. I particularly note here his contribution to *The Four Gospels 1992: Festschrift Frans Neirynck,* entitled "Le Commentaire d'Éphrem sur le Diatessaron. Réflexions et suggestions," 2.2358–67. For me, he was above all the indefatigable collaborator and the unfailing friend of the Association pour l'étude de la littérature apocryphe chrétienne (AELAC). At the seminar we agreed to offer our work in his memory. Let these pages be to him a posthumous homage.

[2] Over the years, my reflections on literary matters have been stimulated by the works of Claude Lévi-Strauss, Roland Barthes, Jean Starobinski, Gérard Genette, Frank Kermode, George A. Kennedy, Jean Delorme, and Jean-Noël Aletti; I am grateful to them all. A complete bibliography relative to exegetical matters on Luke 22–23 that I reference here is cited on pages 102–5. Unless otherwise noted, biblical translations are the NRSV.

Jesus, as well as the episodic presence of so many others, such as Judas and Herod. Fourth, care must be taken – and this is so often neglected – to examine the numerous objects mentioned and to imagine their function and circulation. Fifth, the various schemes Luke uses to articulate the life and death of particular characters must be detected. Sixth, we must define both the number and nature of the levels at which this story offers itself to be read. Seventh, and finally, passing from the story to the narrator and his point of view, we must mark the conscious distance between the voice Luke grants to the characters and the opinion he makes flow from his own pen.

Firm composition and supple movement

Initially one might say that, in contrast to the rest of his Gospel, Luke's narrative of the passion is a continuous story. This assertion represents, however, only a half truth; for this continuous story is in fact an assemblage of distinct episodes, like a wall that draws its beauty from stones that are at once alike and different. For their own part, the individual episodes, such as Peter's denial or Jesus' appearance before Herod, are sufficient unto themselves; yet they also enter into the service of the grand cause, that is to say, of the whole story. Moreover, certain episodes are related to one another, such as preparations leading to a voyage or instructions and their application. Thus, according to a literary device that is based in a social reality, the farewell dialogue (22:14–38) introduces separation and death (22:47ff.). Similarly, since the setting is judicial, it follows that the last stage of Jesus' trial can only be the execution of the penalty, just as the final outcome of the agony is the placement of Jesus' body in the tomb.

This interaction of the whole and the parts can be interpreted. I see here, first of all, a sign of the concomitance between the history of salvation and secular history in the life of Jesus. Next, I perceive a soteriological solidarity between the lot of the Son and that of the children, between the suffering Messiah and his people. Finally, I am struck by the quandary in which the author places his readers: will they admire such a destiny – certainly tragic but also beautiful – of inexorable human grandeur and of providentially divine character? Or, will they revolt against this parody of the law, this miscarriage of justice, thrice consciously done, and this blindness of a people to the recognition of their leader?

The construction of time and place

Both the interaction of time and place as well as the accretion of the sacred and profane in this story cause one to pause and reflect. We will begin with this last pair: Luke locates at Jerusalem not only the passion, which tradition requires him to do, but also its preparations and its auspicious outcome. He is conscious of the sacredness of the city, perhaps being inspired by Isaiah's prophecy of the high mountain from which the Word and the Spirit of God will descend (Isa 2). At the same time, however, Luke works a transformation. At Jerusalem, it was the temple that attested to the protecting presence of God, and certainly Jesus teaches there for a long time. But from the time of the passion forward, sacred space is established outside the temple. Thereafter, the "place that is called the Skull" (23:33) finds its station next to that of the temple and eventually comes to supplant it. According to Luke, for Jesus, and then later for the apostles also, the temple becomes no longer the sacramental place of the mysterious presence but the place, almost profane, where the Word can resound and orient one's gaze toward the site of torture. It is at Calvary, and not at the temple, that the ultimate salvific step of universal import is performed.

An analogous remark can be made regarding time. Luke 22 causes us to enter into the Passover, the most sacred time of year in the Jewish religion. But the decisive event does not coincide with the most sacred moment of that ceremony: to the Passover, Luke adds the Sunday resurrection. When the Sabbath is mentioned (23:54, 56), it is a time of waiting that is brought to fulfillment only in an unexpected – and therefore provocative – manner on the next day and not at the end of time (24:1ff.). For its part, the death of Jesus keeps its profane and historical character that no liturgical veil covers, no paschal typology affects.

If one examines Luke's concrete designation of space and the wording of chronological periods, one discovers a construction that suppresses troublesome coincidences. The most somber moment does not occur in the middle of the night! The time and place of the story draw apart and then rejoin, running in parallel or crossing like the motifs of a Greek frieze, or the movements of a pair of skaters.

We also note that the locations of Luke's story correspond, in the first half, to the will expressed by Jesus[3] and, in the second, to that of his adversaries. This transition from one will to the other takes place between verses 46 and 47 of chapter 22. At this moment, Jesus "falls" from being the grammatical subject and becomes the accusative (in Greek this "declension" is πτῶσις). The only occurrences where Jesus remains the subject of the sentence and the action are the dialogues found, for example, in 22:48, 51, 52; but even these become more rare as time progresses.

Through the will of Jesus, the story leads the readers into a protected space, into the house the Master needs: οἰκία, κατάλυμα, ἀνάγαιον μέγα ἐστρωμένον are the precise terms Luke uses to suggest this space (22:10–12). This is the place that is preordained for the preparation of the Passover, and one will note the importance of the verb ἑτοιμάζω in verses 8, 12 and 13 of this chapter. The Passover itself becomes the prolegomena to the last testament of the Master. The essence of chapter 22 – the scene of farewells – unfolds within this dwelling that has been made providentially available even as homes will later be made available for the earliest churches.

---

[3] This will expresses itself in terms of desire (22:15) and habit (22:39).

From this interior space the will of the hero – underlined by the words "as was his custom" (22:39) – guides him and his disciples toward the Mount of Olives, an exterior place, or τόπος (22:40), where the ultimate temptation (22:39–46; see 4:1–13) and the encounter with the adversary (the arrest, 22:47–51) unfold. If in this exterior place Jesus remains master of the word, he loses control of the action. It is henceforth the pernicious will of humans that is accomplished (23:25: τὸν δὲ Ἰησοῦν παρέδωκεν τῷ θελήματι αὐτῶν). Significantly, the actions of the Jewish authorities as they are led by Judas – himself invaded by the presence of Satan (22:3) – are equally and preemptively a historical inflection that follow another will, that of God; we note here that the word θέλημα appears also in 22:42b.

Within this external space, at the crucial moment when the transfer of wills takes place, one sentence signals to us the quality of the hour that now manifests itself: "your hour," "the power of darkness" (22:53). Henceforth, the story lays hands on the hero and moves him to several places of misfortune: they seize him, lead him, then bring him (the words are banal, but eloquently oppressive in their banality) into the οἰκία of the high priest (22:54). A little later he is directed, under escort, into the συνέδριον, the assembly room of the people (22:66). Then, as a third stage in the trial, the story thrusts Jesus, led by a multitude into the interior of the governor's tribunal to appear before Pilate (23:1). Luke, as one knows, then adds a judicial interlude: from the Roman tribunal the accused is "sent" (ἀνέπεμψεν αὐτόν, 23:7) before Herod, who is in the palace (the word is not mentioned) he occupies during his sojourn at Jerusalem.

Finally, at the end of this meandering and chaotic procedure Jesus is sent back to Pilate. In that place, as already noted, the governor neither imposes his own point of view nor his own will.[4] Rather, he is content to let events happen. Verse 24 conveys a decision, but it is that of doing nothing, or letting happen through others that which one regrets personally: καὶ Πιλᾶτος ἐπέκρινεν γενέσθαι τὸ αἴτημα αὐτῶν (23:24).

From there, the story situates anew the course of history in exterior space. In contrast to the Mount of Olives, where events still depended on the will of Jesus, the Place of the Skull (23:33) is another τόπος, where the adversaries are permitted to accomplish their deadly work. Like the *extra muros* of the Mount of Olives, the *extra muros* of the Place of the Skull becomes a place of obscurity.[5] The temptation and arrest on one side, the crucifixion and death on the other – both belong to the world of darkness. At his death Jesus becomes an inert corpse that takes its own course: it will be doubly enclosed, encased first within a shroud (23:53) and then placed within a tomb (23:53).

In contrast to these events, chapter 24 is one of openings: the opening of the tomb, the breaking free from death toward life and glory, the taking leave of the

---

[4] See 23:20, where Pilate's unstable will is noted: θέλων ἀπολῦσαι τὸν Ἰησοῦν.
[5] See 23:44: καὶ σκότος ἐγένετο ἐφ' ὅλην τὴν γῆν.

city for Emmaus, the opening of minds and the scriptures (24:32). New protecting spaces, comparable to the high chamber of farewells, appear on the morning of Easter: first at the house where the Resurrected One is revealed at table with his two disciples (24:30), then the high chamber where he appears to the reunited Eleven (24:36).

In summary, the Lukan text evokes interior and exterior places; and among the interior places, the communal and protecting houses are set in contrast to the edifices of constricting and excessive power.[6] Moreover, each of these places is a place of passage; verbs of movement are always associated with them. Stages thus alternate with stations.[7] It is in these spaces that the story takes form.

But while attentive to places, the narrative also scans time. The story begins, for instance, "on the day of Unleavened Bread" (22:7): curiously, Luke situates the preparations for the Passover on a Thursday, and on this same day he also prepares for the passion of Jesus, or, more precisely, his last meal (22:7). Then comes the hour, that is, the beginning of the Passover on Thursday evening. From mentioning the day in general, the story thus passes to the precision of "the hour" (22:14). This long evening of communion is carried over into the night at the Mount of Olives, where everything is overturned. The Passover night, the moment of feast and liberation, becomes "your hour" (and no longer God's) and the "power of darkness" (and not that of light) (22:53). Jesus is arrested (22:47–53). The night continues in the first inhospitable house, that of the high priest. Interrogation takes place inside; denial outside (22:63–71; 54–62).

Then comes daybreak: καὶ ὡς ἐγένετο ἡμέρα ("When day came," 22:66). In fact, this day will not correspond to its definition. It will instead be a day of darkness that repeats and continues the preceding night. An intense obscurity, an eclipse of the sun (23:45), will suppress its light from the sixth to the ninth hour (23:44) – an interrupted day, a broken time. In this half day, which will sink into the night, Christ is brought successively into buildings that were constructed in order that justice might reign; but on this day of darkness they will be occupied by beings who mock and abuse innocence. There are three of these places: the Sanhedrin of the people, the tribunal of the governor, and the palace of Herod.

Having been attentive to the preparations of the Passover, we come now to the day of Passover itself, which, according to Luke, falls this particular year on a Friday, the "parasceve," or preparation of the Sabbath. Thus, in Luke's story Jesus on his dominical day will accomplish what has been prepared for by both the Passover and the Sabbath. Luke indicates nothing to us regarding this Sabbath, except

---

[6] The ultimate and provisional resting place, the tomb (23:53, 55), has a neutral and universal valence. All humanity, both protectors and prosecutors alike, is reunited there.

[7] Franz Georg Untergassmair (*Kreuzweg und Kreuzigung Jesu. Ein Beitrag zur lukanischen Redaktionsgeschichte und zur Frage nach der lukanischen "Kreuzestheologie"* [Paderborn: Schöning, 1980] 42, 201) suggests this liturgical notion of stations in relation to the Lukan story of the passion.

its beginning and its end (23:54–56; 24:1). Immobility reigns here and marks the time of the seal of death. Nothing occurs except the waiting of the women (23:54–56). But this waiting is marvelous: it bears witness both to the respect due the dead, according to the way of the traditional religion, and to the ineradicable affection of the women. And it prepares, according to the way of the new religion, for the testimony of the empty tomb and the resurrection.

Luke tells us that on this ambivalent Sabbath, torn between the end of history and the beginning of eschatology – between rite and faith – the Sabbath "breaks forth"; it "begins to shine" (ἐπέφωσκεν, 23:54). But it reveals its light only after the darkness of night has been spread out – since the day actually begins at dusk – and where night maintains its ascendancy in the figurative sense of death's domination.

The melody of time and the accompaniment of space bring the reader to the same quandary: should one celebrate what is happening in a hymn to the cross or should one lament the violence of humans?

The interplay of characters

We have already encountered the conflicting sequence of differing wills: that of Jesus as he plans his Passover – his double Passover one can say – first Jewish and then Christian; that of the adversaries who become determinant from the time of the arrest,[8] leaving Jesus no initiative except freedom of speech. Behind the human will of the Jewish authorities, Luke clearly designates the true culprit, Satan having already entered Judas (22:3); the book of Acts will repeat that the Jews have surely acted albeit through ignorance (Acts 3:17; 13:27). Nevertheless, in order not to let the story escape its providential trajectory, Luke recalls the will of wills; that which takes the risk of not destroying the adversary but which, at this pivotal point is represented by the Garden of Olives, insists on making the well-beloved Son drink the cup. The Son, conscious of the momentum in which he finds himself and of the place where God has decided he should be, expresses his human wish ("remove this cup from me"), but orients – in anticipation and in trust – his will to that of the Father: πλὴν μὴ τὸ θέλημά μου ἀλλὰ τὸ σὸν γινέσθω ("yet, not my will but yours be done," 22:42). For a moment the will of God will be that the will of the devil triumphs. This dramatic reversal takes place against the backdrop of the Mount of Olives and the arrest. The word that the author's pen inscribes is πειρασμός (22:46): "trial" and "temptation" for the disciples, who will not comprehend what is happening; "trial" and "temptation" above all for Jesus, who must let it happen, and who must restrain the divine energy within him that at other times (6:19) was dispensed in order that health and life might triumph. Jesus refuses to defend himself: to the question put to his entourage, "Lord, should we

---

[8] See 23:51: τῇ βουλῇ καὶ τῇ πράξει αὐτῶν.

strike with the sword?"(22:49), the response is "No," manifested narratively by a refusal of violence[9] and a gesture of healing (22:51).[10] The force of life that remains within Jesus is destined for others. Now is the time – the Son here conforms his will to that of the Father – for death to do its work.

The unity of the action in this narrative is assured by one character: Jesus, active and then conscientiously passive, remains at the center of the stage and holds the principal role. But the authorities also play a determining role. They set the action into motion, then disappear progressively from the stage as soon as the desired effect has been obtained. They are referred to no longer, except once after the condemnation: they are the leaders, one reads, who mock the crucified Jesus (23:35).

The role of the people in this drama is more difficult to analyze. At the beginning ὁ λαός or ὁ ὄχλος (22:2, 6), are present in the background and are cast as favorable to Jesus. Thus, one must identify them neither with the "crowd"(ὄχλος, 22:47) that comes to arrest Jesus nor with those who refer Jesus to the tribunal of Pilate (τὸ πλῆθος αὐτῶν, 23:1). On the other hand, it is certainly "the people" (λαός), who are convened officially by Pilate, together with the high priests and the leaders of Israel (23:13). Luke thus integrates them into what will become the final decision. Although Luke does not explicitly acknowledge it, the people let themselves be swept away by their leaders: with them, they cry "Away with this fellow!" (23:18) and then the famous "Crucify, crucify him!" (23:21). Luke underscores this fact by the insertion of the adverb – rare from his pen – παμπληθεί ("together," 23:18). It is also the people, with no mention of their leaders, who accompany Jesus throughout his punishment. They appear this time alongside the weeping women of Jerusalem (23:27). Nothing suggests that the people continue to express hostility. On the contrary, at the cross "the people stood by" mute even as their leaders mocked the crucified one as incapable of saving himself (23:35). And, finally, Luke characterizes their attitude at the death of Jesus as one of quasi-repentance: the people return home, he writes, beating their breasts (23:48; see 23:27).

Above all, Luke wants to make the people eye witnesses.The people have ascertained, perhaps even contemplated, the events (τὰ γενόμενα, 23:48). The evangelist utilizes the verb θεωρῶ with insistence both in 23:35 and 23:48, where he also appeals to the word θεωρία. In this last passage, the people are situated next to the friends and companions of the crucified one. On Jesus' side at the beginning of the story, they return to the side of the disciples at the end, after having followed the authorities, encountered Pilate, then accompanied the women of the city. The succession of these tableaux is not without meaning: it evokes, in narrative fashion, a series of soul states and the evolution of an attitude.

---

[9] There are no armed legions of angels who advance in Luke's narrative (cf. Matt 26:53), but only a consoling angel who approaches (22:43).

[10] When Jesus heals the severed ear he utilizes his divine force for the last time (22:51).

If one examines each episode of the passion in and of itself, one ascertains that Luke follows a convention made known to us through theater and the ancient novel: the Evangelist avoids creating dialogue between more than two persons at a time. Even if more than two actors are on stage, only two express themselves at a time. And if several characters intervene, they do so in turn and not simultaneously.

In spite of the omnipresence of Jesus, some episodes unfold without him. His absence at the beginning and ending of the drama, such as during the conspiracy (22:1–6) and the scenes of mourning (23:50–54, 55–56), serves as a frame. And in two other places the narrator permits a digression: in one case an apostle (and what a one!) 'gives way' (22:54–62), and in the other a disciple becomes engaged 'on the way' (23:26).

In another episode Jesus is confronted by three persons or groups. At the time of the arrest, he speaks first with Judas, then with his disciples, and finally with those who have commissioned Judas (22:47–53). This superabundance is exceptional, and Luke manages it by having three successive dialogues rather than a general conversation. If at this moment Jesus is losing the initiative at the level of action, he still has the last word with each of these interlocutors, such is Luke's belief.

Pilate – as was the case with all judges in antiquity – must confront two parties. The sequence of events with the first audience (23:1–7) is the following: the Jewish leaders address Pilate (Pilate does not respond to them immediately). Pilate turns to Jesus (Jesus returns the question). Pilate speaks to the Jewish leaders, who do not accede to his view. The Jewish chiefs reiterate their complaint to Pilate. Pilate then finds a possible means of escape: their appearance before Herod.

When this solution fails, a second audience proves necessary. The three parties are regrouped, but this time the sequence of events unfolds differently. Jesus no longer intervenes (23:13–25). Instead, everything occurs between Pilate and Jesus' adversaries. This time, Pilate speaks first. The dialogue is extended and marked by the redundant episode with Barabbas. The sequence of interchanges thus runs as follows: Pilate addresses the Jewish leaders (long explication). The leaders respond to Pilate (violent, unanimous intervention). Pilate replies to them (short intervention, but of the same content: liberation); they to Pilate (short and bitter reply: "Crucify, crucify Him!"). Pilate responds to them (new declaration of innocence);[11] they to Pilate (indirect discourse, then great cries). Finally, Pilate replies to them (indirect discourse, decision).

---

[11] According to Luke, Pilate here affirms the innocence of Jesus for the "third time" (23:22). The first time was at the end of the first audience (23:4) and the second at the beginning of the second audience (23:14).

A crescendo builds throughout these two scenes before Pilate. From one scene to the other the violence grows; from one scene to the other the voice of Jesus is more and more hidden; from one scene to the other Pilate emphasizes his certitude of innocence and confirms his steadfast opinion, only to have his will deflate at the moment when the opposition swells. At the end, he abandons Jesus. The passage from direct discourse to indirect discourse encrusts the statement in a lasting and inevitable reality. The narrator and, across from him, the readers silently observe: "See what they have wished. See what he has let happen."

I would like to draw attention again to the scenes that are the most numerous and, in a certain sense, the most paradoxical. These are the face-to-face scenes, where the projector illuminates only two characters, whose features then become so precise and visible that proper nouns and precise titles become necessary. Jesus himself is, of course, already known; he dominates the situation from the beginning. It is therefore no longer necessary to formulate his name. He is the αὐτός ("he"), solemn and admired, or the οὗτος ("this one"), enigmatic and blamed. Attention switches to his interlocutor. And it is here that the paradox resides because this scene should only be a link in a chain, only one functional episode among many others. But, while being this, it is also – and perhaps it is this first of all – an independent, paradigmatic scene with a hero who is not the Master but either a disciple or an adversary. In this way, the good thief, the centurion, Simon of Cyrene, Joseph of Arimathea – not to mention Judas – the daughters of Jerusalem and the group of women each in turn becomes, in the space of an instant, the protagonists. This very skillful literary technique temporarily diverts us from the inevitable, or manifests the inevitable to us from a different angle. It humanizes the drama, shifting it away from absurd solitude towards a subsequent solidarity. Luke's narrative artistry, though focused primarily on one destiny, impacts all through their many-hued and contrasting variety.

Finally, one should not forget two decisive dialogues, meta-narratives one might say: the two prayers of Jesus. In these two invocations, God is called upon as "Father" (22:42; 23:34). In the first, Jesus' request is granted, albeit otherwise than he wished, by the appearance of a beneficent angel (22:43–44). In the second, his request remains in suspense. God does not respond to say whether or not pardon will be granted. This menacing silence on the part of Luke's God persists until the end of Acts: God's pardon will make itself explicit, however, in Luke's second book through the offer of the kerygma and the condition of conversion. This extra-narrative reference to God efficaciously causes the reader to recall that ultimately only one supreme will rules the drama and consciously utilizes the wills of the other characters.

The circulation of objects

It is sufficient to have encountered solitude to understand the importance that certain objects can acquire. The value of an object can vary, depending on its origin, its owner, and the period in life through which its owner is passing. But an object also has its own function; it can, for instance, be useful or not. An object also has its own hour. Finally, the quality of an object can vary according to its degree of novelty and the duration of its use. An object has a life that must be appreciated in the concert, or cacophony, of human relations because it is a part of history, even though it does not itself make history.

Now, the Lukan story of the passion draws attention to a good number of objects.[12] Some of these, such as the jar of water that serves as a point of reference in 22:10, are real objects that are internal to the narrative. Others, such as the sieve in which Simon Peter will be tested (22:31), are allusive objects that are mentioned as metaphors at certain points in the discourse of the characters. This distinction can create ambiguities with which the story sometimes plays: the most famous concerns the swords that are at once metaphors suggested by Jesus and objects held by the anxious disciple (22:35–38, 49).

We will speak first about the real objects in the story. For us, money has become abstract, but for the ancients ἀργύριον was a concrete reality, pieces that had their proper weight. At the beginning of the passion story (22:5) money is put into circulation, passing from the Jewish leaders to Judas as compensation and exchange for another παράδοσις, that is, the delivery of Jesus. The Christian tradition has done well to meditate on this bargaining, this offering of objects in exchange for a subject who is eventually so subjected that in the end he is no more than an inert object, a neuter σῶμα.

At the moment when this transaction takes place Jesus institutes another circulation of objects around a table that is explicitly mentioned (22:21) and that anticipates the table of the kingdom (22:30). Jesus designates a cup that opens onto the coming of the kingdom (22:17–18), then he distributes bread that will not be for exchange, in contradistinction to money, but for the sacramental presence and recollected past of Jesus (22:19). Finally, he circulates the cup that marks communion with the sacrifice of the covenant (22:20).

Two other "object" scenes respond to one another: those of the swords. On one hand, the question arises as to the Christian's equipment, and the text addresses this with the usual attention that Luke brings to means, agency, and mediation (22:35–38); on the other hand, we have the wrong-doing of the anxious disciple, impulsive and overly zealous (22:49–51). The second scene provides the meaning that must be attributed to μάχαιρα in the first scene: the swords the disciples will

---

[12] In this discussion of the Lukan story of the passion I leave aside those things that are not, properly speaking, objects, including parts of the body – ear, hair, abdomen, skull, hand, knee – and vegetable matter, such as as plants and trees.

need when the Master's protection has disappeared are not tangible arms, but a spiritual force that articulates the best of humanity and the splendor of the gift of God; for in the Pauline school where Luke was educated one utilized the metaphor of the sword to describe the Holy Spirit and the word of God (Eph 6:17; Heb 4:12–13); more generally, the Christian life was compared to military service.[13]

But the object *par excellence* in the passion story is obviously the cross. Alluded to since the cries of the leaders and the crowd ("Crucify, crucify him!" 23:21), this object is mentioned at the beginning of the way of the cross (23:26). Curiously, it is then associated with Simon, who carries it so that Jesus will never have its burden. Instead, it is the cross that will carry Jesus (23:33). Here again, a reflection imposes itself: is it too much to say that only Christ confronts the cross in its function as capital punishment ("they crucified," 23:33)? The disciple "behind Jesus" (23:26) encounters the cross in a less dramatic fashion: he is to the cross what Joseph of Arimathea will be to the body of Jesus – one friend, one disciple, who shares to his limit and relieves the fate of his Master as he is able.

Scripture (Ps 22:18) imposes upon the gospel story of the passion the division of garments by casting lots. Luke points this out in passing (23:34), without lingering on the episode's scriptural character. One can ask whether or not the text opposes the garments of the living to those of the dead, the garments torn apart as opposed to the shroud (σινδών) in which the body of the crucified one is wrapped (23:53). We should not forget here the importance that the ancients attributed to clothing as an indication of identity and social status.[14] To take off Christ's clothing was to hasten the end of his life: to cover him with a shroud was to confirm his death. Adversaries who draw lots and partisans who respect the ritual of mourning are in accord in bearing witness to the tragic outcome they cannot grasp.

There could still be other material realities worth mentioning: the vinegar before death (23:36), the aromatics and myrrh afterwards (24:1), the writing hung over the nude body of the crucified one that both betrayed and communicated his royal identity (23:38). We should, above all, speak of the outcome met by another object, that is, the rending of the veil of the temple that deprives it of its reason for being (23:45). The text places this prodigy in relation to another miraculous sign, the darkness that plunges the entire world into obscurity, the eclipse of the sun (23:44–45). It is not enough to say that in ancient writings such prodigies accompany the birth or death of heroes and gods. Rather, this sign has a particular function that confirms what I have suggested above regarding the temple: the sanctuary loses its function from this time forward. The divine presence is henceforth elsewhere, in a place ἀχειροποίητος ("not made of the hand of man," see Acts 7:48).

---

[13] I do not claim to have explicated in this way the enigmatic response of Jesus: ἱκανόν ἐστιν ("It is enough," 22:38).

[14] See Edgar Haulotte, *Symbolique du vêtement selon la Bible* (Théologie 65; Paris: Aubier, 1966).

The interplay of four models

A friend confided to me recently that, in spite of her sadness, she was comforted by the dignity with which her brother had died. This grandeur contrasted, she said, with certain attitudes he had while living.

Life was one way, death will be another. On hearing this diagnostic, I reflected on the presence of what seem to be very ancient schemes in our civilization. I immediately thought about the death of the wicked, most particularly that of persecutors, and observed that with the story of Herod Agrippa's death (Acts 12:20–23), Luke opened the way to Lactantius:[15] as will be his life so will be his death, from sin to its punishment. Then I considered more precisely the words of my friend: in greater contrast, Luke anticipated them in the episode of the good brigand (23:39–43).[16] One who had begun badly came to a good ending. The case of Judas also came to mind as a third mode: his was the miserable death of one who started well, of a renegade disciple (Acts 1:15–20) who prefigures the future *lapsi* of Tertullian and Cyprian's time.

There remains only one case to complete this square of possibilities: the dignified end of a beautiful life. This is the case of Jesus, which surely inaugurates – above all in the Lukan version – the literary genre of the acts of martyrs[17] and prepares the way for other liturgical, homiletic, and theological texts.

What is one to think of these four patterns? Do they exist? Are they as archaic as I suppose? Are they planted in Greece alone, or only in the tradition of Israel, or, as archtypes, do they belong to the social consciousness of all human beings?

Whatever may be the responses to these questions, I can specify several characteristics of the fourth model. In the correspondence between life and death, a foreknowledge of this outcome is required; a dismissal of preoccupation with the self in favor of one's followers; a reason for being that will provide a reason to accept death; a mission to complete that death, which, far from obstructing its realization, actually accelerates it; an aroused jealousy that, before the success of this destiny, holds for this destiny a fatal trap. In addition to Jesus, one thinks of the death of Socrates, nor will we forget the deaths of Simeon (2:25–35) and Stephen (Acts 6:8–8:1).

---

[15] See Lactantius, *De morte persecutorum.* The French edition: Lactance, *De la mort des persécuteurs* (ed. J. Moreau; 2 vols.; SC 39; Paris: Cerf, 1954).

[16] See the story of the good brigand's admittance to Paradise in *Acta Pilati* 26 (= *Descensus Christi ad inferos* 10); *Los Evangelios Apócrifos: colección de testos griegos y latinos, versión crítica, estudios introductorios, comentarios e ilustraciones* (ed. Aurelio de Santos Otero; 6th ed.; BAC 148; Madrid: La Editio al Catolica, 1988) 463–64.

[17] See Hippolyte Delehaye, *Les passions des martyrs et les genres littéraires* (2d ed.; Subsidia Hagiographica 13B; Brussels: Société des Bollandistes, 1966).

The three levels of the work

Much has been written on the theology of Luke's story of the passion. Certain scholars have found there doctrinal tendencies (theodicy, the history of salvation, christology); others have found a historical preoccupation (to confirm the creed); still others a parenetic orientation (the role of the disciples and of the people). The conflict of wills analyzed above has already suggested that we distinguish two levels of reading, which Luke presents simultaneously: a) the narrative level, which suggests a human history – a drama – that Luke, within the schema of contrast, summarizes with these words: "this Jesus whom you crucified" (Acts 2:36); and b) the theological, meta-historical level that sees in the story and its contours the sal-vific design that God has completed properly, which Luke confesses through an al-lusion to "the definite plan and the foreknowledge of God" at Pentecost (Acts 2:23). In my opinion, it is necessary to add to the historical and meta-historical levels, that is to say the narrative and doctrinal levels, an ethical and par-enetic level. Martin Dibelius and Albert Vanhoye have spoken the essentials on this subject:[18] the figure of Christ drawn by Luke is that of the suffering Righteous One, of the rejected prophet, of the martyr. The Righteous One was part of his people, the prophet had a mission, and the martyr acted in communion with his own. In any case, the story of the passion, according to Luke, has been written neither as a simple page of history nor as the statement of a doctrine of expiation or substitution. Its form is destined for readers who have been called, implicitly but truly, to partake in the destiny of Jesus: in the emotion of faith and the gravity of en-gagement. The figures of the disciples should help them keep their bearings, for they are able to identify with Simon of Cyrene and learn to surpass an existence such as that of Judas or Simon Peter. Just as the figure of Jesus sweeps along the path of a subjective soteriology (inclusive of the faith and life of believers), so too the light in which Jesus' companions – be they disciples, women, or passers-by – are cast takes on parenetic coloration in Luke. To the narrative and doctrinal tableaux that Luke offers for our meditation, I would therefore add the moral level.

The narrator

As a narrator, Luke knows what he wishes to accomplish and he never hesitates. He nowhere displays ignorance. He knows the unfolding of the facts, even the

---

[18] See Martin Dibelius, *Die Formgeschichte des Evangeliums* (3d ed., with annex by Günther Bornkamm; Tübingen: Mohr Siebeck, 1959) 178–218; and Albert Vanhoye, *La Passion selon les quatre Évangiles* (Lire la Bible 55; Paris: Cerf, 1981) 18–19, 30–33, 57–61. Vanhoye has corrected his interpretation on one point: he no longer thinks he can rely on verse 62 of chapter 22 (the bit-ter tears of Peter after the denial), but now concedes its inauthenticity; see idem, "L'intérêt de Luc pour la prophétie en Lc 1,76; 4,16–30 et 22,60–65," in *The Four Gospels 1992: Festschrift Frans Neirynck* (ed. Frans van Segbroeck et al.; 3 vols.; BETL 100; Leuven: Leuven University Press and Peeters, 1992) 2.1529–48.

most confidential (22:4) and the most secret (23:45). He is *au courant* with the habits of the characters (22:39), with their spiritual and emotional states (22:5), with their schemes (22:6), with their worth (23:50). He knows the dealings of each, from the most cowardly (22:54–62) to the most heroic (23:34). As the preceding pages have suggested, his is a theological, moral, and literary project.

But if he knows all these things and desires all these things, Luke nevertheless recounts his story without implicating himself in it, and this in contrast to what he does elsewhere in the passages where he speaks of "we" and in the prologues, where he uses the pronoun "I." In the passion account he never judges; even at the worst moments of Judas's betrayal and Peter's denial he maintains perfect reserve. He holds to this attitude because he wishes to give the impression that the facts speak for themselves and that the characters express the meaning that they themselves attribute to events. He himself never utilizes scripture to legitimate or explicate the drama that is unfolding. He simply points out that the hero has established this correspondence (22:37). He does not feel the need to prove personally that the grievances addressed to Jesus are false. He is content rather to recount Pilate's judgment on three successive occasions and let the evidence itself illuminate the reader. The story is, he thinks, made stronger through the arrangement of its own good offices: it thus acquires a sense of objectivity.

The narrator does not stop – one should add – his story at the placing of Jesus' body in the tomb (23:50–54). The narration of chapter 24 constitutes the indispensable exit from the tunnel. It removes the ambiguities and the paradoxes of chapters 22 and 23. In particular and principally, it makes clear that the giving over of Jesus' will is not done out of ignorance, that the lucidity of the hero is not blindness, and that his confidence in events represents the visible surface of a harmonious communion with the One who determines the events of the story. The numbering of the Righteous One among the ranks of the unjust (22:37) can only be provisional. In permitting the will of Satan to be accomplished, Christ let himself become weaker than Satan. In submitting to the will of God, he hoped that God's will would finally prevail and that therefore he had been right to conform freely his own will to God's.[19]

---

[19] I thank the colleagues who, at the time of the Journées Bibliques seminar, reacted to this account. Here are several critical comments I noted: a) Is it not necessary to take into account the status of the readers, who from the beginning of the play know the outcome of the drama? b) Have I sufficiently respected Luke's strategy of avoiding talk about Jesus' condemnation to death? c) Where I spoke – I have since modified this – of the implicit narrator holding himself in reserve, did this contradict earlier paragraphs that insisted on the theological and literary organization of the story? d) Is it not necessary to consider the whole work in order to discover the tendencies and the intentions linked to the structures and effects of composition? e) Is not the effacement of the narrator nothing more than a rhetorical effect? (I have taken this suggestion into account in the definitive version of my text.) f) The Lukan story – this is my conviction – communicates one certainty, that of the innocence of Jesus, the Righteous One.

II. Diachronic Approach: Luke's Sources and their Interweaving

The state of the question

The question each exegete asks himself or herself at one time or another is that of the documentation that Luke had the benefit of when writing chapters 22–23 of his first book. One's interest in this question can be increased for a variety of reasons; Luke's relation to Mark, for example, is here of another nature than during Jesus' Galilean period. In a story nonetheless coherent the sequence of events in Luke's narrative differs from Mark's. For instance, Mark's sequence reads: appearance before the Sanhedrin (Mark 14:53–64), mockings (Mark 14:65), and denial (Mark 14:66–72, foreshadowed in v. 54); but in Luke we find these events in the reversed order of denial (Luke 22:54–62), mockings (Luke 22:63–65), and appearance before the Sanhedrin (Luke 22:66–71). Moreover, when parallel pericopes are placed side by side, the degree of correspondence between the two is less than in the rest of the Gospel. Thus in the story of the trial before the Jewish authorities, Luke ignores the inquiry of witnesses and the logion on the temple but he attests to a doublet, which Mark ignores, regarding the question of Jesus' messiahship (Luke 22:66–71//Mark 14:53–64).

Finally, the Lukan story also diverges in the content of its constituent episodes: Luke omits the anointing at Bethany (Mark 14:3–9; cf. Luke 7:36–50) but transmits Jesus' appearance before Herod (Luke 23:8–12), which is a judicial interlude the other evangelist ignores. To these particulars, it is suitable to add a final finding: although the relationship between the two stories does not reflect literary dependence, Luke shares with the evangelist John certain details in his passion account. Neither John nor Luke have, for example, two meetings of the Sanhedrin, but only one (Luke 22:66–71//John 18:24), which is preceded by a stop at the house of the high priest in both accounts (Luke 22:54//John 18:13–14, 19–23).[20]

The quantitative and qualitative importance of these data explains the immense literature they have engendered. The recent commentaries by Joseph A. Fitzmyer[21] and Wolfgang Wiefel[22] present the major positions.[23] Each admits that Mark is not the creator of the literary genre of "the passion story" and that his story is composed from both tradition and redaction.[24] The *Sitz im Leben*, the so-

---

[20] On the correspondence, or relationship, between John and Luke and the literature this has generated, see Frans Neirynck, "John and the Synoptics (1975–1990)," in *John and the Synoptics* (ed. Adelbert Denaux; BETL 101; Leuven: Leuven University Press/Peeters, 1992) 35–46.

[21] See Joseph A. Fitzmyer, *The Gospel According to Luke* (2 vols.; AB 28 A-B; Garden City: Doubleday, 1981–1985) 2.1365–68.

[22] See Wolfgang Wiefel, *Das Evangelium nach Lukas* (THKNT 3; Berlin: Evangelische Verlagsanstalt, 1998) 12–13, 357–58.

[23] See François Bovon, *Luc le théologien. Vingt-cinq ans de recherches (1950–1975)* (2d ed.; Geneva: Labor et Fides, 1988) 175–81.

[24] For the history of the traditions and the elaboration of a coherent story, see Rudolf Bult-

cial rooting, within the church of such a story had to have been liturgical[25]: it was in order to commemorate the death of Jesus that one strove to recall it, to recount it, and to interpret it (in particular with the aid of scripture). If one supposes a certain plurality among primitive communities, then one must admit that diverse stories of the passion were able to see the light of day. Such a supposition must not, however, favor the hypothesis that the passion stories found in the Gospels enjoyed total autonomy. Literary and frequent verbatim similarities oppose this.

How then are we to imagine and reconstruct this relationship? a) First possibility: as in the rest of his Gospel, here again Luke follows Mark, but he permits himself to modify the story in a more drastic manner than before because of traditions he has heard, or because of a story – possibly oral – that his community has transmitted to him. The divergences in relation to Mark would thus have a *traditionsgeschichtlich* origin. b) Second possibility: this is simply a variant of the first in that Luke intervenes more vigorously than before at the redactional level. He has at his disposal little more than Mark and his imagination, accompanied by his convictions and scriptural references. Thus the disparities in relation to Mark would be explained here in a *redaktionsgeschichtlich* manner. c) Third possibility: Luke here lays down his principal source, which is Mark, and aligns his text with a story, no doubt written, that he prefers for various reasons, doctrinal or practical, emotional or rational.[26] Granted that the Evangelist also knows the Marcan story, he permits himself to interlace the narrative that is special to him with material extracts from the second Gospel. As in the first hypothesis, Luke thus enjoyed two sources but he gave preference to the second. The argument here is *literarkritisch* in its origin, while benefiting from *formgeschichtlich* and *redaktionsgeschichtlich* arguments.

It is not desirable here to present a list of those who advocate for these diverse hypotheses; it is enough to say that the list is long, that is contains many prestigious names, and that it has not been monopolized by any particular nation. Even before the appearance of the history of redaction, certain partisans of *Formgeschichte*, such as Kendrick Grobel[27] and Jack Finegan,[28] maintained that Luke did not have at his disposal any continuous source other than Mark. The originality and the margin of creative liberty accorded to each biblical author by the tenants of the *Redaktionsgeschichte* school have only incited inquirers to attribute to the

---

mann, *Die Geschichte der synoptischen Tradition* (3d ed.; Göttingen: Vandenhoeck & Ruprecht, 1957) 297–303; and Dibelius, *Die Formgeschichte des Evangeliums,* 178–218.

[25] See Étienne Trocmé, *The Passion as Liturgy: A Study in the Origin of the Passion Narratives in the Four Gospels* (London: SCM, 1983).

[26] The story could be either the continuation of the special material that he uses in the story of the journey to Jerusalem or a source particular to the story of the passion.

[27] Kendrick Grobel, *Formgeschichte und synoptische Quellenanalyse* (Göttingen: Vandenhoeck & Ruprecht, 1937).

[28] Jack Finegan, *Die Überlieferung der Leidens- und Auferstehungsgeschichte Jesu* (Gießen: Töpelmann, 1934).

Evangelist more and more of the particularities of his story.[29] Such is the attitude taken by Frans Neirynck,[30] by Martin Rese[31] in an unpublished Habilitations-schrift, by Joseph A. Fitzmyer[32] in the second volume of his commentary, by Marion L. Soards[33] in his analysis of Luke 22, by Franz Georg Untergassmair[34] who from Luke 23 on attributes the Lukan originality to a "spezifisches Verkündi-gungsanliegen,"[35] and by Donald Senior[36] in his recent presentation of the whole story of the passion, to cite only certain ones.

I do not know with whom the opposite hypothesis, that there was a Proto-Luke or a special source particular to the Evangelist for the story of the passion, originated. But in Germany, since the end of the nineteenth century various authors, such as Paul Feine[37] and Bernhard Weiss,[38] have chosen to put this forward. In this linguistic zone the hypothesis, though never very popular,[39] has not disappeared; we encounter it in the works of such eminent exegetes as Adolph Schlatter,[40] Joachim Jeremias,[41] and Eduard Schweizer,[42] without forgetting Frie-drich Rehkopf[43] who reconstructed it with the aid of Luke's Special Source and Q, and Tim Schramm.[44] From the beginning of the twentieth century, and without doubt beforehand, the hypothesis also existed in Great Britain and the United

[29] All are in accord that Luke was able to have at his disposal bits of isolated traditions.
[30] Frans Neirynck, "La matière marcienne dans l'évangile de Luc," in *L'Évangile de Luc. Problèmes littéraires théologiques (Mémorial L. Cerfaux)* (ed. Frans Neirynck; 2d ed.; Gembloux: Duculot, 1973) 109.
[31] Martin Rese, *Die "Stunde" Jesu in Jerusalem*; see Eduard Schweizer, "Zur Frage der Quellenbenutzung durch Lukas," in *Neues Testament und Christologie im Werden: Aufsätze* (Göttingen: Vandenhoeck & Ruprecht, 1982) 46 n. 47.
[32] Fitzmyer, *Gospel According to Luke*, 2.1365–66.
[33] Marion L. Soards, *The Passion According to Luke: The Special Material of Luke 22* (JSNTSup 14; Sheffield: JSOT, 1987) 120–23.
[34] Untergassmair, *Kreuzweg und Kreuzigung Jesu*, 112.
[35] Ibid., 1.
[36] Donald Senior, *The Passion of Jesus in the Gospel of Luke* (Wilmington, Del.: Glazier, 1989) 10.
[37] Paul Feine, "Eine vorkanonische Überlieferung des Lukas," in *Evangelium und Apostelgeschichte: eine Untersuchung* (Gotha: Perthes, 1891).
[38] Bernhard Weiss, *Die Quellen des Lukasevangeliums* (Stuttgart/Berlin: Cotta, 1907).
[39] In their works cited in note 24 above, the two German masters, Rudolf Bultmann and Martin Dibelius, oppose this hypothesis.
[40] Adolf Schlatter, *Das Evangelium des Lukas. Aus seinen Quellen erklärt* (Stuttgart: Calwer, 1931).
[41] See Joachim Jeremias, *Die Sprache des Lukasevangeliums. Redaktion und Tradition im Nicht-Markusstoff des dritten Evangeliums* (Göttingen: Vandenhoeck & Ruprecht, 1980).
[42] Eduard Schweizer, "Zur Frage der Quellenbenutzung durch Lukas," in *Neues Testament und Christologie*, 33–85.
[43] Friedrich Rehkopf, *Die lukanische Sonderquelle. Ihr Umfang und Sprachgebrauch* (WUNT 5; Tübingen: Mohr Siebeck, 1959).
[44] Tim Schramm, *Der Markus-Stoff bei Lukas. Eine literarkritische und redaktionsgeschichtliche Untersuchung* (SNTSMS 14; Cambridge: Cambridge University Press, 1971).

States in the work of John C. Hawkins,[45] Alfred Morris Perry,[46] Burnett Hillman Streeter,[47] and – above all – Vincent Taylor,[48] who rendered it more popular in his own country than in Germany through his personal influence. Today, the hypothesis exists in the United States under the pen of Joseph B. Tyson.[49]

There exist ten or so recent monographs on the Lukan story of the passion![50] What is striking is the disinterest these pay to the question that preoccupies us here. Indeed, through their performance of literary, structural, rhetorical, narrative, and theological readings, certain authors make of it a total non-issue. Anton Büchele[51] presents a *redaktionsgeschichtlich* analysis that has recourse less to the contrast between tradition and redaction than to the analysis of structures, superficial and profound, and motifs,[52] the whole being accompanied by an intertextual effort (the remainder of Luke-Acts constituting the other texts). The same can be said for Robert J. Karris,[53] who supposes that Luke's artistic talent promotes a theological elaboration that can be summarized with these words: faithful God, justice, and sustenance.

Appearing in the same year and from the same American Catholic publisher, a book by Jerome Neyrey[54] is in the same vein. Neyrey envisions Luke as an author to be understood within himself, which leads him to integrate, more than others, the parallels to the story of the passion found in the book of Acts. He focuses on the figure of Jesus on the cross as the Savior saved, the new Adam, the ἀρχηγός ("guide") who leads to salvation, whose courage in the Garden of Olives is contrasted with the λύπη of the disciples (interesting analysis of this term), and whose

---

[45] John C. Hawkins, "Three Limitations to St. Luke's Use of St. Mark's Gospel," in *Studies in the Synoptic Problem by Members of the University of Oxford* (ed. William Sanday; Oxford: Clarendon , 1911) 27–94, esp. 76–94.

[46] Alfred Morris Perry, *The Sources of Luke's Passion-Narrative* (Historical and Linguistic Studies in Literature Related to the New Testament 2, Ser. 4/2; Chicago: University of Chicago Press, 1920).

[47] Burnett Hillman Streeter, *The Four Gospels: A Study of Origins* (London: Macmillan, 1924) 199–222.

[48] Vincent Taylor, *The Passion Narrative of St. Luke: A Critical and Historical Investigation* (ed. Owen E. Evans; London: Cambridge University Press, 1972).

[49] Joseph B. Tyson, "The Lukan Version of the Trial of Jesus," *NT* 3 (1959) 249–358. See also idem, *The Death of Jesus in Luke-Acts* (Columbia: University of South Carolina Press, 1986).

[50] I am not very current on the success of this hypothesis in France and the French-speaking countries. It would be necessary to report on the work of E. Osty, Lucien Cerfaux, Augustin George, Jacques Dupont, Xavier Léon-Dufour, Marie-Émile Boismard, and Albert Vanhoye; bibliographic references for these authors can be found in Joseph Fitzmyer's commentary, *Gospel According to Luke* (see the index of proper names, beginning at 2.1603).

[51] Anton Büchele, *Der Tod Jesu im Lukasevangelium. Eine redaktionsgeschichtliche Untersuchung zu Lk 23* (Frankfurt a. M.: Knecht, 1978).

[52] These motifs are christological, ecclesiastical, and parenetic.

[53] Robert J. Karris, *Luke, Artist and Theologian: Luke's Passion Account as Literature* (New York: Paulist, 1985).

[54] Jerome Neyrey, *The Passion According to Luke: A Redaction Study of Luke's Soteriology* (New York: Paulist, 1985).

faith, which persists to the end, has salvific and exemplary import. Marion L. Soards'[55] objectives and results, while bringing together the quest for sources, look principally toward Lukan redaction and, more particularly, toward the author's own theological orientation, that is, to the author's own christological, eschatological, and ecclesiological tendencies: the work is christological in that in Jesus the plan of God is realized; eschatological in that from the time of the last supper forward the story of Jesus inaugurates the end times; and ecclesiological in that the interactions between Jesus and his disciples offer to the readers of Luke instructions on their proper role in the plan of God.

It is not surprising that the recent monographs that embrace the whole of Luke, that is, of Luke-Acts, themselves participate in this valuing of the Evangelist's ultimate literary form and doctrinal orientation to the detriment of the materials, sources, and traditions that were at his disposal. This statement is valid for the Franco-American quintet: Charles H. Talbert, Robert C. Tannehill, Charles L'Eplattenier, Jean-Noël Aletti, and Roland Meynet.[56]

A hypothesis

In this climate, which can be distinguished on one side by an analysis of redaction that is not interested in tradition and on the other by literary and theological studies, we find ourselves locked into a historical-critical situation concerning the three theories presented above, in which no one takes a position. In an effort to alleviate this situation, I would like to propose a hypothesis that results from my contact with the Evangelist in other sections of his work.[57] From the first third of the Gospel (the Galilean period of the ministry of Jesus) and the first half of Acts, I have ascertained that Luke, in effect, practiced a simple and even rudimentary method in relation to his sources. It seems to me that: a) Luke was content most frequently to have two documents at his disposal, such as, for example, Mark and Q in Luke 3–9, or the traditions of Jerusalem and the traditions of Antioch in Acts 1–15; b) Luke did not like to fuse his sources in the same pericope or the same section: for example, in the sermon on the plain he leaves Mark behind and in the

---

[55] Soards, *Passion According to Luke.*

[56] See Charles H. Talbert, *Reading Luke: A Literary and Theological Commentary on the Third Gospel* (New York: Crossroad, 1982); Robert C. Tannehill, *The Narrative Unity of Luke-Acts: A Literary Interpretation* (2 vols.; Philadelphia: Fortress, 1986); Jean-Noël Aletti, *L'art de raconter Jésus-Christ. L'écriture narrative de l'évangile de Luc* (Paris: Cerf, 1989); Charles L'Eplattenier, *Lecture de l'Évangile de Luc* (Paris: Desclée, 1982); Roland Meynet, *L'Évangile selon saint Luc, analyse rhétorique* (2 vols.; Paris: Cerf, 1988).

[57] My position resembles somewhat that of Taylor, *The Passion Narrative of St. Luke.* Still, the British exegete always reasons with the a priori assumption that one of the sources is dominant over the other. See also Henry Joel Cadbury, *The Style and Literary Method of Luke*, vol. 2: *The Treatment of Sources in the Gospel* (HTS 6; Cambridge: Harvard University Press, 1920) 76: "It is well known that sections of Luke derived from Mark and those of other origin are arranged in continuous blocks and not interspersed as in the Gospel of Matthew."

subsequent stories he ignores Q; c) Luke thus practices an alternation that forbids us to speak of priority given to one source to the detriment of another; and d) whenever possible, Luke prefers a slow alternation that develops through ample blocks rather than a rapid succession of isolated episodes.

Like everyone else, Luke was not looking for difficulties or complications. The practical conditions of his intellectual work, even including the dimensions of his table and the material substrata of his documentation, would not have encouraged Luke to multiply sources, nor would they incline him to utilize them at the same time.[58] For the passage he is writing, everything compels Luke to rely on one document and on one alone, to which he proceeds to return, reformulate, and adapt with great freedom. Whenever it pleases him, Luke abandons the first source in order to direct himself – if necessary by means of a transition – toward the second.

In a good analysis that distinguishes tradition from redaction, Marion L. Soards[59] cites in sequence all of the non-Marcan passages in Luke's passion story, ultimately rejecting the hypothesis of a second continuous source other than Mark. Soards' conclusion is based on the following argument, which he considers infallible: it does not make a coherent story. My response: and for good reason! Because he is a lucid author, Luke detests repetitions; and if the stories are sufficiently close (which, for reasons of ecclesiastical and liturgical deep-rootedness is sufficiently probable), he depends in large part on only half of them, sacrificing without hesitation the other half. He prefers to drop such and such a detail from the other version rather than make the task difficult by searching for a place to insert it in the version presently utilized.

In my view, the alternation – a simple solution the very banality of which accentuates its probability – can be verified easily enough. But the similarity of a passage to its source – Mark being the tangible comparison in half of the cases – should not be evaluated on the basis of only one criterion, such as, for example, the statistics of the vocabulary; it is also necessary to add that the order of the episodes, and the narrative and theological motifs as well, support this. Without taking the time to demonstrate all the reasons for my choices, I will now indicate how I separate the material in chapters 22 and 23 of Luke's Gospel.

To begin, in his second apocalypse Luke seems to rely on two sources. In any case, the parable of the fig tree (Luke 21:29–33) is based on Mark (13:28–31), whereas the final exhortation, which is without Marcan parallel, must derive from another document. The end of chapter 21 (vv. 37–38), where Jesus is at the temple

---

[58] On the conditions, especially the material of intellectual work in antiquity, and the use of sources by classical authors, see George Kennedy, "Classical and Christian Source Criticism," in *The Relationships Among the Gospels: An Interdisciplinary Dialogue* (ed. William O. Walker; San Antonio: Trinity University Press, 1978) 125–55. And naturally, Henri-Irénée Marrou, *Histoire de l'éducation dans l'Antiquité* (2 vols.; 6th ed.; Points Histoire 56; Paris: Seuil, 1981).

[59] Soards, *Passion According to Luke*, 120–21.

during the daytime and on the Mount of Olives at night, the people being attentive to his teachings from the early morning, is Luke's redactional transition.

For the beginning of the story of the passion, the Evangelist manifestly follows Mark, taking into account the omission of the anointing at Bethany, which he considers a doublet of his Galilean story (Luke 7:36–50): plot, treason, preparations for the Passover (Luke 22:1–14//Mark 14:1–2, 10–17). In the story of the last supper, Luke shifts, opting for his own source that places the designation of the traitor after the institution of the communion (Luke 22:21–23) rather than before, as in Mark. Just as Mark's story is formed from two parts, so also Luke 22:15–20 but, here again, in reverse order: the eschatological cup is mentioned at the outset (Luke 22:16–18) whereas in Mark (14:25) it follows the institution. The Lukan formulation of this first unit is, in my view, independent of Mark's Gospel. The same is true – despite its similarity to Mark – of the institution itself (Luke 22:19–20), which I would characterize as "Antiochian" or "Hellenist": εὐχαριστήσας rather than εὐλογήσας; "given for you"[60] after the mention of the body in lieu of any such precision in Mark; the invocation of memory, which is absent in Mark; the eucharistic cup after the meal; "this cup" rather than "this"; "the covenant in my blood" rather than "my blood of the covenant"; blood poured out "for you" rather than "for many." It is this Hellenist formulation that is also known to Paul in 1 Corinthians 11:23–25. Mark and Matthew reflect, in contrast, a version of the communion that I would call "Jerusalemite" or "Aramaic." Although they are close to one another by reason of a well-known liturgical conservatism, the two versions are nonetheless clearly distinct.

From this beginning, Luke pursues the reading and rewriting of his own source in the designation of the traitor (Luke 22:21–23) and the quarrel about "the greatest" (Luke 22:24–30). The similarity to Mark in this last episode can push the exegete to ask himself: Is not Luke referring anew to his other source, Mark, for an instant, that is to say, for one pericope? But, as Luke prefers to pick up alternatively entire blocks rather than isolated units, I reject this hypothesis. It follows – and this is important for exegesis – that the Lukan particularities of this episode, compared to those of Mark, are not all redactional. One part, seemingly the majority, is traditional and born of his own source. If the emblematic word φιλονεικία ("dispute") is perhaps redactional, the contrasting pair μείζων/νεώτερος ("the oldest"/"the youngest") is without a doubt traditional. There is one interesting particularity in this episode: the famous saying "But I am among you as one who serves" (Luke 22:27) is very different from its parallel in Mark 10:45. Luke's independence here, in contrast to Mark, is confirmed by the last verses of the pericope and in particular with regard to the twelve thrones (Luke 22:28–30), which Matthew – to our surprise – also knows and places at the same spot. Matthew and Luke's expressions are, however, rather different.

---

[60] In 1 Cor 11:24, Paul says "that for you," without the verb "to give."

Like Mark, Luke continues with the announcement of Peter's denial (Luke 22:31–34//Mark 14:26–31). Two arguments, however, prevent us from understanding Luke's version as the adaptation of Mark: Mark, who had made the Master and his disciples depart upon singing a hymn and moved them to the Mount of Olives, thus locates the scene outside. But in Luke, Jesus remains inside, in the upper chamber where he carries on his discourse. The two texts differ in other respects as well: Mark cites scripture and mentions the dispersion of the sheep, whereas Luke announces to Peter the trial of the sieve. In contrast to Mark's recounting of the episode with Peter (Mark 14:31), Luke does not have Peter reiterate his promise to die for his master.

In my view, the incident of the two swords (Luke 22:35–38), which is without parallel in the other Gospels, was itself part of the farewell dialogue that belonged to Luke's second source. The Evangelist proceeds with the rereading of this document in the episode that takes place in the Garden of Olives (Luke 22:39–46//Mark 14:32–42), where there are marked divergences from the Markan sequence: Gethsemane, the name of the place, is not mentioned; there is no setting apart of the three preferred disciples; there is no mention of the single desolate soul; the text includes the appearance of a protecting angel, which is absent in Mark; and Luke's ending of the episode is much more compact than Mark's.

In my view, Luke places himself again under the crook of Mark from the time of the arrest (Luke 22:47–53//Mark 14:43–52); there is in these verses a literal kinship that cannot be explained without literary dependence. Luke simply displaces the list of the authorities and their equipment (Mark 14:43b becomes Luke 22:52) and effects two omissions: the explanation of the agreed upon sign of the kiss (Mark 14:44) and the flight of the disciples, including the totally nude young man (Mark 14:50–52). The Evangelist remains faithful to Mark during the following episode: he shifts Peter's denial, placing it – as I mentioned above – before the story of Jesus' appearance before the Sanhedrin (Luke 22:54–62//Mark 14:66–72). It is also from Mark that Luke borrows the derision of Jesus as a prophet (Luke 22:63–65//Mark 14:65), but in Mark the order is simply different: the scene of derision follows, rather than precedes, the audience before the Sanhedrin. Luke also takes the appearance before the Sanhedrin from Mark, that is, he takes his introduction (Luke 22:66) from Mark, but from the second audience (Mark 15:1) rather than the first (Mark 14:53, 55).

In the passage that spans Luke 22:66–71//Mark 14:53–64, the Evangelist omits the false witnesses and the logion on the Temple that are found in Mark 14:56–61a. The principal interventions in Mark's text – one notes again the principle of economy – consist primarily of cuts and omissions. There are also variations in the dialogue, but both Luke and Mark recall the question of the Sanhedrin concerning Jesus' messiahship and the allusion to the Son of Man in his response. Luke refuses – with Matthew, *a minor agreement!* – to incorporate Jesus' affirmative response, which effects a doubling of the question and its response; this, in turn, introduces an exegetical doubling of titles ("Messiah" and "Son of God," 22:67, 70) that is no doubt for the benefit of his Greek audience.[61] Besides, in the explicit refusal of testimony (Luke 22:71) Luke betrays his knowledge of Mark's text (and the episode of the false witnesses, Mark 14:56–61a).

Although Luke expresses the time table in terms different from those of Mark (cf. Luke 22:66 with Mark 15:1) and limits the number of audiences at the Sanhedrin (Mark has two, Mark 14:53, 55 and 15:1; Luke has one, Luke 22:66), he remains attached to Mark in the trial scene before Pilate (Luke 23:1–5//Mark 15:1–5). One might hesitate to say this, however, because Luke transmits the political wrongs that Mark ignores. The pericope is thus one of transition.

For the appearance before Herod, which takes place in the ensuing passage, Luke switches his documentation and follows his own special source (Luke 23:6–12). He continues this resumption of the story in the second appearance before Pilate – a peculiarity of Luke – with the declarations on the part of the governor that Jesus is innocent and the presentation of the exchange between Jesus and Barabbas (Luke 23:13–25).[62] As he has already transmitted two scenes of derision, the one of Jesus as prophet (Luke 22:63–65) and the other at the end of the appearance before Herod (Luke 23:11), where Jesus is mocked as a king, Luke has no reason here to resume his use of Mark, who – as one knows – places his second scene of outrages after the condemnation by Pilate (Mark 15:16–20a). It may be, however, that Luke is inspired by Mark in the mention of Simon of Cyrene (Luke 23:26//Mark 15:20b–21).

In any case, in the dialogue with the women who perform the rites of mourning Luke continues to follow his other source (Luke 23:27–31). He grants priority to this source also in the scene of the crucifixion (Luke 23:32–43), which differs from Mark in several respects: "Father, pardon them …" (Luke 23:34a)[63]; the presentation at this point of vinegar (Luke 23:36b); royal mockeries (Luke 23:37); the mention here of the inscription (Luke 23:38); and the dialogue with the two robbers (Luke 23: 39–43), which is without synoptic parallel.

For the end of the scene, that is to say, the last moments of Jesus, Luke again takes up Mark's account. He is happy to mention two supernatural signs that are

---

[61] One notes the same process at work in the sermon on the plain. There, where Matthew simply states "love your enemies and pray for those who persecute you," Luke paraphrases the saying in a way that splits the single imperative and creates a double (Matt 5:44//Luke 6:27–28); see François Bovon, L'Évangile selon saint Luc (1,1–9,50) (CNT 3a; Geneva: Labor et Fides, 1991) 308–10.

[62] Here we have an indication in favor of my allotting the material between two sources. In Luke 23:21, the Evangelist writes σταύρου, σταύρου αὐτόν, where Mark writes σταύρωσον αὐτόν (Mark 15:13). Because Mark's use of the aorist imperative is correct and Luke's use of the present imperative is not, one must conclude that Luke reproduces here a source other than Mark. He lets pass the awkwardness of his source; otherwise one must imagine the improbability that Luke himself fashioned an improper formulation of a correct Marcan expression.

[63] Is it necessary to see the partition of the clothing in Luke 23:34b as an exception? The closeness here with Mark 15:24 is great.

concomitant with the death of Jesus: the eclipse of the sun and the rending of the veil of the temple, which he presents in two verses borrowed almost literally from Mark (Luke 23:44–45//Mark 15:33, 38). The death of Jesus is also expressed in Marcan terms (Luke 23:46a, c//Mark 15:37). Luke takes, however, two important liberties with Mark's account: he strikes anything connected to the cry of dereliction (Mark 15:34–36) and adds – in its place? – one final, confident phrase spoken by Jesus: "Father, into your hands I commend my spirit" (Luke 23:46b). Curiously, the centurion's confession at the foot of the cross (Luke 23:47//Mark 15:39), which follows, marks the next evident divergence between Mark and Luke. Doubtless, Luke did not invent the expression "Certainly this man was innocent." This saying must be a reminiscence – easy to retain – of the other source. I attribute the presence of the crowd and the women (Luke 23:48–49, 55) to Lukan redaction that is partially dependent on Mark (Mark 15:40–41). I myself cannot explain Luke's silence regarding the identity of the women.[64] In 8:1–3, he exercises no such discretion, nor in 24:10!

In the episode where the body is placed in the tomb, as well as that of the empty tomb, Luke continues to follow Mark (Luke 23:50–56//Mark 15:42–47 and Luke 24:1–11//Mark 16:1–8). For the stories related to the appearance (Luke 24:12–49), however, he returns to dependence on his own special material, happy to find something there when Mark has let him down (Mark 16:8). The scene of the ascension (Luke 24:50–53) is perhaps entirely redactional.

In summary, I delineate below Luke's alternation, back and forth from one source to the other, according to the hypothesis I have advanced here:

Parallel to Mark	Lukan Special Source
21:29–33 The fig tree	
	21:34–36 Be on guard
22:1–14 Conspiracy, Passover preparation	
	22:15–46 Mount of Olives The last supper, farewell dialogue,
22:47–23:5 Arrest, denial, outrages, Sanhedrin, Pilate	
	23:6–43 Herod, Barabbas, condemnation, road to the cross, crucifixion
23:44–24:11 Last moments, centurion, sepulcher, the empty tomb	
	24:12–53 Appearance to Peter, to the disciples at Emmaus, to the Eleven, ascension

---

[64] This silence continues in Luke 23:55//Mark 15:47.

Verifying the hypothesis

The hypothesis I have advanced here, that of alternation, presupposes two sources of which only the first (Mark) is known.[65] Thus it is appropriate to be certain – if indeed this is possible – about the existence of the second source, by arguments other than the dissection performed just now. Two avenues offer themselves for reflection here. The first consists of locating the presence of specific and convergent stylistic and grammatical clues in the passages we have attributed to the special source. I have not yet accomplished this task, which can benefit from the results of certain work[66] and the use of a method that is applied to the Gospel of John.[67] The second path consists of searching for traces of this special Lukan source outside of the canonical Gospel. It could be, in effect, that, among the most ancient patristic witnesses to these episodes, certain ones depended on Luke's source and not on Luke himself.[68]

For example, one Lukan particularity in the scene that takes place in the Garden of Olives is the appearance of the angel and the clots of blood that fall to the ground (Luke 22:43–44). This episode is also attested in a second-century Jewish-Christian gospel as well as in the work of Justin Martyr. The *Historia passionis domini*, a medieval Latin text, notes that the episode of the angel bringing consolation to the agonizing Christ is present in a gospel which that document refers to as "of the Nazarenes."[69] It is possible that this gospel may be dependent on Luke's source. Justin, who notes the "sweat as clots of blood" in his *Dialogue with Tryphon*,[70] surely refers to this gospel and not to Luke's source. The manner in which

---

[65] One can obviously ask which form of Mark Luke had at his disposal.

[66] The method has improved over time with the successive work of John C. Hawkins, Henry J. Cadbury, Heinz Schürmann, Joachim Jeremias, Friedrich Rehkopf, and Tim Schramm. See Frans Neirynck, "La matière marcienne dans l'évangile de Luc," 70–72, and Eduard Schweizer, "Zur Frage der Quellenbenutzung durch Lukas."

[67] See Eugen Ruckstuhl and Peter Dschulnigg, *Stilkritik und Verfasserfrage im Johannesevangelium. Die johanneischen Sprachmerkmale auf dem Hintergrund des Neuen Testaments und des zeitgenössischen hellenistischen Schrifttums* (NTOA 17; Freiburg: Universitätsverlag; Göttingen: Vandenhoeck & Ruprecht, 1991).

[68] Enrico Norelli, my colleague in Geneva, has assisted my methodological reflections on this point, putting forth the hypothesis that the author of the *Ascension of Isaiah* depended not on the Gospel of Matthew in its canonical form, but on the traditions that the first Evangelist had been able to use for the evocation of Jesus' birth. I thank him for having permitted me the knowledge of his study on this subject, which has now appeared; see Enrico Norelli, "Avant le canonique et l'apocryphe: Aux origines des récits de la naissance de Jésus," *RPT* 126 (1994) 305–24.

[69] The text is cited in *Synopsis quattuor evangeliorum. locis parallelis evangeliorum apocryphorum et Patrum adhibitis* (ed. Kurt Aland; 3d ed.; Stuttgart: Württembergische Bibelanstalt, 1965) 457, hereafter cited as *Synopsis*. See Philipp Vielhauer and Georg Strecker, "Judenchristliche Evangelien," in *Neutestamentliche Apokryphen in deutscher Übersetzung* (ed. Wilhelm Schneemelcher; 5 Auflage der von E. Hennecke begründeten Sammlung; 2 vols.; Tübingen: Mohr Siebeck, 1989) 1.127–28, 137.

[70] Justin, *Dialogue with Tryphon* 103.8; text cited in *Synopsis*, 457; Justin, *Dialogue avec Tryphon. Texte grec, traduction française, introduction, notes et index* (ed. Georges Archambault; 2

he introduces this reference, with the allusion to the prologue of the Gospel, proves this indisputably. And it is also possible that the letter to the Hebrews (Heb 5:7), with its dramatization of the prayers and tears of Jesus that probably takes place in the Garden of Olives, knows the same tradition as Luke.

In addition to the Gospel, the canonical Acts (Acts 4:27–28) and the *Gospel of Peter*[71] attest to Herod's participation in Jesus' trial (Luke 23:6–12). Do these passages depend on the Gospel of Luke or on the source that he has at his disposal? Reading them, these two passages do not appear to depend directly on the Gospel of Luke in the fixed form as we know it. Thus do they know the source?

Jesus' reply to the weeping of the women, which is particular to Luke (Luke 23:28–31), has an enigmatic parallel in the *Gospel of Thomas*.[72] In its first half, logion 79 of this text refers back to the beatitude of the woman from the crowd and Jesus' reply, which is another passage special to Luke (Luke 11:27–28). In its second half, it transmits the oracle of misfortune from the story of the passion, but without reference to the death of Christ nor the weeping of the women: "There will come, indeed, days when you will say: 'Happy the womb that has not conceived and the breasts that have not nursed.'" As this is a matter of an apocalyptic topos that has a parallel in Luke 21:23 and an eventual origin in Isa 54:1, it is difficult to be precise as to where the *Gospel of Thomas* obtained its information, and whether or not it depends on Luke or on one of his sources.[73]

A Jewish-Christian gospel appears to have affirmed that Jesus' prayer for the executioners ("Father, forgive them …" Luke 23:34) provoked numerous conversions among the Jews who were present. We know this from both the *Historia passionis domini*[74] and from a medieval commentary on Isa,[75] which both reference, again, the *Gospel of the Nazarenes*; we also find a trace of it, albeit weak, in

---

vols.; Textes et Documents pour l'étude historique du christianisme; Paris: Picard, 1909) 2.140–43.

[71] *Gos. Pet.* 1–5; see *Synopsis*, 479; Maria Grazia Mara, *Évangile de Pierre. Introduction, texte critique, traduction, commentaire et index* (SC 201; Paris: Cerf, 1973) 40–43.

[72] *Gos. Thom.* 79; see *Synopsis*, 482, 527. I use here the translation of H.-C. Puech, *En quête de la Gnose*, vol. 2: *Sur l'Évangile selon Thomas* (Bibliothèque des Sciences Humaines; Paris: Gallimard, 1978) 23.

[73] On *Gos. Thom.* 79, see Robert McL. Wilson, *Studies in the Gospel of Thomas* (London: Mowbray, 1960) 81. Logion 79 of the *Gospel of Thomas* is possibly primitive; Luke would have divided it, placing one part at Luke 11:27–28 and the other at Luke 23:29; otherwise, it is necessary to conclude that the author of the *Gospel of Thomas* has regrouped these sentences using catch-words. See Bertil Gärtner, *The Theology of the Gospel of Thomas* (trans. Eric J. Sharpe; London: Collins, 1961) 252–53; Jacques E. Ménard, *L'Évangile selon Thomas* (NHS 5; Leiden: Brill, 1975) 180–81; Michael Fieger, *Das Thomasevangelium. Einleitung, Kommentar und Systematik* (NTAbh n.f. 22; Münster: Aschendorff, 1991) 218–21.

[74] See *Synopsis*, 484; Vielhauer and Strecker, "Judenchristliche Evangelien," 138.

[75] See *Synopsis*, 484; Vielhauer and Strecker, "Judenchristliche Evangelien," 136. The Isaiah reference is from the *Commentary on Isaiah*, concerning Isa 53:12, which is edited under the name of Haymon de Halberstadt in PL 116, 994. One must, doubtless, attribute this commentary to Haymon of Auxerre.

Jerome.[76] This gospel thus shares the logion with Luke and presents, furthermore, a legendary development. But does it depend on Luke, or on his source?

Regarding the brigands, the *Gospel of Peter*[77] says a little more than Mark and Matthew but a little less than Luke (Luke 23:39–43): "One of the malefactors rebuked them saying: 'We – it is because of the misdeeds that we have done that we are suffering thus; but this one, having become savior of humanity, what wrong has he done to you?'"[78] The *Gospel of Peter* is independent of the Gospel of Luke here; its text appears to be even more archaic than the text of Luke. If it depends on a tradition anterior to Luke, does it know Luke's source?

Luke is the sole New Testament witness to attest to Jesus' final statement: "Father, into your hands I commend my spirit" (Luke 23:46). This logion is cited by Justin in his *Dialogue with Tryphon.*[79] Justin adds "as I have had it this time again from their Memoirs." Following his custom, he must be referring to the gospels in the process of canonization, thus to Luke rather than to his source.

In the only extant Greek fragment of the *Diatessaron*[80] we find a correspondence with the Gospels in the mention of the presence of the women at the beginning of the deposition scene (Luke 23:49; 55–56). This fragment is closely related to the Gospel of Luke: "of Zebedee" refers to Matthew 27:56 and "Salome" to Mark 15:40, but the rest is constructed by fusing Luke 23:49 and 55 (the presence of the women), then Luke 23:54 (the date), Mark 15:42 (the date), Luke 23:50–51 (the appearance of Joseph), Matt 27:57 (the disciple of Jesus), John 19:38 (the secret action for fear of the Jews), and Luke 23:51 (the city of Judea, awaiting the kingdom of God and – in reverse order compared to Luke – nonparticipation in the project of the Jewish leaders). If Tatian works, as it seems, with our canonical Gospels, then this fragment does not attest a direct awareness of Luke's source.

If I may expand my discussion beyond the account of the passion only, in the story of Jesus' appearance to the Eleven, which is special to Luke, the resurrected Christ commands his disciples to touch him in order to distinguish him from a phantom or a spirit that would have neither flesh nor bones (Luke 24:39). It is worth mentioning here that a very similar phrase circulated sufficiently widely in

---

[76] Jerome, *Epist.* 120.8; see *Synopsis,* 484; Saint Jérôme, *Lettres. Texte établi et traduit* (ed. Jerome Labourt; Collection des Universités de France 6; Paris: Les Belles Lettres, 1958) 141.

[77] *Gos. Pet.* 10–16; see *Synopsis,* 484; Mara, *Évangile de Pierre,* 46–49.

[78] *Gos. Pet.* 13 (my translation).

[79] Justin, *Dialogue with Tryphon* 105.5; see *Synopsis,* 489; Justin, *Dialogue avec Tryphon* 2.148–150.

[80] The attribution of this fragment to the *Diatessaron* has been questioned, but it is very probable. This fragment, found at Dura-Europos, is accessible in a photograph, edited with an English translation, in the work of Bruce M. Metzger, *Manuscripts of the Greek Bible* (Oxford: Oxford University Press, 1981) 66–67; on the *Diatessaron,* see William L. Petersen, "Tatian's Diatessaron," in Helmut Koester, *Ancient Christian Gospels: Their History and Development* (Philadelphia: Trinity, 1990) 403–30, esp. 412–13.

antiquity, which, according to Jerome, is attested in a Jewish-Christian gospel ("iuxa Evangelium, quod Hebraeorum lectitant Nazarei").[81] Origen[82] knew of this gospel and attributed it to the *Petri doctrina*, which he rejected. Finally, Ignatius of Antioch also cited it: λάβετε, ψηλαφήσατέ με καὶ ἴδετε ὅτι οὐκ εἰμὶ δαιμόνιον ἀσώματον.[83] These witnesses are precise and could well refer to the source that Luke utilizes in his story of the appearance to the Eleven (Luke 24:39).

From this inventory, it appears that at least one Jewish-Christian gospel shares with Luke various awarenesses that are particular to them. As I cannot easily envision a Jewish-Christian borrowing from a gospel as Gentile-Christian as Luke's, I put forth the hypothesis, certainly adventuresome, that this author had knowledge of Luke's second source. The other witnesses are too few in number and explicitness to apply the same hypothesis to them. In the case of Justin and Tatian, it is necessary even to eliminate it; these two authors must refer to our Gospel of Luke and not to his source. The cases of the *Gospel of Thomas* and the *Gospel of Peter* remain enigmatic.

III. A Provisional Conclusion

Three supplementary tasks await the scholar who ventures here.

1) If there is indeed a document other than Mark's Gospel behind the Lukan story of the passion and if it is a continuous text, then should it be viewed as the continuation of that which is customarily referred to as Luke's special material, the *Sondergut*, that is without a doubt present in the stories of the journey to Jeru-

---

[81] Jerome, *Comm. Is.*, XVIII, praef., and *Vir. ill.* 16; see *Synopsis, 503*.

[82] Origen, *Princ.* I, *prooemium* 8; see *Synopsis, 503*; Herwig Görgemanns and Heinrich Karpp, eds., *Origenes. Vier Bücher von den Prinzipien herausgegeben, übersetzt, mit kritischen und erläuternden Anmerkungen versehen* (Texte zur Forschung 24; Darmstadt: Wissenschaftliche Buchgesellschaft, 1976) 94–97.

[83] Ignatius of Antioch, *Smyrn.* 3.1–3; see *Synopsis, 503*; Ignace d'Antioche, *Polycarpe de Smyrne, Lettres. Martyre de Polycarpe. Texte grec, introduction, traduction et notes* (ed. Théodore Camelot; 4th ed.; SC 10; Paris: Cerf, 1969) 134–35. This passage, like the evidence from Origen and Jerome, has provoked an abundance of literature: see particularly Helmut Koester, *Synoptische Überlieferung bei den Apostolischen Vätern* (TU 65; Berlin: Akademie-Verlag, 1957) 45–56; Henning Paulsen, *Die Briefe des Ignatius von Antiochia und der Brief des Polykarp von Smyrna* (zweite neubearbeitete Auflage der Auslegung von W. Bauer; HNT. Die Apostolischen Väter 2; Tübingen: Mohr Siebeck 1985) 92–93; William R. Schoedel, *Ignatius of Antioch: A Commentary on the Letters of Ignatius of Antioch* (Hermeneia; Philadelphia: Fortress, 1985) 226–29; Antonio Orbe, *Cristología Gnóstica. Introducción a la soteriología de los siglos II y III* (2 vols.; BAC 385; Madrid: Editorial Catolica, 1976) 2.516–17. See Pseudo-Hippolyte, *In sanctum Pascha* 30, which combines John 20:27 (with elements of John 20:25) and Luke 24:39, which is a combination that one also finds in the work of John Chrysostom, *De cruce et latrone homilia* 1.4 (PG 49, 405); see Guiseppe Visoná, *Pseudo Ippolita, In sanctum Pascha. Studio, edizione, commento* (Studia Patristica Mediolanensia 15; Milan: Vita e Pensiero, Università cattolica del Sacro Cuore, 1988) 276, 403. I thank my friend Enrico Norelli for making me aware of this reference.

salem and the mission in Galilee? If the liturgical deep-rootedness of these passion stories seems to oppose this, then a similar literary quality, such as we find in the scenes in the Garden of Olives and the disciples from Emmaus, appears, in contrast, to propose it and even to impose it.

2) If such is the case, then what literary genre must be attributed to this document and what function does it fulfill? I would accord it the genre "gospel" and relate it thus to Mark. On a superior literary level, it would be to Luke what Mark had been to Matthew. In my view, Q was not a part of it; rather, it constituted a distinct document. Whom did it serve? The edification of Christian Hellenists?

3) Why has it disappeared? Because Luke eclipsed it (as Matthew and Luke had rendered Q useless)? Because Marcion had recourse to it? This last hypothesis[84] would have to be verified with the aid of book 4 of Tertullian's *Adversus Marcionem*. Marcion did not attribute explicitly to Luke the gospel that he recognized (this writing, as one knows, began only with the adult ministry of Jesus).

4) The study of Luke's redaction of this source should permit us also to precisely define the literary and theological intentions of the Evangelist. For now, one can insist on the conformity of the destiny of Jesus with the plan of God; on the rejection of the suffering Righteous One and of the authentic prophet; on the fidelity and confidence of the Son relative to his heavenly Father; on the redemptive value of his life and his death, which constitutes a single grand work; on the exhortative function of this fate for the disciples and, in turn, for the believers. All of these Lukan themes, known by the rewritings of Mark and Q, find their ultimate confirmation in the reinterpretation of Luke's special source in the third Gospel. Provided – it is necessary to add – that this source of the passion story really and truly did exist, which is only a hypothesis, remaining as uncertain as the suggestion of a regular alternation between this source and Mark.

Bibliography

Aletti, Jean-Noël. *L'art de raconter Jésus-Christ. L'écriture narrative de l'évangile de Luc.* Paris: Éditions du Cerf, 1989.

Beck, B.E. "Imitatio Christi and the Lucan Passion Narrative." In *Suffering and Martyrdom in the New Testament: Studies Presented to G. M. Styler.* Edited by William Horburg and Brian McNeil. Cambridge: Cambridge University Press, 1981.

---

[84] On the gospel of Marcion, see Adolf Harnack, *Marcion. Das Evangelium vom fremden Gott. Eine Monographie zur Geschichte der Grundlegung der katholischen Kirche. Neue Studien zu Marcion* (Darmstadt: Wissenschaftliche Buchgesellschaft, 1985); R. Joseph Hoffmann, *Marcion: On the Restitution of Christianity: An Essay on the Development of Radical Paulinist Theology in the Second Century* (AARAS; Chico, Calif.: Scholars Press, 1984). This author argues that Marcion utilized an *Urlukas* and that the canonical Gospel of Luke is an anti-marcionite reaction. This work has been criticized and must be read with circumspection; on Marcion, see also Christian Bernard Amphoux, "Les premières éditions de Luc," *ETL* 67 (1991) 312–27 and 68 (1992) 38–48.

Bovon, François. *Luc le théologien. Vingt-cinq ans de recherches (1950–1975)*. Second edition. Geneva: Labor et Fides, 1988.

idem. "Luc-Actes." In *Évangiles synoptiques et Actes des apôtres*. Edited by J. Auneau et al. Petite bibliothèque des sciences bibliques, Nouveau Testament 4. Paris: Desclée, 1981.

Büchele, Anton. *Der Tod Jesu im Lukasevangelium. Eine redaktionsgeschichtliche Untersuchung zu Lk 23*. Frankfurt am Main: Knecht, 1978.

Butin, Jacques D., A. Maignan, and P. Soler, eds. *L'Évangile selon Luc commenté par les Pères*. Paris: Desclée, 1987.

Cousin, Hugues. *Le prophète assassiné. Histoire des textes évangéliques de la Passion*. Paris: Delarge, 1976.

Dibelius, Martin. *Die Formgeschichte des Evangeliums*. Third edition, with annex by Günther Bornkamm. Tübingen: Mohr Siebeck, 1959.

Dorge, Arthur J. and James D. Tabor. *A Noble Death: Suicide and Martyrdom Among Christians and Jews in Antiquity*. San Francisco: HarperSanFrancisco, 1992.

Finegan, Jack. *Die Überlieferung der Leidens- und Auferstehungsgeschichte Jesu*. Giessen: A. Töpelmann, 1934.

Finnell, B.S. *The Significance of the Passion in Luke*. Ph.D. dissertation, Baylor University, 1983.

Fitzmyer, Joseph A. *The Gospel According to Luke*. 2 vols. Anchor Bible 28A-B. Garden City: Doubleday, 1981, 1985.

Ford, Josephine Massyngbaerde. *My Enemy is my Guest: Jesus and Violence in Luke*. Maryknoll: Orbis Books, 1984.

Gormley, J.F. *The Final Passion Prediction: A Study of Luke 22:33 38*. Ph.D. dissertation, Fordham University, 1974.

Green, Joel B. *The Death of Jesus: Tradition and Interpretation in the Passion Narrative*. Tübingen: Mohr Siebeck 1988.

Grobel, Kendrick. *Formgeschichte und synoptische Quellenanalyse*. Göttingen: Vandenhoeck & Ruprecht, 1937.

Jeremias, Joachim. *Die Sprache des Lukasevangeliums. Redaktion und Tradition im Nicht-Markusstoff des dritten Evangeliums*. (Göttingen: Vandenhoeck & Ruprecht, 1980).

Karris, Robert J. *Luke, Artist and Theologian: Luke's Passion Account as Literature*. New York: Paulist Press, 1985.

Keck, Fridolin. *Die öffentliche Abschiedsrede Jesu in Lk 20,45–21,36*. Stuttgart: Verlag Katholisches Bibelwerk, 1976.

Kertelge, Karl, ed. *Der Tod Jesu. Deutungen im Neuen Testament*. Quaestiones disputatae 74. Freiburg: Herder, 1976.

Kloppenborg, John S. "*Exitus clari viri*: The Death of Jesus in Luke." *Toronto Journal of Theology* 8 (1992): 106–20.

Kodell, Jerome. "Luke's Theology of the Death of Jesus." In *Sin, Salvation, and the Spirit*. Edited by Daniel Durken. Collegeville, Minn.: Liturgical Press, 1979.

La Verdiere, E. "A Discourse at the Last Supper." *The Bible Today* 72 (1974): 1540–48.

Léon-Dufour, Xavier. "Passion." *Dictionnaire de la Bible: Supplément* 6. Paris: Letouzey et Ané, 1960. col. 1419–92.

L'Eplattenier, Charles. *Lecture de l'Évangile de Luc*. Paris: Desclée, 1982.

Limbeck, Meinrad, ed., *Redaktion und Theologie des Passionsberichtes nach den Synoptikern*. Wege der Forschung 481. Darmstadt: Wissenschaftliche Burchgesellschaft, 1981.

Marin, Louis. *Sémiotique de la Passion. Topiques et figures*. Paris: Aubier-Montaigne, Éditions du Cerf, Delachaux et Niestlé, 1971.

Matera, Frank J. *Passion Narratives and Gospel Theologies: Interpreting the Synoptics through Their Passion Stories*. New York: Paulist Press, 1986.

Meynet, Roland. *L'Évangile selon saint Luc, analyse rhétorique.* 2 vols. Paris: Éditions du Cerf, 1988.

idem. *Avez-vous lu saint Luc? Guide pour la rencontre.* Paris: Éditions du Cerf, 1990.

idem. "Narrativité et théologie dans le récits de la Passion." *Recherches de science religieuse* 73 (1985): 1–244.

Neirynck, Frans. "La matière marcienne dans l'évangile de Luc." In *L'Évangile de Luc. Problèmes littéraires et théologiques (Mémorial L. Cerfaux).* Edited by Frans Neirynck. Second edition. Gembloux: Duculot, 1989.

Neyrey, Jerome. *The Passion According to Luke: A Redaction Study of Luke's Soteriology.* New York: Paulist Press, 1985.

Rese, Martin. *Die "Stunde" Jesu in Jerusalem [Lk 22, 1–53]. Eine Untersuchung zur literarischen und theologischen Eigenart des lukanischen Passionsberichts.* Habilitationsschrift. Münster: n.p., 1970.

Schneider, Gerhard. "Das Problem einer vorlukanischen Passionserzählung." *Biblische Zeitschrift* NF 16 (1972): 222–44.

idem. *Verleugnung. Verspottung und Verhör Jesu nach Lk 22,54–71.* Studien zum Alten und Neuen Testament 22. Munich: Kösel, 1969.

idem. *Die Passion Jesu nach den drei älteren Evangelien.* Munich: Kösel, 1973.

Schürmann, Heinz. *Der Paschamahlbericht Lk 22, (7–14) 15–18: 1. Teil.* Münster: Aschendorff, 1953.

idem. *Der Einsetzungsbericht Lk 22, 19–20: 2. Teil.* Münster: Aschendorff, 1955.

idem. *Jesu Abschiedsrede Lk 22.21–38: 3. Teil.* Münster: Aschendorff, 1956.

Schweizer, Eduard. "Zur Frage der Quellenbenutzung durch Lukas." In *Neues Testament und Christologie im Werden: Aufsätze.* Göttingen: Vandenhoeck & Ruprecht, 1982.

Senior, Donald. *The Passion of Jesus in the Gospel of Luke.* Wilmington, Del: M. Glazier, 1989.

Sterling , Greg. *"Mors philosophi:* The Death of Jesus in Luke." *Harvard Theological Review* 94 (2001): 383–402.

Soards, Marion L. *The Passion According to Luke: The Special Material of Luke 22.* Journal for the Study of the New Testament: Supplement Series 14. Sheffield: JSOT, 1987.

Sylva, Dennis D., ed. *Reimaging the Death of the Lukan Jesus.* Frankfurt am Main: A. Hain, 1990.

Talbert, Charles H. *Reading Luke: A Literary and Theological Commentary on the Third Gospel.* New York: Crossroad, 1982.

Tannehill, Robert C. *The Narrative Unity of Luke-Acts: A Literary Interpretation.* 2 vols. Philadelphia: Fortress Press, 1986.

Taylor, Vincent. *The Passion Narrative of St. Luke: A Critical and Historical Investigation.* Edited by Owen E. Evans. London: Cambridge University Press, 1972.

Trocmé, Étienne. *The Passion as Liturgy: A Study in the Origin of the Passion Narratives in the Four Gospels.* London: SCM Press, 1983.

Tyson, Joseph. *The Death of Jesus in Luke-Acts.* Columbia: University of South Carolina Press, 1986.

Untergassmair, Franz Georg. *Kreuzweg und Kreuzigung Jesu. Ein Beitrag zur lukanischen Redaktionsgeschichte und zur Frage nach der lukanischen "Kreuzestheologie."* Paderborn: Schöningh, 1980.

Vanhoye, Albert et al. *La Passion selon les quatre Évangiles.* Lire la Bible 55. Paris: Éditions du Cerf, 1981.

idem. "Structure et théologie des récits de la Passion dans les évangiles synoptiques." *La nouvelle revue théologique* 89 (1967): 137–63.

idem. "L'intérêt de Luc pour la prophétie en Lc 1,76; 4,16–30 et 22,60–65." In *The Four*

Gospels 1992 Festschrift Frans Neirynck. Edited by F. Van Segbroeck et al., vol. 2. Bibliotheca ephemeridum theologicarum lovaniensium 100. Leuven: Leuven University Press/Peeters, 1992, 1529–48.

Vööbus, Arthur. *The Prelude to the Lukan Passion Narrative: Tradition-, Redaction-, Cult-, Motif-Historical and Source-Critical Studies.* Stockholm: ETSE, 1968.

Wanke, Joachim. *Beobachtungen zum Eucharistieverständnis des Lukas auf Grund der lukanischen Mahlberichte.* Leipzig: St.-Benno-Verlag, 1973.

Wiefel, Wolfgang. *Das Evangelium nach Lukas.* Theologischer Handkommentar zum Neuen Testament 3. Berlin: Evangelische Verlagsanstalt, 1988.

Winter, Paul. "The Treatment of His Sources by the Third Evangelist in Luke XXI–XXIV." *Scottish Journal of Theology* 8 (1955): 138–72.

The Role of the Scriptures in the Composition of the Gospel Accounts: The Temptations of Jesus (Luke 4:1–13 par.) and the Multiplication of the Loaves (Luke 9:10–17 par.)*

I

What formative part did the Hebrew Scriptures, which were the sacred scriptures of the first Christians, play in the development of the gospel stories? In answering this question I shall set aside at the outset two extreme solutions. According to the first, the prophetic texts of the scriptures played so normative a role that they made inevitable a particular, and necessarily fictitious, formulation of the New Testament narratives. According to the second, the gospel events and the first narratives of them had such a solid historical basis that the Hebrew Scriptures exerted no influence at all; only later was the correspondence between promise and fulfillment underscored by scriptural references or citations.

II

In my judgement, the relationship between history and the scriptures is not one-directional; it resembles rather the gropings and subsequent corrections that we see in cybernetics. To take the temptations of Jesus as an example[1]; the event that takes place is individual and unique (Matt 4:1//Luke 4:1). But the happening on this occasion resembles other, earlier events that have already been described in religious terms; the likeness is evident because a theological consciousness is at

---

* These pages were offered in homage to Father Emilio Rasco, S.J., whose friendly welcome has always touched me, both at Rome and at the various meetings of the Society for New Testament Studies. Common theological interests and, in particular, a similar focus on Luke the evangelist helped give rise to this friendship, as did also Dom Jacques Dupont, whom I take this occasion to remember.

[1] On the temptations of Jesus and the vast bibliography to which they have given rise, see Ulrich Luz, *Das Evangelium nach Matthäus (Mt 1–7)* (EKKNT 1/1; 2d ed.; Zürich: Benzinger Verlag; Neukirchen-Vluyn: Neukirchener Verlag, 1989) 158–67; ET: *Matthew 1–7: A Commentary* (trans. Wilhelm C. Linss; Edinburgh: T&T Clark, 1989); François Bovon, *Das Evangelium nach Lukas (Lk 1, 1–9, 50)* (EKKNT 3/1; Neukirchen-Vluyn: Neukirchener Verlag; Zürich: Benzinger Verlag, 1989) 191–204.

work that is alert to the element of continuity and therefore to the fidelity of the one same God. The story of what is specific and unique – that is, Jesus, who is neither Moses, nor Aaron, nor Elijah – is thus brought into harmony with a story that precedes it, namely, the presence of the lawgiver on Sinai (Exod 19–20; 24; 32–34). The withdrawal of Jesus into the wilderness is therefore not the first such action; the guidance of the Spirit displays continuity; the devil is not here tempting someone for the first time; and the length of the withdrawal (forty days) matches that of Moses' ordeal in the wilderness (Exod 34:28).

But the interaction does not involve only two poles, namely, the event of Jesus' temptation and the scriptures. It also includes the gospel story – as distinct from the Jesus event that makes its own demands – as well as something too often forgotten: the ongoing reading and actualization of the Hebrew Scriptures as seen first in Jewish and then in Christian exegesis. In short, we are dealing with a passage that has four sharply defined points of reference: *the historical event* in the life of Jesus, that is, his withdrawal and sojourn in the wilderness; *the biblical echo* of Moses' forty-day stay on the mountain; *the narrative logic* of the gospel stories that show lack (fasting) being followed by desire (hunger); and finally, *Jewish exegesis*, which, in the form of midrash is a good translation and the end result of long term meditation on the scriptures, and which considers the fruit of its reflections to be legitimate commentary, namely, that what is encountered in the wilderness is not only the "biblical" God but also the "intertestamental" devil who seeks to bring about the downfall of believers.[2]

III

Life is made up of countless incidents, and the scriptures of countless stories. How is the selection from these two sources made? Who establishes the correspondences? Christian tradition has kept alive the memory of an incident from the beginning of Jesus' ministry because people like beginnings to be sharply defined, and this has kept alive the temptation story in particular, because they admire the tests that certify and empower heroes.[3] This selection of incidents ist therefore neither fortuitous nor arbitrary. Neither is the selection of scriptural correspondences: Jesus is the mediator of a new order; was not Moses at the source of the former blessings, namely, the covenant and the law? In order to give expression to what is new, the first Christians turned instinctively to the past. The New Testament story, which is an irreducibile *ephapax*, is altered by being brought into

---

[2] See Jean Steinmann, *Saint Jean Baptiste et la spiritualité du désert* (Maîtres spirituels; Paris: Seuil, 1955) 155–57; ET: *Saint John the Baptist and the Desert Tradition* (trans. Michael Boyes; Men of Wisdom 5; New York: Harper, 1958).

[3] For a semiotic analysis of the temptation stories and their commentaries see Louis Panier, *Récit et commentaires de la tentation de Jésus au désert. Approche sémiotique du discours interprétatif* (Paris: Cerf 1984).

correspondence and connection with the scriptures (resemblance, crescendo, and antithesis). If Jesus is to be understood, he must be like someone already known, in this case Moses since knowledge increases only through comparison of the object to be known with objects already known and through the discovery of likenesses.[4]

In the final analysis, this is what the typological exegesis of antiquity and the Middle Ages saw very clearly. But if the correspondences between Adam and Christ, or between the high priest and Christ, are now part of the Christian inheritance, this is due not to the gospel stories but to the reflections of the first theologians: the apostle Paul and the author of the Letter to the Hebrews. As for the evangelists, the point that caught their attention in the inexhaustible store of the Hebrew Bible is chiefly the comparison with Moses.[5]

IV

The gospels often set a prophetic figure alongside the typical image of Moses as a leader and legislator. According to the gospel story Jesus was a prophet – a new Elijah or the prophet like Moses – as well as the son of David and the royal messiah.[6] The gospel account of the multiplication of the loaves (Matt 14:13–21//Mark 6:32–44//Luke 9:10–17//John 6:1–13) makes it possible to check this claim; but this example also reminds us not to forget the points of reference listed earlier, namely, the constraints proper to the literary genre of the miraculous gift[7] which are: Jewish exegesis, which sometimes interprets the quail from the sea (Num 11:31) as flying fish and thus explains the presence here of the two fish (Luke 9:13 par.)[8]; the event that is the starting point but is difficult to define; and, finally, the scriptures. But which passage of scripture? The stories of Elijah and Elisha multiplying meal and oil (1 Kgs 17 and 2 Kgs 4). These stories represent, of course, only

---

[4] See Bertil Edgar Gärtner, "The Pauline and Johannine Idea of 'To Know God' against the Hellenistic Background: The Greek Philosophical Principle 'Like by Like' in Paul and John." *NTS* 14 (1968) 209–31.

[5] For a bibliography on Moses in the New Testament, and especially in the work of Luke, see François Bovon, "La figure de Moïse dans l'œuvre de Luc," in *La figure de Moïse. Écritures et relectures* (ed. Richard Martin-Achard; Publications de la Faculté de Théologie de l'Université de Genève 1; Geneva: Labor et Fides, 1978) 47–65; reprinted in idem, *L'œuvre de Luc. Études d'exégèse et de théologie* (LD 130; Paris: Cerf, 1987) 73, 96.

[6] See Felix Gils, *Jésus prophète d'après les Évangiles synoptiques* (Orientalia et Biblica Lovaniensia 2; Louvain: Publications Universitaires, 1957).

[7] See Gerd Theissen, *Urchristliche Wundergeschichten. Ein Beitrag zur formgeschichtlichen Erforschung der synoptischen Evangelien* (SNT 8: Gütersloh: Gütersloher Verlagshaus Mohn, 1974) 111–14: *Miracle Stories in the Early Christian Tradition* (trans. Francis McDonagh; Edinburg: T&T Clark, 1983).

[8] See Jean-Marie van Cangh, *La multiplication des pains et l'eucharistie* (LD 86; Paris: Cerf 1975) 105–09.

stages in a tradition of faith according to which God satisfies the hunger of his people, as attested in the proverb cited in the story of Elijah: "The jar of meal will not be emptied and the jug of oil will not fail until the day that the Lord sends rain on the earth." Nevertheless, one of these stories, that of Elisha, did provide the gospel account with its structure and development.

2 Kings 4:42–44	*New Testament*
A man comes to Elisha; there are numerous spectators	The crowds come to Jesus
The man brings bread	People in the crowd have bread
The prophet's servant is present	The disciples of Jesus are present
The prophet orders that the people be fed	Jesus (immediately or after discussion) orders that these people be fed
Reaction of the servant	Reaction of the disciples
New order from the prophet	New order from Jesus
Carrying out of the order (distribution)	Carrying out of the order (distribution)
There is bread left over	There is bread left over

Understood in the context of the scriptures, the New Testament story emphasizes the fact that God continues to feed his people and that God is still faithful; that he makes use of an intermediary, a prophet – who in this case is Jesus; that the food, though material, is a manifestation of salvation and even anticipates the blessings of the eschaton; that Christian worship and the ecclesial community are the present locales, or settings, for this anticipation.[9] The biblical model is thus related to the gospel story, even as the Lord's supper is related to the banquet of the kingdom.[10]

V

Let me return to the story of the temptations, especially as told by Matthew. We read in Matthew 4:12–13a that after this test Jesus returns to Galilee, going first to Nazara (Luke 4:16 has the same strange form of the name Nazareth), and then to Capernaum. The evangelist's intention is to show Jesus' first preaching as following upon the certifying trial, as Mark has done before him and as Luke does contemporaneously. The two poles of reference, conversion and kingdom (which are

---

[9] For a bibliography on the multiplication of the loaves see Bovon, *Das Evangelium nach Lukas*, 465–66.

[10] On imitation of the Hebrew Scriptures see Thomas Louis Brodie, "Towards Unravelling Luke's Use of the Old Testament: Luke 7, 11–17 as an *imitation* of 1 Kings 17, 17–24," *NTS* 32 (1986) 247–67; James H. Charlesworth, "The Pseudepigrapha as Biblical Exegesis," in *Early Jewish and Christian Exegesis: Studies in Memory of W. H. Brownlee* (ed. Craig A. Evans and William F. Stinespring; Homages Series 10; Atlanta: Scholars Press, 1987) 139–52.

in reverse order here as compared with Matt 1:15), are regarded by Matthew as an adequate summary of this preaching (Matt 4:17). Matthew then continues, as Mark does, with the call of the first disciples (Matt 4:18–22).

Between the return to Galilee and these two events, however, Matthew seeks to convince us, almost to force our hand – me in any event – to prove a truth to us, to *tell* us something about a *reality*, or more accurately, to prove the conformity of a prediction to a fact (Matt 4:13b–16). The prediction took the form of a prophetic oracle, τὸ ῥηθέν, which originally lacked substance but has now been filled πληρῶ. There is here a different relation to the scriptures than at the beginnig of the chapter, at the time of the sojourn on the mountain, and also later at the multiplication of the loaves. We have here an instance of a citation (Isa 8:23–9:1) that has a tremendous effect.[11] The citation first universalizes, then dramatizes, and finally sets free. It universalizes by describing the encounter between Jesus and the Galileans as a manifestation of God to all of his people. It dramatizes by situating all Galileans, like it or not, in darkness. Finally, it sets free by offering the salvation it describes, or, more specifically, by an anticipatory interpretation of the preaching of Jesus (Matt 4:17) as the dawning of a saving light (Matt 4:16). For all Jewish readers, and even all Greek readers, were aware of the connection between light and salvation.[12]

Matthew the evangelist, who can in other respects be so conservative, becomes even bolder than he has been in offering this application of the scriptures (4:15–16): He does not hesitate even to intervene in the living reality of history; I mean, of course, the history that he is narrating. He makes Zebulun and Naphtali the rivets that attach history to scripture and scripture to history. Jesus must betake himself not only to Nazara and Capernaum in Galilee but also to the "land of Zebulun, land of Naphtali, on the road by the sea" (Isa 8:23, cited in Matt 4:15). If he must, then he will. This explains Matthew 4:13b and the movement it describes as intimated by the scripture, which is felt to be achieving its fulfillment (with the help of an entertaining ambiguity: in the Hebrew Scriptures, the sea to which Isaiah refers is the Mediterranean; in the gospel citation of that passage the sea can only be the Lake of Gennesaret).[13]

VI

If we look now at the scriptural content of the temptations (Luke 4:1–13; Matt 4:1–11), we will note first of all that the superhuman wrestling between the Son of God and the devil is located at the level of human beings and takes the form of a

---

[11] On the concept of citation, see Françis Bovon, "'Schön hat der Heilige Geist durch den Propheten Jesaja zu euren Vätern gesprochen' (Act 28, 25)," *ZNW* 75 (1984) 226–32; reprinted (French) Bovon, *L'œuvre de Luc*, 145–53; see below, pp. 113–19.

[12] See Hans Conzelmann, "φῶς," *TDNT* 9.10–58.

[13] On the episode of Zebulun and Naphtali see Luz, *Das Evangelium nach Matthäus*, 169–74.

rabbinical dialogue between protagonists who strike blows with verses from the Bible. Alongside the imitation of the scriptures, which draws its inspiration from narrative forms and biblical prophecy in search of fulfillment, there is here a third usage of the scriptures. The latter are seen here as a norm that applies not just now and then, but permanently. The future tense used in the citations is the future not of prophetic promise but of concrete obedience.

Both parties accept the scriptures as law. Jesus recalls the passages that fit the circumstances and shows his adversary how to use them properly. Against the devil's misuse of scripture Jesus appeals to Moses, whereas in the multiplication of the loaves he imitates and completes Elijah and especially Elisha. In the episode of the temptations the scriptures do not provide the form of the story as they do in the passage on Zebulun and Naphtali, but they do serve as an explicitly cited norm for the decisions and actions of Jesus, who is presented as a hero of faith and obedience. The tempter's formal fidelity, which is really infidelity, to the scriptures is met by the faithful fidelity of Jesus, a fidelity characterized by trust and dedication. Thanks to the passages he chooses, Jesus outlines the behavior, based on faith, that the people should have demonstrated at the exodus: reliance on the word of God (Deut 8:3), determination to adore God and God alone (Deut 6:13), and refusal to put God to the test (Deut 6:16)

This is an obedience that is not so much moral as theological. The Son of God chooses to use neither the miracle-working power he possesses (he refuses to transform the stones into loaves), nor the political power that is his inheritance (he renounces the kingdoms of this world), nor the immunity bestowed by his divine origin, which is attested by the princely escort at his disposal (he does without the help of the angels' wings). The story of the temptations is messianic but also ethical and theological, and it can be read as christological as well as parenetic. It leads us to the scriptures, as well as to other areas, by reason of new events and experiences. Here on this still unknown terrain of spiritual experience and testing, Jesus, the principal protagonist who is located – if we may so put it – in his own time and context, refers to scripture as the norm of faith and life. This is what the evangelists Luke and Matthew are saying in the story of the temptations.

VII

At the close of this short analysis I may conclude that the evangelists, Luke and Matthew in particular, have a vital relationship with the scriptures, a relationship that refuses both haughty rejection of them and servile dependence on them. Desirous of respecting the scriptural record of the first fulfillments, the ancient promises, and the constant will of God, the evangelists establish numerous correspondences of various kinds between the sacred scriptures and the saving event that is ultimate and decisive in their eyes as believers, namely, the life, death, and resurrection of Jesus, the Messiah and Son of God, whose story they are carefully reporting and whose significance they want to define.

The stories they tell of the temptations of Jesus and the multiplication of the loaves enable us to uncover at least three uses of scripture: imitation of the biblical story, fulfillment of prophecy, and understanding in faith the scriptural norm.[14]

---

[14] On the part played by the Hebrew Bible in the work of Luke, see François Bovon, *Luc le théologien. Vingt-cing ans de recherches (1950–1975)* (2d ed.; Le Monde de la Bible 5; Geneva: Labor et Fides, 1988); Jacob Jervell, "Die Mitte der Schrift. Zum lukanischen Verständnis des Alten Testaments" in *Die Mitte des Neuen Testaments. Einheit und Vielfalt neutestamentlicher Theologie. Festschrift E. Schweizer* (ed. Ulrich Luz and H. Weder; Göttingen: Vandenhoeck & Ruprecht, 1983); Jack T. Sanders, "The Prophetic Use of Scriptures in Luke-Acts," in *Early Jewish and Christian Exegesis*, 191–98.

"Well Has the Holy Spirit Spoken to Your Fathers through the Prophet Isaiah" (Acts 28:25)*

For Eduard Schweizer on his seventieth birthday

The aim of this short article is to shed light on the art of quotation, interpret the citation formula, and draw a few conclusions regarding the Lukan understanding of Scripture. I hope to offer something new here, for studies of the closing verses of Acts[1] have dealt either with the citation itself or with the narrative surrounding it; they have treated neither the citation formula nor the art of citation.

The literary context of the citation is as follows: The Jews of the capital city come for the second time (in larger throngs) to Paul, who tries all day long to "persuade them concerning Jesus from the Law of Moses and the Prophets" (v. 23). Because they are divided in their response, Paul adds another word as they are leaving. In this short speech he inserts the famous Isaiah citation before concluding the argument with the following sentence: "So now you should know: this salvation of God is sent to the Gentiles, and they will listen" (v. 28). Then Luke himself adds one more sentence, in which he notes Paul's two years in Rome.

---

* This short article was delivered on April 16, 1983, at the celebration of E. Schweizer's seventieth birthday. English translation by James D. Ernest. Copyright © Baker Book House Company, 2005.

[1] Joachim Gnilka, *Die Verstockung Israels. Isaias 6, 9–10 in der Theologie der Synoptiker* (SANT 3; München: Kösel-Verlag, 1961), 119–54; Traugott Holtz, *Untersuchungen über die alttestamentlichen Zitate bei Lukas* (TU 104; Berlin: Akademie-Verlag, 1968), 33–37; Jacques Dupont, "La conclusion des Actes et son rapport à l'ensemble de l'ouvrage de Luc," in *Les Actes des Apôtres: Traditions, rédaction, théologie* (ed. J. Kremer; BETL 48; Gembloux: J. Duculot; Leuven: Leuven University Press, 1979), 359–404; Hermann J. Hauser, *Strukturen der Abschlußerzählung der Apostelgeschichte (Apg 28, 16–31)* (AnBib 86; Rome: Biblical Institute Press, 1979), esp. 35–39, 69–75, 99–102, 200–202, 235–42, literature 251–64; and B. Prete, "L'arrivo di Paolo a Roma e il suo significato secondo *Atti* 28 16–31," *RivBib* 31 (1983): 147–87, esp. 173 n. 51. The reader will find an overview of contributions to the Lukan understanding of Scripture in my book, *Luke the Theologian: Thirty-three Years of Research (1950–1983)* (trans. Ken McKinney; Princeton Theological Monograph Series 12; Allison Park, Penn.: Pickwick, 1987), 85–117.

I. The Art of Citation

As is already apparent from this summary, we have here not just one but two citations, i.e., a citation within a citation: an Old Testament citation (of a written text) within a New Testament citation (of an oral saying). The first is marked as such by "that" (ὅτι, v. 25b), the other by "saying" (λέγων, v. 26). Isaiah's statement is packed into Paul's saying like a smaller Russian doll inside a larger one. In the setting, since the Jews depart "in disagreement with each other" (ἀσύμφωνοι, v. 25), the agreement in the Christian camp between the old and new covenants stands out in contrast. Just as the various dissonant utterances of the Jews hint at the fracturing of Israel, so Luke in Paul's speech registers by way of contrast the unity, unanimity, and clarity of the Christian truth. On the last page of his twofold literary opus, Luke expresses the one word, rooted in divine inspiration, of the two complementary witnesses, Isaiah and Paul.

Let us linger a little longer with the phenomenon of citation (which has been analyzed by the French critic Antoine Compagnon).[2] "Citation" is not easy to define. One thing is clear: "citation" means more than its usual dictionary definition, "a passage cited from an author or from a famous person (generally to illustrate or support one's point)."[3] This definition envisions only the result, ignoring the act; citation is in the first instance an action, or even a double action, that is similar to surgery or to sewing: cutting out, then implanting in a foreign setting. Like surgery or sewing, it is an exacting, difficult, subjective, and indeed dangerous work. Only secondarily is "citation" the result of this transposition, i.e., the quoted bit of text itself.

If we inquire into the reasons for making citations, we should proceed phenomenologically and historically.

Phenomenologically speaking, the beginning is always with the desire, the will, or the need to cite. I cite because it suits me or is appropriate to do so. Of course it sometimes happens that I cite precisely that with which I disagree: *he or she* says it, not I. Or I cite because for me the cited author or thinker constitutes an authority: if *he or she* says it, it is surely true. We can think of other motives for citing, ranging from pleasure taken in ornamentation to showing off one's own erudition. The author can insert the citation without introduction if the reader can be assumed to have a certain education. Usually,

---

[2] Antoine Compagnon, *La seconde main ou le travail de la citation* (Paris: Seuil, 1979); cf. Gérard Genette, *Palimpsests: Literature in the Second Degree* (trans. Channa Newman and Claude Doubinsky; Stages 8; Lincoln: University of Nebraska Press, 1997). I thank both of these critics for their important contributions.

[3] "Passage cité d'un auteur, d'un personage célèbre (généralement pour illustrer ou appuyer ce que l'on avance)," in Paul Robert, *Dictionnaire alphabétique et analogique de la langue française* (nouvelle éd.; Paris: Société du Nouveau Littré, 1979), s.v. "citation."

however, the author prefers to give a signal that allows the reader to note the presence of the citation.

To the writer's work, with its two-fold responsibility—achieving elegance and correctness, and transmitting sense and meaning—citation adds another, namely, the responsibility to mark the citation as a citation. The cited extract thereby acquires a meaning or force apart from its own content.[4] As exegetes we must pay attention not only to *what* is cited but also to *how* it is cited, and even prior to that, to the fact *that* a citation is being made.

We must also investigate the basis of the citation historically, for today citation as act takes on a different nuance than in antiquity or the Renaissance. Therefore I often miss, in studies of Hebrew Bible citations in the New Testament, a form-critical investigation of the literary art of citation in the primitive church. In the time of the Renaissance, citation became separated from the authority of Scripture and the principle of *auctoritas.* Montaigne freely selected quotations with which he decorated the walls of his study. Often drawn from secular wisdom, these quotations were emblems: on the one hand almost as personal companions;[5] on the other hand as a key to his own personality. In the Middle Ages the situation was completely different: freedom resided in fidelity, and fidelity in repetition. In the Middle Ages, the age of citation, this art was something like a chain of endless commentary on the given revelation. Within pagan antiquity, the situation was again somewhat different. There were two kinds of citation. In rhetoric, a secularized sort of citation, under the influence of Aristotle, was predominant. In the framework of *mimesis*, the γνώμη took on a twofold function: as testimony (either from ancient times or from the recent past) and as metaphor (in the third division of rhetoric, i.e., *elocutio,* which followed *inventio* and *dispositio*). But with the resurgence of religion in the first and second centuries CE, the Platonic religious kind of citation also reappeared, aimed less at proving or persuading than at revealing the wonderful effect of the Word.[6]

In my opinion, the relationship of this latter kind of citation (in religious discourse) to the Jewish system of citation deserves another study. As far as I can see, the development of the Jewish teaching on inspiration[7] may be seen as a polemical imitation of the Greek religious art of citation. In both cases *auctoritas* stands at the center; in Judaism and in the early church this *auctoritas* is the authority of divine *Scripture.*

How then do things stand in Luke? From a phenomenological point of view, Luke enjoys expressing his agreement with a tradition that he regards as sacred.

---

[4] Cf. Compagnon, *La seconde main,* 69, 106–109.

[5] Cf. Compagnon, *La seconde main,* 284; and Jean Starobinski, *Montaigne in Motion* (trans. Arthur Goldhammer; Chicago: University of Chicago Press, 1985), 6–9.

[6] For this historical discussion of citations, see Compagnon, *La seconde main,* 95–336.

[7] Str-B 4.1:415–51.

He does this polemically, in agreement with what he treats as the true tradition, whose main witnesses are Paul and Isaiah. The basis of this agreement lies for him in the divine subject of this twofold witness, namely, the Holy Spirit. The pleasure and pride Luke takes, and his triumphal tone, must not blind us to that which is highly subjective, even biased, and therefore suspect in the Lukan project: he takes a brief excerpt out of Scripture and, with a good conscience over against the Jews, annexes it. To be sure, Luke is not the first Christian to lay claim to this Isaiah citation.[8] But compared with the Synoptic tradition, our citation makes (if you will permit a house-moving image) a second move. The first move transferred the saying from Scripture into the mouth of Jesus (i.e., in the Synoptic tradition);[9] the second, accomplished by Luke, transfers the saying from the mouth of Jesus (in the parable of the sower,[10] where Luke, unlike Mark, does not explicitly present this saying as a Scripture quotation) to the mouth of Paul. This transposition thus moves it from the beginning of the Gospel to the end of Acts. As T. Holtz[11] plausibly suggested, Luke, just to be safe, checked the quotation in Scripture itself (i.e., in a Septuagint codex): this explains the first part of the quotation, which is special to Luke and which has the situation of the people in view (πορεύθητι πρὸς τὸν λαὸν τοῦτον καὶ εἰπόν) .

Luke is saying: Scripture belongs to us Christians. The last word in my work goes to Paul and the Christian understanding of Scripture: Scripture gives definitive testimony regarding Israel's hardening of heart. Luke carefully laid the groundwork for this conclusion through Paul's admonitions in Acts 13:46 and 18:6, where he warns the Jews that after their rejection of the gospel he will turn to the Gentiles. Luke's aim in citing Isaiah at this point and in this way is thus polemical, arising from the failed dialogue with the synagogue. The cry of victory is therefore at the same time evidence of a Christian defeat.

The conversions to Christianity that Luke nevertheless hopes for will therefore come primarily from Gentile circles: "So let it be known to you: this salvation of God is sent to the Gentiles, and they will listen" (v. 28). Nonetheless these words, like the whole final speech of Paul, including the Isaiah citation, are directed to *Israel* ("So let it be known to you," γνωστὸν οὖν ἔστω ὑμῖν, v. 28a). And perhaps a residual glimmer of hope for Israel appears in a discreet *double entendre* that I detect at the end of the citation: Luke has not forbidden us to take the words "and I will heal them" (καὶ ἰάσομαι αὐτούς) and perhaps also "and turn" (καὶ ἐπιστρέψωσιν, where the reading ἐπιστρέψουσιν, "and they will turn," occurs in many manuscripts—confusion between ου and ω is common) independently of "lest" (μήποτε) (v. 27), i.e., positively, as expressing a last hope for Israel. So his joy

---

[8] Cf. Gnilka, *Die Verstockung.*
[9] Mark 4:12 par.
[10] Luke 8:10.
[11] Holtz, *Untersuchungen*, 35.

in triumph is something entirely different from *Schadenfreude*. If we now locate the Lukan citation within the *history* of citation, we can provisionally establish the following: with the exception of Acts 17:28 (the Aratus citation), they are exclusively passages from the prophets. Thus Luke unambiguously aligns himself with the Jewish tradition. Not until the second century, when dialogue with the Greek tradition comes to life—for example, in Clement of Alexandria—do Christians begin to turn to the secular kind of citation. In Luke neither the citation formulae nor the manner of citation has any philosophical or rhetorical coloring. The Lukan art of citation is naturally related to early Christianity and recalls Jewish tradition, e.g., the Qumran *Community Rule*[12] or the first two books of the Maccabees,[13] where, as in Luke, the citations testify to a harmony, sometimes even an eschatological correspondence, between the Scripture and the history of God's people.

II. The Citation Formula

From Luke's intention, as expressed in quotation as act and as text, I would now like to move on to the citation formula, because the way citations are introduced has great importance for the Lukan theology of Scripture. Luke calls Paul's last speech, a mixture of quotations and his own words, a "word" (ῥῆμα). ῥῆμα ἕν is here not simply "one word"; it sounds solemn and formal. The word here is the biblical ῥῆμα,[14] not λόγος. Luke reserves ῥῆμα for Hebraic tradition, for the word of God, and for human speech inspired by God. For him ῥῆμα ἕν is exhortation, promise, confidence rooted in God, a dynamic word tightly connected with deed, a firm promise that includes sure fulfillment.

More interesting is the meaning of καλῶς ("well"), which by itself would be banal. It seems as though the early church wished to use this adverb to designate what is correct over against the Synagogue as well as the earliest heresies—that is, what is correct in a Christian way, and specifically in the realms of ethics, church government, exegesis, and preaching. Wherever Christians had to choose what was right—right deeds and right thoughts—at the end of the first century adverbs like καλῶς and ἀληθῶς appear. We think at once of *good* works (1 Pet 2:12), the *good* fight (2 Tim 4:7), doing good (καλῶς ποιεῖν, Matt 12:12), and diaconal ministry ("those who serve well as deacons," οἱ γὰρ καλῶς διακονήσαντες, 1 Tim 3:13) and on the elders who rule well (οἱ καλῶς προεστῶτες πρεσβύτεροι, 1 Tim 5:17).

In Scripture interpretation this καλῶς shows up in an especially impressive way in the course of the Synoptic tradition: καλῶς ἐπροφήτευσεν Ἡσαΐας (Mark

---

[12] 1QS V, 15, 17
[13] 1 Macc 4:24; 7:17; 9:21, 41; 2 Macc 7:6.
[14] Cf. Walter Radl, "ῥῆμα," *EDNT* 3:210–11.

7:6; Matt 15:7). Then it shows up in Luke (in the text under discussion here) and somewhat later in the *Letter of Barnabas*. The author of *Barnabas* cites Lev 11:3 in its entirety, provides first a literal interpretation, and then reaches a preliminary conclusion with these words: "he spoke well, looking to the commandment" (καλῶς εἶπεν βλέπων τὴν ἐντολήν). Then he gives an allegorical meaning, especially of the divided hoof, and comes to his conclusion: "Do you see how well Moses has given the law?" (βλέπετε, πῶς ἐνομοθέτησεν Μωϋσῆς καλῶς, *Barn.* 10:11).[15] Christians may express their admiration for Scripture if they are willing to understand it in their own way and appropriate it for themselves.

So embedded in this καλῶς are (1) the recognition of the Scripture that the Christians share with the Jews; (2) the conviction that this Scripture contains the meaning that they believe they alone possess (this is the truth component of the καλῶς). (3) In connection with this claim, καλῶς naturally strikes a polemical point against Jewish biblical interpretation. (4) Since Scripture as promise has become concrete and has been fulfilled in a historical reality, there appears, apart from the truth component of the καλῶς, a component of nobility—a nobility emerging not so much from Scripture alone as from the harmonious interplay between promise and fulfillment. (5) The fifth component of the καλῶς, really the most important, is the theological: we are informed that the one who made the promise is not Isaiah himself but the Holy Spirit. Even here Luke has not undertaken anything new, since Jewish and Christian tradition at Luke's time already knew the inspiration of Scripture. But what is amazing is that Luke gives credit ("has spoken well," καλῶς . . . ἐλάλησεν) not to the human transmitter of the truth, i.e., the prophet Isaiah, but to the divine source of the truth: thus in reading this "has spoken well" we should think less of the awarding of a gold medal than of the sort of praise expressed by the psalmists.

The divine origin of Scripture is expressed even more clearly in two other citations in Acts that simultaneously underline the mediating role of human utterance: "No, this is what was spoken through the prophet Joel . . . God declares" (ἀλλὰ τοῦτό ἐστιν τὸ εἰρημένον διὰ τοῦ προφήτου Ἰωήλ . . . λέγει ὁ θεός, Acts 2:16–17) and "It is you who said by the Holy Spirit through our ancestor David, your servant" (ὁ τοῦ πατρὸς ἡμῶν διὰ πνεύματος ἁγίου στόματος Δαυὶδ παιδός σου εἰπών, Acts 4:25; here, through this supernatural linkage between divine and human activity, even grammatical rules are broken).

Without getting into the question of the origins of the Jewish and Christian doctrine of inspiration, I would instead note the following conclusions with regard to our verse: (1) According to Luke, the Spirit has not written but spoken (as for Jewish tradition, so also for the Evangelists, the human form in which the Spirit is given is more important than the written form). (2) God's sovereign authority

---

[15] Trans. Bart D. Ehrman, *Apostolic Fathers* (LCL 25; Cambridge, Mass.: Harvard University Press, 2003), 2:51.

over against human cooperation is expressed grammatically through "the Holy Spirit" (τὸ πνεῦμα τὸ ἅγιον) as subject. We should not forget that the Greeks see declension as a decline[16] and when possible put their gods and rulers in the nominative case in their sentences. (3) Speech inspired by the Holy Spirit is not timeless truth or instruction: it sounds once, in the past, for particular ears (see the aorist ἐλάλησεν and the fathers as recipients at that time). But since for Luke the sons are like the fathers and yet again take their stand against the Holy Spirit (Acts 7:51), the contextual saying can again be repeatable, "quotable." Then as now the divine word applies: The Holy Spirit has spoken so well because the word spoken at that time remains applicable now. With Luke, a typology of judgment always accompanies the promise-fulfillment schema. In other words, in parallel with the history of salvation runs a history of ruin.

The Gospel of Luke and the Acts of the Apostles themselves became Scripture. And Christians today have inherited from Paul and Luke the task of understanding and explaining these Lukan writings. In this chain of Scripture interpretation we are bidden to hear how the Holy Spirit has already spoken through Luke. Perhaps the canon is closed; but we nevertheless believe that the Holy Spirit remains active in his church, even in the work of the reader.

---

[16] The Greeks viewed each case, apart from the nominative, as a πτῶσις (literally, a "fall"). I became aware of this phenomenon through the work of Gerald Mussies (*The Morphology of Koine Greek as Used in the Apocalypse of St. John: A Study in Bilingualism* (NovTSup 27; Leiden: Brill, 1971), 93.

II. New Testament Theology

Parable of the Gospel—Parable of the Kingdom of God[*]

"Ainsi le visible dit plus que le visible"
Michel Serres, *Les cinq sens* (Paris, 1985), 23

A century has passed since the appearance of the first volume of Adolf Jülicher's monograph.[1] The work was groundbreaking, as we know, in its rigorous introduction of a strict historical-critical method, and in its attack on both allegorical and dogmatic interpretation. Since then, his method has been applied and refined. Other methods, more literary, rhetorical, or theological, have gone in various directions. Is this diversity of approach a sign of weakness, or does it enrich our understanding of the words of Jesus? Does it have something to do with the polysemy inherent in Jesus' own language? This is what the following pages seek to clarify.

I.

In the language of a parable, John the evangelist has Jesus say the following: "Look around you and see how the fields are ripe for harvesting," and "the reaper is already receiving wages and is gathering fruit for eternal life" (John 4:35 and 36). One of the most ancient commentators on the Fourth Gospel, the gnostic Heracleon (second century), sees in these words a description of those "who are ready for the harvest and already ripe for gathering into the barn—that is, ready through faith for rest and for the receiving of the word" (text handed down in Origen, *Comm. Jo.* 13.44 § 294 [GCS 10:270, 30–34]). The earliest Christian exegesis of the parables was allegorical, following the lead of the first narrative and intratextual interpretation ascribed to Jesus himself. Note how in the parable of the Sower, for example, Mark 4:13–20 is an interpretation of Mark 4:3–9; likewise, in the parable of the Wheat and Tares, Matt 13:36–43 is an interpretation of Matt 13:24–30. This line of exegetical development was the reflection of a Christian conviction that the true meaning of a parable is provided through a second sense of Scripture, which emerges from the deciphering and elucidating of the literal account. This effort

---

[*] English translation by Ronald James Marr. Copyright © Baker Book House Company, 2005.
[1] *Die Gleichnisreden Jesu*, vol. 1 (Freiburg: J. C. B. Mohr [Paul Siebeck], 1888).

to amplify the received text—word by word, in an instructive, edifying way—is, at the same time, a personal construction. Christian readers of Greek or Jewish background were of one mind in believing that metaphorical language points to a spiritual reality, which calls for such expression. They were also influenced by the traditional Christian use of the word παραβολή, a metalinguistic marker for this doctrinally significant narrated reality.

The exegetes of the nineteenth and twentieth centuries, on the other hand—with similar determination—read the parables from an historical-critical perspective and discovered other things. They suspected, for example, that the Matthean parable of the Talents (Matt 25:14–30) and the Lukan parable of the Entrusted Pounds (Luke 19:12–27) are derived from a single, traditional story in spite of their differences. They convincingly trace a process whereby isolated reports pass from mouth to mouth over time, before being used regularly by the church. In the Lukan parable, for example, they conclude that the nobleman departing to receive a kingdom constitutes a specific, historical allusion (to the fall of Archelaus), while also corresponding to a general change of religious consciousness (in regard to the delay of the Parousia).

Of course, exegesis is also, and perhaps first of all, an explication of words. Before one's gaze is directed from the text out to the world to which it points, it is essential that the text itself be well examined and understood. In this regard, the philological tradition has had its high and low points. In antiquity, it was bound up with allegorizing; since the Renaissance, however, historical exegesis has led the way and bolstered the discipline. So, for example, while the account in Luke 12:16–20 of a rich man who foolishly dreams of new barns is clear enough, the lesson drawn from it in verse 21 is not so obvious. In particular, what do the words καὶ μὴ εἰς θεὸν πλουτῶν indicate? Are they referring to a spiritual or to a material wealth? Does the verb πλουτῶ mean "to be rich" or "to enrich oneself?" Finally, does εἰς θεόν suggest a beneficiary or custodian of the accrued treasure (in symmetry with ἑαυτῷ), or does it indicate the highest profits of spiritual enrichment (in which case, there is no dative parallel to the ἑαυτῷ in the first clause)? Philology, better than the allegorizing or historical approaches, can pose these questions and—frequently—solve them. Philology is also more decisive at this point than semiotic analysis.

Still, semiotic analysis can achieve a different goal, through its sensitivity to coherence and function. By attending to narrative program, thematic peculiarities, and affective connections, it can elicit manifest points that habit or inattention would otherwise have left obscure. In the parable of the Good Samaritan (Luke 10:30–37), it rightly draws our attention to the fact that "the story comes to a close before the complete restoration of the robbers' victim to health takes place" and "the debate ends without the lawyer reacting to Jesus' final words." This analysis offers the theological, almost homiletical, but in any case exegetical conclusion that "the disappearance of the lawyer after Jesus says 'Go and do likewise' leaves vacant the receiver's past in this speech for the sake of anyone who would care to accept it."[2] This, in effect, is a semiotic analysis of the reader (i.e., ourselves), according to which we enter into the pragmatic and dialogical power of the parable.

Every close study of the text uncovers something genuine, even if different. Of course, each method also has it limitations, peculiarities, and blind spots. Adolf Jülicher was right to fulminate against the allegorizing of the church fathers and the moralistic interpretations of the pietists. Contemporary exegetes most oriented toward a literary approach are right to attack a historical criticism that interests itself only in the content of an *Urtext* or an oral tradition—which may lie beyond our reach. An interpreter sensitive to metaphorical language will properly maintain that a literary preoccupation with the dramatic casting (i.e. who is saying what lines) will obstruct the inner thrust of a parable, when its function is to go beyond this surface, demanding that the reader leave it behind for the sake of a different theme. In spite of all this, however, every reading of the text also has its own advantage and legitimacy. It is one point of viewing. Just as the same mountain appears to be different when viewed from the north or the south, so the same parable presents different faces and a changing profile, according to whether we view it within the framework of history, aesthetics, or theology.

II.

Does this diversity of possible approaches arise out of the nature of the parable? Out of an intentional polysemy? I will try to clarify this question in two different ways: by analyzing the evangelical setting in which Jesus preached in parables, and by tracing the meaning of the word "parable" itself.

To begin with, let us look at the way Jesus proceeds in the parables, according to the Gospel of Matthew. At the end of Matt 12:46–50, the Matthean Christ contravenes the bonds of blood kinship, which is to say that he speaks critically of literal "family relations" in order to redefine them in the secondary, figurative sense of a spiritual order. At the same time, this spiritualizing is not without a certain incarnation. Jesus does not raise his hand toward heaven to indicate his new relations there; rather, he stretches his hand toward the assembled company of disciples: "See, there are my mother and my brothers!" (Matt 12:49). Moreover, this new sense of things can be expanded; its new claim no longer depends on physical creation, but on an active submission to the will of God (Matt 12:50).

The contrast between inside and outside in this pericope is suggestive. The family of Jesus remains outside the house (cf. "outside" in both v. 46 and v. 47), while Jesus and his disciples, on the other hand, are gathered inside. The second

---

[2] The Entrevernes Group, *Signs and Parables: Semiotics and Gospel Texts* (trans. Gary Phillips; Pittsburg Theological Monograph Series 23; Pittsburg: Pickwick, 1978), 53–54.

sense of "family" reveals itself on the inside. Exegetes often overlook another character—anonymous and remaining in the background—whose importance may be gauged by the connection he makes between the inside and outside, between the literal and the metaphorical. Not that he defined the connection. At first, he was only aware of a literal state of affairs, but he came to apprehend significance in what followed from this. When this person says by his own authority, "Look, our mother and your brothers are standing outside" (v. 48), he will understand Jesus' answer and interpretation: "Here are my mother and my brothers" (v. 49). The anonymous person inside the text is the exegete, whose path from verification to interpretation we — readers looking in from outside the text — are invited to follow.

After the evangelist has said this, he describes Jesus leaving the house not for a walk (Matt 13:1), but to seat himself (a verb suggesting the position of a teacher). The venue Jesus establishes by the seashore is neither for an ancestral nor for a church family, but rather — broader in scope than the first and less distinctive than the second — for "great crowds" (Matt 13:2).

Matthew continues his role as narrator, by reporting that Jesus was going to speak (Matt 13:3); however, as he specifies that Jesus spoke in parables, Matthew is switching from narrator to guide (Matt 13:3). After rendering the parable of the Sower (Matt 13:3–9), Matthew assigns the disciples to the role of the anonymous exegete of Matt 12:47. They are amazed, as they recognize a metaphorical dimension to what Jesus says of the visible, the literal, and the corporeal (Matt 13:10). As Jesus presses them from the outside to the inside, from the letter to the Spirit, from the parable to the kingdom of God, he is designating his disciples as pilgrims, for whom it is possible to make the crossing from one meaning to another: from language to God, from secrets embedded in the parables to a spiritual understanding of them (Matt 13:11). "To you" be it "added" to receive the figurative, as well as literal meaning. "For to those who have, more will be given, and they will have an abundance" (Matt 13:12a), "but from those who have nothing, even what they have will be taken away" (Matt 13:12b)—especially the parables. In the preceding pericope (Matt 12:46–50), those who remain outside are represented by the consanguine family, and this parable pictures them as the ground where the seed fails to flourish (Matt 13:4–7).

The "you" of disciples who understand—not by themselves, but under the tutelage of Christ—are praised (Matt 13:16–17). Blessed are the disciples in what they see and hear, because they are able to move from the visible to the invisible, from human words to divine reality. The others also have opportunity to see and hear, but do not understand.

Jesus concentrates on the "you" in this division as the only members of his true family. After giving the parable to both groups in mysterious, cryptic language, he further gives the second, deeper, decoded meaning to his disciples alone. The interpretation is allegorical in the intrinsic meaning of the word, therefore, which is to say that it leads "to another place" (Matt 13:18–23).

The entire scene has a double function: (1) it highlights Jesus' most important parable (the Sower) as a summary of the whole gospel, and (2) it demands, magisterially, that the function of parables generally and an interpretation appropriate to them be understood in the horizon of faith.

III.

The use of the word "parable" by the evangelists themselves confirms a theological intention that was rooted in the historical person of Jesus and came to flourish in the synoptic tradition. It sent a signal that this form of human language is directed at a divine reality that is beneficent, impatient, and demanding.

The Greek word παραβολή is translated from the Hebrew māšāl. But as a concept, how does it stand in relation to several other forms of figurative speech (from proverb to riddle, from parable to fable)? The word is derived from the verb παραβάλλω, which even in the transitive can have a great number of meanings: "throw alongside of," "cast in one's teeth," "confide, entrust," "throw out of the right way," "bring alongside," "heave to," "compare," "set in parallel with."[3] The parable is a "discarding," and a "comparison," but also an "encounter," a "shock" (as in the clash of a battle), a "deviation from the right way," a "radiating" (of light), a "parabola" (in relation to a cone), a "parallelogram," or "divison" (in arithmetic). In the Gospels, the word has a semantic field with protean boundaries, just as in Hebrew; however, it does not take on the whole scope of possible Greek meanings. A recent dictionary records the meanings that are close to the Semitic māšāl, specifying the following: "maxims," "metaphorical saying," "general rules," "parable," "parabolic stories," "paradigmatic illustrative stories."[3] With these different possibilities, the word παραβολή itself in the Gospels signals that the significance of the Jesus' teaching may require searching beneath the surface of the most readily apparent meaning.

IV.

To speak in parables implies, therefore, something other than to speak as usual; it means to choose a mode of expression in which the listener's attention is first stimulated by the surprise of something novel and then directed from the literal toward another reality. The surprise is this subsequent discovery that the first, astonishing pronouncement refers to something else. In this regard, the difference

---

[3] Günter Haufe, "παραβολή κτλ.," *EDNT* 3:315–16, esp. 315.

between a simile, in which a comparison between two entities is stated up front, and a metaphor, in which the identity of the other reality is "concealed" within language is doubtless exaggerated. Many parables begin with the formula of a simile (see Mark 4:26, 30; Matt 13:24, 31, 33, 44, 45, 47; Luke 13:18, 20), which should suffice to make us carefully consider the following: (1) apart from a narrow, nominalist definition of language, the simile participates in the being of the entity of comparison, and conversely (2) one may not overrate the metaphor, as if it will generate a satisfactory force simply through its form of expression.

V.

The difference between parable and allegory should also not be overvalued. There is a not unreasonable chance that the first redacted collections of the traditional parables of Jesus were of an allegorical type (e.g., Mark 4:13–20 and Matt 13:36–43). Certainly, the integrity of the parable as a whole, though it contains more than one punch line, does not allow the simple appropriation of individual parts as if they were semantically equivalent—as for example in the sentence: "But as for what was sown on good soil, this is the one who hears the word and understands it . . ." (Matt 13:23). It is also no accident, of course, that the first heterodox exegetes of the second century read the parables of the Gospels from an allegorical perspective. By contrast, though, the parables of Jesus were characterized by being concrete, prosaic, rural, near to the people, and embedded in a cultural tradition for which "the shepherd" and the "sower" had long been great figures in a symbolic world of religious meaning. And not just images and metaphors, but also story lines told by Jesus and the evangelists belong to this world: a departure and a return, loss and recovery, the duty of hospitality to strangers or the duty to familiar relations, such matters were occasions for stories whose theological forcefulness had impressed spirits for a long time. Everyone, even Jesus, must accept certain limitations in order to make himself understood. In order to convey something new, only the old stands at one's disposal. An arrangement of the given words, motifs, and themes is alone what makes it possible for the appearance of something novel. For this reason, all the parables of Jesus contain a certain share of the allegorical. In spite of this, Jesus and the first Christians activated a notable break, not at the level of the symbolic world, but in regard to practices relating to exegesis of the Torah. For in contrast to various Jewish parables, those of Jesus no longer look back on in order cleverly to illustrate a normative, biblical text (". . . The parable is not something trivial in your eyes, for through a parable one is able to obtain comprehension of the Torah," *Midr. Cant.* 1,1[79a]),[4] but forward

---

[4] See Str-B, 653–54.

to the kingdom of God, of which they speak with power (in the double sense of the word as both virtual and active power).

The analysis of the connections between parable and allegory must overcome the formal aspects. It is appropriate in carrying it out to consider the pragmatic process of communication. Originally, with its first use, the hearers of parable are "shocked" or "astounded" (do these words still convey something of the meaning they had in our Gospels?). Actually, the parables were first employed in crisis situations (which can be confirmed through socio-linguistics). If the use of other kinds of language is prevented, the parable offers an indirect, circuitous, but sure way to communicate. (David allowed himself to be drawn into the language of Nathan's delicate topic, because Nathan spoke of a lamb instead of a woman and of someone else instead of David himself [2 Sam 12].)[5] The scenario that Luke sets up in chapter 15 of his Gospel illustrates this conclusion: the three parables of mercy—the Lost Sheep (Luke 15:3–7), the Lost Coin (Luke 15:8–10), and the Lost Son (Luke 15:11–32)—are not presented by the evangelist as enjoyable instructions, but as answers to criticism. It is not required that the historicizing introduction of Luke 15:1–2, in which criticism of the Pharisees and scribes arises against Jesus' way of life, be exactly historical; it is enough that Luke suggests that every parable is part of a larger dialogical or polemical process of communication.

Shocking, calling urgently for decision, self-realizing of its own message — this is the unique effect of the parable on those who first heard it. But its power does not cease here. Every text that has impressed us becomes our companion, and we turn to it again and again. We meditate on it, touched and troubled, and through its absolute penetration, its coherence, and its pointed message, we come to experience all its details, inner workings, and overtones. We let a certain word continue to resonate in us; we read of a certain situation as it relates to our own personal or cultural memories; we associate a certain response with a certain message.

In short, the parable is in the first instance an interpellation, a calling, which with repeated telling becomes an instruction or a revelation. Initially a metaphor, it turns into allegory. The father in the parable of the Lost Son was *not* God at first, but became so after a second reading. Such a development is not illegitimate.

VI.

The parables may not be isolated from their biblical context. They are an integral part of the gospel documents, not something that appears for a moment acciden-

---

[5] Cf. Bertolt Brecht, *Mann ist Mann* 5, in *Gesammelte Werke* 1.1, (Frankfurt am Main: Suhrkamp, 1967), 322: "The *bonze Wang* uses a drawing and a kind of parable as a roundabout way of communicating a matter dangerous for him."

tally or without reason in the text. The central placement of Luke 15, for example, must be viewed like the Jerusalem conference in Acts 15, to which it corresponds in Luke's second volume. Indeed, the parables are a compressed version of the gospel, a summary and picture of Jesus' message.

The παραβολή, which in its literary texture is a parable of the gospel, is also by virtue of its persuasive truth a parable of the kingdom of God. At the intersection of Letter and Spirit, a meeting place for humans and God, it offers itself to us in its weakness and strength. We must read it with all the energy of our heart and mind. The parable speaks of a treasure hidden in a field (Matt 13:44) and of a costly pearl (Matt 13:46); from inside the narrative, the parable itself is this treasure and pearl. Whoever would discover it follows the hard and painful way of the man who went out and sold all he had in order to buy it (Matt 13:44 and 46). This means that he deployed all the means of the spirit and the heart ("all that he had") in order to acquire it, to understand it. To understand the parable is to gain the kingdom of God. The understanding of a text that speaks of treasure and pearl signifies finally the comprehension of what connects the parable with the kingdom of God. The readings of the spirit and of the heart complete each other. Philological, historical, literary, psychological, and sociological observations help to illuminate aspects of every parable, because the need for all means of understanding applies to linguistic attestation as to every other human reality. In faith, however, the Christian reader hopes that God gives God's own self to be recognized in these human forms. Or, to put it another way, it is hoped that these texts from antiquity will adumbrate the divine. If this is not so, then we must despair, in cynicism and disappointment.

Bibliography

Bovon, François, and Grégoire Rouiller, eds. *Exegesis: Problems of Method and Exercises in Reading (Genesis 22 and Luke 15).* Translated by Donald G. Miller. PTMS 21. Pittsburgh: Pickwick, 1978.

Crossan, Jon Dominic. *In Parables: The Challenge of the Historical Jesus.* New York: Harper & Row, 1973.

———, ed. *The Good Samaritan. Semeia* 2 (1974).

———, ed. *Polyvalent Narration. Semeia* 9 (1977).

Dupont, Jacques. *Pourquoi des paraboles? La méthode parabolique de Jésus.* Lire la Bible 46. Paris: Cerf, 1977.

Harnisch, Wolfgang. *Die Gleichniserzählungen Jesu.* Uni-Taschenbücher 1343. Göttingen: Vandenhoeck und Ruprecht, 1985.

———, ed. *Gleichnisse Jesu: Positionen der Auslegung von Adolf Jülicher bis zur Formgeschichte.* Wege der Forschung 366. Darmstadt: Wissenschaftliche Buchgesellschaft, 1982.

————, ed. *Die neutestamentliche Gleichnisforschung im Horizont von Hermeneutik und Literaturwissenschaft.* Wege der Forschung 575. Darmstadt: Wissenschaftliche Buchgesellschaft, 1982.

Haufe, Günter. "παραβολή, κτλ." *EDNT* 3:315–16.

Jeremias, Joachim. *The Parables of Jesus.* Translated by S. H. Hooke. 3d. ed. London: SCM, 1972.

Jülicher, Adolf. *Die Gleichnisreden Jesu.* 2d ed. 2 vols. Freiburg: J. C. B. Mohr (Paul Siebeck), 1910.

Kjaergaard, Mogens Stiller. *Metaphor and Parable: A Systematic Analysis of the Specific Structure and Cognitive Function of the Synoptic Similes and Parables qua Metaphors.* ATDan 20. Leiden: Brill, 1986.

Klauck, Hans-Josef. *Allegorie und Allegorese in synoptischen Gleichnistexten.* NTAbh NF 13. Münster: Aschendorff, 1978.

Via, Dan O. *The Parables: Their Literary and Existential Dimension.* Philadelphia: Fortress, 1967.

Weder, Hans. *Die Gleichnisse Jesu als Metaphern: Traditions- und redaktionsgeschichtliche Analysen und Interpretationen.* FRLANT 120. Göttingen: Vandenhoeck und Ruprecht, 1978.

The Church in the New Testament, Servant and Victorious

Introduction

The way churches understand themselves today varies considerably from one theologian to another, from one pastor to another, and from one church member to another. Some think that a church that does not bring people to conversion cannot be the church of Jesus Christ. Others think of the church in connection with a particular confessional tradition and its history. A defense of the church understood this way is at the same time an apology for a tongue and for a nation. Still others neglect the structures and their inevitable power to embed the church in the radical gospel: if Christians forget the social trend of the good news and omit giving priority to the needs of the poor, they do not belong to the true church. Finally, many church leaders consider their task to be the edification of the congregation: to preserve what exists, to help members in their struggles, and to build a lively congregation. To the impressive multiplicity of emphases we have to add the doctrinal diversity of numerous Christian denominations, which is no less formidable. Churches with similar goals may diverge widely in their understanding of Christ and in their conception of the sacraments.

In a famous paper delivered first in English, in 1955 and published in Canada, Rudolf Bultmann proposed a new understanding of the New Testament church.[1] Instead of a harmonious origin, he proposed a polemical development. He considered four phases in the self-understanding of the primitive church. First, the early church thought of herself as the holy congregation of the last time. In this stage Christians were still Jews; no break with Judaism had yet occured. Second, the incorporation of Gentiles into the church expressed a first transformation. The church became a holy community gathering Jews and Gentiles into its unity. Because it was a body, what counted was no longer the eschatology, but the anticipation through the Holy Spirit of the kingdom in the reality of the church. Third, a second transformation occurred, according to Bultmann, when the people of God were no longer constituted by history (the event of Christ) but by the sacraments. Before this transformation the church was the "People of God"; with it she became the "Body of Christ." As the many members have different duties in a

---

[1] Rudolf Bultmann, "The Transformation of the Idea of the Church in the History of Early Christianity," *CJT* 1 (1955) 73–81.

single body, the numerous Christians had to be organized into a single institution. Ministries were established and a hierarchy emerged. The future of the individual soul overtook collective eschatology. The delay of the parousia played a large role in this evolution. The church became an institution of salvation, and the minister became a priest. Fourth, in the last stage, according to Bultmann, the Christian faith became a new religion and the church a worldwide institution (the "third race" beside Jews and Gentiles). Therefore it became possible to write a history of the church as, for example, in the canonical Acts of the Apostles.

Some years later, at an ecumenical meeting of the Commission for Faith and Order in Montreal (1963), Ernst Käsemann agreed with his teacher that there is no one single canonical and authoritative ecclesiology in the New Testament, but he offered a different view of the origins of Christianity.[2] Instead of a historical linear evolution, Käsemann proposed a sociological picture. Diversity was not successive, but contemporaneous. The unity of the church (which was the goal of the Montreal gathering and is still the objective of the World Council of Churches) had not been a historical reality, but an imperative objective for which it was necessary to fight. What was concrete and real in the first century were tensions, struggles, and divisions among Christians. This reality was created by different religious backgrounds, social contexts, and personal realities. But this plurality of church experiences did not eliminate a strong common belief. After all, these fighting congregations regarded themselves as Christian, meaning that they all descended from the same Jesus and they all believed that he was the Messiah, resurrected from the dead by God his father.

I consider myself to be in the line of Ernst Käsemann with regard to ecclesiology. I believe that in the beginning there were several different Christian groups: the circle of the Twelve,[3] the so-called Hellenists,[4] the members of Jesus' family including James the brother of the Lord, the Johannine congregation under the patronage of the mysterious beloved disciple, and the radical itinerant missionaries and prophets.[5] These groups all had reasons to disagree because of their divergent roots in Judaism, because of their conflicting social worlds (urban versus rural, wealth versus poverty, education versus ignorance, freedom versus slavery). At the same time, these groups shared a common spiritual treasury. This common faith, grounded in the love of God, nevertheless gave rise to divisions and struggles. The paradox is a true paradox and not a softened contradiction. It

---

[2] Ernst Käsemann, "Unité et diversité dans l'ecclésiologie du Nouveau Testament," *ETR* 48 (1966) 253–58. See also "The Canon of the New Testament and the Unity of the Church," in *Essays on New Testament Themes* (trans. W.J. Montague; SBT 41; Napierville, Ill.: Allenson, 1964) 95–101.

[3] Under the leadership of Peter.

[4] Under the leadership of the Seven, particularly Stephen and Philip, and later of Paul.

[5] There are several reconstructions of the early churches. Among them see François Vouga, *A l'aube de christianisme, une surprenante diversité* (Aubonne, Switzerland: Moulin, 1986).

will be my intention in these pages to respect first the *differences*, but also to see that in the reactions of the various groups as well as in their given reality, there were common Christian elements that could be shared in a true church experience. In a world of divisions, oppression, and hatred, different groups and various individual believers could constitute – because of their faith, hope, and love, because of God's will, Christ's intercession, and the Holy Spirit's presence – the visible and invisible, the holy and the sinful, the present and the eschatological church that was full of memory and hope, of sharp awareness of the presence of evil as well as knowledge of God, "the one apostolic and universal church."

The Common Faith

In this section I am dependent on what I have learned as a student from teachers such as Oscar Cullmann, Franz J. Leenhardt, and Eduard Schweizer, and from Roman Catholic exegetes such as Lucien Cerfaux and Rudolf Schnackenburg.[6] Because of the intellectual influence of the Roman Catholic tradition in France, it is logical that the question of ecclesiology has been widely discussed among French speaking exegetes. The spirit of that time also contributed to the discussion; it was the time of Vatican II and of the ecumenical movement. A description of the common faith of the early church should include at least four elements.

1. Some Jews, touched by Jesus' teaching, came to believe after his capital punishment that he had been vindicated by God. Resurrected and exalted, Jesus had, according to them, been designated as the Messiah of Israel and the Son of God. A new relation to him emerged, which they called "faith." These believers were the true remnant of the people of God, the calling of the lost sheep of Israel. They were dependent on God's call and on Christ's mediation. The emphasis was on unity, cohesion, common belief, and communion in love (what Luke expresses retrospectively in Acts 2:46). Several terms were used by the Christians themselves to designate what they had in common: "disciples" (Acts 6:2); "the holy ones" (Acts 9:3); the "brothers" (Acts 10:23); the "elected" (Luke 18:7; Mark 13:20); and later the "Christians" (Acts 11:28; 1 Pet 4:16). This last name had not been a self-designation, but was bestowed by non-Christians in Antioch to designate the new religious movement.[7] But the most important name that was chosen was the Greek

---

[6] Cf. Oscar Cullmann, *La foi et le culte de L'Église primitive* (Bibliothèque théologique; Neuchâtel: Delachaux & Niestlé, 1963); Franz J. Leenhardt, *L'Église: Questions aux protestants et aux catholiques* (Lieux théologiques 1; Geneva: Labor et Fides, 1978); Eduard Schweizer, *Church Order in the New Testament* (trans. Frank Clarke; SBT 32; London: SCM, 1961); Lucien Cerfaux, *The Church in the Theology of Saint Paul* (trans. Geoffrey Webb and Adrian Walker; New York: Herder, 1959); Rudolph Schnackenburg, *The Church in the New Testament* (trans. W.J. O'Hara; New York: Herder, 1965).

[7] Cf. François Bovon, *Luke the Theologian: Thirty-Three Years of Research (1950–1983)* (PTMS 12; Allison Park, Pa.: Pickwick, 1987) 320–21.

word ἐκκλησία. This term was convenient because it was neglected by the Jews, who prefered the word συναγωγή ("synagogue"), and, it was used by the Greeks as a political term. (it meant the political assembly of the citizens of a πόλις, of a city). So the Christians avoided any syncretistic connotation; religious associations in Greece were called religious guilds, clubs, or confraternities, but not churches.[8]

In the word ἐκκλησία, as well as in its Hebrew and Aramaic equivalents, the "calling" (καλῶ) carries the main meaning. The church feels herself called by God's initiative and God's power; she understands herself to be brought together and established as a unity. A divine and invisible force unifies and founds the church in spite of material distances and visible differences. Do not forget that in the term ἐκκλησία is the preposition ἐκ ("out of"). To be a church means to come "out of" some place – material and spiritual – in the world. The term ἐκκλησία, used normally in the singular,[9] is not easy to translate. If we translate the word as "community," we miss the universality of the one church. If we choose to translate the word as "church," we are in danger of projecting into first-century Christianity legal and institutional categories that were absent at this early stage.

2. There is an early Christian theological structure that provides a second characteristic of the New Testament church. Besides the Christ event there is the apostolic responsibility. Using Paul's terminology, besides the "reconciliation" in Christ, there is and must be the "service of reconciliation."[10] The early Christians not only believed in what God had done by reconciling the world through Christ, but they immediately shared this religious knowledge with others through preaching and witnessing in words and deeds. The centripetal force (which is acknowledged in the very word ἐκκλησία is balanced by the centrifugal missionary activity. The oldest ministry was called "the apostolate."[11] As we know, etymologically, an apostle is a witness for Christ, who is "sent" by his Lord to testify of the historical and suprahistorical truth. There is a similarity, an analogy between the life of the church and the life of its Lord: Jesus had been sent by God, the apostles in turn were sent by the Lord; Jesus had tried to bring Israel to repentance, the first Christians tried to bring first Jews, and then Gentiles, through Jesus back to God the Creator and Redeemer; Jesus had given witness by words and deeds, the disciples preached and gave concrete signs of God's love for the world; Jesus refused to compromise and died as a victim of human reluctance; the church also has to suffer opposition and repulsion.[12]

---

[8] Cf. Karl-Ludwig Schmidt, "καλέω," *TDNT* 3 (1965) 487–536; and Wayne A. Meeks, *The First Urban Christians: The Social World of the Apostle Paul* (New Haven: Yale University Press, 1983) 74.

[9] Cf. 1 Cor 1:2 for example: "The church of God which is in Corinth".

[10] 2 Cor 5:18–21. Cf. François Bovon, *L'Évangile et l'Apôtre. Le Christ inséparable de ses témoins* (Aubonne, Switzerland: Moulin, 1993).

[11] Cf. Karl Heinrich Rengstorf, "ἀποστέλλω," *TDNT* I (1964) 398–447.

[12] Cf. John 15:18.

3. Jesus preached the imminent coming of the kingdom. This apocalyptic atmosphere[13] remained determinant for the early Christians. The resurrection of Christ – resurrection meant the beginning of the last days – supported and confirmed this eschatological understanding of the present situation and of the nature of the church. Like the people who preserved the Dead Sea Scrolls, the early Christians understood their existence as eschatological[14]. They gave to Christ the Lord the title πρωτότοκος ("firstborn") of the new creation,[15] which infers that others will be taken into the procession of the newly born of the redemption. They interpreted the historical event of Good Friday and Easter in a typological way as the fulfillment of the first exodus, the eschatological antitype of the protological type. The death of Jesus, particulary shocking at first glance, can be seen not as a misfortune, but as the sacrifice and sealing of the new convenant. The ritual as well actualizes this event and expresses the covenant. Baptism is viewed as individual redemption. Eucharist is seen as the collective link with God and the communion of Christians together. Finally, the coming of the Holy Spirit, first as a reality perceived, then as a reflection over that experience, confirms the eschatological dimension of the church and confronts her with the new image of God: Father, Son, and Spirit.

4. The gathering of the early Christians was at the same time a pleasure and a duty, a material reunion, when possible, and a spiritual convention in any case. They ate together and shared their resources: no poor should remain in need, which was already an ideal of the old Israel.[16] Money could be a demonic reality, but it could also be a benediction, a spiritual power. They prayed together. As long as possible they went to the synagogue to pray and share the word of God, but they came together for meetings at Easter and during the night from Saturday to Sunday, perhaps twice, once Saturday night and then on Sunday morning, the evening with the death of Jesus in mind, the morning with his resurrection on the heart. Their common prayer was first a eulogy, a benediction, a thanksgiving for the Creator of life who is also the Redeemer, the Father of Jesus, the beloved Son who was sent for us. But prayer also had other dimensions, such as petition and intercession. Together these people shared information (a factor New Testament scholars tend to forget) about one another and from congregation to congregation.[17] The *communio sanctorum* was not an empty expression. Baptism introduced new converts to the people of God: Christians were now sealed with the Spirit, consecrated by God, put into Christ's possession, and introduced and in-

---

[13] The present tendency in the United States to replace this apocalyptic orientation with a wisdom perspective does not seem correct to me. It is perhaps dependent more on the present situation of Christianity than on the original meaning of the texts of the New Testament.

[14] The Christian congregation believed themselves to be the true remnant of Israel and to be living in the last days; see Gal 6:16.

[15] See Heb 1:8; Col 1:15, 18.

[16] See Acts 4:34, which is dependent on Deut 15:4.

[17] See François Bovon, "L'origine des récits concernant les apôtres," *RTP* 1 (1967) 345–50.

corporated into the church. The eucharist expressed the new congregation's unity, faith, mutual love, and expectations of victory over death. Like the idealized image of Israel in the desert where she was dependent only on God, the Christians were "holy," the "saints," devoted to God, separated from Egypt, from the world.[18] This characteristic of the church – her holiness – is an ecclesiological category, and a cultic category, but also an ethical one. As the "saints," the Christian congregations shine in the night of this world, giving a good witness, attracting the attention of "those from outside."[19]

Three Early Christian Churches

1. The Church of Q

A great deal of discussion has taken place over the so-called source of the logia, the Q document.[20] It is my opinion that this document did exist and was used by both Matthew and Luke. Q was a collection of Jesus' words that were collected by anonymous Christians, who should be identified neither with the group of the Twelve nor with the Hellenists. Those who carried these words were radical Christians, trying to apply Jesus' requirements literally; they were itinerant missionaries with apocalyptic expectations, who had left behind their families and their jobs, "everything." They tried to "follow" Jesus, to "confess" his lordship and to "suffer" for his name. They may have walked in Galilee, then in Syria, speaking Aramaic, and then Greek. They were Jews, but their acknowledgment of Jesus as the Son of Man brought them into conflict with the Pharisees and their radical evangelism with the Zealots. They may still have been observant of the Mosaic law and consequently responsible for a kind of ritual regression from Jesus' freedom into Jewish obedience. But they were Christians as is shown by their interest in Jesus, not only as a wise man or an apocalyptic visionary but also as God's only Son and the expected Son of Man. Their theology was marked by one Jewish tradition, which originated in the deuteronomistic historiography: they believed that Israel constantly resisted God, that only a few authentic prophets would be faithful, and that these prophets would be persecuted as many others before them – remember the understanding in Q of Jerusalem as the city that kills the prophets (Matt 23:37; Luke 13:34). Several of Jesus' sentences that they transmitted help us comprehend their understanding of God's people, their "ecclesiology": the words about following Jesus (Matt 8:19–22//Luke 9:57–60),

---

[18] The typology of the Exodus is used effectively in preaching at Easter, as can be seen in the patristic treatises. See, for example, *The Homily "On the Passover"* by Melito of Sardis.

[19] Matt 5:14–16 and Phil 2:15.

[20] John Kloppenborg, *The Formation of Q: Trajectories in Ancient Wisdom Collections* (SAC; Philadelphia: Fortress Press, 1987).

the teaching on mission (Matt 10//Luke 9–10), the Lord's prayer (Matt 6:9–13//Luke 11: 1–4), the attack on the Pharisees (Matt 23//Luke 11), and the so-called Johannine logia (Matt 11:25–27//Luke 10:21–22).

They were pleased to remember Jesus' prayer, "I thank you, Father, Lord of heaven and earth, because you have hidden these things from the wise and the intelligent and have revealed them to infants; yes, Father, for such was your gracious will" (Luke 10:21). In this single verse a full theology and a peculiar ecclesiology are beginning to take root:[21] a discovery of God as Creator ("Lord of heaven and earth") but also, and first of all, as Redeemer (as "Father" with a "gracious will"). The Q community believed that Jesus had been the mediator between that God and themselves: "All things have been handed over to me by my Father; and no one knows who the Son is except the Father, or who the Father is except the Son and anyone to whom the Son chooses to reveal him." But particularly important for our topic is the way the Christian community, the church, is described here. First the church is presented in a polemical way. The sentence expresses first what she is not. She is not "wise" and she is not "intelligent." The church is not constituted from below by human resources, like wisdom or intelligence. She is created from above by God himself. The Q community was not hostile to wisdom, but refused any human quest to obtain divine knowledge. Revelation that comes from grace is the only source of faith and wisdom. The Q congregation fought against the religious and intellectual power of the Jewish leaders – Sadducees, Pharisees, or Essenes – who were sure of the validity of their theology. The Q congregation was also "sure and confident," but her strength was in her weakness, her intelligence was in her humility, and her maturity was in her childhood. "Infants" (νήπιοι) was her ecclesiological title.[22] There is in the synoptic tradition an enhanced valuation of the child that is exceptional in the antique world. This attention to children was embedded in the teaching of the historical Jesus, but the Q congregation was keen to claim this heritage for herself. They were children of God who had received – better than a science – a revelation (you "have revealed them to infants," Luke 10:22). In their view Jesus' teaching was the revelation of God.

2. The Church of the Book of Revelation

With the book of Revelation[23] we leave Christianity in Syria and discover another one, a Johannine one, in Asia. The Jewish War brought Jews and Christians from

---

[21] For a bibliography and a full explanation, see François Bovon, *L'Évangile selon saint Luc (9,51–14,35)* (CNT 2/3b; Geneva: Labor et Fides, 1996) 67–79.

[22] Etymologically, the word νήπιος, like the Latin *infans*, means a child who cannot yet speak. On this word, see Simon Légasse, *Jésus et l'enfant. "Enfants," "petits" et "simples" dans la tradition synoptique* (Études bibliques; Paris: Gabalda, 1969).

[23] On Revelation, see Pierre Prigent, "Apocalypse de saint Jean" (2d ed.; CNT 2/14; Geneva: Labor et Fides, 1988).

Palestine to Asia. The Johannine group that was formerly in Samaria was scattered, and some members settled in Ephesus. It is probable that two distinct Christian congregations existed in Ephesus at the dawn of the first century C.E., a Pauline one and a Johannine one. The time may be the end of Domitian's reign, about 93–96 C.E. To enter the world of these Christians we need to read the beginning of the book of Revelation. Verses 1–3 of the first chapter express the ambition and authority of the author. He is sure to have received a revelation (like the "infants" in Q) from Jesus Christ, who is (as in Q) the mediator: "The revelation of Jesus Christ, which God gave him." The author believed himself to be an authorized and inspired prophet. The function of a prophet after the apostles was decisive in this kind of community, as it was in the congregation of the Hellenists (cf. Acts 13:1–3) and in the congregations of Pauline churches (see 1 Cor 12:28). He believed he was the servant of Jesus, God's mediator. His responsibility was to bring the revelation to the congregations. According to the New Testament structure I have mentioned, beside the divine event comes the communication; a human witness is needed, which in this instance is John's witness, his μαρτυρία. The divine revelation is not uniform in the New Testament: at times it is a revelation about the immediate future, such as "the time is close" (Rev 1:3); elsewhere it is related to the immediate past as in "these things" (Luke 10:21) that are realized by Jesus himself.

The prophet has the responsibility not just to be secretly pleased with himself but to express in human words what has been disclosed to him. In so doing the prophet is at the same time weak (compared with powerful human leaders: Jewish scholars in Luke 10:21 or Roman emperors in Revelation) and triumphant (in that he has received God's message, God's wisdom, and God's revelation).

The prophet's religious strength becomes evident in the letter that follows. In fact this epistle – actually the whole book of Revelation (Rev 1:4–22:21) – is the framework within which he will bring the divine revelation. He inserts into this framework the letters to the seven churches (Rev 2–3), where we have exceptionally the plural form ἐκκλησίαι. The dialectic between the singular and plural corresponds to the interaction between divine unity and human diversity. In an archaic form John – such is the name of the prophet (cf. Rev 1:1 and 1:9) – first greets the addressees. His extension of the grace of God in 1:4 is made according to the Jewish understanding of Exod 3:14. The present God ("who is") is the same as the God of the holy past ("who was") and of the coming future ("who shall come"). This grace comes also from the Spirit. Strangely enough, the Spirit is seen in its richness and is identified with the angels who are at God's court ("the seven spirits, which are in front of his throne," Rev 1:4). Finally, grace comes from Jesus Christ; the trinitarian order Father – Son – Spirit has not yet been established. The prophet has to explain the nature and the function of his Christ by saying that Christ is the witness, the faithful one, and the firstborn from the dead. He reminds his readers of the three steps in Jesus' life: the ministry through the word, the passion, and the resurrection. Saying that Christ loves us (note the present) and that he has delivered us, John affirms that the future cannot threaten the soteriological fact. On the contrary, the future of the church can only be a participation in the Lamb's triumph. As he is himself the winner, his people are not only liberated from the sinful past but are also established in the present and for the future as heirs of God's kingdom and priests of his spiritual temple. This holy past and this divine present can only merge into an eschatological, imminent, future. According to Rev 1:3b the received revelation means that the time is short, because the winner comes to celebrate his victory. His troops will experience triumph, but his adversaries will encounter defeat (v. 7b).

This was the address and the greeting of the long letter that constitutes the book of Revelation. Next comes the narrative, the story explaining and justifying how, when, and where John received this divine message: "I, John, your brother who share with you in Jesus the persecution and the kingdom and the patient endurance, was on the island called Patmos because of the word of God and the testimony of Jesus" (1:9). Historically, this means that the prophet had been put on trial by a Roman court for spreading religious propaganda and had been condemned to deportation and slave labor. But through his faith John learned how to look at history through God's eyes. This is a case of prophecy: the deportation and slave labor are real, but there is space for Sunday prayer, religious experience, and contact with God through the Spirit (1:10). What he experienced on Patmos was not the privilege of an exquisite believer, but the destiny of each Christian and the destiny of the church in society: suffering and winning, servanthood and triumph. John did not use his proximity with Christ and his prophetic ministry to establish a hierarchical authority. As prophet he did not become the father of the Asian churches, but remained a brother. He was so little an exception that he called himself a companion, someone literally "who is a companion sharing with you" (note the redundance συγ-κοινωνός. What he shares is exactly the topic of this paper; the θλῖψις (the "tribulation," the "suffering") and the βασιλεία (the "kingdom," the "triumph").

This tension between humility (humiliation) and glory (kingship) is the human condition, the present destiny of the church. It is also an ethical tension, where Christ's will must be in harmony with the children's decisions. The communion between John and the Asian churches is a communion of ὑπομονή a word well-translated by "patient endurance." There is both a passive side in ὑπομονή, what you suffer from someone else, and an active side, which is the resistance or endurance you offer with all your might.

In this autobiographical presentation of John, we also have a theological definition of the church according to the book of Revelation: servant on one side, bride on the other; suffering in the world, but promised the imminent triumph of the Lamb. In confrontation with the world and its powers, the church aims for the welfare and future salvation of the whole world.

3. The Pauline Church

The usual way of dealing with Pauline ecclesiology is to turn to the Pastoral Epistles, or to the Epistles to the Ephesians and Colossians. That is, to appeal to later developments, to institutional or ideological solutions given at a time when the church had to be stabilized in order to survive. The *notae ecclesiae*, the marks of the church, as they appear in the main authentic epistles are often neglected or distorted. And when the genuine letters are under scrutiny, 1 Corinthians normally falls under the spotlight.[24] I propose to consider here primarily the Epistle to the Romans. For even if the word ἐκκλησία ("church") does not occur in this letter, its author manifests constant ecclesiological care.[25] I concentrate our attention on the famous ending of Romans 8, verses 31b–39: "If God is for us, who is against us? ... For I am convinced that neither death, nor life, nor angels, nor rulers, nor things present, nor things to come, nor powers, nor height, nor depth, nor anything else in all creation, will be able to separate us from the love of God in Christ Jesus our Lord." Of great interest here is the use of "us" for the first person plural pronoun, which represents the whole company of the believers, the glorious Christian "church."

But the reader must be careful. When the apostle wrote this epistle from Corinth in the year 56 or 57, he was far from being victorious. On the contrary, he had three main sources of anxiety.[26] First, in Corinth, where he was staying, he was not sure that the dangerous enthusiasm he tried to eradicate some time earlier would not re-emerge. In order to prevent such a risk he wrote chapters 14–15 on the relationship between the so-called "strong" and "weak." Second, he was not sure what would happen in Jerusalem, where his path would soon lead him. Paul was taking to the "saints" of the Jewish capital the collection for which he accepted organizational responsibility at the closing session of the famous Jerusalem conference (in approximately 48, cf. Gal 2:10). Because he knew of judaizing opposition against his understanding of Christian freedom, he feared that the Jerusalem mother church would refuse the gift of the Gentile Christian congregations of the diaspora. Behind this tension between two wings of the Christian movement he felt the broader problematic of the connections between Judaism, which was the genuine olive tree, and Christianity, the wild olive tree. The apostle wrote chapters 9–11 in order to

---

[24] There are, nevertheless, good studies on Paul's ecclesiology. Cf. for example, Josef Hainz, *Ekklesia: Strukturen paulinischer Gemeinde-Theologie und Gemeinde-Ordnung* (Biblische Untersuchungen 9; Regensburg: Pustet, 1972); and Gosnell L.O.R. Yorke, *The Church as the Body of Christ in the Pauline Corpus: A Re-examination* (Lanham, Md: University Press of America, 1991).

[25] In his introduction to his commentary on Romans, Franz J. Leenhardt has insisted on this point. See *The Epistle to the Romans: A Commentary* (trans. Harold Knight; Cleveland: World Publishing Company, 1961) 13–23.

[26] Cf. Günther Bornkamm, "Der Römerbrief als Testament des Paulus," in *Geschichte und Glaube, zweiter Teil, Gesammelte Aufsätze* (BEvT 53; München: Kaiser, 1971) 4.120–33.

clarify his own position on the relation between Israel and the church. In so doing he hoped to help the Roman congregation gain a sound understanding of this relationship. Third, Paul kept to his goal of reaching Rome after stopping in Jerusalem and before going to Spain (Rom 15:22–29). What was the situation of the Roman congregation? Was her internal life firmly harmonious in its relations between Christians of Jewish origin and Christians of Gentile origin? The apostle gave his attention first to this question and attempted in chapters 1–8 to present a clear theological teaching on this interrelation between Jews and Gentiles within the people of God. But he did not develop his thought without fear.

If Paul speaks often of "us," of the "Christians" (Rom 8:31b–39), in spite of the triumphant tone of his voice he does not have in mind a victorious church without problems, nor a congregation abundant in charity and well-rooted in the faith and sealed in unity. What makes this "us" "far more than conquerors" (Rom 8:37) is not the quality of church administration, nor the unity of doctrine, nor the splendor of the liturgy, nor the success of missionary campaigns, nor the authenticity of spiritual experiences, but only – as the text states it – the one God who loves us: therefore "in all these things we are more than conquerors through him, who loved us" (Rom 8:37).

In Rom 8:18–28 Paul has shown that Christians share in suffering and finitude with the rest of humanity. They complain and they groan, as everyone else, because if they are to be saved, it is still in hope (Rom 8:24). With this observation, the apostle seems to have reached an end: "What then are we to say about these things" (Rom 8:31). But he was not pleased to conclude merely with this recording of a global frustration, the misery of this world and the suffering of the church. He was also eager to mention a difference between the present situation of the world and that of the church. He liked to recall what he had said at 8:1: "There is therefore now no condemnation for those who are in Christ Jesus." So he reminded his Roman readers that Christians already belong to the new world, to the new creation. And this eschatological privilege, the old world, the old society, cannot bear without polemical reaction.

Here, then, is the paradox of Rom 8:31–39. Nowhere else does Paul mention more diligently the victory of the Christian believers, their justification, and their glorification. But nowhere else either is the opposition of the world to the true church mentioned more boldly. If the tension between this triumph and this defeat of the church – of the "us" – can be finally suppressed, it is because the origin of the church's victory does not lie in human power, but is only possible through God's action. Left alone, the church, like any other human institution, can only waste away and finally perish. Only Christ's victory under God's leadership has overcome sin, finitude, and death.[27]

---

[27] On Rom 8:31–39, cf. Ernst Käsemann, *Commentary on Romans* (trans. Geoffrey W. Bromiley; Grand Rapids: Eerdmans, 1980) 245–52.

Conclusion

There are marks of the church that I have not sufficiently underscored, in particular preaching and the sacraments. There are ecclesiological themes that I have only mentioned, notably the divine calling and the gathering of God's people after the Easter victory, the gift of the Holy Spirit and the new life it makes possible, the organization and growth of Christ's body, and the truly Christian actions inside and outside the organized church. There are other Christian groups I have not described, including the most venerable one, the church of the Twelve in Jerusalem. But I have tried to show here that in spite of sociological, ideological, and cultural discrepancies, the churches of the first century – as far as we can reach them through a critical exegesis of the New Testament – all had a common specificity that designated them as Christian. They possessed in Christ a richness, a power and a wisdom that no one could steal from them because it was not from this world, but was already beginning to transform this world. Certainly distinct from the others, "aside," the Christians would soon suffer from contempt, then from persecution. Rom 8:36 summarizes well what I wish to bring into light: "As it is written, 'For your sake we are being killed all day long; we are accounted as sheep to be slaughtered.'" Because God let us share in his Kingdom, because we have received divine strength, we can fulfill a stewardship and take over responsibilities that will lead us into trouble and pains. Our existence as church members will therefore conform to Christ's destiny.

There was a christomorphy in the church's life, a christomorphy that was grounded in the fact that Christians had been incorporated into the body of Christ (see 1 Cor 6:15–17; 12:12–31; and Rom 12:4–5). Just as Christians had received Christ in themselves, they bore him.[28] They had clothed themselves with him (Gal 3:27). Through Christ, the death of Christians, as well as their life, could receive a positive meaning. The theological structure I have tried to highlight with its two poles, glory and service, was embedded in the dialectic (more than the succession) of Good Friday and Easter. In different words, it was present in the three traditions we have discussed. In Paul, it was the tension between the present justification and the present tribulation. In the book of Revelation, it was the reign of the believers who could not escape the persecution of beasts. For the Q congregation, it was God's revelation given to vulnerable infants. Such an ecclesiology in its strength and weakness can be found in other parts of the New Testament, from Luke to 1 Peter. It was a common conviction held by all the first Christians, from Peter to Timothy, from Mary to Lydia.[29]

---

[28] The adjective *christophoros* ("Christ-bearing") is used first by Ignatius of Antioch, *Ephesians* 9.2; then it is applied to martyrs, in a letter written by Phileas of Thmuis and quoted by Eusebius of Caesarea, *Hist. eccl.* 8.10.3.

[29] After completion of this paper I received Eduard Schweizer's review (*TLZ* 119 [1994] 665–68) of Jürgen Roloff, *Die Kirche im Neuen Testament* (GNT 10; Göttingen: Vandenhoeck & Ruprecht, 1993).

These Christians Who Dream: The Authority of Dreams in the First Centuries of Christianity*

Introduction

At the beginning of this inquiry,[1] I would like to set forth a fact and a question. The fact is that dreams are omnipresent, both in past civilizations and today. The question is one that is both theological and existential: Does God still communicate through signs? If yes, then does God do so through dreams?

Those who are hostile to dreams have long refused to admit their prominences, and have obscured the question as to whether or not God communicates through signs such as dreams. Partisans of the Enlightenment and defenders of religion, hand in hand, reduced to a minimum the theological authority that was rightly accorded dreams. The former considered dreams to refer to nothing but ourselves, to our distresses or our desires. The latter, whether Roman Catholic or Orthodox, claimed that the revelation of God was entrusted to magisterium and the tradition and, if they were Protestant, claimed that dreams were in subversive competition with holy scripture. For the Roman Catholic church, God still continues to manifest Godself today, but visions and dreams must be authenticated by an official authority. A kind of allergy to the supernatural compels Protestant theologians,

* With this study, I wish to honor Professor Martin Hengel on the occasion of his seventieth birthday. I also wish to express my gratitude to Laura Nasrallah, who translated this paper into English.

[1] The bibliography concerning dreams in antiquity is immense. The following articles or works give access to innumerable titles: Ernst Ludwig Ehrlich, *Der Traum im Alten Testament* (BZAW 73; Berlin: de Gruyter, 1953); Robert Gnuse, "Dream Reports in the Writings of Flavius Josephus," *RB* 96 (1989) 358–90; G. von Grunebaum and Roger Caillois, eds., *The Dream and Human Societies* (Berkeley: University of California Press, 1966); John S. Hanson, "Dreams and Visions in the Graeco-Roman World and Early Christianity," *ANRW* 2.23. 2 (Berlin/ New York: de Gruyter, 1980) 1395–1427; A. Oepke, "ὄναρ," *TDNT* 5 (1967) 220–38; Serge Sanneron, ed., *Les songes et leur interprétation* (Sources Orientales 2; Paris: Seuil, 1959) (this work does not discuss Christianity); "Sogni, visioni e profezie nell'antico cristianesimo (XVII incontro di studiosi dell'antichità Cristiana Roma, 5–7 Maggio 1988)," *Aug* 29 (1989) 1–612. I read the following three studies only after the editing of this article: P. Gibert, *Le récit biblique du rêve. Essai de confrontation analytique* (Lyon: Profac, 1990); Christoph Morgenthaler, *Der religiöse Traum. Erfahrung und Deutung* (Stuttgart: Kohlhammer, 1992); Patricia Cox Miller, *Dreams in Late Antiquity: Studies in the Imagination of a Culture* (Princeton: Princeton University Press, 1994).

as an a priori, always to believe that subsequent manifestations add nothing to the revelation of Christ.

The resurgence of interest in dreams should thus be welcomed, even if it corresponds a bit too much to today's sometimes troubling return to the irrational. There are certainly illusions and insane hopes in the attention our contemporaries bring to their dreams, voices, and other messages from beyond the grave. Nevertheless, scientific pretensions as disparate as sleep medication and Freudian psychoanalysis also prove to be illusory, or at least reductionist. Is there not some wisdom in believing that sleep can bring us closer to the divine world? In antiquity, this view was the most widespread and – to the chagrin of ecclesiastical authorities – it continued for many centuries as part of the Christian tradition.

Greek and Roman Antiquity

True and false dreams

Like its great Oriental sisters, Greek civilization was interested in dreams. It did not, however, approve of them without reservation. Homer had already distinguished truth from illusion, describing the gate of horn that opened out onto authentic dreams and the gate of ivory that led to false dreams.[2] Lucian, many centuries later, led dreamers to an island where the visitor encountered two temples, that of ἀλήθεια ("truth") and that of ἀπάτη ("deception").[3] According to Artemidorus, a specialist in dream interpretation, two sorts of dreams exist: on the one hand, the ὄνειρος is a true dream; on the other, the ἐνύπνιον is a simple dream that reveals nothing.[4] Thus not every nocturnal manifestation was to be taken seriously. Opinions vary, moreover, from author to author. Many philosophers, from Artistole to Cicero, played the skeptic[5] despite opposition from guilds – and especially priests – that supported dream interpretation and despite resistance from conservative intellectuals in late antiquity, when belief in the importance of dreams again flowered.

The "science" of dreams

Just as today science has its devotees, religion of long ago had its scholars. Oracles, prophecies, haruspicy, and dreams demanded experts; these were proud of their knowledge and concerned to establish disciples who would then be called upon to preserve this knowledge and its mysteries. The science of dreams (the

---

[2] Homer, *Od.* 19.562–67.
[3] Lucian of Samosata, *Vera historia* 2.33.
[4] Artemidorus of Ephesus, *Onirocritica* 1.1.
[5] See Oepke, "ὄναρ," *TDNT* 5 (1967) 222.

queen of the sciences) was called ὀνειροκριτικόν (*oneirokritikon*); its objective, naturally, was the gathering of information regarding dreams, the classification of this information, the examination of the dreamer in order to learn about his or her life and temperament, and, finally, the offering of insights gained from the interpretation of dreams.

As is attested by the survival of books of interpretation – both manuals and monographs – that have reached us from Babylon and Egypt, this science took written forms. We know of the existence, or the titles, of about forty Greek works in this area, all lost except for that of Artemidorus of Ephesus (also called Artemidorus of Daldis, in Lydia, the homeland of his mother).[6] This text has traversed the centuries and has awakened the curiosity of many, from Rabelais to Seferis.[7] Artemidorus lived under the emperor Commodus, who reigned from 180 to 192 C.E.

For purposes of our discussion here I offer a few pertinent observations from my reading of Artemidorus. First, there is a distinction, to which I have already alluded,[8] between the dream (ἐνύπνιον) and the true dream (ὄνειρος). The former is concerned with the present and reflects the dreamer's physical state (of lack or excess) or psychic state (of fear or hope). The true dream, in contrast, is concerned with the future.

Second, it is also interesting to note the artificial etymology of the word "dream" (τὸ ὄν εἴρει, "it says what is")[9]: "*Oneiros* is a movement or condition of the mind that takes many shapes and signifies good or bad things that will occur in the future."[10] There is, however, a distinction between theorematic dreams, in which one sees directly what will happen, such as a drowning, and allegorical dreams, in which a reality is announced through the image of another reality.[11] Within the second set of dreams, that is, the allegorical, five categories exist: personal (about the dreamer), impersonal (about someone else), common (about the dreamer and someone else), political, and cosmic.[12]

Artemidorus also asserts that some dreams are sent by the gods because humans have requested them, while others are sent without any prior request.[13] For

---

[6] See André J. Festugière, *Artémidore, La clef des songes. Onirocriticon, traduit et annoté* (Bibliothèque des textes philosophiques; Paris: Vrin, 1975). All English translations are taken from Artemidorus, *Interpretation of Dreams* (trans. and comm. Robert J. White; Park Ridge, N.J.: Noyes, 1975).

[7] François Rabelais, "Le tiers livre des faicts et dicts héroïques du bon Pantagruel," in idem, *Œuvres complètes* (Bibliothèque de la Pléiade; Paris: Gallimard, 1955) 377; and G. Seferis, Δοκιμές (Athens: Ikaros, 1984) 316–17. Seferis's essay first appeared in Italian as a preface to the edition of Artemidoro Daldiano, *Dell'interpretazione dei sogni* (Rome: Edizioni dell'Elefante, 1970). I thank Bertrand Bouvier for this reference.

[8] See above, p. 145 n. 4.

[9] Artemidorus, *Onir.* 1.1.

[10] Ibid., 1.2.

[11] Ibid.

[12] Ibid.

both kinds, he presents a system of interpretation, a key for understanding their meaning; thus, for example, "If a man dreams that he is drinking vinegar, it signifies that he will quarrel with the members of his household, because of the contraction of the mouth."[14]

Typical dreams

Typical dreams can include cult dreams in which a divinity dictates the founding of a sanctuary and indicates his or her desire to inhabit it. A passage from Lucian of Samosata is illustrative of this type:

> This Stratonice, while she was still living with her first husband, had a dream. In it Hera ordered her to build her a temple in the Holy City and threatened her with many dire consequences if she disobeyed. Stratonice paid no attention at first, but afterwards, when a serious illness afflicted her, she described the vision to her husband, propitiated Hera, and promised to erect the temple. Immediately she became healthy, and her husband sent her to the Holy City. Along with her he sent funds and a large escort, some members of which were to do the building while others were for security.[15]

Within the category of cult dreams, we must also include those linked to therapeutic processes, such as incubation and healing in a sanctuary. An example of this type would be the blind man who thanked Asclepius by offering him two stelae, since he had two dreams (δοιοὺς ὀνείρους) that announced his healing. After having these dreams, the man recovered his sight.[16]

Political dreams are also quite frequent, and the premonitory dreams that announce the brilliant reign of many princes and sovereigns are recorded for us. Suetonius, for example, records this story about Augustus: "Having reached this point, it will not be out of place to add an account of the omens which occurred before he [Augustus] was born, on the very day of his birth, and afterwards, from which it was possible to anticipate and perceive his future greatness."[17] Then, after enumerating some of these signs, Suetonius continues:

> I have read the following story in the books of Asclepias of Mende entitled *Theologoumena*. When Atia had come in the middle of the night to the solemn service of Apollo, she had her litter set down in the temple and fell asleep, while the rest of the matrons also slept. On a sudden a serpent glided up to her and shortly went away. When she awoke, she purified herself, as if after the embraces of her husband, and at once there appeared on her body a mark in colours like a serpent, and she could never get rid of it; so that presently she

---

[13] Ibid., 1.6.

[14] Ibid., 1.66 (trans. White, p. 50).

[15] Lucian of Samosata, *De syria dea* 19, in *The Syrian Goddess (De Dea Syria) Attributed to Lucian* (trans. Harold W. Attridge and Robert A. Oden; SBLTT 9; Missoula, Mont.: Scholars Press, 1976).

[16] *Epigrammata Graeca ex lapidibus conlecta* 839 (ed. Georg Kaibel; Berlin: Reimer, 1878; Hildesheim: Olms, 1965); cited by Oepke, "ὄναρ," *TDNT* 5 (1967) 224.

[17] Suetonius, *De vita Caesarum* 2.94 (Divus Augustus) (trans. J.C. Rolfe; 2 vols.; LCL; London: William Heinemann; New York: Macmillan, 1914) 1.262.

ceased ever to go to the public baths. In the tenth month after that Augustus was born and was therefore regarded as the son of Apollo. Atia too, before she gave him birth, dreamed that her vitals were borne up to the stars and spread over the whole extent of land and sea, while Octavius dreamed that the sun rose from Atia's womb.

The day he was born the Cataline conspiracy was before the House, and Octavius came late because of his wife's confinement; then Publius Nigidius, as everyone knows, learning the reason for his tardiness and being informed also of the hour of the birth, declared that the ruler of the world had been born.[18]

Finally, personal dreams can concern an individual's future as well as that of his or her family. There is, for instance, the account of Croesus's dream in which the king saw his son Atys impaled on a spear. Alas, for him, this theorematic dream was realized despite all of Croesus's efforts to protect his son.[19]

From experience to story

The experience of a dream is not accessible to others except by the mediation of language. In antiquity as now, this act of setting experience into discourse could be more or less stylized; we encounter diverse kinds of dream accounts, from the most rough to the most literary. Among the latter, certain ones became famous, such as Scipio the African's dream that Cicero recorded. Having appeared in a dream to his grandson, the old Roman taught him the ideal form of political power.[20] Dream accounts are also found in the historical novels of antiquity; as premonitions, they direct the thread of the account or confirm the providential nature of the events.

The structure of dreams[21]

In a recent article, John S. Hanson asserts that dream accounts in antiquity all manifest the same fundamental structure.[22] Although Hanson overstates his case somewhat, his observations are often correct. He sets forth the following schema:

---

[18] Ibid., 263–67.

[19] Herodotus, *Hist.* 1.34, 38–40, 43.

[20] Cicero gives this account at the end of *De republica*, which is for the most part lost. The account is, however, preserved in Macrobius's *Commentary on the Dream of Scipio* (trans. William Stahl; New York: New York University Press, 1990).

[21] Carl G. Jung attempted to determine the fundamental structure of dreams; he thought that their structure resembles that of theatrical dramas. Dreams unfold as drama does: an exposition is followed by a muddled situation, which culminates in a third act before the resolution takes place. See Carl Gustav Jung, *Lexikon Jungscher Grundbegriffe. Mit Originaltexten von C.G. Jung* (ed. Helmut Marks; Olten-Freiburg im Breisgau: Walter Verlag, 1988) 177–79, which suggest as further reading "Allgemeine Gesichtspunkte zur Psychologie des Traumes," in idem, *Die Dynamik des Unbewussten* (Gesammelte Werke 8; Zürich/Stuttgart: Rascher Verlag, 1967) 335–75, § 561–64. In fact, the entire study, which first appeared in 1928 under the title *Über die Energetik der Seele*, is about dreams.

[22] Hanson, "Dreams and Visions," 1405–13.

1) The *mise en scène* situates the dreamer in time and place, then signals his or her mood.

2) The *mention of the dream* is marked by precise terms, the most frequent being ὄναρ ἰδεῖν ("to see in a dream").

3) The *content of the dream* is supplied by naming the visible elements, the audible elements, or both. Most often, this is done by a person – more often divine rather than human – who appears, for example, standing at the bedside of the sleeper and communicates to him or her a message, a revelation, or a command, before withdrawing.

4) The *reaction of the sleeper* manifests itself as an abrupt or gradual wakening and by a lively desire for understanding and interpretation.

5) A *follow-up* to the dream is sometimes mentioned; the reaction naturally varies from case to case.

This schema, which is general enough to absorb the evidence of most dream accounts, conveys the nature of events and their particularities. Because of narrative habits, aided by natural conservatism and the principle of economy, this pattern of relating events would be formalized, and, over time, the very narrative structure of dreams became fixed. The exegete will do well to discover the content and the specific function of each ancient dream, however, in order not to become a mere cataloguer of structural similarities.

Ancient Judaism

Judaism of antiquity, in both Palestine and the diaspora, conferred upon the phenomena of dreams and ecstasy a greater importance than ancient Hebrew traditions had previously done. Three examples illustrate the increasing importance of dreams.

In the Septuagint, the Greek version of the book of Esther varies in more than one way from its original Semitic form. The two accounts diverge from one another at both the beginning and end of the book: the text of the Septuagint adds a premonitory dream at the beginning of the work, and the conclusion recalls the existence and significance of this first dream, thus forming a well-organized *inclusio*.[23] The dream is that of Mordecai, who hears cries upon the earth and sees two great dragons ready to battle one another. From the cries they utter, a small spring gushes forth and becomes a great river. As we know, the book of Esther, in both of its versions, recounts the death of the evil Haman and the triumph of the pious Mordecai. For the author of the Greek version, this is exactly what the dream had predicted: at the end of the account Mordecai says, "These things have come from

---

[23] See *The HarperCollins Study Bible: New Revised Standard Version with the Apocryphal/ Deuterocanonical Books* (ed. Wayne A. Meeks et al.; New York: HarperCollins, 1993) 1481–96.

God; for I remember the dream that I had concerning these matters, and none of them has failed to be fulfilled. ... The river is Esther, whom the king married and made queen. The two dragons are Haman and myself. The nations are those that gathered to destroy the name of the Jews."[24]

A second example is found in the *Genesis Apocryphon*, an Aramaic text discovered at Qumran that recounts anew the adventures contained in the first book of Moses. The passage that concerns us here is the report of Abraham's sojourn in Egypt (par. Gen 12:10–20) and the subterfuge contrived by the patriarch while there. In lieu of the statement Abraham makes to his wife Sarah in the canonical Genesis account ("Say, I beg you, that you are my sister"), the apocryphal account inserts a dream and its interpretation:[25]

And on the night of our entry into Egypt, I, Abram, dreamt a dream; [and behold], I saw in my dream a cedar tree and a palm tree ... men came and they sought to cut down the cedar tree and to pull up its roots, leaving the palm tree (standing) alone. But the palm tree cried out saying, "Do not cut down this cedar tree, for cursed be he who shall fell [it]." And the cedar tree was spared because of the palm tree and [was] not felled.

And during the night I woke from my dream, and I said to Sarai my wife, "I have dreamt a dream ... [and I am] fearful [because of] this dream." She said to me, "Tell me your dream that I may know it." So I began to tell her this dream ... [the interpretation] of the dream ... "... that they will seek to kill me, but will spare you ... [Say to them] of me, he is my brother, and because of you I shall live, and because of you my life shall be saved."

And Sarai wept that night on account of my words ...[26]

A similar emphasis on dreams can be found in the work of Josephus. Like the authors of the Hebrew scriptures, and like his own Greek and Latin contemporaries, the Jewish historian mentions dreams that presaged certain destinies – here, the decline of Archelaus, son of King Herod:

Archelaus, on taking possession of his ethnarcy, did not forget old feuds, but treated not only the Jews but even the Samaritans with great brutality. Both parties sent deputies to Caesar to denounce him, and in the ninth year of his rule he was banished to Vienna, a town in Gaul, and his property confiscated to the imperial treasury. It is said that, before he received his summons from Caesar, he had this dream: he thought he saw nine tall and full-grown ears of corn on which oxen were browsing. He sent for the soothsayers and some Chaldaeans and asked them their opinion of its meaning. Various interpretations being given, a certain Simon, of the sect of the Essenes, said that in his view the ears of corn denoted years and the oxen a revolution, because in ploughing they turn over the soil; he would therefore reign for as many years as there were ears of corn and would die after a che-

---

[24] Greek Esther Addition F 10:4–8.

[25] The author of the *Genesis Apocryphon* was no doubt inspired by the parallel account found in Genesis 20:3, 6–7; there, however, it is Abimelech who, before committing the irreparable deed, is prevented from doing so by a dream.

[26] *Genesis Apocryphon* 19.13–23; see *The Dead Sea Scrolls in English* (trans. Geza Vermes; 4th ed.; New York: Penguin, 1995) 453–54.

quered experience of revolutionary changes. Five days later Archelaus was summoned to his trial.[27]

The Hebrew scriptures mention dozens of dreams, from those of Abimelech, of Jacob, Joseph, and Pharaoh and his attendants, which are all found in Genesis, to those recorded in the book of Daniel, not to mention the dreams recorded during the time of Gideon, the prophet Samuel, and King Solomon.[28] The scriptures also contain severe warnings regarding the phenomenon of dreams.[29] Therefore, while a persistent exegetical tradition maintains that the scriptures are distrustful toward all dreams, I maintain instead that they are merely hostile toward illusory dreams, as all were in antiquity. Similarly, the scriptures do not at all doubt the existence and importance of prophecy, but only condemn false prophecy.

The Hebrew faith admits, in effect, that God manifests Godself through dreams and that God is concerned to furnish the key to dreams through inspired interpreters.[30] Samuel and Solomon both received nocturnal revelations while sleeping.[31] Thus we find in 1 Kgs 3:5, "At Gibeon the Lord appeared to Solomon in a dream by night; and God said, 'Ask what I should give you.'"

We discover the same support for dreams inspired by God in Jewish literature of the second temple period.[32] It could be, moreover, that there was less fear of il-

---

[27] Josephus, *Bell. Jud.* 2.111–13 (trans. H. St. J. Thackery; 9 vols.; LCL; Cambridge: Harvard University Press, 1961) 2.365.

[28] Gen 20:3, 6–7 (God reveals to Abimelech that Sarah is Abraham's wife); Gen 28:11–19 (Jacob sees the ladder); Gen 31:10–13 (Jacob contemplates the streaked, speckled, or spotted goats); Gen 37:5–11 (two dreams of Joseph: the largest sheaf and the stars who prostrate themselves); Gen 40:4–23 (the cupbearer and the baker recount their dreams to Joseph, who interprets them); Gen 41:1–43 (the dreams of Pharaoh regarding the cows and the ears of grain, which Joseph interprets): Judg 7:13–15 (the dream of the bread that tumbled, interpreted by a companion of Gideon); 1 Kgs 3:4–15 (at the high place of Gibeon, Solomon dreams during the night, and he and God engage in dialogue); Dan 2:1–49 (the dreams of Nebuchadnezzar; he requires not only an interpretation of his dreams, but also that the contents of the dream be recounted; Daniel alone, thanks to God's help, satisfies this double demand); Dan 4:1–23 (dream of Nebuchadnezzar, the great tree which is felled, a dream interpreted by Daniel); Dan 7:1–28 (dream or vision of Daniel, who sees the four beasts and a Son of Man); see also Num 12:6. What Zechariah sees (Zech 1:8–6:15) are better described as nocturnal visions than dreams. The same is true of Amos, Isaiah, and Ezekiel, who have ecstatic visions.

[29] Deut 13:2–6; Jer 23:16–32; 27:9–10; 29:8–9; Zech 10:2; Ps 73:20.

[30] See Gen 40:8; 41:16, 39; Num 12:6; Dan 2:28.

[31] Samuel (1 Sam 3:1–18) heard a voice, a call reiterated by the Lord, during his stay in the sanctuary of Shiloh, while Solomon contemplated a dream (1 Kgs 3:4–15) in the high place of Gibeon.

[32] The thematic index of J.-M. Rosenstiehl is invaluable here; see André Dupont-Sommer and Marc Philonenko, eds., *La Bible. Écrits intertestamentaires* (Bibliothèque de la Pléiade: Gallimard, 1987) 1889, see "songe." This index allows one to find references and allusions to numerous dreams found in second temple literature. Concerning dreams in rabbinic literature, see Maurice Hayoun, *La littérature rabbinique* (Que sais-je? 2526; Paris: Presses universitaires de France, 1990) 94–100.

lusory dreams at this time. Contrary to one modern translator,[33] I do not believe that Philo of Alexandria was disinterested in dreams in themselves, only paying attention to them if they were evoked in a biblical text, and that even then he was only concerned with the allegorical sense of the text. For this would suggest that exegesis was more important to him than prophecy and inspiration. We find proof to the contrary in Philo's expressed conviction that God communicates with pure souls by means of dreams.[34] We find proof, above all, in the treatise he wrote concerning dreams, of which two of the five books have survived.[35] In this work, Philo distinguishes three sorts of dreams sent by God: those in which God expresses Godself immediately and without ambiguity through images (the dreamer does not play any role)[36]; those in which God inspires the spirit toward dream activity that predicts the future[37]; and, finally, those in which the symbolic form corresponds to the will of God but the interpretation depends upon a well-trained expert.[38] For Philo, biblical dreams have a normative value, and his intention is to be inspired as he gives his interpretations, but he does not believe that exegesis is the only appropriate task for the present time. The divine breath can still stir up new dreams.

Ancient Christianities

What was Jesus' attitude and that of the first Christians concerning dreams and other omens? Here it is interesting to note the opinion expressed by A. Oepke, who states that "for all its scientific aspirations the ancient interpretation of dreams is little more than a mixture of fatalism, superstition and filth."[39] Oepke also asserts that the Hebrew scriptures knew of the phenomenon of dreams, but refined their content and interpretation; they became less egotistical, less individualistic, and less erotic. In contrast, in the New Testament, according to Oepke, "the line found in the O[ld] T[estament] is now fully developed."[40] Thus, to use a

---

[33] Pierre Savinel, *Philon d'Alexandrie, De somniis, I–II, introduction, traduction et notes* (Les œuvres de Philon d'Alexandrie 19; Paris: Cerf, 1962) 11–12.

[34] See Philo of Alexandria, *Migr.* 190; and *Contempl.* 26; Émile Bréhier, *Les idées philosophiques et religieuses de Philon d'Alexandrie* (Études de philosophie médiévale 8; Paris: Vrin, 1950) 179–205.

[35] See the bibliographical reference to this treatise above (p. 151 n. 32). See also the following essays, which all appear in K.H. Richards, ed., *Society of Biblical Literature 1987 Seminar Papers* (Atlanta: Scholars Press, 1987) 394–402, 403–28, and 429–32, respectively: Earle Hilgert, "A Survey of Previous Scholarship on Philo's *De Somniis* 1–2"; Robert M. Berchman, "Arcani Mundi: Magic and Divination in the *De Somniis* of Philo of Alexandria"; David M. Hay, "Politics and Exegesis in Philo's Treatise on Dreams."

[36] The portion of the treatise that examines these dreams has been lost.

[37] This study actually occupies the first book of Philo's treatise concerning dreams.

[38] Philo speaks about this in the second preserved book of the treatise.

[39] Oepke, "ὄναρ," *TDNT* 5 (1967) 228.

[40] Ibid., 235.

metaphor from the Hebrew scriptures, a pagan worshiper who had unclean feet was only permitted to enter into the outer court of the temple, but in the New Testament he enters into the purity of the sanctuary. But during the course of ancient Christianity, according to Oepke, the situation declined and dreams were again regarded with favor: "Thus the muddy waters of antiquity, not without a misuse of holy things, nor without the guilt of the Church, debouch into the sink of new superstition."[41]

Although we certainly find impressive erudition in this article, the author defends a position that is ideological and even a caricature of itself: in his opinion, the New Testament discovered the ideal solution in that it is critical of dreams,[42] and even in those he retains as significant, it tones down the individualistic and erotic elements while accentuating the themes of community, the person of Jesus Christ, and the history of salvation.

New Testament evidence

A close reading of the New Testament itself reveals a certain ambiguity between dreams and visions. According to Luke, the centurion Cornelius and the apostle Peter both received a vision (ὅραμα) at the same moment of the day, at noon.[43] This is the same word Luke uses to define the nocturnal apparition of the Macedonian, which certainly occurred during a dream.[44] The Pauline epistles do not explicitly evoke dreams, but incline more toward revelations (ἀποκάλυψις in Gal 2:2; ὀπτασίαι καὶ ἀποκαλύψεις in 2 Cor 12:1) and ecstasies (2 Cor 12:2–5). If the evangelists mention certain supernatural manifestations (appearances of angels, celestial voices, intervention of the Holy Spirit, visions[45]), they conceive of them more as immediate phenomena. As for the author of the Apocalypse, he views his written visions not as dream accounts, but as his communication of an ecstatic ascent and sudden rapture by the Spirit.[46]

Two gospel writers pay some attention to dreams. In his nativity account Matthew records several dreams; in each instance the beneficiary of the providential dream is called by name and perceives an angel who addresses him with a precise and explicit message.[47] This phenomenon is described by the expression κατ᾽ ὄναρ ("in a dream") and the dreamer responds in an appropriate manner, given the supernatural message addressed to him: in a dream, Joseph receives the order not

---

[41] Ibid., 238.

[42] Evidence from the Bible prevents the author from claiming that scripture is hostile to dreams.

[43] Acts 10:3, 17, 19.

[44] Acts 16:9.

[45] Luke 1:11, 26; 2:9, 13; 24:4 (par.); Mark 1:10–11 (par.); Mark 9:7 (par.); Mark 1:12 (par.); Luke 10:18.

[46] Rev. 1:10–20.

[47] The angel is not mentioned each time, nor even the name of the addressee.

to cast Mary off (Matt 1:20–15); the magi are told not to visit Herod again (Matt 2:12); Joseph is told to leave for Egypt (Matt 2:13) and, later, to return to Palestine (Matt 2:19), and again, more precisely, to go to Galilee (Matt 2:22).[48] Matthew mentions yet another dream more cautiously: that of the wife of Pilate, which causes her to plead with her husband that he be prudent in judgment (Matt 27:19).[49] The concentration of these dreams in only two locations in the Gospel can be explained by the nature of the sources used by the writer and by the function dreams performed at crucial periods in life – in this case, at birth and at death.

Luke is the other gospel writer attentive to the phenomena of dreams and visions; he does not, however, distinguish between these two with any precision. In the Acts of the Apostles, these manifestations proliferate, and this accords well with the prophecy of Joel that is cited at Pentecost: "'In the last days it will be,' God declares, 'that I will pour out my Spirit upon all flesh, and your sons and your daughters shall prophesy, and your young men shall see visions, and your old men shall dream dreams'" (Acts 2:17). It is in a dream that Christ manifests himself to Paul in order to encourage him: "One night, the Lord said to Paul in a vision, 'Do not be afraid, but speak and do not be silent'" (Acts 18:9); "That night, the Lord stood near him and said, 'Keep up your courage! ...'" (Acts 23:11).[50] The most fully developed dream is found in Acts 16:9–10: "During the night Paul had a vision: there stood a man of Macedonia pleading with him and saying, 'Come over to Macedonia and help us.' When he had seen the vision, we immediately tried to cross over to Macedonia, being convinced that God had called us to proclaim the good news to them." The author of Acts is so open to dreams and premonitory visions that he understands God to be the force behind Paul's nocturnal experience, and he views the content of the dream as a decisive divine command for the future of Christianity[51]: inspiration, ecstasies, dreams, and visions have to do with the future of the gospel in the world, and they orient the history of the Church according to God's plan. If they determine individual destinies, they do so only within the larger perspective of the providential extension of the Christian movement as a whole. They signal that God has abandoned God's silence and again begun to work. As Luke adds to the citation from Joel, we have, accordingly, entered into the last times (Acts 2:17).

---

[48] Concerning these dreams, see the remarks of Raymond E. Brown, *The Birth of the Messiah: A Commentary on the Infancy Narratives in Matthew and Luke* (Garden City: Doubleday, 1979) 129, 176–77.

[49] The expression used (κατ' ὄναρ) is the same as that used in the nativity accounts. The content of the dream, however, is not indicated.

[50] See also Acts 27:23–24.

[51] See the remarkable exegesis and excursus of Alfons Weiser, *Die Apostelgeschichte. Kapitel 13–28* (ÖTKNT 5.2; Gütersloh: Gütersloher Verlaghaus Gerd Mohn; Würzburg: Echter, 1985) 402–15.

The ancient church

First- and second-century Christian literature is often apocalyptic in nature. Ecstasies, more often than dreams, are the source of the visions this literature transmits, although the difference between these two phenomena is not always evident. This is the case in the grand depiction of the *Ascension of Isaiah* and the visions that Hermas, the author of the *Shepherd*, receives.[52]

Alongside these visions, which reveal necessary truths to all believers, we find dreams by which the divinity guides the fate of individuals. In the *Acts of Thomas*, for example, a woman, Mnesara, tells her husband Vazan how Christ appeared to her in the night in order to lead her to the prison where the apostle was being kept.[53] In the *Acts of John*, the apostle relates how he saw in a dream what he should do the next day: he must walk out and leave the city, an act that leads him to a decisive meeting with a parricide.[54] The narrative thus demonstrates that the man of God is not only a believer who knows the Christian message;[55] he must also still live, act, repent, and be willing to die. The Lord's assistance in the course of his ministry is vital, and this support manifests itself in diverse ways and at many points, in particular in dreams and visions. After the ἐφάπαξ, the "once for all"[56] of the revelation of Christ, after the decision of faith – that is, conversion – life and its constraints, ethics and its exigencies, again become actuality, as was the case under the first covenant. One returns to the everyday, and hopes for dreams and visions, whether they be theorematic, following the example of the *Acts of John*,[57] or allegorical, as in the case recorded in the canonical Acts, where the apostle Peter receives a vision of animals that symbolize humans.[58]

---

[52] *Ascen. Isa.* 6.1–11.43; the edition and commentary of this text appear under the responsibility of Enrico Norelli and others in the Corpus Christianorum Series Apocryphorum 7–8 (Turnhout: Brepols, 1995), under the title *Ascensio Isaiae*. The first part of the *Shepherd of Hermas*, 1–25 (Vis. 1–5) consists of five great visions. One can also point to the visions in Christian apocalyptic literature, such as the scenes depicted in the *Apocalypse of Peter* and the *Apocalypse of Paul*; see Wilhelm Schneemelcher, ed., *New Testament Apocrypha*, vol. 2: *Writings Relating to the Apostles: Apocalypses and Related Writings* (ET: ed. Robert McL. Wilson; Cambridge: Clarke; Louisville: Westminster/John Knox, 1991–92) 620–38; 695–748.

[53] *Acts Thom.* 154.

[54] *Acts John* 48; see Éric Junod and Jean-Daniel Kaestli, *Acta Iohannis* (2 vols.; CCSA 1–2; Turnhout: Brepols, 1983) 1.230 n. 1; 2.516.

[55] The message here is principally for the soul and is unconcerned about the quotidian life of the body. The narrative ignores the involvement of the Son of God in human history and also neglects the incarnation and passion of Christ.

[56] Heb 7:27; 9:12; 10:10; Hebrews differs from the *Acts of John* insofar as it stresses the importance of the incarnation and crucifixion.

[57] See above n. 54.

[58] The vision is not allegorical except at the level of the Luke's redaction; the tradition that underlies the redaction is theorematic and is directed at dietary laws; see François Bovon, "Tradition et rédaction en Actes 10, 11–11, 18," *TZ* 26 (1970) 22–45; reprinted in idem, *L'œuvre de Luc. Études d'exégèse et de théologie* (LD 130; Paris: Cerf, 1987) 97–120, esp. 107–13.

Writing in the platonic tradition, Cicero[59] had already observed that the time of death is favorable for an encounter with the divine. Christians appropriated this idea in their conviction that God sustains the one who enters into death pangs, particularly the martyr. In addition to the case of Stephen, the protomartyr who saw "the Son of Man standing at the right hand of God" (Acts 7:55–56), we can point to the famous case of Polycarp: "And while he was praying he fell into a trance three days before he was arrested, and saw the pillow under his head burning with fire, and he turned and said to those who were with him: 'I must be burnt alive.'"[60] We find another example in the *Passion of Marianus and James*: in a dream, James sees two belts that Christ throws to two victims, thus enjoining them to follow him without hesitation.[61]

The most striking case,[62] however, is undoubtedly that of Perpetua and Felicitas. The *Passion* contains both an account of their martyrdom and the personal testimonies of Perpetua and Saturus, her spiritual teacher.[63] These testimonies primarily consist of the visions that are granted to the two believers in the days preceding their martyrdom. Perpetua, for example, is conscious of her visionary gift, which is linked to her status as a martyr. She also senses the authority this situation confers upon her, as the following fragment attests:

Then my brother said to me, "Dear sister, you are greatly privileged; surely you might ask for a vision to discover whether you are to be condemned or freed."

Faithfully I promised that I would, for I knew that I could speak with the Lord, whose great blessings I had come to experience. And so I said: "I shall tell you tomorrow." Then I made my request and this was the vision I had.

I saw a ladder of tremendous height made of bronze, reaching all the way to the heavens, but it was so narrow that only one person could climb up at a time. To the sides of the ladder were attached all sorts of metal weapons: there were swords, spears, hooks, daggers, and spikes; so that if anyone tried to climb up carelessly or without paying attention, he would be mangled and his flesh would adhere to the weapons.

At the foot of the ladder lay a dragon of enormous size, and it would attack those who tried to climb up and try to terrify them from doing so. And Saturus was the first to go up, he who was later to give himself up of his own accord. He had been the builder of our strength, although he was not present when we were arrested. And he arrived at the top of the staircase and he looked back and said to me: "Perpetua, I am waiting for you. But take care; do not let the dragon bite you."

"He will not harm me," I said, "in the name of Christ Jesus."

---

[59] Cicero, *Div.* 1.63.

[60] *Martyr. Pol.* 5.2; see *The Apostolic Fathers* (trans. Kirsopp Lake; 2 vols.; LCL; Cambridge: Harvard University Press, 1992) 2.319.

[61] *Passion of Marianus and James* 7.

[62] There is also the case of Cyprian who, through a dream about his court proceedings, indirectly learns that he is condemned to death and that he will obtain a stay of execution for one day after discussion. Relieved, he then wakes up. The dream comes true step by step; see the *Life of Cyprian* 12–13.

[63] Pierre de Labriolle, *Histoire de la littérature latine chrétienne* (Collection d'études anciennes; Paris: Les Belles Lettres, 1947) 156–59.

Slowly, as though he were afraid of me, the dragon stuck his head out from underneath the ladder. Then, using it as my first step, I trod on his head and went up.

Then I saw an immense garden, and in it a grey-haired man sat in shepherd's garb; tall he was, and milking sheep. And standing around him were many thousands of people clad in white garments. He raised his head, looked at me, and said: "I am glad you have come, my child."

He called me over to him and gave me, as it were, a mouthful of the milk he was drawing; and I took it into my cupped hands and consumed it. And all those who stood around said: "Amen!" At the sound of this word I came to, with the taste of something sweet still in my mouth. I at once told this to my brother, and we realized that we would have to suffer, and that from now on we would no longer have any hope in this life.[64]

The author, who may have been Tertullian himself, recounts both the testimony of the martyrs and their end; he confers a great deal of authority upon these documents by defining them as *instrumentum ecclesiae*, "instruments of the Church." For Tertullian, the word *instrumentum* frequently designates the holy scriptures. In the eyes of certain Christian readers, then, the visions of Perpetua and Saturus, as new prophecies, assume an authority comparable to that of the Bible itself. Such a position seems to be an echo of Montanism, the prophetic movement of the mid-second century that awaited and experienced present-day interventions of the Paraclete. Although a connection to Montanism is possible, granting such authority to dreams and visions was not the exception: rather, it was an extreme expression of a general tendency among Christians at that time. Their living God, their risen Lord, manifests his love in the present as much by the message of the gospel as by ecstatic and oneiric manifestations. In all cases, these are inspired.

It is well known that the social and political triumph of the Christian cause put an end to persecutions. It did not, however, put an end to dreams or ecstasies, which then became frequently associated with the ascetic, the martyr substitute. Hermitages and monasteries often served as a refuge for oneiric activity of a religious character. The best example is certainly that of Jerome. In his famous dream, the Christian scholar saw himself accused of not having renounced the charms of pagan literature, of Cicero and Plautus, in order to devote himself to the reading of sacred writings. In his dream, Jerome is told, "Thou art a follower of Cicero and not of Christ."[65]

Monastic literature – hagiography in particular – is peppered with visions, dreams, and miracles; these are found elsewhere in Christian historiography as well. Just as at an earlier time dreams had highlighted the suffering of the martyrs, some dreams would eventually come to punctuate the triumph of the church. Certain accounts of the conversion of Constantine and his victory over Maxentius at the Milvian Bridge in 312 attest to this. Eusebius of Caesarea's *Life of Constantine* records the account of the Emperor's premonitory dream that promised

---

[64] *Martyrdom of Perpetua and Felicitas* 4.

[65] See Jerome, *Letter to Julia Eustochium* 22.30 (ed. Philip Schaff and Henry Wace; trans. W.H. Fremantle et al.; NPNF 2/6; Peabody, Mass.: Hendrickson, 1994) 35.

victory ("Conquer by this [sign, the cross]") and enjoined him to decorate the military emblems of his troops with the cross:

> He [Constantine] said that about noon, when the day was already beginning to decline, he saw with his own eyes the trophy of a cross of light in the heavens, above the sun, and bearing the inscription, "Conquer by this." At this sight he himself was struck with amazement, and his whole army also, which followed him on this expedition, and witnessed the miracle.
>
> He said, moreover, that he doubted within himself what the import of this apparition could be. And while he continued to ponder and reason on its meaning, night suddenly came on; then in his sleep the Christ of God appeared to him with the same sign which he had seen in the heavens, and commanded him to make a likeness of that sign which he had seen in the heavens, and to use it as a safeguard in all engagements with his enemies.[66]

Dreams were not, however, the exclusive privilege of saints and emperors. For the believing Christian of the first centuries, God could provoke dreams in all God's children if such were God's pleasure and particular design. The dream even occupied a place so decisive in the lives and consciousness of its members that the church felt the need to channel these streams, by determining their theological validity and authority. Ecclesiastical law points to the pains with which the church grappled with dreams, while the work of Augustine reveals the theological struggle.

As various ministries came to be delineated in early Christianity, widows received a role from the very beginning. Diverse canonical and liturgical texts point out that a ministry of prayer was conferred upon these women. Certain texts even specify the two types of prayer the church could expect from them: intercessions, so that the community would avoid temptations, and – significant for our study – requests for obtaining visions. The canonists of the church, those from whom one expects the least amount of concessions for enthusiastic charisms, were only able to limit this activity. Since dreams were inescapable, the canonists incorporated them within a ministry as a means of controlling the effects of such spiritual gifts. These experts unfortunately do not specify for us either the nature or the content of these charisms.[67]

The history of interpretation of Peter's vision recorded in the canonical Acts (Acts 10:9–16) – and thus, for the church, an inescapable account of a vision – attests to the prudence of theologians. They were forced to admit the possibility of

---

[66] Eusebius of Caesarea, *Life of Constantine* 1.28–29 (ed. Philip Schaff; trans. Ernest Cushing Richardson; NPNF 2/1; Peabody, Mass.: Hendrickson, 1994) 490. See Marcel Simon and André Benoît, *Le judaïsme et le christianisme antique d'Antiochus Épiphane à Constantin* (Nouvelle Clio 10; Paris: Presses universitaires de France, 1968) 308–34 (on the so-called conversion of Constantine).

[67] See *Ecclesiastical Constitution of the Apostles* 21 (also called *Apostolic Ordinance* or *Apostolic Canons*, not to be confused with the *Apostolic Constitutions*, nor with the *Apostolic Tradition*). It is Cephas – a figure distinct from Peter – who speaks here. Alexandre Faivre, "La documentation canonico-liturgique de l'Église ancienne," *RevScRel* 54 (1980) 204–19, 173–97. The Greek text of this work can be found in Adolf von Harnack, *Die Lehre der Zwölf Apostel* (TU 2.1–2; Leipzig: Hinrichs, 1884) 225–37.

visions inspired by God because scripture itself constrained them to do so. In their orthodox eyes, however, a minimum of order was needed to regulate the unfolding of these visions and dreams: only ecstasies in which the believer retained his or her consciousness in an awakened state were considered to be inspired manifestations. Fits and hallucinations marked by the overthrow of consciousness would be disqualified from the very beginning.[68]

How were dreams understood in theoretical reflection? A treatise of Augustine of Hippo[69] allows us to respond to this question, at least in part.

Augustine of Hippo

It was in approximately 414–415 that Augustine composed the twelfth and last book of his detailed commentary on the first chapters of the book of Genesis, *De Genesi ad litteram*.[70] In this work he develops his reflections concerning mystical knowledge and spiritual experience. At that time, he no longer believed in the natural knowledge of God. Instead, he asserted that in order to know God, supernatural grace is necessary (this idea thus extricates him from a platonic theory of memory). Such is his biblical realism: the soul can pose questions about God but, in order to find a response, the soul must be purified (but not detached from the senses through philosophical exercises). The response will only have an effect through the inhabitation of God within us. The process is better called hyper-rational than irrational.

Augustine, in discussing consciousness in general, distinguishes three modes: in order of increasing importance, these are perceptible consciousness, rational consciousness, and intelligible vision. All three of these modes are required for entering into full consciousness. They survive at the time of the resurrection, and the prophets have already appealed to them in the past. Augustine thus refuses to

---

[68] See François Bovon, *De Vocatione Gentium. Histoire de l'interprétation d'Acts 10, 1–11, 18 dans les six premiers siècles* (BGBE 8; Tübingen: Mohr Siebeck, 1967) 145–47.

[69] Synesius of Cyrene also wrote a treatise entitled *On Dreams*, although all of its references seem to relate to pagan tradition. This treatise, which is number 5633 in Maurice Geerard, *Clavis Patrum Graecorum* (5 vols.; CC; Turnhout: Brepols, 1979) 3.99, is also accessible in the Patrologia Graeca of J.P. Migne (vol. 66: cols. 1281–320); it exists in French translation in the work of Henri Druon, *Œuvres de Synésius, évêque de Ptolémaïs, dans la Cyrénaïque au commencement du Vᵉ siècle, traduites entièrement, pour la première fois, en français et précédées d'une étude biographique et littéraire* (Paris: Hachette, 1878). Concerning Synesius and his work, see Johannes Quasten, *Patrology* (4 vols.; Utrecht/Brussels: Spectrum; Westminster, Md.: Newman, 1950–1986) 3.106–14. The treatise concerning dreams should be dated 403 or 404.

[70] Augustine, *De Genesi ad litteram* 12. The edition that should be consulted first is that of Joseph Zycha, *Sancti Aureli Augustini De Genesi ad litteram* (CSEL 28.1; Vienna: Tempsky, 1894). There is a more recent edition, accompanied by a French translation and excellent notes, by Paul Agaësse and A. Colignac that is found in *Œuvres de saint Augustin* (Bibliothèque Augustinienne 4; Paris: Desclée de Brouwer, 1972). I use here the introduction and German translation of M.E. Korger and Hans Urs von Balthasar, *Aurelius Augustinus, Psychologie und Mystik (De Genesi ad litteram 12)* (Sigillum 18; Einsiedeln: Johannes Verlag, 1960).

associate religious consciousness with a special place in, or a particular organ of, the body. In descending order, he also defines what is known by God, the angels, the demons, the resurrected, and finally, humans. For humans with a pure heart, there is the possibility of knowledge of God. Knowledge, language, and love go hand in hand; indeed, they must go hand in hand, a fact very few men and women come to realize because of the sin that menaces them.

In the twelfth book of *De Genesi ad litteram*, Augustine distinguishes four types of prophecy, as he had eighteen years earlier in his response to Simplicianus.[71] First, there is prophecy that comes by way of the formation of images in the mind, which is visited by a dream (thus Nebuchadnezzar or Pharaoh), or transported in ecstasy (thus the prophet Daniel or the apostle Peter). Second, there is prophecy by the illumination of reason. The true meaning of the images is revealed only to an interpreter. The patriarch Joseph and the prophet Daniel come to mind here as authentic interpreters of dreams. Joseph, by his interpretation of dreams, became a greater prophet than Pharaoh, who had the dreams but did not understand them. Thus the νοῦς ("mind," or "intelligence") of the interpreter prevails over the πνεῦμα ("spirit") of the charismatic (cf. 1 Cor. 14:15).

Third, if the first type of dream corresponds to an event and the second to its interpretation, the third combines the two, as is the case in the Apocalypse of John, the seer of Patmos. A fourth type of dream must be set forth separately: it consists of inspiration or prophecy that occurs without the knowledge of the one who prophecies, as in the case of Caiaphas (cf. John 11:49–52), an involuntary prophet of the salvific death of Jesus.

Augustine thus considers human beings to be so different from God that a natural knowledge of the Creator is excluded, but in other respects the humans are so close to God that they immediately apprehend and understand God's manifestation. Among the visionaries and prophets, Moses and Paul were the greatest: in their lifetimes, they attained to the vision of God. Augustine expressed this view in the course of an analysis of 2 Cor 12:1–5, the passage in which Paul affirms that he was carried up into the third heaven. While most prophets and visionaries see God by the mediation of images or the illumination of the mind, these two heroes of the faith achieve a more immediate consciousness of God by the purification of their minds. Numbers 12:6–8 demonstrates this for Moses: "With him I speak face to face." The journey to the third heaven demonstrates the same for Paul (2 Cor 12:1–5).

As we can see, Augustine is concerned about the connections between God and human capacities for perception and intelligence. He thinks that divine revelation is possible. The features of human psychology are such that humans have the privilege of triple access to reality: through the body, through the senses, and through the mind. These three correspond to the three parts of a person's being that can re-

---

[71] Augustine, *De diversis quaestionibus ad Simplicianum* 2.1.

ceive messages communicated from God. If God does not show Godself directly, God can send the Spirit to stir up images through dreams or utter sacred words to worshippers in ecstasies. All dreams are not divine messages, however. On the contrary, Augustine insists on the banal and natural character of dreams and prefers ecstatic visions. But he does not deny the possibility that God uses such mediation in order to transmit an order or formulate a prediction. Scripture attests that, at several points, God had recourse to dreams, even as God also inspired prophets through ecstasies.

Conclusion

The first Christians lived in an age of great credulity. Nevertheless, they did not allow themselves to be caught in a trap of facile apologetic; they did not claim for themselves special powers of thaumaturgy or particular mantic practices. Neither did they yield to a rationalistic spirituality that would censure all claims of dialogue with the beyond, consign manifestations of God to the past, or dissociate faith from the body and from history. They believed in a God who was still living, whom the scriptures attested, and who was manifested in Jesus Christ, a God who continues to communicate with God's people. They did not hesitate to add dreams and ecstasies to cult and prayer as a means of establishing actual connections between the divine and human. These were not understood as routes followed by humans, but as channels accessible to the will of God. In this matter as in others, the discernment of spirits was granted both to the community and to the individual believer, in order that they might determine whether the dream or ecstasy was true or illusory. Certain members of the community, widows in particular, received the ministry of addressing requests to God, that God should manifest God's plans and advice by the intermediary of dreams or visions. The church, attentive to the decisive moment of death, attributed great significance to the last messages and last dreams of its martyrs. The faithful one who was at the threshold of death concentrated his or her attention upon that which was essential, upon his or her imminent meeting with the Lord. This believer was not suspected of demagoguery, nor of a lust for power, nor of an optical illusion. Dreams, as an anthropological reality, do not necessarily open onto the transcendent world. Nevertheless, by reason of analogy with the world of God, which first overlaps with word and spirit, dreams can serve as a vehicle for divine intentions. Individual believers and local communities can be guided, encouraged, and instructed by what is demonstrated, heard, and comprehended.

How can we come to appreciate this attitude, which in the end welcomes dreams? This question is all the more real since our contemporaries debate the nature and the authority of dreams. Recently, the ambitions of parapsychology have been added to the psychological perspective. If one holds to psychoanalysis,

Freudians[72] and Jungians[73] present different perspectives on the problem, as we know. According to Jung, the unconscious is less fixed, more open to possibilities, and associated with collective aspirations. For him, we appear to be in our dreams what we are in reality, and not merely what we seek to manifest in our waking lives. Moreover, during our sleep, and thanks to our dreams, our problems can gestate and the symbolic images that appear can give us guidance. In the end, our dream activity joins us – beyond ourselves and our present situation – to our origins and to the legitimate passions and symbolic expressions of humanity. Thus our dreams are not only an expression of our repressed urges.

If I were to formulate a critique here, it would be directed less toward Jung's optimism and more toward the established associations of his thought with a syncretistic spirituality. Jung is undoubtedly to be blamed for declaring that the symbolic function of our dreams is transcendent. I nevertheless acknowledge the strength of some of his ideas: it is certain that our dreams tell us about reality and sometimes suggest solutions. But in order to decide if God expresses Godself through them,[74] one needs an external authority, a judgment of the spiritual order, a link between the content of dreams and the assurance of the faith, a gospel faith – that is to say, rooted in the event of Jesus Christ and connected to the reality of the church. But even if dreams are subject to examination, they should not be brought under the sole control of this external authority or judgment, for this would be to put shackles upon God and to risk extinguishing the Holy Spirit.

---

[72] Concerning Freud's interpretation of dreams, see Sigmund Freud, *Introduction à la psychanalyse* (trans. S. Jankélévitch; Paris: Payot, 1922) 83–249; idem, *Die Traumdeutung* (Frankfurt: Fischer, 1972).

[73] See the various concepts related to dreams (*Traumdeutung, Traumdichtung, Traum-Ich, Trauminkubation, Traumserie, Traumstruktur,* and *Traumsymbol*) which are explained in the important *Lexikon Jungscher Grundbegriff* (see above, p. 148 n. 20), and illustrated with long citations. I must mention Jung's last work, a popularizing one that he composed before his death. Jung accorded a privileged place to his reflection on dreams, as is indicated by J. Freeman in his introduction to this work (pp. 12–13): see Carl G. Jung and Marie-Louise von Franz, Joseph L. Henderson, Jolande Jacobi, Aniela Jaffé, *L'homme et ses symboles* (Paris: Laffont, 1987). The original appeared in English as idem, *Man and his Symbols* (Garden City: Doubleday, 1964).

[74] Jung courageously affirms this at the end of his contribution in *L'homme et ses symboles*, 102–3 (see n. 73 above).

The Canonical Structure of Gospel and Apostle

In the pages that follow I would like to illustrate a theological structure that proved decisive for early Christian faith, that of gospel and apostle.[1] An analysis of several New Testament passages reveals the contours of this structure, its importance and universality. Once detected and understood, this structure may explain the formation of a two-part canon in the second century without assigning priority to the role of outside forces in shaping it. Clearly there was interaction between Christians, Jews, and pagans with regard to their sacred texts. The Christian communities on their way to orthodoxy and heresy were influenced by these changes. But I wish to challenge the prevailing thesis that credits Marcion with the beginnings of New Testament canonization.[2] In my opinion, while Marcion may have contributed to the process, he was responsible neither for the idea of a collection nor for its bipolar structure. A "New Testament" containing Gospels and Epistles is the logical outgrowth and materialization of a revelation that articulates an event and the proclamation that follows, that is, of Jesus and his disciples. Thus the need for a New Testament and its two-part configuration is inscribed in the very nature of the Christian faith from the beginnings of Christianity.

I.

Embroiled in a controversy with his adversaries in Corinth, the apostle Paul refers in his Second Epistle to the salvific plan of God, which he formulates in terms of reconciliation. Significantly, he carefully outlines not just one, but two acts: salvation consists of both reconciliation itself as event and the "ministry," or "service," (διακονία) of reconciliation. In other words, the proclamation communicates the event.[3] For Paul, Jesus Christ is the very heart of the event. As an

---

[1] I advanced this thesis in my farewell lecture at the University of Geneva in 1993, a lecture that was published in a small book entitled *L'Évangile et l'Apôtre: Christ inséparable de ses témoins* (Aubonne: Moulin, 1993). I summarize it here with additional material; it was first published in French under the title "La structure canonique de l'Évangile et de l'Apôtre," *CNS* 15 (1994) 559–76. I wish to thank Laura Beth Bugg for her work in translating this paper.

[2] Cf. Hans von Campenhausen, *Die Entstehung der christlichen Bibel* (BHT 39; Tübingen: Mohr Siebeck 1968); ET: *The Formation of the Christian Bible* (Philadelphia: Fortress, 1972).

[3] 2 Cor 5:18: "All this is from God, who reconciled us to himself through Christ, and has given us the ministry of reconciliation." Note the side by side placement of "Christ" and "us," that is to say, the apostles.

apostle, Paul himself is responsible for the proclamation of the gospel. God acts through the gift of sending and resurrecting his Son, who needs human collaboration to proclaim God's program. The apostolic word becomes the indispensable complement to the act of redemption. The gospel has two faces: one represented by Jesus and the other represented by the apostles.[4]

The Epistle to the Galatians contains direct evidence of this structure with respect to Christ and the apostles. The functioning of each is seen in the central part of Paul's autobiographical passage: "But when God, who had set me apart before I was born and called me through his grace, was pleased to reveal his Son to me, so that I might proclaim him among the Gentiles, I did not confer with any human being..." (Gal 1:15–16). The divine origin of this endeavor is evident from this encounter: this is God's project. The salvific role of this appearance of the Son to the apostle may also be seen. It takes place so that the Gentiles will be touched by the good news and thus come to faith and saving grace. While the Son is revealed in his Easter glory, with an implicit reference both to his origin and his divine mission, Paul is at the same time depicted as both a believer and a messenger. The fate of one becomes the other's object of proclamation.[5]

In spite of different tasks and responsibilities, a profound analogy stands between the Lord and his apostle. In effect, the vocation of apostle aligns the fate of the one who practices it with the one who is preached. The Pauline imitation nevertheless does not imply a slavish copy, but the participation of one's entire being. The apostle urges the same imitation of himself in return. He says to the Corinthians, "Be imitators of me, as I am of Christ" (1 Cor 11:1). In order to understand Christ, to truly hear the gospel, one must not only listen to the apostle but also see and discover in him a model to imitate. The structure of Gospel-Apostle has salvific value, because Christ, at the heart of the good news, is the image of God (2 Cor 4:4; Rom 8:29; cf. Col 1:15). The gift of divine origin, therefore, extends to Christians by means of both the Gospel and the Apostle.[6]

Early Christianity did not spread the idea of several messiahs but of a multifaceted Christ: the one Messiah was at the same time King, Priest, and Prophet, Savior and Lord, Son of Man and Son of God, proclaimed by the witness of many servants and disciples. The apostle Paul did not attempt to diminish the importance of the Twelve and the other witnesses. On the contrary, while persuaded of

---

[4] Cf. Victor Paul Furnish, *II Corinthians, Translated with Introduction, Notes, and Commentary* (AB 32a; Garden City: Doubleday, 1984) 305–37.

[5] Cf. Hans Dieter Betz, *Galatians: A Commentary on Paul's Letter to the Churches in Galatia* (Hermeneia; Philadelphia: Fortress, 1979) 64–74.

[6] On imitation in Paul, see Hans Dieter Betz, *Nachfolge und Nachahmung Jesu Christi* (BHT 37; Tübingen: Mohr Siebeck, 1967); Elizabeth A. Castelli, *Imitating Paul: A Discourse of Power* (Louisville: Westminster/John Knox, 1991). Paul refers quite often to these other apostles in his epistles; cf. 1 Cor 9:5; 15:7–10; Gal 2:8–9.

the value of his own direct and personal christological experience, he nevertheless gave great recognition to the existence and authority of "the apostles before me."

The Pauline school, as we see it in the deutero-Pauline and Lukan writings, seeks to maintain and clarify the theological position of its teacher. In the prologue to his work, Luke urges his readers to remember "the events that have been fulfilled among us" (Luke 1:1). For the evangelist Luke as for the apostle Paul, Christianity rests neither on an abstract revelation nor on a mystical experience. It rests instead on a story, an intervention by God in time and place. In order to be effective, this salvific event needs to be expressed and attested. This is why Luke is eager to add that the observers of these events became both "eyewitnesses and servants of the Word" (Luke 1:2). The two poles are inseparable, but they should not be confused. The first is bound to an event, the coming of Jesus Christ, and the second to the proclamation, the apostolic witness. The first pole, of which Luke is immediately aware, is also related to language and, similarly, the second is also related to action. Jesus Christ himself is also a witness to the word of God, and the gospel preached is by flesh-and-blood apostles. The gospel has two faces: the gospel as christological event and the gospel as apostolic proclamation. Each face, in turn, has two sides: a historic aspect and a linguistic aspect. These aspects and faces are not to be confused nor are they to be separated.[7]

In the same way that Pauline faith articulates the reconciliation and the ministry of reconciliation, Luke records the memory of the apostles alongside those of the founding Messiah. The coexistence of the book of Acts and the Gospel is not an anomaly, but the concretization of a theological conviction shared by Paul and his disciples.[8]

The authors of the deutero-Pauline epistles essentially shared the views of their teacher and of Luke. The author of the Epistle to the Ephesians in particular sees the matter in foundational terms. While Paul himself considered Christ the sole foundation of Christianity (1 Cor 3:11), the author of Ephesians, remaining faithful to Pauline theology, demands a further foundation, that of the apostles and prophets (Eph 2:20). The point is not to have two juxtaposed or successive foundations, but one double foundation: the interweaving of the event and its meaning, of Christ and his attestation by the apostles.[9]

This articulation was not easy to develop, express, or maintain. It could be poorly received and poorly expressed. The foundational event could be eclipsed by the weight of the witnesses, and the apostolic witness could be adulterated.

---

[7] Cf. François Bovon, *L'Évangile selon saint Luc (1,1–9,50)* (CNT 3a; Geneva: Labor et Fides, 1991) 32–44.

[8] Cf. François Bovon, *Luc le théologien: Vingt-cinq ans de recherches (1950–1975)* (Le Monde de la Bible 5; 2d ed.; Geneva: Labor et Fides, 1988) 83–84.

[9] Cf. Maurice Goguel, "Tu es Petrus (Mt 16,17–19)," *Bulletin de la Faculté libre de théologie protestante de Paris* 15 (1938) 1–13. On the passage from Ephesians, cf. Michel Bouttier, *L'épître de saint Paul aux Éphésiens* (CNT 9b; Geneva: Labor et Fides, 1991) 124–31.

Such dangers appear on the horizon of the Pastoral Epistles. In order to defend his teacher, the author privileges the Pauline witness to the detriment of the other apostles, who are consigned to obscurity, and he overestimates the apostolic function relative to the role of Christ himself.[10] But these moves, which were provoked by a specific ecclesial situation, have not obscured the presence of the structure being examined here. At the heart of the theology of these epistles, the two-part structure of Gospel and Apostle is once again found.[11]

II.

A comparison of the prologues to the Fourth Gospel and the First Epistle of John reveals the presence of the same schema in another current of early Christianity, namely, the Johannine movement. The prologue to the Gospel proclaims the coming of the Word, while that of the Epistle, shaped by an interpretive element, adds the force of an indispensable complement: the apostolic witness. Alongside the incarnation of the Logos and the manifestation of his divine glory stands the physical presence of the apostolic witnesses.[12] In the same way that the Pauline school skillfully maneuvered to find the proper place for its hero in the choir of witnesses, the Johannine community exercised theological diplomacy to defend the legitimacy of its beloved disciple. For the purposes of this study, the main item of interest is that in the Johannine movement as well we find the role of apostle next to that of revealer. Through the force of metaphor, Johannine theology illustrates the initial course of the revelation: from the Father to the Son and from the Son to the beloved disciple. As the Word rests in the Father's bosom in knowing intimacy (John 1:18), in the Johannine hermeneutic the beloved disciple rests his head on Jesus' bosom (John 13:25). The revelation is a religious one in that it comes from God, but it is also a historic and human one, since it passes through persons and their words. As expressions of witness, the Johannine Epistles are to the Gospel what the Acts of the Apostles is to Luke and what the Pauline words are to reconciliation in Christ.[13]

---

[10] Compare Yann Redalié (*Paul après Paul: Le temps, le salut, la morale selon les épîtres à Timothée et à Tite* [Le Monde de la Bible 31; Geneva: Labor et Fides, 1994] 242), who is less affirmative than I am.

[11] Cf. 1 Tim 2:5–7; 2 Tim 1:8–12.

[12] On the prologue to the First Epistle, compare Hans Conzelmann, *"Was von Anfang war,"* in *Neutestamentliche Studien für R. Bultmann* (ed. Walther Eltester; Berlin: Töpelmann, 1954) 194–201; reprinted in idem, *Theologie als Schriftauslegung: Aufsätze zum Neuen Testament* (Munich: Kaiser, 1967) 207–14; and Raymond E. Brown, *The Epistles of John: Translated with Introduction, Notes, and Commentary* (AB 30; Garden City: Doubleday, 1982) 149–88.

[13] Cf. François Bovon, "The Gospel According to John, Access to God, at the Obscure Origins of Christianity," *Diogenes* 146 (1989) 37–50.

Doubtless being part of the sacred collection of writings belonging to the Johannine community, the Gospel and the Epistles attest to the second-century tendency to concretize the theological structure of Gospel and Apostle in canonical form.[14] Marcion responds to the same internal demands and draws on a similar arrangement, although he uses undeniably different methods.

III.

The narrative tradition that collected, adapted, and conveyed the memories of Jesus until the time of the evangelists, in particular Mark and Matthew, also attests to a two-part structure, in spite of its focus on the Master. It also specifies how individual roles should be distributed within the arrangement as well.

In retaining the accounts of the institution of the Twelve (Mark 3:13–19 and par.), of their commissioning (Mark 6:7–13 and par.), and of the appearances of the Resurrected One (Matt 28:16–20; Luke 24:36–53; cf. Acts 1:1–8), the bearers of these traditions established this strong relationship between the Lord and his disciples. The apostles constitute a group of officials who, though they are weak, have been made strong by the power of Christ. Sent out two by two, they carry out the work of Jesus, preaching the gospel of the kingdom of God and restoring life through exorcisms and healings.

At the end of Matthew's Gospel, on Easter day, the disciples receive from the risen Christ a mission founded on a promise: "Jesus came to them and said these words" (Matt 28:18a). If divine authority belongs to Christ ("All authority has been given to me in heaven and on earth," Matt 28:18b), the act of witnessing belongs to the apostles ("Go, therefore and make disciples of all nations," Matt 28:19). Thus there is a distinction of roles just as there is a distinction of periods. Because Christ will leave that place, the apostles will have to act. But, as in the prologue to the First Epistle of John (1 John 1:3), the communion of Christ and his disciples will not end in spite of their physical separation: "I am with you always, to the end of the age" (Matt 28:20).[15]

Therefore, for the bearers of these traditions, the apostles represent a living link to the Resurrected One. The Lukan account of Pentecost (Acts 2:1–41) and the Johannine Christ's farewell discourse (John 14:15–21, 26; 15:26; 16:7) give a name to the facilitator of this link: the Holy Spirit, or Paraclete. According to Luke, the risen Christ receives from the Father the power of communion and life: "Being

---

[14] Cf. Jean-Daniel Kaestli, Jean-Michel Poffet, and Jean Zumstein, eds., *La communauté johannique et son histoire: La trajectoire de l'Évangile de Jean aux deux premiers siècles* (Monde de la Bible 20; Geneva: Labor et Fides, 1990).

[15] On the ending of Matthew, cf. Jean Zumstein, "Matthieu 28, 16–20," *RTP* 3/22 (1972) 14–33; reprinted in idem, *Miettes exégétiques* (Le Monde de la Bible 25; Geneva: Labor et Fides, 1991) 91–112.

therefore exalted by the right hand of God, and having received from the Father the promise of the Holy Spirit, he has poured out this that you both see and hear" (Acts 2:33). Christ has passed the Spirit on to his disciples, and by it they are transformed. Formerly hesitant, Mary Magdalene goes boldly to the disciples to confess her faith (John 20:11–18); formerly a renegade, Peter proclaims a message of assurance (Luke 22:61–62; Acts 2:14–41). Though at one time a persecutor, Paul is made the apostle to the nations (Gal 1:23; 2:7–8); once eager for reward, James wears the mantle of martyrdom (Mark 10:35–37; Acts 12:1–2).

IV.

The gospels differ from ancient biographies on at least one point: they must be read on two levels. On one level, the gospels are the recollection of the pre-Easter life of Jesus. On a second level, they are windows through which the post-Easter life of the apostles and churches can be seen. These two planes can take many forms. In a temporal schematic, the mission of Jesus who proclaims the gospel (Mark 1:14–15) precedes the apostolic preaching to the nations (Mark 13:10). If the significance of this reality is broadened, the authority to forgive sins, which is in the first instance the prerogative of the Son of Man (Mark 2:10), is then handed on to humans (Matt 9:8). In other words, this authority is transferred to the church and its apostles and ministers (cf. Matt 16:19; 18:18; John 20:23). Because of a hermeneutic that demands relevancy for a new situation, the message of Jesus becomes the Christian proclamation. While Luke maintains the parable of the lost sheep in a historical context (Jesus defends his missionary efforts in the face of the Pharisees' criticism, Luke 15:1–7), Matthew appropriates the story and integrates it into a chapter he has constructed on the theme of communal life (Matt 18:10–14). Consequently, the parable no longer illustrates the seeking of sinners but the responsibility of ministers to claim those among their flock who are lost. The shepherd, who in Luke represents God or Christ, becomes in Matthew the figure of the apostle or pastor. Operating in both the realm of reference (to the former time of Jesus) and the realm of relevance (to the present work of the church), the gospels confirm the existence and importance of the Gospel-Apostle structure.[16]

---

[16] Pierre Bonnard, "Composition et signification historique de Matthieu 18," in *De Jésus aux évangiles: Tradition et rédaction dans les Évangiles synoptiques* (ed. Ignace de la Potterie; 2d ed.; BETL 25; Gembloux: Duculot, 1967) 130–40; reprinted in idem, *Anamnesis: Recherches sur le Nouveau Testament* (Cahiers de la Revue de théologie et de philosophie 3; Geneva: Revue de théologie et de philosophie, 1980) 111–20.

V.

Another early Christian reality to consider is the emergence of narratives concerning the life, ministry, and destiny of the apostles. Protestant theology, which has always insisted on the unique role of Jesus Christ, has often refused to accord the apostles the place they have earned in the economy of salvation. Thus several Protestant exegetes of the nineteenth and twentieth centuries considered the book of Acts an anomaly, a theological mistake.[17] For them, Acts was unseemly and even sacrilegious, because it focused attention on the type of witnesses that ought to vanish behind the christological message. This opinion, which was rooted in Protestant polemic against the Catholic doctrine of apostolic succession, ignored the two-part structure of Gospel and Apostle and tipped the scales in favor of the spiritual and the divine.[18]

Luke is not alone, however, in his interest in the fate of the apostles. The Epistles and even the Gospels give them a place in the transmission of the good news. Paul understands the cult to be the social and ecclesial *Sitz im Leben* of the Christian "news." Joined in prayer, the first communities praised God for the work of Christ, but they also rejoiced in the universal spread of the gospel (cf. 1 Tim 3:16; Rom 1:8). And they pleaded with God to protect and accompany the apostles and the missionaries (cf. Acts 13:3; 20:36–38). The early communities also recounted the edifying narratives of the pilgrimages of the missionaries and apostles and their success (cf. 1 Thess 1:6–10). Thus we can explain the origin of the cycles of travel narratives reworked by Luke in the book of Acts,[19] such as the dealings of Philip in Samaria and his setbacks with Simon the magician (Acts 8:4–40), the missionary work of Peter and the foundation of the Caesarean community at the time of Cornelius's conversion (Acts 9:32–11:18), and the missionary expedition of Paul and Barnabas from Antioch as an official delegation (Acts 13–14). The narrative is driven by allegiance to the faith and shaped by Christian affection both for Jesus Christ the Savior and for his apostles, heralds, and missionaries.[20]

This interest in the apostles persisted into the second century and explains the continuation of narratives concerning them. The often unorthodox, or sectarian,

---

[17] See especially Franz Overbeck, *Christentum und Kultur: Gedanken und Anmerkungen zur modernen Theologie* (ed. C.A. Bernoulli; Basel, 1919; reprinted Darmstadt: Wissenschaftliche Buchgesellschaft, 1973) 78–80.

[18] Cf. François Bovon, "L'origine des récits concernant les apôtres," *RTP* 3/3 (1967) 345–50; reprinted in idem, *L'œuvre de Luc: Études d'exégèse et de théologie* (Paris: Cerf, 1987) 155–62.

[19] Jacob Jervell, "Zur Frage der Traditionsgrundlage der Apostelgeschichte," *ST* 16 (1962) 25–41; ET: Jacob Jervell, *Luke and the People of God: A New Look at Luke-Acts* (Minneapolis: Augsburg, 1972) 19–39.

[20] On the cycle of traditions contained in the book of Acts, cf. Gerhard Schneider, *Die Apostelgeschichte, I. Teil. Einleitung. Kommentar zu Kap. 1,1–8,40* (HTKNT 5; Freiburg: Herder, 1980) 82–94.

orientation assumed by authors of the so-called "apocryphal" acts, with their avid asceticism and occasional docetic tendencies, evoked prejudice against these remembrances that had been expanded by legendary imagination. The church, the emerging "great church" or "catholic church," was at first distrustful of these apostolic traditions, but after it had established a system of apostolic authority it attempted to recover and harness them. The church succeeded, and these narratives, though not integrated into the canonical scriptures, were nevertheless preserved as religious works; they became integrated into hagiographic collections along with remembrances of martyrs and saints.[21]

VI.

Everyone agrees that a New Testament canon did not appear before the middle of the second century and that there is no evidence before this date of a collected grouping of the Gospels and Epistles.[22] In my opinion, the Gospel-Apostle structure, manifest from the first generation of Christians, prepares the way for the formation of a new body of scriptures as a complement or counterpart to the Holy Scriptures (the Septuagint) inherited by the church. The formation of a New Testament canon was therefore the logical materialization of this theological structure. The presence of the Gospel-Apostle pair during the time of the Apostolic Fathers and the apologists assured the transition from the parameters set by Paul, Luke, and John to the body of witnesses to the New Testament that developed from the time of Irenaeus of Lyon and beyond.

The church that would become the "great church" of the second and third centuries simultaneously rejected idolatrous veneration of the apostles at the expense of Christ and refused a revelation that omitted human mediation. It also opposed a privileged position for any one apostle. In effect, it recognized the importance of these two elements, Gospel and Apostle, Christ and his disciples. The *First Epistle of Clement* of Rome (ca. 95–98) clearly defines this demarcated structure: "The apostles received the good news for us from our Savior, Jesus Christ; Jesus, the Christ, was sent by God. Thus Christ comes from God and the apostles come from Christ; the two were sent out in good order by the will of God" (*1 Clem.* 42:1–2).[23]

---

[21] François Bovon et al., *Les Actes apocryphes des apôtres: Christianisme et monde païen* (Publications de la Faculté de théologie de l'Université de Genève 4; Geneva: Labor et Fides, 1981).

[22] Of the recent works on the New Testament canon, see particularly Bruce M. Metzger, *The Canon of the New Testament: Its Origins, Development, and Significance* (Oxford: Oxford University Press, 1987); *Le Canon des Écritures: Études historiques, exégétiques et systématiques* (ed. C. Theobald; LD 140; Paris: Cerf, 1990); and *The Canon Debate* (ed. Lee Martin McDonald and James A. Sanders; Peabody, Mass.: Hendrickson, 2002).

[23] Translated after the French of Annie Jaubert, *Epître aux Corinthiens. Introduction, texte, traduction, notes et index* (SC 167; Paris: Cerf, 1971) 168–69.

For his part, Ignatius of Antioch (ca. 115) encourages the Magnesians to remain firm "in the teachings of the Savior and the apostles." He urges the presbyters and deacons to support the bishop as their invaluable spiritual leader; as leader, the bishop in turn must submit to the apostles of Christ.[24]

Some years later, between 110 and 130, Papias of Hierapolis insisted on an apostolic mediation that would bring the Christians of his time into contact with the early manifestation of truth in Jesus. He preferred an oral testimony, verified by persons deemed worthy of faith, over writings of uncertain validity. To that end he sought direct contact with ancients who had known the apostles. In his own way, Papias attests to the Gospel-Apostle structure by attaching validity both to "the commandments given by the Lord" and to "those who recall them."[25]

In his *Apology,* Aristides (ca. 140) inscribes the faith of Christians within the structure of gospel and apostle. After presenting Christ in rather confessional terms, he evokes the memory of the twelve disciples who were called to record Jesus' salvific work (his "dispensation") and to make it known to all the earth.[26]

Bipolarity is also decisive for Justin, who emphasizes both the biblical prophecies realized in Jesus and the teachings of Christ transmitted by the apostles. Thus in the *First Apology* he presents the institution of baptism as an act required by Jesus Christ and known from "the doctrine that we have learned from the apostles" (*1 Apol.* 61.9).[27]

Around 180 C.E., Irenaeus of Lyon definitively expressed the schema examined here. In his preface to *Adversus haereses,* he speaks of "the one true and living faith, which the church has received from the apostles and transmitted to its children." He continues, "The Lord of all things has in effect given to his apostles the power to proclaim the gospel, and it is through them that we have known the truth, that is, the teaching of the Son of God. It is also to us that the Lord said, 'Who listens to you listens to me, and who rejects you rejects me and the one who sent me.'"[28]

---

[24] Ignatius of Antioch, *Magn.* 13.1–2; see Th. Camelot, ed. and trans., *Lettres, Ignace d'Antioche, Polycarpe de Smyrne. Martyre de Polycarpe. Texte grec, introduction, traduction et notes* (4th ed.; SC 10; Paris: Cerf, 1969) 90–91.

[25] Cited by Eusebius, *Hist. eccl.* 3.39.3. On Papias, see Ulrich H.J. Körtner, *Papias von Hierapolis: Ein Beitrag zur Geschichte des frühen Christentums* (Göttingen: Vandenhoeck & Ruprecht, 1983).

[26] Aristides, *Apol.* 15.1–2; see E.J. Goodspeed, ed., *Die ältesten Apologeten: Texte mit kurzen Einleitungen* (1914; Göttingen: Vandenhoeck & Ruprecht, 1984) 19–20. The Latin text is a modern version of the German restoration of the text by J. Geffcken, but this does not appear clear in Goodspeed's introduction. The Greek text that appears in the apparatus is that of the *Life of Barlaam and Ioasaph,* which often builds on the *Apology* of Aristides. It speaks here of "that which among themselves [the Christians] is called the holy and evangelical scripture" (p. 19 n. 9).

[27] See André Wartelle, trans. and ed., *Saint Justin. Apologies. Introduction, texte critique, traduction, commentaire et index* (Paris: Études augustiniennes, 1987) 182–85, 289–91.

[28] After the French translation of Adelin Rousseau, *Irénée de Lyon, Contre les hérésies* (Paris: Cerf, 1984) 275–76.

In the East as well as in the West, the structure of Gospel and Apostle hence-forth became the unshakable foundation of the church. In the fourth century, when Christianity was imposed throughout the Roman Empire, Eusebius of Caesarea vigorously reaffirmed this structure in his *Ecclesiastical History* (1.1.1).[29] His continual reference to episcopal succession demonstrates the normative role of the bipolar organization of Gospel and Apostle. Apostolic succession was mediated through the didactic and governmental device of bishops. But the ecclesiastical hierarchy that was put in place in correlation with the Gospel and Apostle structure – with the bishops in the highest position, the priests below, and then the deacons – left out the prophets, healers, and women who, in the first century, had all been standard witnesses of the Christian message.[30]

VII.

The theological structure of Gospel and Apostle that underlies the progressive organization of ministries promoted the birth of a New Testament canon with two distinct parts. This structure was doubtless formed imperceptibly, yet irresistibly. During the formation of the great church, everyone was pleased to see the confirmation of doctrine and ecclesial organization. In my opinion, Marcion's choice of a gospel and some epistles as a source and standard for doctrine was no innovation.[31] Marcion's canon, alongside the others, testifies to the structuring force of Gospel and Apostle. Ecclesiastical authors around the year 200 knew such a juxtaposition of Gospels and Epistles as a sacred collection for a new economy. It must be said, however, that the theological structure of Gospel and Apostle mattered more to them, in general, than the formal outline of a canon. Nevertheless, when the proconsul demanded the surrender of Christian books during the reign of Commodus (July 180), it was the *libri* – probably the Gospels – and the Epistles of

---

[29] Cf. François Bovon, "*L'Histoire ecclésiastique* d'Eusèbe de Césarée et l'histoire du salut," in *Oikonomia: Heilsgeschichte als Thema der Theologie* (ed. Felix Christ; Hamburg-Bergstedt: Reich, 1967) 129–39; published here in English translation pp. 271–83; see also Harold W. Attridge and Gohei Hata, *Eusebius, Christianity, and Judaism* (Leiden: Brill, 1992).

[30] On the growing marginalization of the prophets, see Adolf von Harnack, *Die Mission und Ausbreitung des Christentums in den ersten drei Jahrunderten* (2 vols.; 4th ed.; Leipzig: Hinrichs, 1924) 1.332–79, esp. 362–64; Enrico Norelli, "L'Ascensione di Isaia nel quadro del profetismo cristiano," in *Il profetismo da Gesù di Nazareth al montanismo: Atti del IV Convegno di studi neotestamentari, Perugia, 12–14 Settembre 1991* (ed. Romano Penna; published as *Ricerche storico-bibliche* 5/1 [1993]) 123–48, esp. 147–48.

[31] On Marcion's canon, cf. Adolf von Harnack, *Marcion: Das Evangelium vom fremden Gott. Eine Monographie zur Geschichte der Grundlegung der katholischen Kirche. Neue Studien zu Marcion* (Leipzig: Hinrichs, 1924; Darmstadt: Wissenschaftliche Buchgesellschaft, 1985) 35–73 and 40*–255* respectively; Enrico Norelli, "La funzione di Paolo nel pensiero di Marcione," *Rivista biblica* 34 (1986) 543–97.

Paul that were handed over, according to the account of the Scillitan martyrs.[32] Moreover, the Muratorian canon, from the second century of our era, enumerates the Gospels, then the Epistles.[33]

Consequently, it is not surprising that in the Christian liturgy the system of biblical readings is based on the model of our theological structure. From the time of Justin[34] and the *Acts of Peter*[35] Christian worship has included readings from the Hebrew Bible, in addition to those drawn from the Gospels and the Epistles. In the West it was usual to speak of the Gospel and Epistle, while in the East it was the Gospel and the Apostle, yet both referred to the same reality. The title of this article suggests that I find the formulation used by the Orthodox East especially helpful here.[36]

VIII.

Thus far we have followed the path that led to the great church. At the same time, however, there is evidence of a parallel track traveled by other Christian communities and movements. What is striking about these other texts, be they gnostic, Jewish-Christian, or apocryphal, is that they also are aware of the bipolar structure of Gospel and Apostle, even if they occasionally ordered them in different ways.

Certain New Testament traditions focus upon a particular apostle as Christ's successor and counterpart. The Gospel of Matthew accords, for example, a special place to Peter (Matt 16:18) without diminishing the role of others. The Pastorals claim an almost exclusive connection with Paul. And a diverse group of traditions that do not find a place in the New Testament canon tend to valorize other apostolic figures. Thomas and James, the brother of the Lord, become the leading figures of certain gnostic and Jewish-Christian movements, as we learn from Epiphanius of Salamis,[37] the apocryphal *Gospel of Thomas*,[38] the *Apocryphon of James*,[39] as well as the two *Apocalypses of James*.[40] The *Letter of Peter to James*, the

---

[32] *Passio sanctorum Scilitanorum* 12, in Gustav Krüger and G. Ruhbach, eds., *Ausgewählte Märtyrerakten: Neubearbeitung der Knopfschen Ausgabe* (Tübingen: Mohr Siebeck, 1965) 29.

[33] On this list, compare the article by Jean-Daniel Kaestli, "La place du *Fragment de Muratori* dans l'histoire du canon: A propos de la thèse de Sundberg et Hahneman," *CNS* 15 (1994) 609–34, and the bibliography found there.

[34] Justin, *1 Apol.* 67.3; see Wartelle, *Saint Justin. Apologies*, 45–48 and 297–98.

[35] *Acts Pet.* 20; Léon Vouaux, *Les Actes de Pierre. Introduction, textes, traduction et commentaire* (Les apocryphes du Nouveau Testament; Paris: Letouzey et Ané, 1922) 339 n. 7.

[36] Cf. H. Leclercq, "Évangéliaire," *DACL* 5, 1 (1922) 775–845; G. Godu, "Évangiles," *DACL* 5, 1 (1922) 853–923; Godu, "Epîtres," *DACL* 5, 1 (1922) 245–344.

[37] Epiphanius, *Pan.* 88.7.7–9.

[38] *Gos. Thom.* title and 12.

[39] NHC I,2.

[40] NHC V,3 and V,4.

Formal Agreement, and the *Letter of Clement to James*, preserved at the beginning of the *Pseudo-Clementine Homilies*, also bear witness to the presence of this structure.[41]

The pseudo-Clementine literature reveals yet another arrangement of gospel and apostle. Here the apostolic circle becomes broken. The good apostles, especially Peter, must confront a negative figure, Simon the magician, who probably represents the apostle Paul. Here the system of pairs, of two people "yoked together" *(syzygoi)*, takes the form not of Christ and his apostles, but of a false messenger of God confronting the figure of a true apostle. For the authors, that is what happened in the apostolic age. In fact, this alternation between the apostate and the true believer is an ancestral opposition that goes back to the rivalry between Cain and Abel.[42]

In certain circles, an apostle was invested with such power and deemed the beneficiary of such revelation that Christ himself was neglected. In the apocryphal *Acts of Andrew*, for example, Jesus is present only as one of the names of God.[43] He represents the spiritual divinity who invites the soul to reach a superior world. Here below, the entire earth is occupied by the apostle. It is he who possesses the words of life.[44] The memory of the ministry of Jesus, of his acts and speeches, is completely erased. It is in the presence of the apostle, not of Christ, that salvation blossoms and death retreats.[45]

In the desire to privilege a particular apostle or apostolic circle one may omit certain witnesses, as happened with the women apostles. We may begin with Mary Magdalene, mentioned in the Gospels of Matthew and John (Matt 28:1–10; John 20:11–18).[46] But already Paul and many authors of the second century have erased her from memory. Mary Magdalene does not figure, for example, in the list of the appearances of the Resurrected One (1 Cor 15:5–8). At most, the Apostle to the Gentiles knows of pairs of apostles made up of a man *and* a woman, such as

---

[41] Cf. *Die Pseudoklementinen*, vol. 1: *Homilien* (ed. Bernhard Rehm and Georg Strecker; 3d ed.; GCS; Berlin: Akademie-Verlag, 1992).

[42] Georg Strecker, *Das Judenchristentum in den Pseudoklementinen* (Berlin: Akademie-Verlag, 1981) 188–91.

[43] Jean-Marc Prieur, *Acta Andreae: Praefatio-Commentarius* (2 vols.; CCSA 5–6; Turnhout: Brepols, 1989) 1.344–67.

[44] François Bovon, "Les paroles de vie dans les *Actes de l'apôtre André*," in *Apocrypha: Le champ des Apocryphes* 2 (1991) 99–117; reprinted in idem *Révélations et écritures: Nouveau Testament et littérature apocryphe chrétienne* (Monde de la Bible 26; Geneva: Labor et Fides, 1993) 271–87. English translation, see below pp. 238–52.

[45] On the second-century image of the apostles, cf. Wolfgang A. Bienert, "Das Apostelbild in der altchristlichen Überlieferung," in *Neutestamentliche Apokryphen in deutscher Übersetzung*, vol. 2: *Apostolisches, Apokalypsen, und Verwandtes* (ed. Wilhelm Schneemelcher; 5th ed.; Tübingen: Mohr Siebeck, 1989) 6–28.

[46] Cf. François Bovon, "Le privilège pascal de Marie-Madeleine," *NTS* 30 (1984) 50–62; reprinted in idem, *Révélations et écritures*, 215–30.

Priscilla and Aquila[47] and Andronicus and Junia.[48] The institutionalization of the circle of the twelve apostles coincides with the marginalization of the role of these women. Some heterodox Christian circles, however, venerated their memory.

IX.

Having noted the enormous diffusion of the two-part structure of Gospel and Apostle, we turn to its function. This structure was not put in place during a period of religious calm, nor in a spiritual desert. Instead, it existed at a time when Christians were confronted with diverse propaganda accompanied by claims of authority. In this context, the Christians drew upon Jewish theology to present their new claims: a new instance of revelation, a kind of ultimate "deuteronomic" work, a new and final testament. Claiming authority, they hoped this structure would be normative and have polemical value.

In fact, the Gospel-Apostle pattern was confronted with contemporary religious expressions that were both polytheistic and pantheistic. It also spread during an age that the Christians, marked by apocalypticism, decried as a period of decay. The image was one of a humanity marked by hatred, division, and violence, a world passing away and reaching its end (1 Cor 7:31).

It is against this background that the first Christian communities framed a revelation that proclaimed Christ's victory over evil, a triumph that destroyed hatred, demolishing it like a wall (Eph 2:14). These communities testified to this victory with conviction and efficacy through the voices of their apostles and messengers. Without the interpretive voice, those events remain brute facts that offer some evidence but that need the persuasive influence of the message. And without the harshness of the facts – the scandal of the Cross, the enigma of the Word incarnate – the apostolic language is just another cheap form of spirituality in the religious "supermarket" of antiquity.

Although the event of Christ occurred in the past, in the history of God and his people the apostolic word is unfurled, fragile yet effective, in the present. Shaken by the voices of other religions and other philosophies without, this word is also threatened by sectarian and heretical tendencies within the church. The structure of Gospel-Apostle thus allows for the communication of the message but also serves in a polemical fashion to defend the truth and to criticize other models.

---

[47] Rom 16:3–5; 1 Cor 16:19; 2 Tim 4:19; Acts 18:2, 18, 26.

[48] Rom 16:7. Contemporary feminist exegesis insists rightly on "Junia" as the true name, a woman's name; cf. Bernadette Brooten, "Junia ... hervorragend unter den Aposteln, Röm 16,7," in *Frauenbefreieung: Biblische und theologische Argumente* (ed. Elisabeth Moltmann-Wendell; 3d ed.; Munich: Kaiser, 1982) 148–51. This view was expressed earlier by Marie-Joseph Lagrange, *Saint Paul: Epître aux Romains* (Études bibliques; Paris: Gabalda, 1916) 366.

To the kerygmatic and apologetic functions we can add a third, which is useful within the Christian community. Through its bipolarity, the normative structure of Gospel and Apostle allows the community to grow in faith. A free faith expresses itself through the practice of love. The Gospel and Apostle pattern call for the ethic required by God, or expressed through both the two-part love command and the words of Zechariah's hymn, the *Benedictus*, "to serve him without fear in holiness and righteousness" (Luke 1:74–75).

The Christian consciousness is further enlightened by the joining of gesture and the word, thus echoing the events of the gospel and the message of the apostles. Believers can grow in faith when they remember, as Luke says, both what Jesus has *done* and what he has *taught* (Acts 1:1). They must also arrange their ecclesial life according to this two-part principle, which finds expression in the diaconate of the word and the diaconate of the table, the founding of which is evoked by the author of Acts (Acts 6:2–4).

The language of edification recalls the metaphors of the house and the foundation. That the foundation of the church is in one place said to be Christ (1 Cor 3:11) and in another place the apostles (Eph 2:20) suggests an indispensable complementarity of these two entities.

X.

The plurality of gospels might have posed a problem for first-century Christians[49] and putting their opinions and remembrances into writing may have had unsettling consequences.[50] But the formation of a two-pronged collection, made up of gospels and epistles, does not seem to have upset them. Clearly, the theological structure of Gospel and Apostle had prepared them for this development. Various events had cleared the way: Paul added his epistles to the oral gospel; Matthew, following Mark, compiled the memories of Jesus in the form of a book that stressed the foundational role of the apostles, and of Peter in particular; Luke's narrative relates both the story of Jesus and the story of the witnesses of the resurrection; the Johannine community channeled the revelation addressed through the Son to the beloved disciple and added epistles to their gospel; following the same principles, the orthodox communities in the middle of the second century formed a collection of gospels and numerous epistles. At the same time Marcion, too, honored the structure of Gospel and Apostle.

---

[49]　Cf. Helmut Merkel, *Die Pluralität der Evangelien als theologisches und exegetisches Problem in der Alten Kirche* (Traditio Christiana 3; Bern: Lang, 1978).

[50]　Lukas Vischer, "Die Rechtfertigung der Schriftstellerei in der Alten Kirche," *TZ* 12 (1956) 320–36.

The New Testament canon, faithful to the underlying theological structure, binds revelation to history following a logic proper to Christianity; it closely associates the gospel as the foundational event and the gospel as good news. In so doing, it proclaims not only a historic beginning but also claims an indispensable apostolic mediation.

Israel in the Theology of the Apostle Paul*

For the past fifty years German exegesis of the New Testament has been intensely preoccupied with the fate of Israel, and one can understand why. German scholars have thoroughly expounded Romans 9–11, and many prefer to stress the continuity of the church with the people of Israel rather than the sudden discontinuity found in Christ. If the church did not "succeed" Israel, then what is the respective status of them both today? In France, the situation is different: the memory of the French Resistance Movement against the Germans during World War II often engendered sympathy for the Jewish cause, but the catholic hostility toward the Jews, though now in the past, has never been forgotten. In the United States, one witnesses a vigorous passage of arms between the adversaries of "successionism" and the fundamentalists, who make use of those statements in the Gospels and the Epistles that so violently oppose the Pharisees and the Jews in general.[1]

As for me, I propose the following three-step approach. First, we shall confine ourselves to those Pauline texts that concern Judaism by endeavoring to respect

---

* I thank David Warren for translating this paper into English.

[1] Besides the commentaries on the Epistle to the Romans, especially those of Charles E.B. Cranfield, Ernst Käsemann, Franz J. Leenhardt, Ulrich Wilckens and Joseph A. Fitzmyer, I here restrict the essential bibliography to the following: Richard H. Bell, *Provoked to Jealousy: The Origin and Purpose of the Jealousy Motif in Romans 9–11* (WUNT 2.63; Tübingen: Mohr Siebeck, 1994), which contains a rich bibliography on pp. 363–416; François Bovon, "Paul aux côtés d'Israël et des Nations (Rm 9–11)," *BullCPE* 44 (1992) nos. 7–8, 6–16; Lorenzo De Lorenzi, ed., *Die Israelfrage nach Röm 9–11* (Benedictina, Section biblico-œcuménique 3; Rome: Abbey of St. Paul outside the Walls, 1977), a collection of articles in several languages; Stanislas Lyonnet, "Le rôle d'Israël dans l'histoire du salut selon Rom 9–11," in *Israelfrage nach Röm 9–11,* 42–47, 161–67, 174 (reprinted in Stanislas Lyonnet, *Études sur l'épître aux Romains* [AnBib 120; Rome: Editrice Pontificio Istituto biblico, 1989] 264–73); Christian Müller, *Gottes Gerechtigkeit und Gottesvolk. Eine Untersuchung zu Römer 9–11* (FRLANT 86; Göttingen: Vandenhoeck & Ruprecht, 1964); Franz Mußner, *Tractate on the Jews: The Significance of Judaism for Christian Faith* (trans. with an introduction by Leonard Swidler; Philadelphia: Fortress Press, 1984); Heikki Räisänen, "Römer 9–11: Analyse eines geistigen Ringens," in *ANRW* 2.25.4 (ed. Wolfgang Haase and Hildegard Temporini; Berlin: de Gruyter, 1987) 2891–939 (there is a bibliography in the last four pages); François Refoulé, "*... et ainsi tout Israël sera sauvé,*" *Romains 11,25–32* (LD 117; Paris: Cerf, 1984); Karl Hermann Schelkle, *Israel im Neuen Testament* (Darmstadt: Wissenschaftliche Buchgesellschaft, 1985); Christophe Senft, "L'élection d'Israël et la justification (Romains 9–11)," in *L'Évangile, hier et aujourd'hui* (Mélanges offerts au professeur Franz-J. Leenhardt; Geneva: Labor et Fides, 1968) 131–42; Folker Siegert, *Argumentation bei Paulus, gezeigt an Röm 9–11* (WMUNT 34; Tübingen: Mohr/Siebeck, 1985).

the historical dimension, ancient Judaism having become variegated in the course of its formation; we shall examine the vocabulary, the categories and the texts. The second step, more hermeneutical in nature, shall attempt to construct a comprehensive picture of Paul's theology of Israel in order to understand on what basis the Pauline structure rests. The third step shall deal with that which German theology calls the *Sachkritik*. Modestly, but firmly, I will confront the Pauline theology of Israel, and I invite you to take part in the debate.

Inventory and Description of the Texts

To begin, there are a number of expressions whose degree of synonymy is unknown, but whose polysemy can be established. There is, for example, the term "Israel," whose ethnic component the apostle retains in Rom 9:31 ("But Israel, who did strive for the righteousness that is based on the law, did not succeed in fulfilling that law"), but which he claims without hesitation for the church in Gal 6:16 ("peace be upon them, and mercy, and upon the Israel of God"). In Romans 9, Paul meditates on the identity of the true Israel when he writes "For not all Israelites truly belong to Israel" (Rom 9:6). Nevertheless the Israelites (Rom 9:4) do exist as a social reality: these are those whom the apostle calls his "brothers," a term he defines with the words "my kindred according to the flesh" (Rom 9:3); they are recognizable by the blessings they possess (see the impressive list in Rom 9:4, "to them belong the adoption, the glory, the covenants, the giving of the law, the worship, and the promises"). There is no reason to believe that Paul has put this enumeration in the past.

The ancients – as we may recall – were fond of distinguishing between peoples and took pleasure in characterizing them by using generalizations. These peoples would at times instill fear, at other times admiration, sometimes jealousy, and at other times contempt. Subdivisions were added to the biblical distinction between Israel and the Gentiles and the Hellenic difference between the Greeks and the barbarians. The Greeks obviously knew to distinguish the Egyptians from the Persians, and the Jews did not confuse the Babylonians with the Romans.[2] From this point of view, the Pauline assessment is simple. True to the categories of his people, Paul distinguishes between Israel and the nations, the Jews and the Greeks (see 1 Cor 1:22). He does not even mention the Romans as a people. As for the Egyptians, they figure as personages of the past who were associated with the Exodus.

It is, moreover, always interesting to examine the name, or names, that peoples are fond of applying to themselves. Paul – as we have just seen – employs the term

---

[2] On the notion of placing one people above another, particularly the Greeks, see Arnaldo Dante Momigliano, *Alien Wisdom: The Limits of Hellenization* (Cambridge: Cambridge University Press, 1975).

Israel for his people. But when he proudly parades himself before the Philippians and Corinthians, he chooses yet another name, that of "Hebrew": "a Hebrew of Hebrews" he boasts, in addition to being "of the race of Israel, of the tribe of Benjamin" (Phil 3:5; cf. 2 Cor 11:22: "Are they Hebrews? So am I. Are they Israelites? So am I. Are they the seed of Abraham? So am I." – translations mine). Here the terms must be taken in a literal sense to designate a social and historical grandeur. Unless I am mistaken, the title "Hebrew" is never employed by Paul in a figurative sense, as he continues to hold onto the First Dispensation.[3] But on the other hand, just as the term "Israel" can have a figurative meaning (see, for example, Gal 6:16), the expression "seed of Abraham" can also be used in a second, figurative sense: the σπέρμα 'Αβραάμ is the Christ, and then by reason of filial adoption it becomes the Christians (see Gal 3:15–18). The apostle appears to be sufficiently free to use either the literal or figurative sense at his convenience. The categories of "flesh" and "spirit" (σάρξ and πνεῦμα) allow him to establish a theological distinction between the two manifestations of "Israel" and the "seed of Abraham."[4] In Rom 9:3, which we have just read, Paul explains that the "brothers" in question here are not Christians but his "kinsmen according to the flesh."

How, then, does Paul use the term Ἰουδαῖος? On one occasion (Rom 2:28–29), he constructs a wordplay and distinguishes between the Jew "manifest" and the Jew "in secret," that is to say, the Jew of the Christian.[5] Nevertheless, usually in those passages where he elaborates his doctrine, he is thinking of Jew in its more literal, racial sense, his brother according to race. Thus in Rom 2:17, when – in a flight of rhetoric – he employs the pattern of the diatribe and begins to question his imaginary challenger, he uses the word "Jew" literally: "But if you," he says to him, who "call yourself a Jew ..." (εἰ δὲ σὺ Ἰουδαῖος ἐπονομάζῃ κτλ., Rom 2:17).[6] The same observation holds true for the expression "the circumcision" and "those of the circumcision": it nearly always concerns Jews or Christians of Jewish origin (see Gal 2:8). In one instance, however, Paul applies the title "circumcision" to Christians (whoever they may be, even including pagan Christians). In one passage of extreme violence he writes: "Beware of the dogs, beware of the evil workers, beware of the incision [κατατομή]. For it is we who are the circumcision

---

[3] On the term "Hebrew" as Paul applies it to himself, see Joachim Wanke, "Ἑβραῖος," *EDNT* 1.369–70; Niels Peter Lemche, "Hebrew," *ABD* (1992) 3.95.

[4] On the Pauline distinction between the flesh and the spirit, see Robert Jewett, *Paul's Anthropological Terms: A Study of Their Use in Conflict Settings* (AGJU 10; Leiden: Brill, 1971).

[5] See Ernst Käsemann, *Commentary on Romans* (trans. and ed. Geoffrey W. Bromiley; Grand Rapids: Eerdmans, 1980) 71–77.

[6] One may wonder, among other things, if Ἰουδαῖος always signified a "Jew," whether from Rome or Alexandria, or if on occasion the term could also designate an inhabitant from Judea, hence the "Judean." The sense of "Judean" seems exceptional to me, and I see only 1 Thess 2:14 where this meaning can be justified by reason of the mention of Judea. Elsewhere it is necessary to translate the term as "Jew." See Horst Kuhli, "Ἰουδαῖος," *EDNT* (1991) 2.193–97.

[περιτομή], we who adore God in spirit, we who glory in Christ Jesus and have no confidence in the flesh" (Phil 3:2–3, translation mine).[7]

According to Paul, every human being belongs to a γένος, to a race, to a "people" (ἐκ γένους Ἰσραήλ, Phil 3:5), and every human being has ancestors. The apostle himself is a descendant of Abraham according to the flesh (Rom 11:1; 2 Cor 11:22). This people is organized into tribes, and Paul is proud of being a member of the tribe of Benjamin (Rom 11:1; Phil 3:5). Certain outward marks characterize this people: the law (ἡ νομοθεσία, "the legislation," Rom 9:4), the cult (ἡ λατρεία, Rom 9:4), and the relationship with the One who is confessed as the only true God (adoption, glory, convenants, promises, according to the list cited earlier, Rom 9:4). It is, he hastens to state, from this people, from this ancestry, that the Christ proceeded "according to the flesh" (Rom 9:5). There is, then, a boundary between Israel and other peoples, between Israel and the nations. This separation is objective: it corresponds to the reality of facts, but it does not have to be appreciated immediately in terms of worth, that is, in terms of the superiority of a chosen people. In the second part of this paper, we shall examine the "usefulness" (with some restrictions) Paul confers on the reality of Judaism; for now let us simply say that, as a son of this people, Paul recognizes and respects those favors that historical Israel had at its disposal.

As one knows, this respect for the principle of reality, this legitimate affection for his people (see Rom 9:3; 10:1), lived in the apostle's thought along with a violent criticism of Israel. Paul does not lay the blame on the favors received from God as such, but on the usage Israel made of these. At the root of his vehemence, there is no juvenile reaction, no revolt against his parents, no being "fed up" with all of his social and cultural heritage. Rather, there is the new way in which Paul views the world since the religious experience he had on the road to Damascus. At that time his encounter with the resurrected Christ taught him the new direction God has given to history. The fullness of time having arrived (Gal 4:4), obedience to the law must henceforth be qualified. But if obedience to the law is not rooted in faith, if it is only seeking its own fulfillment, if it obscures the distinction between the letter and the Spirit, or between the flesh and the Spirit, and if it manifests itself outside the realm of freedom, then in reality such outward obedience actually becomes disobedience: "Christ," he writes to the Galatians, who were tempted to fall back under the yoke of the law, "redeemed us from the curse of the law" (Gal 3:13).

Even if there is a difference between Israel and the nations, Paul realizes that all humans are basically alike in their being and moral attitude. They all share, each in

---

[7] On this passage, see Jean-François Collange, *L'épître de saint Paul aux Philippiens* (CNT 10a; Neuchâtel: Delachaux et Niestlé, 1973) 109–13; Helmut Koester, "The Purpose of the Polemic of a Pauline Fragment," *NTS* 8 (1961–1962) 317–32; François Bovon, "The New Person and the Law according to the Apostle Paul," in idem, *New Testament Traditions and Apocryphal Narratives* (PTMS 36; Allison Park, Pa.: Pickwick, 1995) 15–25, 183–86.

his or her own way, the very same tragic guilt. Romans 1–3 establishes this truth: regardless of whether it is the law written on stone or in the heart, both Jews and Gentiles have sinned and lost the brilliance of the Adamic glory that existed before the Fall (Rom 3:23). In the same way, belonging to the people of God – that is, the church – no longer depends on a physical belonging to historical Israel. It depends on the work of God in Jesus Christ and his acceptance by faith. In Christ, truly "There is no longer Jew or Greek, there is no longer slave or free, there is no longer male and female" (Gal 3:28). All are dead in Adam; all return to life in Christ (Rom 5:12–21).

Paul's criticism of Israel can, at times, take on an offensive tone and an intolerable violence. In ridicule, "circumcision" becomes "incision" (Phil 3:2, translation mine), and the blessings of Israel are considered "rubbish" that the apostle is only glad to be rid of (Phil 3:8). As for the descendants of Abraham, those children of Israel, Paul disqualifies them and calls them the children of the slave Hagar, children then of Ishmael (Gal 4:21–31). Such a condemnation, let us state, does not proceed from the exterior of Israel. It springs from its center. As is characteristic of prophetic vehemence, it draws on scripture (Rom 2:17–24).[8] In the passage from the Epistle to the Galatians to which I have just referred, with respect to the two cities Paul begins his reasoning with the following irony: "Tell me, you who desire to be subject to the law, will you not listen to the law?" (Gal 4:21). The victory of Christ and the presence of the Spirit provide the hermeneutical criteria to understand the scriptures. He does not need to wear the veil that once hid the face of Moses from the Israelites: it is with an uncovered face that the Christians reflect the glory of God (2 Cor 3:12–18).

The opposition of the flesh and the Spirit, as I have already stated, comes to Paul's aid in a decisive way. He himself belongs to a Judaism that, in Alexandria and the dispersion, thought it best to understand the biblical anthropomorphisms and ritual commandments in a spiritual sense. He is part of the stream of Jewish spiritualists who do not deny their patriotic heritage.[9] In his eyes, his personal journey is characteristic of his people as a whole. His life before the road to Damascus corresponds to the state of fleshly Israel that still does not accept the gospel. To hold to the letter of the commandments in a servile observance represents, in his opinion, a way to satisfy the flesh. The dualism of 2 Corinthians 3 is inescapable. The ministry of the new covenant is a ministry of the Spirit and of righteousness, whereas the old dispensation is called "the ministry of death" (ἡ διακονία τοῦ θανάτου, 2 Cor 3:7): "For the letter kills, but the Spirit gives life" (2 Cor 3:6). The transformation that took place in him on the road to Damascus[10] never-

---

[8] Isa 52:5 is cited in Rom 2:24: "The name of God is blasphemed among the Gentiles because of you."

[9] On Paul's social, intellectual, and spiritual origin, see Martin Hengel, "Der vorchristliche Paulus," *ThBei* 21 (1990) 174–95; and Bell, *Provoked to Jealousy*, 286–301.

[10] On this event, see Philippe H. Menoud, "Revelation and Tradition: The Influence of Paul's

theless leaves hope for those of his race. For, it is God who acts. It is God's right to mold the vases. It is God's right to choose and to make alive. For a time, God molds Israel from two kinds of vessels, vessels of choice and vessels of wrath, just as in former times God hardened Pharaoh but took pity on Israel – or formerly – loved Jacob but hated Esau. This dualism is not, however, the last word from God: it involves a spectacle in which one waits for the cathartic jolt – Israel, all Israel, shall be saved (Rom 11:25–26).

If the Pauline criticism of Israel is Jewish in nature, drawing inspiration from the prophets and Deuteronomy (the hardening of the people, the rejection of God's messengers), then the positive theological categories to which Paul appeals are also highly biblical, deriving from the Hebrew Bible, an intrinsic part of the Jewish heritage. Even the apostle's christology can be understood as a re-reading of Jewish Messianism. The Jewish literature we refer to as "intertestamental" attests to a succession of divine figures, of hypostases: the Wisdom, the Name, the Presence, the Righteousness, the Word, and the Spirit were all functioning as mediators between the transcendent God and the creation.[11] But these also indicate the presence of a plurality in the unity of the Divine. Some esoteric Jewish milieux, such as that of *3 Enoch* with its mention of Metatron even go so far as to give to God an angelic companion.[12]

Another great theme in Paul's theology of Israel is the calling of the nations. Trained in Jewish exegesis, Paul does not cease manifesting the biblical roots of his thesis. He manages to convince his readers by spiritualizing the concept of Israel, by redefining obedience in terms of hearing and faith and interpreting the death of Jesus as a covenantal sacrifice. While one may reproach Paul for his exegesis, in his own mind he believes that he is being faithful to his Jewish heritage in thinking the way he does. His new definition of the people of God (there is no longer a difference between Jew and Greek, Rom 10:12) rests on a biblical citation, Joel 3:5, that in the Septuagint reads: "Everyone who calls on the name of the Lord shall be saved" (Rom 10:13).

The same can be said for the other great Pauline themes, such as the new covenant, the promise, election, creation, redemption, faith, and obedience. Nevertheless, Paul is not so concerned to root these in scripture, and he neglects Jewish traditions. He does not, for instance, write down the spiritual gifts or the organ-

---

Conversion on His Theology," *Int* 7 (1953) 131–41, reprinted in idem, *Jesus Christ and the Faith: A Collection of Studies* (PTMS 18; Pittsburgh: Pickwick, 1978) 31–46.

[11] For bibliography on this process of personification, see François Bovon, "The Christ, the Faith and Wisdom in the Epistle to the Hebrews (Hebrews 11 and 1)," in idem, *New Testament Traditions*, 127–29, 222–23.

[12] See Philip S. Alexander, "3 (Hebrew Apocalypse of) Enoch: A New Translation and Introduction," in *The Old Testament Pseudepigrapha* (ed. James H. Charlesworth; 2 vols.; New York: Doubleday, 1983–1985) 1.223–302, esp. 241–45; Philip S. Alexander, "Enoch, Third Book of," *ABD* (1992) 2.522–26; cf. Marinus de Jonge, *Christology in Context: The Earliest Christian Response to Jesus* (Philadelphia: Westminster, 1988).

ization of ministries in Israel's past. Similarly, he rarely occupies himself with the Mosaic law when he delineates the limits of Christian ethics, with the exception of the commandment to love one's neighbor, which in his eyes constitutes the heart of the matter (see Gal 5:14; Rom 13:8–10).[13] The moral catechism of 1 Thess 4 is eloquent and approximates more the moral philosophy of Paul's time than the Mosaic regulations. And yet, for all that, Paul considers himself faithful to scripture, just as someone like Philo of Alexandria or the Tannaim believed themselves to be. Actually, he was not wrong. The historicity of the truth forces such reconstructions. Without a reformulation of the biblical heritage in new constellations, there is no survival of the traditional blessings.[14]

By now we have identified the major texts relating to our subject, which are those found in Rom 1–3, 9–11; 2 Cor 11; Gal 4; and Phil 3.

Interpretation

Just as Rabbi Akiba believed in the second century that he had found the Messiah in the person of Simon bar Kokhba,[15] so also Saul the Pharisee was convinced that Jesus of Nazareth was the Messiah and that he had encountered him alive on the road to Damascus (cf. Gal 1:15–17). By reason of this event, Paul reoriented his own religion, and to accomplish this he availed himself of his Jewish-Hellenistic origin and education.

For Paul, the whole past pales and grows old before this present Deliverer. A discontinuity has set itself up between the law of old and the Christ of today, between the old covenant and the new. From now on, the only thing that counts is Christ: "For to me, living is Christ and dying [i.e., to be reunited with Christ] is gain" (Phil 1:21). Those things that are valued by Paul the new Christian are also valued by the entire Christian community as a whole. Though the church had its very origin within Israel, its validity does not depend on historical continuity with Israel, but only on theological continuity, thanks to the work of Christ from his preexistence, and thanks to the intervention of the Spirit since the time of the prophecies. Paul understands that it is God's benevolent initiative, and not national patrimony, that has saved and continues to save every human being. It is the

---

[13] On this commandment in Paul, see Hans Hübner, *Law in Paul's Thought* (Edinburgh: Clark, 1984).

[14] On the Hebrew Bible in Paul, see Edward Earle Ellis, *Paul's Use of the Old Testament* (5th ed.; Grand Rapids: Baker, 1991); Moisés Silva, "Old Testament in Paul," in *Dictionary of Paul and his Letters* (ed. Gerald F. Hawthorne, Ralph P. Martin and Daniel G. Reid; Downersgrove: InterVarsity, 1993) 630–42.

[15] First stated in *y. Taan.* 4.7 or 5 (6) (68d); see Robert Goldenberg, "Akiba, Rabbi," *ABD* (1992) 1.137–38, who points out that some scholars have questioned whether Akiba was an enthusiastic supporter of Bar Kokhba. See also Moïse Schwab, *Le Talmud de Jérusalem* (12 vols.; Paris: Maisonneuve, 1871–1890; reprinted in 6 vols., Paris: Maisonneuve, 1977) 4.189.

Word of God and not the religious heritage of Israel that gives birth to and sustains the church.

In opposition to one prevalent thesis,[16] I do not think that this divine strategy began with the incarnation of the Son. Actually – and the Pauline exegesis of Genesis in Romans 9 demonstrates this very point – the divine method is as old as the world itself. If Isaac was born in spite of Sarah's sterility, this was by reason of the free act of God (Rom 9:6–9). If Jacob, the younger, was preferred over Esau, the firstborn, this was by reason of God's free choice (Rom 9:10–13). If Abraham was at the origin of God's people, this was not by reason of his works and merits, but by reason of the God who imputed to him his faith as righteousness (Rom 4:1–25).[17] According to my reading of the apostle Paul, the working of God remains constant. If it happens that a grandfather Abraham, a father Isaac, and a son Jacob have constituted the people of God, then this is by reason of divine election that was repeated to each generation, and not by a transmission of familial privileges. If historical and social continuity existed for the people of God, then this was for theological reasons by virtue of the faithfulness of the election.

It is necessary, then, that Paul state in what way this election (ἐκλογή, see 1 Thess 1:4; Rom 9:11; 11:5, 7, 28) is carried out. The election is realized by a selection: Israel is chosen from among the nations, the Christ is chosen from within Israel, Christians are chosen from among Israel and then from among the nations. In order to show the divine origin of this election, Paul uncovers in each case a surprising choice. Those who are selected are neither the most powerful nor the richest, neither the most intelligent nor the most beautiful. On the contrary, God is pleased to shock the onlookers and to choose without taking outward appearances into account. He indicates in this way that the continuity of Israel is established from on high. The Word of God has not failed. God's plan remains the same (Rom 9:6). Rather, it is the humans who have broken faith and become hardened. Not all of Israel is Israel!

This principle is valid not only for the time period following the coming of Jesus Christ but was also the principle that God adopted from the very beginning. The proof is found in Isaac, who was elected not because he was Abraham's son,

---

[16] This would be the traditional Catholic position; see Gervais Dumeige, ed. and trans., *Textes doctrinaux du magistère de l'Église sur la foi catholique* (2d ed.; Paris: Orante, 1975) 284: "God formerly had chosen for himself a specific people with whom he had made a covenant. The new covenant with the new people has been made in Christ. The deeply historical aspect of the church is thus underscored" ("Dieu s'était choisi jadis un peuple particulier avec lequel il avait conclu une alliance. L'alliance nouvelle avec le peuple nouveau a été conclue dans le Christ. L'aspect profondément historique de l'Église est ainsi souligné").

[17] There was a controversy between Günter Klein (*Rekonstruktion und Interpretation. Gesammelte Aufsätze zum Neuen Testament* [BEvTh 50; Munich: Kaiser, 1969] 145–69) and Ulrich Wilckens (*Rechtfertigung als Freiheit. Paulusstudien* [Neukirchen-Vluyn: Neukirchener Verlag, 1974] 33–76). As for me, I align myself with the latter: Abraham is not just a *witness* for the faith; he is the *father* of the believers. In Romans 4 the component of salvation history must not be underestimated.

but because God had *called* him to become his son. The true lineage of Abraham was spiritual from its inception. It is on this basis that the following phrase, which, though curiously constructed, is decisive: "And not all of Abraham's children are his true descendants" (Rom 9:7a).[18] It is also on this basis that the citation of Gen 21:12 acquires its special meaning according to the Septuagint: "It is through Isaac that descendants shall be named for you" (Rom 9:7b). Your descendants – Paul here is making God the one who addresses Abraham – will exist only thanks to my will, my power, and my efficacious calling.

During the whole dispensation from Abraham to Christ, God was pleased to elect from within the people of Israel. In doing this, however, Paul sees no lack of fairness on God's part: "Is there injustice on God's part? By no means!" (Rom 9:14). This divine constancy clearly confers value on the course of history. Paul, who knows how to reject the fleshly lineage and material heritage when it concerns obtaining salvation, also knows how to recognize its value on another level. It is appropriate now for us to examine this matter further.

According to my reading of the Pauline Epistles, the lasting value of the people of Israel is easily understood from social and historical realities. Paul calls this level the level of the "flesh" (σάρξ), taken here in the positive sense of historicity. Let us observe that the apostle does not argue solely by opposition. With subtlety, he locates another condition, the human condition, between the positive life in Christ and the negative life caused by sin. If the expression ἐν πνεύματι defines life in God and if the expression κατὰ σάρκα defines the sinful life, then the expression ἐν σαρκί defines a third category where one can become either righteous or unrighteous. Thus Paul writes to the Corinthians, "For if we walk in the flesh, we do not fight according to the flesh" (2 Cor 10:3, translation mine).

The blessings of Israel belong to this last category, and in order to define their value Paul resorts to the vocabulary of "usefulness." This point does not appear to me to have received the attention it deserves until now; but what kind of "usefulness" is involved here? As I have said over and over again, these privileges are of no benefit for salvation. They can, however, be useful as signs: "Then what advantage has the Jew? Or what is the value of circumcision? Much, in every way. For in the first place the Jews were entrusted with the oracles of God." (Rom 3:1–2). These lines are indeed difficult to understand, but they appear to me to answer the question. Upon receiving the law and the land, the people of Israel likewise received the promise of future blessings. They have been able to capture the voice of

---

[18] The following translation is that of Louis Segond, *La Sainte Bible* (3 vols.; Geneva: Cherbuliez, 1874–1880; Paris: Société biblique britannique et étrangère, 1910; reprinted, 1931): "Et, pour être la postérité d'Abraham, ils ne sont pas tous ses enfants." According to *The Jerusalem Bible* (Garden City, N.Y.: Doubleday, 1966): "Not all the descendants of Abraham are his true children." According to the *Traduction œcuménique de la Bible* (integral ed.; Paris: Alliance Biblique Universelle/Cerf, 1988): "Et pour être la descendance d'Abraham, tous ne sont pas ses enfants."

God and hear the divine prophecies. They get to keep, then, the privilege of knowing the rules of the game and the route that leads to the ultimate goal. Israel knows that God is truthful and powerful, and that human disobedience does not put in jeopardy the power of God's word: "What if some were unfaithful? Will their faithlessness nullify the faithfulness of God? By no means!" (Rom 3:3–4a). God's good deeds remain in force and retain their value as a sign. From this point of view, even the events that marked the life of Israel in the desert are "useful" – useful as signs. Having become narrative texts in the scripture, they aid in understanding eschatological realities; a good example is found in 1 Cor 10:1–13: the miracle at the Red Sea, the crossing of the desert, and the water gushing forth from the rock help us understand Christian baptism, the vigilance expected of Christians, and the spiritual presence of Christ. It is also profitable to recount the exodus from Egypt, for it helps us grasp the redemption offered by Christ, "our Passover" (1 Cor 5:7). As long as asking for signs is done in faith, Israel does not err in making this request (1 Cor 1:22).

Historical Israel is a reality blessed by God as well as set apart and made holy by God. Paul deeply believes this; does he not spontaneously express this in statement such as "But if the first fruits are holy […] and if the root is holy […]" (Rom 11:16, translation mine)? Such exclamations allow us to discover a second "usefulness" of these good deeds, of these privileges of Israel: in accordance with the image of the graft, they will have permitted the integration of the nations into the people of God. God has planted Israel, and he has grafted the nations onto the old trunk of Jesse. The old olive tree, the ungrafted tree, is thus useful in that it receives the graft from the wild olive tree, the new tree. Here again the "usefulness" of Israel, the ungrafted olive tree, results from God alone and not from the tree itself or from its merits. Moreover, God has been compelled to deal severely with this olive tree: the branches that belonged to the tree by nature were not spared (Rom 11:21).[19] While appealing to another image, the apostle states in the same chapter 11 that Israel has undergone a "diminishing" or a "lessening" (Rom 11:12, translation mine). This "diminishing" promoted the "augmentation" of the people of God through annexation of the nations, that is to say, the "riches" of the Gentiles. Such is the second "usefulness" of Israel and the good deeds that belong to them: they serve as a valuable tool in the hands of God for the realization of his universalistic design.[20]

Paul considers yet a third usefulness of the divine blessings accorded to Israel. This usefulness, however, has some rather paradoxical aspects; the evil use of these privileges breeds evil and thereby speeds redemption: "But law came in, with the result that the trespass multiplied; but where sin increased, grace

---

[19] On the famous allegory of the two olive trees, see Siegert, *Argumentation bei Paulus,* 167–71; and William S. Campbell, "Olive Tree," in *Dictionary of Paul and His Letters,* 642–44.

[20] On this passage (Rom 11:11–15), see Bell, *Provoked to Jealousy,* 107–67.

abounded all the more" (Rom 5:20). Without sin, the law would have been on par with life and salvation. Circumcision itself would have cooperated with obedience (Rom 2:25). But then "You that boast in the law, do you dishonor God by breaking the law?" (Rom 2:23). Israel, who had wanted to be a guide for the blind, closed her eyes (see Rom 2:19). This human failing has its meaning; *felix culpa* ("O fortunate fault"), it encourages God to bring help to his people and to all peoples.[21]

Paul does not stop with the negative side of this declaration. He knows that a remnant of Israel perceived the signs and passed from the old covenant to the new. He knows that God has not abandoned his people (see Rom 11:1). He even dares to affirm that he has received a revelation: "I want you to understand this mystery: a hardening has come upon part of Israel, until the full number of the Gentiles has come in. And so all Israel will be saved" (Rom 11:25–26). Consequently, the fate of Israel will not be that of a shagreen skin. There will be no extinction of historical Israel, but a "fullness" (πλήρωμα) will follow the "diminishing" (Rom 11:12). This difficult expression probably receives its commentary from verse 26 cited above: "And so all Israel will be saved" (Rom 11:26).[22] Such is the content of the divine "mystery" that was revealed to the apostle. It eases the fears raised by the provisional hardening of Israel.

Appraisal of Paul's Theology of Israel

The uncertainties of exegetes, and my own hesitations as well, result in part from Paul's own obscurities; the reader of the Epistles sometimes wavers over whether to bestow a literal or a figurative meaning to the term "Israel" and its equivalents. At other times, the reader wonders whether the apostle does not excessively disqualify the old dispensation in spite of being so proud that he belongs to it.[23] Most likely, Paul did not work out his theology of Israel in one sitting. Chapters 9–11 of the Epistle to the Romans, as well as the "mystery" now revealed (Rom 11:25), attest to the slow clarification Paul the Jewish Christian was striving to attain.[24] Yet on the whole, and bearing in mind the occasional nature of some developments, it

---

[21] On the function of the law, see Bovon, "New Person," 15–25, 183–86.

[22] On this verse and the various interpretations it has been given, see Mußner, *Tractate on the Jews*, 28–38; and Refoulé, "Tout Israël," 25–30 and passim.

[23] Some of the traditional statements Paul receives, and then reuses with joy, stress the new dispensation that begins at the end of time, thanks to the work of Jesus Christ, thus Gal 1:4–5 and 4:4–5; see Bovon, "A Pre-Pauline Expression in the Epistle to the Galatians (Gal 1:4–5)," in idem, *New Testament Traditions*, 1–13, 177–83.

[24] According to Senft ("L'élection d'Israël," 131), when Paul was composing Romans 9–11 he did not have a ready-made solution. He was gradually developing his own thought as he proceeded.

seems to me that the Pauline position is well-constructed and that it works out rather clearly.

There is a history of God and his people made from love and disillusionment. There is a steadfast plan of God that abides by his election and his concrete good deeds. In this history, there is the past of the people, whose faithfulness is determined by the grace of God and the unfaithfulness that falls under the stroke of wrath.[25] And above all, there is the manifestation present in Christ at the end of time that clarifies the true identify of the people. The last situation results from God: It is God who chooses and calls the church. The Holy Spirit allows the true Israel to be recognized. All these truths are loaded with theological force and blend together numerous thoughts that are scattered throughout the gospels.[26]

In a study more than a century old,[27] Ignaz Döllinger, a Catholic historian and theologian, distinguished two periods in the Christian attitude toward Judaism. The first attitude was the one manifest by the apostles and the early Christian writers, that is, by Paul and Origen. These Christians saw the Jews as temporarily lost brothers and sisters who were going to return to their home, and they considered that the people of Israel continued to be the bearers of irrevocable traditions. This attitude of patient affection, which Döllinger judges favorably, was later followed by another attitude of fierce and aggressive polemic in the age of Constantine, in Byzantium as well as in the West during the Middle Ages. The church from that time forward interpreted the fact that Israel had remained distant from her as a hardening stained with ill will. It goes without saying that this second attitude, already rejected by Döllinger, must be severely criticized today more than ever, and this all the more as anti-Semitism has reemerged in several quarters from which it perhaps never entirely disappeared.

Personally, I wonder whether Döllinger's solution, which is also the one that triumphed at the Council of Vatican II,[28] is truly supportable today. At a time of inter-religious dialogue, is it not dangerous to assume for oneself the position of the Apostle? Is it still possible to adopt an attitude that is so paternalistic? Must one not criticize the apostle for having conceived as positive not the existence of Israel, but its stage in history? Historical Israel, according to the apostle, has

---

[25] On the manifestation of the "righteousness" and the "wrath" of God, see Rom 1:17–18 and, more generally, Rom 1:16–3:31.

[26] See, for example, Matt 11:25–27//Luke 10:21–22; Matt 23:37–39//Luke 13:34–35; Mark 12:1–12//Matt 21:33–46//Luke 20:9–19; Luke 13:23–30; Matt 8:11–12//Luke 13:28–29; Luke 18:7–8, 9–14; Matt 8:5–13//Luke 7:1–10; Mark 13:10; John 1:1–18; 5:19–29; 6:36–40, 44; 12:20–32; 14:16, 26; 15:1–8; 17:1–26.

[27] Johann Joseph Ignaz von Döllinger, "The Jews in Europe," *Studies in European History Being Academical Addresses* (3 vols. in 2; London: Murray, 1890–1894) 1.214–15. It was Karl Hermann Schelkle (*Paulus Lehrer der Väter. Die altkirchliche Auslegung von Römer 1–11* [2nd ed.; Düsseldorf: Patmos, 1959] 422–23) who drew my attention to this study.

[28] *Nostra aetate*, 4; see John T. Pawlikowski, "Judentum und Christentum," *TRE* 17 (1988) 386–403, esp. 391; Rolf Rendtorff and Hans Hermann Henrix, eds., *Die Kirchen und das Judentum. Dokumente von 1945 bis 1985* (Paderborn: Bonifacius; Munich: Kaiser, 1988) 39–44.

value, but this value must now become obsolete. Judaism is a "sign" of Christianity, or rather the people of Israel are a bridge to the Christian church. Indeed, being a Jew himself, Paul is unable to conceive of an Israel by itself, distinct from that which it had become since the incarnation of the Son of God. Must we not, here at the end of the twentieth century, consider Judaism in itself as a legitimate continuity of the Hebrew religion? Judaism and Christianity, in my view born almost at the same time, are both descended from the old trunk of Jesse. The argument from antiquity,[29] besides the fact that it is hardly a suitable theological question, is dangerous to handle, since the Christian church descended from Israel and since ancient Judaism formed itself in reaction against Hellenism and Christianity. Jews and Christians, for different reasons but both of them valid, can claim to be Abraham's heirs.[30]

Could it not be envisioned in our so-called "postmodern" period that theologians propose to their churches the acceptance of a new position: to renounce the hope of Israel's conversion by releasing its neck from christological strangulation? Have not missionary societies that minister to the Jews radically revised their practices since the Holocaust?[31] The Pauline position, however, does not have to be rejected as if we must inadvertently throw out the baby with the bath water. With its coherence and theological beauty, it can still find a place in the church, but only with internal application; it can serve to comfort and edify the faithful, and remind them of Christianity's Jewish roots and of God's benevolent love in election. From this theological position, admittedly imperfect but at least free of doctrinal imperialism, Christians could look on the Jewish community in a new way. Instead of regarding the synagogue as either an obsolete or lost entity, Christians would discover in it a venerable and legitimate religious expression. I have always been surprised by the absence of any proselytism, paternalism, or judgmental spirit directed toward Christians on the part of any Jews. Should not churches imitate this attitude and likewise accept a side by side posture that, by mutual interest, could eventually become a positive face to face relationship?

There is of course the formidable obstacle of the New Testament canon. The violence that early Christians directed toward the Pharisees and the Jewish authorities in the first century can be easily understood. It happened because the earliest Christian communities represented Jewish minorities that had been marginalized and often mistreated by those who were considered wise and intelligent in Israel. By these same excesses, they expressed how their love had been disap-

---

[29] It is known that this argument played a considerable role in the earliest period of Christianity in the apostolic fathers, particularly in Theophilus of Antioch. See Karl Baus, *Von der Urgemeinde zur frühchristlichen Grosskirche* (special edition; Handbuch der Kirchengeschichte 1; Freiburg: Herder, 1985) 209–10.

[30] See Alan F. Segal, *Rebecca's Children: Judaism and Christianity in the Roman World* (Cambridge: Harvard University Press, 1986).

[31] See Paul Gerhard Aring, "Judenmission," *TRE* 17 (1988) 325–30.

pointed. The canonization of some of their writings, gospels and epistles, has, however, made this violence normative.[32] Later, when political power fell into Christian hands, an anti-Semitic use of the New Testament became – alas – commonplace in the Orthodox Church of the East as well as in Catholic and Protestant churches of the West.[33] This situation is a tragic one for the New Testament, which through the centuries has become something other than a fountain of faith and illumination; it has also become a watering hole for religious and racial hatred.[34]

---

[32] On the canon of the New Testament and its fixation, see François Bovon and Enrico Norelli, "Dal kerygma al canone. Lo statuo degli scritti neotestamentari nel secondo secolo," *CNS* 15 (1994) 525–40 (this entire issue of *Cristianesimo nella storia* is devoted to the formation of the canon of the New Testament in the second century).

[33] On the anti-Semitic use of the New Testament, see Heinz Schreckenberg, *Die christlichen Adversus-Judaeos-Texte und ihr literarisches und historisches Umfeld (1.–11. Jh.)* (2d ed.; Frankfurt: Lang, 1990); Rainer Kampling, "Neutestamentliche Texte als Bausteine der späteren Adversus-Judaeos-Literatur," in *Christlicher Antijudaismus und jüdischer Antipaganismus. Ihre Motive und Hintergründe in den ersten drei Jahrhunderten* (ed. H. Frohnhofen; Hamburger Theologische Studien 3; Hamburg: Steinmann & Steinmann, 1990) 121–38.

[34] Curiously, the analytical index of proper names for the *Textes doctrinaux du magistère de l'Église sur la foi catholique* (no. 16) contains no reference to either Israel or election.

III. Apocryphal and Patristic Literature

Jesus' Missionary Speech as Interpreted in the Patristic Commentaries and the Apocryphal Narratives

I. Introduction

The sending out of the apostles and Jesus' missionary speech (Matt 10//Mark 6//Luke 9 and 10) form both the background and the focus of this paper.[1] The usual treatment of this pericope is to make a comparison between the synoptic Gospels, to detect the oldest, traditional elements and establish the missionary scheme of Jesus in the context of first-century Jewish life, a backward direction in time. But my intention here is the contrary, that is, to inquire into the *subsequent* life of the Gospels, into the reception and interpretation of these texts in patristic times, not only to understand the historical effects of these particular canonical texts but also to draw some conclusions about the time of Jesus and the early church through a retrospective deduction; this implies looking ahead, beyond the events themselves.

Between the second and fifth centuries C.E., Christian theologians gave a full account of Jesus' missionary speech in their interpretations of the synoptic Gospels and, in a simultaneous development, Christian novelists attempted to tell the stories of the apostles' missions and martyrdoms. As a result of this twofold effort, we have on one side the patristic commentaries on the Gospels, those of Origen, Jerome, Ambrose and Cyril of Alexandria; and on the other side, the so-called apocryphal acts of the apostles, those of Peter, John, and Philip.

It is my intention to compare these two contemporaneous productions, to inquire into their functions, and finally, to test the following hypothesis: are these two kinds of literature not two legitimate ways of interpreting the teaching of Jesus, the one intellectual and theological, the other imaginative and narrative? I would even suggest that these two streams of Christian literature are two logical products of a first-century reality: that is, they are the simultaneous interpretation of Jesus' teachings on a *reflective* level, as attested in the hermeneutics of the Pauline letters, and on a *narrative* level, through the telling of stories that provide

---

[1] These pages are dedicated to Professor Lars Hartman on the occasion of his sixty-fifth birthday. He has demonstrated his exegetic acumen and his theological wisdom for many years with modesty, brio and humor. I express my thanks to him for deepening the connections between exegetes of different cultural and religious spheres.

an interpretive fulfillment of the prophecies and prescriptions of Jesus as attested
in the Acts of the Apostles. Theological interpretation and narrative verification
were probably two complementary ways of receiving the Christian legacy.

In the first section of this paper, I will characterize several patristic commentaries on Jesus' missionary speech; in the second, I will focus on the noteworthy
points in the apocryphal novels devoted to the apostles; and in the third, I will
make a critical comparison between these two strands of Chistianity in order to
test my own hypothesis.

But before that, let us briefly recall the biblical situation: the sending of the disciples is told in such a similar way by Mark and Q (the second synoptic source)
that we may presume it was based on a single, original literary unit. To quote Ferdinand Hahn: "Part of this primary redaction was first the sending, then the question of equipment, then the prescriptions about the stay in the houses, finally the
behavior in the cities."[2] This primitive version was probably a Christian post-
Easter construction with archaic, pre-Easter, independent elements. Both Mark
and Q received and adapted this literary unit. Matthew then merged these two
versions of Mark and Q into a single episode (Matt 10) whereas Luke reproduced
them separately, making out of Mark the sending of the Twelve (Luke 9) and of Q
the sending of the Seventy-two (Luke 10).

2. The Patristic Commentators

The reader of patristic commentaries – whether Eastern or Western – encounters
several surprises. First, whereas the biblical pericope is in *our* eyes a missionary
text, the Church Fathers treat it in the context of their ecclesiological concerns. In
what can be considered the first commentary on Luke's Gospel, the fourth book
of the *Adversus Marcionem* by Tertullian – a passionate and polemical interpretation to be sure – the African writer offers strangely little on the sending itself (in
his pages on Luke 9).[3] Similarly, Ambrose, in his *Homilies on Luke's Gospel*,
understands the lambs and wolves metaphor not as the situation of Christian
missionaries in the midst of pagans, but as the dramatic and actual tension between Catholics and heretics (the Arians).[4] Along the same line, the Venerable
Bede in his commentary on Luke, makes a twofold ecclesiological equation: the
Twelve of Luke 9 are to be understood as the bishops, whereas the Seventy-two
are to be seen as predecessors of the priests.[5]

---

[2] Ferdinand Hahn, *Das Verständnis der Mission im Neuen Testament* (WMANT 13; Neukirchen-Vluyn: Neukirchener Verlag, 1963) 34. A more recent study is Dorothy J. Weaver, *Matthew's Missionary Discourse: A Literary Critical Analysis* (JSNTSup 38; Sheffield, Eng.: JSOT,
1990).

[3] Tertullian, *Marc.* 4.21.

[4] Ambrose of Milan, *Exp. Luc.* 7.44–53.

[5] Bede the Venerable, *In Lucam* 3.1871–74.

There is a second surprise. Whereas the modern preacher is concerned to show the necessary implementation of Jesus' prescriptions in *real* life, an exegete of antiquity has a different preoccupation: he seeks to underline the harmony between Jesus' prescriptions and the Old Testament. This is particularly true for the strange obligation, present only in Luke, to refrain from greeting people on the road (Luke 10:4b). An explanation, which persists from Tertullian into modern times (Calvin for example), is to justify this rule by comparison with Elisha, who ordered his servant Gehazi to give no greeting on his way (2 Kgs 4:29).[6]

This strong presence of the Hebrew Bible is particularly manifest in the numerous homilies Cyril of Alexandria dedicates to Jesus' sending of the disciples.[7] Cyril cites Jer 23:16, 21 and 14:14 to distinguish the disciples sent by Christ from false prophets.[8] The instructions given to Christian missionaries are consistent with instructions and prophecies found in the Hebrew Bible. Cyril, for instance, quotes Ps 55:22 ("Cast your burden on the Lord and he will sustain you")[9] and Exod 12:11 ("This is how you shall eat it: your loins girded, your sandals on your feet, and your staff in your hand ..."). Cyril connects the gesture of shaking the dust to the oil of anointment in Ps 141:5 ("never let the oil of the wicked anoint my head").[10] The apostolic power over demonic forces is endorsed by two Hebrew scriptures: Isa 10:14 (according to the Septuagint, "I will hold the whole world in my hand as a nest ...") and Hab 2:7 ("That suddenly they shall arise that bite thee ...").[11]

Particularly interesting is the question of the missionaries' remuneration. Like other Greek and Latin Fathers, Cyril operates through a chain of authorities: from Paul's opinion (1 Cor 9:11), he takes the solution he himself chooses for the salary of Christian priests and ecclesiastical workers. He feels that this is faithful to the rule established by Jesus in his missionary speech, which in turn is nothing other than the biblical regulation of Deut 25:4.[12] Again and again, Christian commentators look back to the time of Moses and the Hebrew prophets.

Third surprise: when the sending of the disciples or apostles is not cast in the light of the Hebrew Bible, neither is it connected to any historical application in the life of the apostles, *but rather to other teachings of Jesus himself.* Concerning the equipment of the apostles and their dedication to God, Cyril quotes two famous sayings of Jesus: "You cannot serve God and Mammon" (Luke 16:13) and "For where your treasure is, there your heart will be also" (Matt 6:21).[13]

---

[6] Tertullian, *Marc.* 4.24; John Calvin, *Harmonie évangélique* ad Lc 10.1–12.

[7] Cyril of Alexandria, *Hom. Luc.* 47 (on Luke 9:1–5) and 60–64 (on Luke 10:1–16).

[8] Ibid., 64.

[9] Ibid., 47. In the Septuagint, to which Cyril refers, Ps 54:23.

[10] Ibid. In the Septuagint, Ps 140:5.

[11] Ibid.

[12] Ibid., 62.

[13] Ibid., 47.

From the patristic commentaries I have read, I know of only a few firm connections made with the canonical Acts of the Apostles, that is, with the historical fulfillment of Jesus' promises: 1) explaining the poverty Jesus requires, Ambrose cites Acts 3:6, where Peter, accompanied by John, proclaims that he has no money, neither gold nor silver, as proof of the apostles obedience.[14] 2) Cyril, elaborating on apostolic strength and confidence, quotes from Acts 4:33 to indicate the great power and authority of the apostles.[15] 3) In another place,[16] the same Cyril wonders how the Christian mission to pagan unbelievers can co-exist with the strict rule of Jesus "not to give holiness to dogs, nor again to cast pearls before swine" (Matt 7:6). He recalls Paul's awkward position in Athens, when the Greek philosophers laughed (Acts 17:32), while discussing the risk of expounding the Christian message to unbelievers. For Cyril, the laughter was brought on not by the message of the resurrection but by the presentation of a spiritual God who does not dwell in temples built by human hands.

There are, however, a few noteworthy exceptions. In his first *Homily on Matthew 10*, John Chrysostom encourages his audience to compare the starting point, namely the words of the Lord Jesus, with the following events, which are the application of these words to the life of the apostles.[17] Cyril, when he dares to remember the fate of the apostles as the fulfillment of promises and prescriptions of the Lord, is another exception:

> Let us see whether they [the pagans] too also were not at one time beasts of prey, and fiercer than wolves against the ministers of the Gospel message of salvation, but were transformed into the gentleness and guilelessness which are by Christ's help. They too persecuted the holy apostles, not so much like men struggling with wolves, as like beasts of prey, raging savagely against sheep. And though they wronged them not, but rather called them to salvation, they stoned them, they imprisoned them, they persecuted them from city to city.[18]

That is all the reader learns; there is no concrete description of the Christian mission, no single story of one apostolic martyrdom, no itinerary of an apostolic expedition. Even the canonical lives of Peter and Paul are very poorly used as proof of the validity of Jesus' prophecy and prescriptions for mission. The only concrete notice I have found in patristic commentaries that is not taken from the canonical scriptures is an allusion by Bede to the tragic death of apostates who abjure the Christian faith: the well-known death of Judas is placed side by side with the non-canonical death of Simon the magician.[19]

---

[14] Ambrose of Milan, *Exp. Luc.* 7.54.

[15] Cyril of Alexandria, *Hom. Luc.* 64.

[16] Ibid., 62.

[17] John Chrysostom, *Hom. Matt.* 33.

[18] Cyril of Alexandria, *Hom. Luc.* 61 (trans. R. Payne Smith).

[19] Bede, *In Lucam* 4.185–86. This may in fact be an allusion to the story of Simon, which is recounted in Acts 8:9–24. But in that passage the fate of Simon is not yet sealed.

At the end of this first look at early Christian commentaries, let me draw some preliminary conclusions. Although written for colleagues or for people of the congregation, commentaries and homilies are in fact the products of theologians, scholars who are preoccupied with the doctrinal unity of the two Testaments and the adequacy of their interpretation for the Christian creed, and who are prepared to use these interpretations in a polemical way. They do not feel the modern need to see the historical application of the text in the life of the apostles, nor do they dare to communicate their delight in telling the fate of the disciples in a narrative genre. It is also possible that in some places the "commentary" genre prevented them from following a narrative interpretation. Finally, the existence of heretical acts of the apostles must surely have confirmed their reluctance.

3. The Apocryphal Narratives

The reader of the so-called apocryphal acts of the apostles[20] also has cause for amazement. On one hand, the reader notices an extreme affinity between these texts and Jesus' missionary speech, and on the other (the difference between the two kinds of documents is evident) the scarcity of explicit references to the canonical Gospels.

The motif of sending out of the apostles appears in several apocryphal texts: as a post-Easter appearance narrative, it develops texts such as Matthew 28 in a very free fashion and actualizes the first pre-Easter sending found in Matthew 10// Luke 9.[21] Attention is given to a single apostle. In the earlist acts, the apostle travel alone, but in the later compositions, such as the *Acts of Andrew and Matthias*,[22] there are often two apostles and the canonical rule is observed. It is interesting to note that orthodox re-writings of apocryphal literature give to a lonely apostle a strong companion – the person of Peter himself. In this case, the intention is two-fold: to respect the rule of the two messengers and to provide doctrinal protection

---

[20] On these, compare Eckhard Plümacher, "Apokryphe Apostelakten," in *Pauly-Wisowa Realenzyclopädie*, Sup. 15 (Munich: Druckenmüller, 1978) cols. 11–70; François Bovon, ed., *Les Actes apocryphes des apôtres: Christianisme et monde païen* (Publications de la Faculté de théologie de l'Université de Genève 4; Geneva: Labor et Fides, 1981); Dennis Ronald MacDonald, ed., "The Apocryphal Acts of the Apostles," *Semeia* 38 (1986); Richard I. Pervo, *Profit with Delight: The Literary Genre of the Acts of the Apostles* (Philadelphia: Fortress, 1987). Maurice Geerard's *Clavis Apocryphorum Novi Testamenti* (CC; Turnhout: Brepols, 1992) provides the necessary indications for the study of the apocryphal *Acts* of the apostles (publications, monographs, etc.) and attributes a reference number to each document.

[21] See, for example, *Acts Thom.* 1: Jean-Daniel Kaestli, "Les scènes d'attribution des champs de mission et de départ de l'apôtre dans les Actes apocryphes," in *Les Actes apocryphes des apôtres*, 249–64.

[22] For publication and study of these acts, see Dennis Ronald MacDonald, *The Acts of Andrew and the Acts of Andrew and Matthias in the City of the Cannibals* (SBLTT 33; Christian Apocrypha Series 1; Atlanta: Scholars Press, 1990).

by the Prince of the apostles! In any case, the names of these apostles correspond to the list we have in our canonical Gospels and Acts: Peter, John, Thomas, and so on.

The possible situations that Jesus' missionary speech envisages are all illustrated in the travel narratives of the apocryphal acts. The apostolic peregrinations on sea and land are recounted in a very novelistic style, with dangers and adventures, shipwrecks and terrifying monsters. The entrance to cities and houses, which are situations examined in Matthew 10 and Luke 10, are illustrated with talent. In a newly published document,[23] one writer tells us the story of the arrival of Philip, Bartholomew and a third companion, a woman named Mariamne who is the sister of Philip, in the city called Ophioryme. In a dramatic way, we are told that at the city gates, the guards wear cruel snakes on their shoulders. Whenever travellers are worshippers of the Adder, the goddess of the city, then the snakes let them enter without harm. But if travellers, such as Philip and his companions, worship other gods, then their lives are in danger. Without any explicit quotation from Matthew or Luke, this narrative interprets the coming of the apostles and the descent of peace onto the town, which is then liberated from the demonic oppression of the Adder goddess and her snakes.

The same is true of the prescribed entry into homes. In a charming, novelistic episode, the author of the *Acts of Paul and Thecla* tells us how the apostle meets the young Thecla. On his way to Iconium, he is welcomed by a man who is very eager to invite him to his home. Responding to the greeting of Onesiphorus, Paul salutes him with the words "Grace be with you and with your house." This house – following the Christian rule attested by the missionary speech – becomes the meeting place of a newly founded congregation. Prayers and liturgy take place here. In a neighboring house lives young Thecla, who falls under the charm of Paul's voice (she has not seen him but only heard him speak). Several episodes bring Thecla to faith and the apostle to prison, before they finally meet one another.[24]

The theme of financial remuneration (that is, in return for the gracious gift of the gospel a minimum compensation in the form of daily food is accepted) plays a role in the apocryphal novels in a way that is descreet and in harmony with Christian usage and Gospel prescriptions (Matt 10:8: gratuity; Matt 10:9: "Take no gold, no silver, no coppers in your belts"). We have already recalled Peter's saying in the canonical Acts of the Apostles: "Silver and gold have I none; but such as I have give I thee: In the name of Jesus Christ of Nazareth rise up and walk" (Acts 3:6). We might also remember here some of the reactions of the apostles in the apocryphal acts: Philip, for example, refuses to take a large provision of bread for

---

[23] *Acts Phil.* 13.
[24] *Acts of Paul and Thecla* 1–43.

his journey[25] and John pushes aseticism so far as to be nourished sufficiently by a single date for a full week![26] The Christian apostles often refuse gold and silver, pretentious banquets, luxurious furniture, and expensive clothing.[27] All of these illustrations which are easy for the pagan reader to understand, are didactic and delightful, free and faithful interpretations of the Gospel prescriptions.

Important also is the *power* of the apostle. We remember that, according to the canonical Gospels, Jesus gave power and authority to his twelve disciples (Matt 10:1//Luke 9:1//Mark 6:7). The speeches, miracles, sovereign knowledge, and many qualities of the heroes in the apocryphal acts are like musical, narrative variations of this theme. Let us give ear to these words of the apostle Peter in his own legendary acts:

For this is not only to convince you with words that it is the Christ that I am preaching, but also by deeds and marvellous powers I urge you through the faith in Jesus Christ ...[28]

The following passage from the *Acts of Andrew*[29] suggests the prestige that this supernatural power bestows upon the apostle; thus a servant of the Roman governor Aegeates informs his master:

There is a foreigner who sojourns here and became famous not only in this city, but in all Achaea. He accomplishes great miracles and healings which are above human capacity, as I can partly testify because I was present when dead people were resurrected by him.[30]

Just as the assumption that divine forces empower the disciples is perhaps the most constant motif throughout the apocryphal acts, so also suffering and martyrdom, which the canonical Jesus announced to his disciples, are also integral parts of the apocryphal scene. The dramatic death of the apostle is prepared for by his ascetic way of life. Accustomed to the renouncement of pleasure, the apocryphal apostle is free to renounce – masterfully I would say – his own life. In agreement with an aretalogical tendency, the authors do embellish the dreadful tortures, but it is important to note that at no time is martyrdom removed from the picture. The Christian necessity to testify not only with words, but also with deeds (in the giving of life both through miracles and through sacrificing one's own life) runs throughout the apocryphal acts, and its origin lies in the canonical Gospels, in the Beatitudes (Matt 5:1–12//Luke 6:20–23) and in the missionary teachings of Jesus (Matt 10:17–20//Mark 13:9–13//Luke 21:12–19).

---

[25] *Acts Phil.* 7.7 (93).

[26] *Acts of John in Rome* 5–6. These acts, to be distinguished from the early acts, bear the number 216 in Geerard's *Clavis Apocryphorum*.

[27] See, for example, *Acts Phil.* 5.14–22 (56–60).

[28] *Acts Pet.* 7. ET: see *New Testament Apocrypha* (ed. Edgar Hennecke and Wilhelm Schneemelcher; trans. Robert McL. Wilson; 2 vols.; Philadelphia:Westminster, 1965) 2.289.

[29] See the edition by Jean-Marc Prieur, *Acta Andreae* (2 vols., CCSA 5–6; Turnhout: Brepols, 1989).

[30] *Acts Andr.* 25.

But it is not only the fate of the apostle, his successful mission and his acceptance of suffering that accomplish the promises of Christ; his disposition and character are also important. There is a kind of apostolic *normative psychology*, be it Peter or Thomas, Paul or John. Indeed, the repetitious, sometimes tedious, style of these works is explained, beyond the similarity of the narrative motifs, by this normative Christian behavior. The apostle is never too tired to preach; his fortitude is endless. He is never openly anxious, and if once he is, particularly at the moment of departure for mission, he is briskly chastised by the Lord. This absence of cowardice is particularly evident in the public scenes. Before the most impressive Roman legate, even before the most ruthless Emperor (Nero in the *Acts of Paul*[31]), our apocryphal apostle fulfils the words of the canonical Jesus: "And ye shall be brought before governors and kings for my sake, for a testimony against them and the Gentiles. But when they deliver you up, take no thought how or what ye shall speak: for it shall be given you in that same hour what ye shall speak. For it is not ye that speak, but the spirit of your Father which speaketh in you" (Matt 19:18–20). Do we not read a narrative echo of this promise at the end of the *Acts of Paul*?

And, among the many, Paul also was brought bound; to him all his fellow prisoners gave heed, so that Caesar [i.e. the emperor Nero] observed that he was the man in command. And he said to him: "Man of the great king [the Lord Christ who just resurrected the friend of the emperor, Patroclus], but (now) my prisoner, why did it seem good to thee to come secretly into the empire of the Romans and enlist soldiers from my province?" But Paul, filled with the Holy Spirit, said before them all: "Caesar, not only from thy province do we enlist soldiers, but from the whole world."[32]

The apostle is always modest. According to the evangelical rule, he never asks for better equipment or more powerful means. An episode of the *Acts of Philip* is devoted to the dictum of not returning evil for evil. During his martyrdom, Philip remembers the evangelical temptation to punish the Samaritans (Luke 9:54); he justifies himself and from the cross castigates his oppressors, sending them into the engulfing earth. But the heavenly Lord rectifies the situation and promises to his boiling apostle a temporary punishment *post mortem*! Such a negative vision of an apostle who still has time *ante mortem* to repent![33]

Even when he is a man of the lower class, the apostle is never ashamed when confronted by aristocratic ladies or political authorities: he is "wise as a serpent and harmless as a dove" (Matt 10:16). He is the narrative incarnation of the apodictic prescription. In this way, the apocryphal acts are novelistic commentaries on the canonized Gospels.

And of course, the apostle is ready to die as a witness for his God. If he is powerful and sovereign because of the divine force that dwells within him, he is

---

[31] *Acts Paul Mart.* 1–5.
[32] Ibid., 3. (trans. Wilson, *New Testament Apocrypha*, 2.384).
[33] *Acts Phil. Mart.* 23–48 (127–45).

also obedient and submissive to his master (the difference between God the Father and the Lord Jesus Christ is not always clearly noticed by the apocryphal acts). This bipolarity of strength and weakness, of moral standing and existential defeat, which is unique in the literature of the antique world, forges a strong connection between the apocryphal acts and the canonical Gospels.

At the end of this second part, let me conclude with some formal observations. First, in my opinion, the apocryphal acts constitute clear evidence for the *reception* of Jesus' missionary speech as attested in the canonical Gospels. They manifest a narrative – though not necessarily popular – understanding of Jesus' teachings. The intellectual acumen of the various writers may be markedly different, from the philosophical author of the *Acts of Andrew* to the prosaic and uneducated Christian who wrote the *Acts of Peter*. Nevertheless, all of them – independently of their more or less ascetic and encratite ideal – believe that the missionary will of Jesus has been empowered by the concrete commitment of his disciples. To remember with details and delight the ups and downs in the disciples' lives is for these writers a legitimate form of taking the canonical text into Christian consideration.

Second, like all commentators, the authors of the apocryphal acts make certain choices and omissions and express their preferences. They simply "forget" Jesus' prescription to restrict their mission to the lost sheep of Israel and avoid the road of the Samaritans and the pagans (Matt 10:5–6). They also substitute their spiritual and personal belief in a generous – though a little narrow-minded – divinity for the eschatological and universal kingdom of God (Matt 10:7 and par.: "And as ye go, preach saying, 'The kingdom of heaven is at hand'" plays no role at all in this apocryphal literature).

Third, the subsequent development of Gospel metaphors is also interesting to consider. On one hand, we observe a certain flexibility: as possible fulfillment of the saying about the sheep and the wolves, we find the reconciliation of a leopard and a kid in the *Acts of Philip*.[34] In this instance, the apocryphal narrative commentary is not the usual sort of meta-text,[35] that is, a commentary, but an unusual – in any case a not sufficiently recognized – narrative extension. Through this new metaphor ("new" compared with the "old" canonical Gospel), the author supplements the Gospel metaphor of the sheep and the wolves telling us more than the Gospel: not only will the Christian mission be painful and dangerous (canonical metaphor) but it will emerge in an eschatological peace (apocryphal metaphor). Though explicitly quoting neither the Hebrew Bible nor the New Testament, our subtle author clearly alludes to the prophet Isaiah who – we remember – expects paradisiac peace between lambs and wolves, leopards and kids, in the eschatologi-

---

[34] *Acts Phil.* 8. 15–21 (96–101).
[35] On this terminology, see Gérard Genette, *Palimpsestes. La littérature au second degré* (Collection poétique) (Paris: Seuil, 1982) 10–11.

cal future (Isa 11:6). So the *newer* apocryphal metaphor of the leopard and the kid proves to be as biblically old as the new, Gospel one.

Finally, another aspect of the fate of the metaphors is their transformation from image into reality. If this is already visible in the story of the leopard and the kid, which are real animals and real converts in the *Acts of Philip*, it is even more evident in the *Acts of Peter and Andrew*, where the apostle Peter is strong enough to let a real camel go through a needle that is no less real.[36] This concretization of the metaphor coincides with a historization of the prescription of Jesus. What he *said* has become *deeds* through the work and lives of his apostles. Such is the apocryphal conviction, whereas the theological commentaries are eager to demonstrate rather that the sayings of Jesus are in harmony with other sayings, the written prescriptions of the Law.

4. The Comparability of the Patristic Interpretations and the Apocryphal Narratives

I shall limit my comparison of these two kinds of early Christian literature to three main topics: a) the endowment of divine power to the apostle; b) the strict limitation of means; and c) the readiness to face pain and death. These are the most relevant aspects forming the background of a general confrontation. Christology and the image of God may differ extensively. Ecclesiology and questions of ministry or ethics are often substantially distinct, as appears for example in the orthodox re-writing of our apocrypha at a later date: the docetic Christology of apocryphal discourses is rectified in the later versions, and the condemnation of marriage and the proposing of encratic behavior softened. It was the theology of the Fathers that imposed these doctrinal improvements.

In contrast, the activity of the apostle was treated similarly by both the Church Fathers and the apocryphal writers. Both *admired* the first disciples of Christ. Both were convinced that the mediation of the apostles was an indispensable benediction. Whereas the New Testament refuses any hagiographical interest in the disciples (their picture disappears behind their message), patristic and apocryphal literature both draw iconic images of the apostles. Through their deeds, their wisdom, and even their person, the power of Christ can reach a human world that expects and needs this beneficial influence.[37]

In his *Homily on Luke 9*,[38] Cyril of Alexandria speaks again and again of the apostolic powers. Christ, he says, remunerates the believers, particularly the apostles, for their faith. He gives them strength to overcome demonic powers.

---

[36] *Acts Pet. Andr.* 13–21; see Geerard, *Clavis Apocryphorum*, no. 237.
[37] Cf. Bovon, *Les Actes apocryphes des apôtres.*
[38] Cyril of Alexandria, *Hom. Luc.* 47.

These specific gifts that the apostles receive are to be admired, for they are a parallel and a continuation of the divine force that God transmitted to Christ himself. Indeed it would have been useless to be appointed an apostle only to be deprived of divine power. This thaumaturgic gift brings the skeptics to reason, which, for Cyril, means to the faith. The Bishop of Alexandria's conclusion is that we must *venerate* the apostles, because through them we can venerate the *Christ* who sent them.

These patristic witnesses are in complete harmony with the picture drawn by the apocrypha. Already in 1932 Rosa Söder distinguished what she called the "aretalogical element" (ἀρετή – Phil 4:8; 2 Pet 1:5: virtue as a manifestation of divine power in current Greek) as the most important motif in the apocryphal acts of the apostles.[39] A few examples of this manifestation of power include the following: 1) in the Coptic fragment of the original *Acts of Peter*, the apostle performs a double miracle on his own daughter[40]; 2) the Latin *Acts of Peter* recounts a "fight" (ἀγών) between the apostle Peter and Simon the magician, in which Peter establishes his superiority by being able to perform several resurrections[41]; 3) in the *Acts of Thomas*, the cupbearer of the king from Andrapolis must undergo dreadful punishment at the hands of the apostle because he laughed at him[42]; 4) in the *Acts of Andrew*, preserved in the *Life* of this apostle by Gregory of Tours,[43] we find a typical repetitive sequence of persuasive miracles. Whereas the miracles performed by the apostles in the New Testament are limited and concentrated on the healing of human beings, the apocryphal miracles concern both animals and humans, as well as material objects (stones, plants etc.).[44]

In a world where belief in the irrational was strong,[45] the divine power of the apostle – whether proclaimed as commentary on New Testament teaching or depicted as apocryphal illustration – had the same function: to validate the truth of the Christian message by miracles and healings, that is, by the very activity of a victorious God. In the *Acts of John* the Ephesians proclaim: "We are converted, now that we have seen thy marvellous works!"[46] To this missionary function, we

---

[39] Rosa Söder, *Die apokryphen Apostelgeschichten und die romanhafte Literatur der Antike* (Würzburger Studien zur Altertumswissenschaft 3; Stuttgart: Kohlhammer, 1932; Darmstadt: Wissenschaftliche Buchgesellschaft, 1969) 51–102.

[40] Cf. Michel Tardieu, *Écrits gnostiques: Codex de Berlin* (Sources Gnostiques et Manichéennes 1; Paris: Cerf, 1984) 217–22, 403–10.

[41] *Acts Pet.* 23–29.

[42] *Acts Thom.* 6–8; cf. André-Jean Festugière, *Les Actes apocryphes de Jean et de Thomas: Traduction française et notes critiques* (Cahiers d'Orientalisme 6; Geneva: Cramer, 1983) 47–49.

[43] Cf. Prieur, *Acta Andreae*, 2.551–651.

[44] Cf. Söder, *Die apokryphen Apostelgeschichten*, 60–65, 109–12.

[45] Cf. Eric Robertson Dodds, *The Greeks and the Irrational* (Sather Classical Lectures 25; Berkeley: University of California Press, 1951); and idem: *Pagans and Christians in an Age of Anxiety: Some Aspects of Religious Experience from Marcus Aurelius to Constantine* (Wiles Lectures 1963); Cambridge: Cambridge University Press, 1965).

[46] *Acts John* 42. Cf. Éric Junod and Jean-Daniel Kaestli, *Acta Iohannis* (CCSA 1–2; 2 vols.; Turnhout: Brepols, 1983).

may add a double apologetical intention: a) to counter-balance the social weakness of the Church with spiritual strength; and b) to prove the divine – and not the demonic – origin of the thaumaturgic success of the Christians. In so doing, both patristic exegesis and apocryphal narratives lost sight of an important element in the Gospel of Jesus and Paul: the strength of God is no longer shown by the weakness of human reality; on the contrary, the theology of the cross is overshadowed by a theology of glory and triumphalism. But this evolution did not start in the time after the New Testament: it is present from the very beginning, traces of it being already visible in the canonical Acts of the Apostles and in the Gospel of John.[47]

As to the equipment of the apostles, to the poverty of means at their disposal, we find a similar understanding in both the patristic interpretations and the apocrypha. Christ's rules are open to a description and portrayal of apostolic behavior that awakens admiration. Such a description could be tempered by a stoic tone, as in Cyril's idealized interpretation, which underscores the simplicity and disinterestedness of the apostles. This infers an internal disposition to cast one's burdens on the Lord (Ps 55:22) and results in a practical advantage for the Church Father.[48] Bede follows the same line: to be confident in God and not lose time with worldly affairs is an expression of human wisdom.[49] But in the apocrypha, apostolic poverty, or the apostolic limitation of means, according to Jesus' missionary speech is *not* an emphasized element. The refusal of provisions and money, when it is mentioned at all, is not connected with the prescriptions of Jesus, but with the encratic intention of the apostle himself.[50] The effect, however, is the same. Through little means the apostle will have much to show and offer. The disciple of Christ needs the help of divine power, but scorns the usual human capacities and material means.

This observation becomes pertinent when we consider the apostolic martyrdoms. In the case of the apocryphal Andrew, for example, the crowd pleads: "He has hung there for two days and he is still alive. He has eaten nothing but has nourished all of us with his words."[51]

As prophesied by the canonical Jesus, the disciple is persecuted by political authorities, in the case of Andrew by Aegeates, the Roman governor of Achaea.[52] Even if Matthew 10 is not explicitly quoted, it is certainly the events prophesied in Matthew 10 that are taking place ("And ye shall be brought before governors and

---

[47] Cf. Acts 5:15; 13:9–12; 14:3, 8–10; 19:11–17; John 2:11; 5:19–47; 9:1–7; 11:4–16, 38–44.

[48] Cyril of Alexandra, *Hom. Luc.* 47.

[49] Bede, *In Lucam* 3.1921–26.

[50] Cf. *Acts John* 56–57; *Acts of John in Rome* 5–6; *Acts Phil.* 8. 7 (93); cf. François Bovon, "Les Actes de Philippe," *ANRW* 2.25.6 (Berlin/New York: de Gruyter, 1988) 4492.

[51] I cite the second Greek version of the *Passio sancti Andreae Apostoli*, also called *Epistle of the Presbyters and Deacons of Achaea* 12. On this, see Prieur, *Acta Andreae*, 13–14; Geerard, *Clavis Apocryphorum*, 138 (no. 226).

[52] *Acts Andr.* 51–65.

kings for my sake ... v. 18). Two narrative detours give a theological and ethical interpretation to the prophesied event: first, a demonic force is presupposed to be behind the decision of the governor (the author explains that the devil inspires the prince, according to a Jewish and Christian belief)[53]; and second, pagan hostility arises out of frustration. It is not so much the conversion of the wife of Aegeates that provides reason for persecution, but the new sexual ethics of the converted Maximilla, that is, her sudden chastity.[54]

As Jesus had foretold, "whoever does not take up the cross and follow me is not worthy of me" (Matt 10:38). In the apocryphal acts, Andrew is logically condemned to this very torment. And as the canonical Jesus promised, "when they hand you over, do not worry about how you are to speak or what you are to say; for what you are to say will be given to you at that time; for it is not you who speak, but the Spirit of your Father speaking through you" (Matt 10:19–20), it may be said – *cum grano salis* –that on that occasion the Holy Spirit was very loquacious. For the dying apostle speaks in long discourses to the cross itself, to the converted people, to the crowd, and so on.[55] There is, however, a major difference between the canonical prophecy and its apocryphal fulfillment, a difference that is also perceptible in the Church Fathers' theology of glory: whereas the New Testament does not eliminate the reality of suffering and agony, the apocryphal apostle is smiling on the cross, showing to everyone that the human punishment does not reach him in a painful way.[56] This docetic touch in the apocrypha is confirmed by the content of the apostolic teaching: "In one word you left away every transitory thing: let yourselves now be taken away with me."[57]

The martyrdom of Andrew is a sublime trip, the passing away from material to spiritual reality. In a sense – for us in a very strange sense – this death is a narrative interpretation of the sentence of Jesus that is also preserved in the Matthean missionary speech: "Do not fear those who kill the body but cannot kill the soul; rather fear him who can destroy both soul and body in hell" (Matt 10:28). Indeed, Andrew has no fear of the governor, but he fears the God who holds body and soul at his disposal.[58]

This theological interpretation of martyrdom is not peculiar to the apocrypha. We find it also in several commentaries on Matthew 10 and Luke 10. One example is the first homily that John Chrysostom devotes to Jesus' missionary speech (Matt 10). Concerning Matt 10:22 ("You will be hated by all because of my name. But the one who endures to the end will be saved"), the famous preacher says that the Christian apostles outmatch pagan heroes by far; for finding their human ad-

---

[53] Ibid., 45.
[54] Ibid., 51.
[55] Ibid., 54–59 (note that the apostle addresses his eulogy to the cross before mounting it).
[56] Ibid., 55.
[57] Ibid., 57.
[58] Ibid., 62.

versaries like devils, they do not slay them. On the contrary, they transform them into companions (rivals in goodness) of angels. And all this, the apostles accomplish through their martyrdom.[59]

5. Conclusion

Just like neighbors who ignore one another yet share the same sunshine and water, the patristic interpretations and the apocryphal narratives have stood side by side throughout the centuries. My hypothesis is that this strange phenomenon has biblical roots: the Pauline Epistles and the synoptic tradition also stand side by side, ignoring one another. Both are, nevertheless, in the New Testament because both are legitimate witnesses and legitimate heirs of the gospel. Patristic interpretation, like the canonical Epistles, is a theological, intellectual, and pastoral reception of the message of Jesus. The apocryphal novels, like the canonical Acts of the Apostles, are narrative implements and commentaries on the prescriptions and prophecies of Jesus. Both the patristic commentaries and the apocryphal novels are necessary because together they testify to the complementarity of words and deeds. To speak and to act – the words and the deeds of Jesus constitute the structural bipolarity of the Good News. Without words, the deeds look like mute and unintelligible events; without narratives, the words sound like unreal and unbelievable promises. The Christian faith rests in these two pillars.

What I have defended thus far is the legitimacy of two kinds of reception. My demonstration was made primarily within a formal framework. The content of the stories as well as the intrinsic quality of their interpretation must also be tested. I have not, however, forgotten the inherent danger in a theology of glory. One could also challenge in the patristic commentaries the use and abuse of allegorization, and condemn in the apocrypha a gospel message that is based more on the apostle and his spiritual God than on the Christ and his historical life and death. But here let us limit ourselves to the content of the form (to use the terminology of some linguists), for in it we find the inspiring support for action and meditation. Have we not had in our century an ecumenical confirmation of these two complementary elements, with the movement of "Life and Work" and the meetings of "Faith and Order"?[60]

---

[59] Chrysostom, *Hom. Matt.* 33.

[60] Other elements of the *Wirkungsgeschichte* of Jesus' missionary speech can be found in Ulrich Luz, *Das Evangelium nach Matthäus* (EKK 1; 4 vols.; Neukirchen-Vluyn: Neukirchener Verlag; Zürich: Benziger, 1985–2002) 2.74–161 and pass. I would like to thank my former assistants, Isabelle Juillard and Eva Tobler, for their help. I would also like to express my gratitude to Jane Haapiseva-Hunter, who applied her talents of translation in giving English form to these pages.

The Synoptic Gospels and the Noncanonical
Acts of the Apostles[*]

Introduction

At the end of the second century, four gospels became canonical. Today they are present everywhere in the world at the beginning of the New Testament and at the heart of the Christian Bible, side by side and in the same order, endowed with the same authority. The text of these four Gospels has been fixed for a long time, notwithstanding the existence of thousands of textual variants that have troubled European scholars since the eighteenth century.[1] Today no one dreams of publishing interpolated versions of these Gospels or of doctoring our holy books. Biblical scholarship devoted to the study of these Gospels now occupies a firm place in the programs of numerous theological faculties and departments of religious studies.

In contrast, with respect of the Christian apocryphal literature, no one knows exactly even what writings should belong to this corpus. The text of these documents has never been fixed. At the same time that Konstantin von Tischendorf was preparing his critical edition of the martyrdoms and apocalypses of the apostles,[2] a Greek monk from Palestine[3] was retelling in his own style the same stories that Tischendorf, Richard Lipsius, and Maximilien Bonnet[4] were editing. No special scientific discipline has arisen that is devoted to the study of these

---

[*] Lecture delivered at the annual meeting of the Society of Biblical Literature in Atlanta, 24 November 1986, and at the Divinity School, Harvard University, 5 February 1987. I wish to thank Ken McKinney for translating my French text into English.

[1] The John Mill edition of *Novum Testamentum cum lectionibus variantibus* (Oxford, 1707), by setting out numerous variants, troubled many minds in Europe, including Johann Albrecht Bengel. Cf. Werner Georg Kümmel, *Das Neue Testament. Geschichte der Erforschung seiner Probleme* (2d ed.; Freiburg/Munich: Alber, 1970) 50–51; ET: idem, *The New Testament: The History of the Investigation of Its Problems* (London: SCM, 1973) 47–48.

[2] Konstantin von Tischendorf, *Acta apostolorum apocrypha* (Leipzig, 1851); idem, *Apocalypses apocryphae* (Leipzig, 1866; Hildesheim: Olms, 1966).

[3] I am referring to the monk Joasaph of the S. Sabba monastery, who ended his days on Mount Athos. His work, calligraphed in a large folder, is dated 2 May 1879. It bears the figure Z 59 in the Library of the Megisti Lavra in Athos.

[4] Concerning the Tischendorf editions, cf. n. 2. The nineteenth-century investigations culminated in the Richard Adelbert Lipsius and Maximilien Bonnet edition, *Acta apocrypha* (3 vols.; Leipzig, 1891–1903; Darmstadt: Wissenschaftliche Buchgesellschaft, 1959).

texts; students of the New Testament, patristic scholars, and historians are the guardians of this orphaned literature.

I propose to modify our perspective. We must learn to consider the gospels of the New Testament canon, in the form in which they existed before 180 C.E., in the same light in which we consider the apocrypha. At this earlier time the gospels were what the apocrypha never ceased to be. Like the apocrypha, the gospels of the New Testament were not yet canonical; they did not circulate together,[5] and when they did, they did not always appear in the same sequence.[6] Moreover, these gospels were not the only ones in circulation: other gospels had been born. Furthermore, their texts were subject to scholarly recension (especially Luke-Acts). Readers improved them, harmonized them (Tatian), pruned them, and supplemented them. Many made them into sacred writings in ways not necessarily desired by their original authors. Certain people would soon enshrine them in a canon which, according to Franz Overbeck,[7] resulted in a loss of meaning. Orthodox and heterodox theologians from Marcion to Origen, partisans as well as adversaries of Christianity from Celsus to Porphyry, all attest to the transformation of these gospels in their early period of transmission. They were not secured until the time of Irenaeus.[8] Familiarity with texts that were never made sacred, like the apocryphal acts of the apostles, will be fruitful for the study of documents such as the canonical gospels as they existed for more than a century prior to their eventual canonization.

Such a new perspective will also allow us to focus our attention on these gospels during the period before their general circulation, on their redaction, and on the time at which their sources were written. This change of view will force us, perhaps unwillingly, to notice that the Evangelists freely practiced what heretics were later accused of doing by the Church Fathers, that is, of manipulating the sources that told about Jesus and dipping into earlier documents before these were left to oblivion. We know that they adapted and modified their sources, but because their writings are now canonical we deem their deliberate interventions as faithful, successful, and legitimate. After all, it was necessary to adapt earlier texts to

---

[5] To take one example, the codex of the papyrus $\mathfrak{P}^{75}$ contained but two of our four Gospels. Cf. the edition of Victor Martin and Rodolphe Kasser, *Papyrus Bodmer XIV-XV*, vol. 1: *Évangile de Luc, chap. 3–24*; vol. 2: *Évangile de Jean, chap. 1–15* (2 vols.; Bibliotheca Bodmeriana; Cologny-Geneva: Bibliothèque Bodmer, 1961).

[6] The bilingual (Greek and Latin) codex Bezae (D = 05), as well as several of the most ancient witnesses of the Latin versions, the Palatinus (2 = e), Vercellensis (3 = a), Veronensis (4 = b), codices contain the Gospels in what is called the Western order: Matthew, John, Luke, Mark. Cf. Léon Vaganay and Christian-Bernard Amphoux, *Initiation à la critique textuelle du Nouveau Testament* (Études annexes de la Bible de Jérusalem; Paris: Cerf, 1986) 37–39, 51–62.

[7] Cf. Franz Overbeck, *Zur Geschichte des Kanons. Zwei Abhandlungen* (Chemnitz: 1880; Darmstadt: Wissenschaftliche Buchgesellschaft, 1965) 1.

[8] Irenaeus, *Adv. haer.* 3.1.1. Cf. Helmut Merkel, *La pluralité des Évangiles comme problème théologique et exégétique dans l'Église ancienne* (trans. J.-L. Maier, Traditio Christiana 3; Bern: Lang, 1978) 4–5.

new contexts. Although we realize that legends about Jesus were already developed in these very gospels, our judgment remains generally favorable. But why
are Matthew's modifications of Mark legitimate and Marcion's modification of
Luke disastrous? Obviously, our judgments concerning these documents are colored by a certain notion of canon.

It is not my intention to be an iconoclast, or to threaten the integrity of the
canon. I simply want to underscore the historical fact that the corpus of the canonical gospels did not exist until the end of the second century. The constitution
of this corpus was a slow process.[9] In their arguments for the integrity of the canonical writings, the Fathers obscured the memory of these elaborate beginnings,
the alterations of older sources made by the Evangelists, as well as the subsequent
modifications of their work made by those who come later. One and the same literary practice is shared by the Evangelists and by their successors. It is by observing the successors at work – and the workshop is still open – that we will be able to
reconstruct the practice of the Evangelists whose workshop is now closed.

In order to assess the advantages and hazards of the suggested change of perspective, I have chosen examples from fields which I myself have been tilling for a
long time, namely, the work of Luke and the noncanonical acts of the apostles,
particularly the *Acts of Philip (Acts Ph.)*.

The Packaging and the Product

Biblical scholars spend most of their time in front of a modern edition of the New
Testament. I propose that exegetes, in particular editors of apocrypha, return to
the manuscripts themselves. Nothing can replace direct contact with these documents or access to the *modus operandi* of the scribes and the demands that influenced their work. One need not be a codicologist to become infected by the
virus: it is enough simply to be interested. I was convinced, not by hundreds of
erudite pages but by a visit to the library of Lavra (Mt. Athos), of the importance
of the lectionaries, written in capital letters, which New Testament textual criticism has neglected far too long.[10]

One must consider the external structure of the manuscript. It is necessary to
establish connections of the scriptorial practices of the Christian scribes with

---

[9] Outside the canon histories, I know of no studies concerning the formation of the first collections of the Gospels like Kurt Aland's study, "Die Entstehung des Corpus Paulinum," in
idem, *Neutestamentliche Entwürfe* (ThB 63; Munich: Kaiser, 1979) 302–50. I did not gain access
to E. Preuschen's *Zur Vorgeschichte des Evangelienkanons* (Darmstadt: Jahresbericht des Ludwig-Georgs-Gymnasium, 1925).

[10] While in the United States there had been long-term interest in the lectionaries, European
scholars only began to pay attention to them after Jean Duplacy. Cf. Jean Duplacy, "Les lectionnaires et l'édition du Nouveau Testament grec," in Albert Descamps and André de Halleux, eds.,
Mélanches bibliques en hommage au R.P. Béda Rigaux (Gembloux: Duculot, 1970) 509–45.

their theological convictions on the one hand and with the ecclesiastical constraints under which they were working on the other.[11] To alter our perspective implies that we remind ourselves of what is still a "curious thing"[12] – that only five of the 274 uncial manuscripts transmit the New Testament in its totality. While "New Testament" suggests a fixed corpus, its constituent parts belong to a more fluid manuscript tradition of the first two centuries.

To study a manuscript containing a collection of hagiographic or homiletical writings involves establishing the table of contents, the listing and identifying of its parts, observing incipit, desinit (termination), inscriptio, subscriptio and all other indicators (colophon, etc.). For instance, the subtitles of the Epistles of Peter, in the margin of $\mathfrak{P}^{72}$ will strike anyone who has seen the manuscript as a third-century interpretation[13]. Yet these subtitles have been overlooked until now: they do not appear in the Nestle-Aland *Novum Testamentum Graece* nor in the UBS Greek New Testament,[14] which show little interest in these indicators. The title at the end of the work, the subscriptio, was important in antiquity; why do the editors fail to mention the titles at the end of the Gospel of Luke and the Acts of the Apostles?

Turning to the noncanonical acts of the apostles, one notes that these works, which are preserved most often in fragmentary form, are inserted into hagiographic compilations and lives of the saints. The titles these documents bear ("act" or "acts," "travels," "life and martyrdom") appear in turn. The ancient numbering of the acts (e.g., in the *Acts Phil.*) is generally eliminated whenever a scribe copies just one of the acts from his source (be it *Acts Phil.* 2 or more often, the martyrdom; *Acts Phil.* 8 is an exception).[15] This inconsistency demonstrates the instability of the notions of canon and text – a weighty argument against the reassuring statement by Martin Hengel, who points to the stability of the titles in the manuscript tradition of the New Testament.[16] Because of the simple fact that we have no codices (with inscriptio and subscriptio) of these Gospels predating their canonization, the variety of titles no longer appears. The Gospel of Matthew could have been called "Origin" (γένεσις) or "Life" (βίος), just as Luke-Acts

[11] Cf. Colin H. Roberts and Theodore C. Skeat, *The Birth of the Codex* (London, 1983; reprinted London: Oxford University Press, 1985).

[12] Vaganay and Amphoux, *Initiation*, 35.

[13] Cf. Michel Testuz, *Papyrus Bodmer VII-IV. VII: L'Épître de Jude; VIII: Les deux Épîtres de Pierre; IX: Les Psaumes 33 et 34* (Cologny-Geneva: Bibliothèque Bodmer, 1959).

[14] Cf. Nestle-Aland, *Novum Testamentum Graece* (27th ed.; Stuttgart: Deutsche Bibelstiftung, 1993) 246, 408; Kurt Aland, Matthew Black, Bruce M. Metzger, and Allen Wikgren, eds., *The Greek New Testament* (Stuttgart: United Bible Societies, 1966) 319, 528.

[15] Cf. Bonnet, "Acta Philippi" in Lipsius and Bonnet, *Acta Apocrypha*, 2.1–90; and François Bovon, "Les Actes de Philippe" in idem, ed., *Les Actes apocryphes des apôtres. Christianisme et monde païen* (Publications de la Faculté de théologie de l'Université de Genève 4; Geneva: Labor et Fides, 1981) 301–05.

[16] Cf. Martin Hengel, *Die Evangelienüberschriften* (SHAW.PH 1984, 3; Heidelberg: Carl Winter, 1984).

could have borne the title "Narrative" (διήγησις), or Mark that of "Memoirs" (ὑπομνήματα). At the end of the canonical Acts of the Apostles a manuscript could have preserved the original title of the entire two-volume work. The example of the *Acts of Andrew*[17] leads to the following two-fold conclusion: the Gospels of the New Testament, in their earliest manuscripts, had titles; but the titles they now have are the result of stabilization efforts and are therefore secondary.

The Selection and the Elimination of Sources

One should not underestimate the constraints weighing on the scribes and limiting their freedom. Redaction is a deliberate process: whether or not a text is reproduced, discarded, partially preserved, or eliminated, is not unintentional. Theological orientation, literary sensitivity, ecclesiastical pressures, and material constraints govern such decisions.

Consider the example of the *Acts of John*, which survived severe condemnations by Eusebius of Caesarea, the Second Council of Nicaea, and the Patriarch Photius.[18] Why was this work preserved? Despite its proclaimed heretical character, the *Acts of John* transmitted valuable accounts concerning this venerated apostle, especially the story of his death.

Sections of the original *Acts of John* have survived in texts containing accounts of the apostle, especially in the *Acts of John* of Ps-Prochorus. How were these sections incorporated into other writings? Two main procedures, substitution and interpolation, can be discerned. In certain cases, the older story of the death of John, the *Metastasis*, was simply substituted for the story appearing in the *Acts* of Ps-Prochorus.[19] In other cases, entire sections were inserted into the text of Ps-Prochorus's work.[20] The compiler, who implanted large extracts of the original *Acts of John* into his copy of the *Acts* of Ps-Prochorus, was forced to recast the entire outline of the latter.[21]

---

[17] This concerns the conclusion of the Greek *Acts of Andrew* (AAGr 65, according to the numbering of Jean-Marc Prieur). See Jean-Marc Prieur, *Acta Andreae* (2 vols.; CCSA 5–6; Turnhout: Brepols 1989) 2.549.

[18] Photius, Bibliothèque, Codex 114. Cf. René Henry, *Photius Bibliothèque*, vol. 2 (Paris: Les Belles Lettres, 1960) 84–86; Éric Junod, "Actes apocryphes et hérésie: le jugement de Photius," in Bovon, ed., *Actes apocryphes*, 11–24. Another text, the *Acts of John* by Ps-Prochorus, survived the centuries unmenaced. A recent study, as yet unpublished, of the Greek manuscript tradition on this text has allowed the indexing of about 150 manuscripts. Cf. Éric Junod and Jean-Daniel Kaestli, *Acta Iohannis* (2 vols.; CCSA 1–2; Turnhout: Brepols, 1983) 1.3–8.

[19] New York, Morgan Library, Coptic MS 576 and Paris, Bibliothèque Nationale, Coptic MS 129[17].

[20] See for instance, *Acts John* 18–55, 58–86, 106–15, inserted into the *Acts of John* by Ps-Prochorus, according to several manuscripts edited by Junod and Kaestli, *Acta Iohannis*, 1.4–7.

The case of the *Acts of John* illuminates what must have happened in the process of the production of the canonical gospels. The authors of the Synoptic Gospels intentionally saved all or parts of their sources dear to them. Matthew preserved almost all of the content of Mark, but he sometimes rearranged the order and apparently wanted to render Mark dispensable.[22] In canonizing Mark, the church disregarded Matthew's intentions as well as his disapproval of some of Mark's wording and order. Luke, who alternated his sources in the composition of his gospel,[23] was obliged to adapt the sequence of these sources in order to create greater continuity. Luke 6:12–19, where the inversion of Mark 3:7–12 (summary of healings) and Mark 3:13–19 (calling of the Twelve), appears just before the insertion of a section from the Synoptic Sayings Source (Q). Our understanding of the transmission of the apocrypha in ancient manuscripts enhances our ability to analyze the Synoptic Gospels. It forces those of us who were raised in the seraglio of *Formgeschichte* to pay renewed attention to the use of written sources (source criticism) in these gospels.

In late antiquity, the preservation of certain works often required the discarding of others. Liturgical constraints demanded the abridgment of longer texts. The accounts of the apostles' martyrdom, most valuable for the reader, were frequently extracted at the expense of the less moving *peregrinatio*. A precious colophon[24] specifies that the *Martyrdom of Philip* was to be read in church, whereas the narratives of his life were considered appropriate distraction for monks during their frugal meals. In this instance, however, the latter narratives did not disappear from the mauscript but were moved to a secondary position.

Statements of this kind are confirmed for the canonical gospels through the existence of lectionaries. However, we can apply such observations *mutatis mutandis* at an earlier period to the gospels themselves and their relationship to their sources. The practice of extraction and selection would have shaken the confidence of men such as Herder and Gunkel[25] for whom the shortest text was the oldest and purest. Constraints that we are not aware of or can only surmise may have caused amputations of the most beautiful biblical stories. Evolution does not always proceed from the simpler to the more complicated. Mark

---

[21] Cf. Junod and Kaestli, *Acta Iohannis* 1.5: "The compiler who took the initiative to add large extracts of the primitive AJ [= *Acts of John*] to the text of AJPr [= *Acts of John* by Ps-Prochorus] was constrained to rework the outline of the latter."

[22] This naturally rests on a hypothesis, but a very likely hypothesis, which is defended by Merkel, *Pluralité des Évangiles*, viii.

[23] Cf. Burnett Hillman Streeter, *The Four Gospels: A Study of Origins Treating of the Manuscript Tradition, Sources, Authorship, and Dates* (London: Macmillan, 1924) 199–200, who notes this alternation and supposes the existence of a "Proto-Luke."

[24] See manuscript of Athos, Xenophontos, 32, fol. 29[v].

[25] Cf. Hermann Gunkel, "Literaturgeschichte, 2," RGG[2] III 1678. Citations of Johann Gottfried Herder in Kümmel, *Das Neue Testament*, 97–98.

must be the oldest Gospel not because it is the shortest of the three Synoptic Gospels, but because it is the most simple from a literary perspective.

Any insertion from a source into a more comprehensive document requires a corresponding rearrangement of the text into which the insertion is made. An example from the *Acts of Philip* is instructive. The adapter who extracted the martyrdom account from another source had to make sure that what thus became a new document had a beginning.[26] He furnished this by writing a historical account which he provided with an imposing synchronism, thus betraying a historicizing concern as well as literary claims. Should we not interpret the synchronism of Luke 3 in the same way? It would indicate the use of a new source, commencing at this point, the creation of an "effect of reality" by providing a date, and it would reveal literary pretensions with respect to the style of the account.

The Use of Sources

Another phenomenon in the use of sources frequently occurs alongside selection and elimination: adaptation. Lou Silberman's work on Jewish literature[27] and Pierre Vidal-Naquet's study of Flavius Josephus[28] have taught us that ancient historians frequently arranged and rearranged the material of their sources on the basis of doctrinal or ideological criteria. In the case of the apocrypha and the canonical gospels, it is necessary to distinguish between citation, imitation, and adaptation. The *Acts of Philip Martyrdom* cites the story of the daughter of Peter from the *Acts of Peter*, which the *Acts of Philip* 2 manifestly imitates: the description of Philip in Athens bears the features of Paul's appearance in that city as described in Acts 17.[29] *Acts of Philip* 5–7, on the other hand, adapts a long section from the *Acts of Peter* (a scriptural quotation).[30] All three techniques – citation, imitation, and adaptation – are methods which reveal the use of written documents.

Applying these observations to the Synoptic Gospels reintroduces attention to the use of written sources, alongside our continuing application of form-critical analysis. One wonders, for example, what Luke's appraisal of Mark was. What status did he give to his source? It should not surprise us that Luke could attribute the same saying in one case to John the Baptist (Luke 3:16) and in another instance

---

[26] This concerns *Acts Phil. Mart.* 1–2 (107–8) in the Bonnet edition "Acta Philippi," 41.

[27] Lou Silberman, "'Habent Sua Fata Libelli': The Role of Wandering Themes in Some Hellenistic Jewish and Rabbinic Literature," in W. O. Walker, ed., *The Relationship among the Gospels: An Interdisciplinary Dialogue* (San Antonio: Trinity University Press, 1978) 195–218.

[28] Pierre Vidal-Naquet, "Du bon usage de la trahison," in Flavius Josephus, *La Guerre des Juifs* (trans. Pierre Savinel; Paris: Minuit, 1977) 7–115.

[29] *Acts Phil.* 2.6–29 and *Acts Phil. Mart.* 36 (142), collections Θ and Δ; cf. Bonnet, "Acta Philippi," 81.

[30] *Acts Phil.* 6.64–86; cf. Bonnet, "Acta Philippi," 26–34; *Acts of Peter* 23–28 (*Acta Vercelli*).

to Jesus (Acts 1:5; 11:16), nor that the same story (e.g., the purification of the temple, Mark 11:15–17 and par.) could appear in such dissimilar forms in the different Gospels, nor that Mark and Q present similar and yet very different stories about John the Baptist (Mark 1:1–11; Luke 3:1–22).

The process of adaptation is best illuminated when one observes the rewriting of the same document by several adapters. With respect to the Alexandrian and Western text of the canonical Acts of the Apostles, the current tendency, at least in France, is to consider both texts as different examples of the adaptation of the same document.[31] And if one accepts the two-source hypothesis and compares the parallel sections, one can discern the different ways in which Matthew and Luke adapt their common sources Mark and Q. Their work, of course, cannot be understood as a simple compilation of sources, but both writings still belong to the same category of literature as their sources. The modern editor of apocryphal literature is confronted with the same phenomenon of adaptation. Since this work is less burdened by theological presuppositions, the biblical scholar can learn from it to reflect on the merits and deceptions of the arrangement of related texts in parallel columns (synopses). I want to consider here in more detail the example of the *Martyrdom of Philip,* which, like the *Metastasis of John,* circulated in three different forms or recensions. The following passage from the *Acts of Philip* can be presented in the form of a synopsis, analogous to the customary presentation of the Synoptic Gospels.[32]

The section I have selected (see the following pages) tells how the apostle John enters the city where his companion Philip is being martyred. Ignorant of what is going on, he asks the people the reason for this agitation (θόρυβος). A citizen, surprised by his ignorance, tells him the story of Philip's stay in the city, his missionary activities, and his trial.

Even a first glance at this synopsis shows that the recensions Γ and Δ are neighbors: both omit lines 11–16, the allusion to sexual continence, and they ignore lines 24–30, the recollection of the miraculous healing of Stachys by the saliva of Mary (just as Matthew and Luke have omitted Mark 8:22–26, the healing of a blind man by the spittle of Jesus). Stricter than Δ, Γ also omits lines 30–40, the section concerning the animal converts. In this case, Δ comes close to Θ and even adds to it. One can discern the relationship between these versions and also sense

---

[31] Several have gone so far as according priority to the Western text; see Marie-Émile Boismard and Arnaud Lamouille, *Le texte occidental des Actes des apôtres. Reconstitution et réhabilitatio* (2 vols.; Synthèse 17; Paris: Recherche sur les Civilisations, 1984). Cf. Vaganay and Amphoux, *Initiation,* 41, concerning the 0171 manuscript, which is close to D (= 05).

[32] The ties between the three forms of the *Martyrdom of Philip* have been examined by Joseph Flamion, "Les trois recensions grecques du Martyre de l'apôtre Philippe," in *Mélanges d'histoire offerts à Charles Mœller à l'occasion de son jubilé de 50 années de professorat (1863–1913)* (Université de Louvain Recueil de travaux publiés par les membres des conférences d'histoire et de philologie 40; Louvain/Paris: Bureau du Recueil, 1914) 1.215–25. In the case of the *Acts of John* 106–15, cf. Junod and Kaestli, *Acta Iohannis,* 1.317–43.

their tendency: Γ and Δ are dependent upon the same source, which is distinct from Θ. But Γ presents an even more purified stage of the narrative, while Δ incorporates elements (lines 33–40) originating from another source (the prayer of the animals) – or even invents this additional section. If one reads the redactional parts of the Synoptic Gospels, one must ask the same question: do the evangelists create new materials or do they draw additional materials from a different source?

The tradition-redaction phenomenon is verified when the common source of Γ and Δ is compared to Θ. The tradition existed in written form, but did not exclude oral elements. Moreover, the redaction also allows us to identify its tendency: it edits the text in an orthodox direction. What is important in the judgment of the redactor of Γ is not the question of historical truth, as seen by modern exegetes, but an ideological orientation. We must, therefore, conclude that also for the authors of the Synoptic Gospels their editing (even in the case of Luke) was less motivated by historical exactitude than by their doctrinal orientation. Furthermore, it is by no means certain that one of the three Synoptic Gospels served as *Vorlage* for the other two. In the case of *Acts of Philip* it is necessary to assume a common *Vorlage* for two of the three recensions, which must then be compared with the third recension. Their minor agreements are so striking that it is necessary to assume their dependence upon another document which is not preserved. Father Boismard's overly complicated Synoptic source hypothesis,[33] his joy and my irritation, may prove to be correct after all. Perhaps there were intermediary stages of written sources; perhaps Matthew and Luke used a version of the Gospel of Mark that was earlier than, and different from, our canonical Mark.

The Transmission of the Sayings

In the canonical gospels as well as in the apocrypha one must treat the sayings and speeches differently from the narrative sections. In the case of the sayings, the wording is more durably and, in general, more scrupulously preserved in the oral tradition. However, this is also the place where certain forms (the parable, for example) offer such evidently solid types that they stimulate creations of analogous materials. As far as sayings are concerned, the contributions of the noncanonical acts go well beyond purely methodological interests. Because of the stability of the transmission of the sayings, it is quite possible that the noncanonical acts preserved archaic sayings; the genetic method (*Überlieferungsgeschichte*) could allow us to trace such sayings back into the apostolic or pre-apostolic times.

Three different types can be discerned that are analogous to the techniques observed in the narrative materials. Again, adaptation is the most frequent tech-

---

[33] Cf. Pierre Benoit and Marie-Émile Boismard, *Synopse des quatre Évangiles en français* (Paris: Cerf. 1972) 2.15–59.

Acts of Philip Martyr: 22 (128)

(According to Athos Xenophontos 32, fol. 97ᵛ–98ʳ)

Γ

ὡς δὲ ταῦτα ἦν λέγων ὁ
Φίλιππος, καὶ ἰδοὺ Ἰωάννης εἰσ-
ῆλθεν εἰς τὴν πόλιν ὡς συμ-
πολίτης αὐτῶν· καὶ διακινῶν
5 ἐν τῇ πλατεία ἠρώτησεν· τίνες
οὗτοι οἱ ἄνθρωποι, καὶ διὰ τί
τιμωροῦνται; οἱ δὲ λέγουσιν
αὐτῷ· μὴ οὐκ εἶ ἐκ τῆς πόλεως
ἡμῶν, καὶ ἐρωτᾷς περὶ τῶν
10 ἀνθρώπων τούτων;

οἵτινες πολλοὺς ἠδίκησαν, ἔκλεισαν
δὲ καὶ τοὺς θεοὺς ἡμῶν,
καὶ ἐν τῇ μαγεία αὐτῶν
ἄνειλον καὶ τοὺς ὄφεις
15 καὶ τοὺς δράκοντας· πολλοὺς
δὲ καὶ νεκροὺς ἤγειραν, οἵτινες κατέπληξαν ἡμᾶς πολ-
20 λὰς κολάσεις ἐξηγούμενοι.

Θ

καὶ ταῦτα λέγοντος τοῦ
Φιλίππου ἰδοὺ Ἰωάννης εἰσ-
ῆλθεν εἰς τὴν πόλιν διακαι-
νῶν ἐν τῇ πλατεία, καὶ ἐξή-
ταξεν τοὺς ἐν τῇ πόλει· τίς
ἐστιν ὁ θόρυβος καὶ τινες οἱ ἄνθρωποι οὗτοι; καὶ λέγουσιν αὐτῷ·
τιμωροῦνται; καὶ λέγουσιν αὐτῷ·
οὐκ ἧς ἐν τῇ πόλει ταύτη, οὔτε
ἔγνως ἕνεκα τῶν ἀνθρώπων τούτων,
ὅπως ἐτάραξαν τοὺς οἴκους ἡμῶν
καὶ τὴν πόλιν δὲ πᾶσαν; ἔτι γε
μὴν καὶ τὰς γυναῖκας ἡμῶν
ἀποστῆναι ἀνέπεισαν ἀφ' ἡμῶν προ-
φάσει θεοσεβείας ξένον ὄνομα
καταγγέλλοντες Χριστοῦ. ἔκλεισαν
δὲ καὶ τὰ ἱερὰ ἡμῶν ἔχοντές
τινα μαγείαν μεθ' ἑαυτῶν
ὄντας ἐν τῇ πόλει διὰ ξένων
ὀνομασιῶν μὴ ἐγνωσμένων ἡμῖν
ποτε.

Δ

ὡς δὲ ταῦτα ἦν λέγων ὁ
Φίλιππος, ἰδοὺ Ἰωάννης εἰσ-
ῆλθεν εἰς τὴν πόλιν ὡς εἰς
τῶν πολιτῶν διακινῶν εἰς
τὴν πλατείαν, καὶ ἠρώτησεν·
τίνες οὗτοι οἱ ἄνθρωποι, καὶ
διὰ τί τιμωροῦνται; οἱ δὲ
λέγουσιν αὐτῷ· μὴ οὐκ εἶ ἐκ τῆς
πόλεως ἡμῶν, καὶ ἐρωτᾷς περὶ τῶν
ἀνθρώπων τούτων;

οἵτινες πολλοὺς ἠδίκησαν, ἔκλεισαν
δὲ ἡμῶν καὶ τὰ εἴδωλα, καὶ
ἐν τῇ μαγεία αὐτῶν
ἄνειλον καὶ τοὺς ὄφεις
καὶ τοὺς δράκοντας, πολλοὺς
δὲ καὶ νεκροὺς ἤγειραν, οἵτινες κατέπληξαν ἡμᾶς πολ-
λὰς κολάσεις ἐξηγούμενοι.

25 τὸ δὲ κατοικητήριον ἔπηξεν ἐν
τῇ οἰκίᾳ Στάχυος τοῦ τυφλοῦ,
ὃν καὶ ἐποίησαν ἀναβλέψαι διὰ
πτύματος γυναικὸς ἀκολουθούσης
αὐτοῖς· ἐκείνη δέ ἐστι τάχα ἡ
ἔχουσα ἐν ἑαυτῇ ὅλην τὴν μα-
30 γείαν. ἀκολουθοῦσιν δὲ αὐτοῖς
λεόπαρδος καὶ ἔριφος λαλοῦντες
ὡς ἄνθρωποι.

ἔχουσιν δὲ
καὶ λεόπαρδον καὶ ἔριφον, καὶ
φωνῇ ἀνθρωπίνῃ βοῶσιν
κατὰ μικρὸν λέγοντες· Χριστὸς
μερὶς ἡμῶν ἡ ἁγία. καὶ τοῖς
ὀπισθίοις ἱστάμενα ποσὶν
τοῖς ἐμπροσθίοις τὰ πρόσωπα
κατασφραγίζονται καὶ πρὸς
ἄλληλα λέγουσιν· ἡ εἰρήνη
τοῦ Χριστοῦ καὶ ὁ σταυρὸς
αὐτοῦ μεθ' ἡμῶν.

35
εἰ δὲ καὶ σὺ τοιαῦτα πράγματα
40 ἑωράκεις, οὐκ εἶχες ταραχθῆναι
ἐπὶ τούτοις;

θέλουσιν δὲ καὶ κρεμάμενοι
45 οὗτοι οἱ ξένοι πῦρ αἰτῆσαι
ἐξ οὐρανοῦ καὶ καταχαῦσαι
ἡμᾶς καὶ τὴν πόλιν ἡμῶν.

ἔχουσιν δὲ κρεμάμενοι
καὶ οὗτοι οἱ ξένοι πῦρ αἰτῆσαι
ἐξ οὐρανοῦ καὶ καταχαῦσαι
ἡμᾶς.

nique. In order to write the speech of an apostle, an author would adapt a discourse from another apocryphal book. One such example is the conclusion of *Acts of Philip* 11: during a Eucharistic ceremony "Philip" adapts without warning the famous hymn of Christ from the *Acts of John*.

The second instance concerns a citation. During an appearance to Philip, the Savior speaks words that recall the style of the sayings in the Synoptic Gospels, particularly that of Q:

At that moment, the Savior appeared and said to Philip: "Who is the one that puts his hand to the plow, then looks back and makes his row straight? Or who is the one who gives his lamp to others, and then himself remains sitting in the darkness? Or who is the one who lives on a pile of manure and leaves his habitation to foreigners? Or who is the one who undoes his clothes, and goes into the hard winter? Or which enemy rejoices in the joy of the one who hates him? Or which soldier goes into the war well-armed and does not put on the vestment of victory? Or which slave, having fulfilled the service of his master, will not be invited by the latter to the meal? Or which athlete runs with ardor in a stadium and does not receive the prize, O Philip? Here, the wedding chamber is ready, blessed is the guest of the spouse, for rich is the harvest of the fields and blessed is the worker who is able."[34]

Surprisingly, these sayings of sapiential character do not correspond to any known gospel. A new area of research is opening up here: to complete the collection of Agrapha by Alfred Resch, who was not yet able to use Bonnet's edition of the *Acts of Philip*.[35] The relevance of these sayings for the study of the Synoptic Gospels depends upon the degree to which they can be established as "traditional." The apocrypha of the fourth century may indeed quote ancient texts that have not survived. The sayings in this speech of Jesus are no doubt quotations – "invented" speeches of the Savior or an apostle have a completely different flavor. But from which work are these quotations drawn? from which older collection of logia?

The third instance concerns imitation: a certain type of saying that is characteristic for the sayings of Jesus in the Synoptic Gospels is attributed to an apostle in the noncanonical acts. One might consider, for example, the beatitudes. A passage from the *Acts of Philip* permits us to substantiate that the beatitude survived as a literary genre in apocryphal writings. As in the *Acts of Paul*, these beatitudes are not attributed to Jesus, but to an apostle, in this case to Philip:

Hearing these words, Philip began to teach: "Blessed are those who follow uprightly the word of Jesus, for they will inherit the earth; blessed are those who repudiate the glory of

---

[34] I translate from a manuscript of Athos, Xenophontos, 32, fol. 100ᵛ–101ʳ, from *Acts Phil. Mart.* 29 (135), collection Θ; cf. Bonnet, "Acta Philippi," 66–67.

[35] Alfred Resch, *Agrapha. Aussercanonische Schriftfragmente gesammelt und untersucht in zweiter völlig neu bearbeiteter durch alttestamentliche Agrapha vermehrter Auflage herausgegeben* (T 21 n.s. 15.3–4; Leipzig: Hinrichs, 1906) 279–81. These quotations from the *Acts of Philip* come from the editions which were aware of only a part of the *Acts of Philip* and are older than Bonnet, "Acta Philippi."

this world, for they will be glorified; blessed are those who welcome the word of God, for they will inherit incorruptibility." With these words from Philip, all were filled with joy.[36]

What date should be given to these beatitudes? In what kind of milieu did they originate? The expression "word of Jesus" is surprising: is it an archaism? The phrases "follow uprightly" and "repudiate the glory of this world" evoke a rigorous type of Christianity that is familiar to Matthew ("inherit the earth"), John ("be glorified"), possibly Luke ("welcome the word of God"), and Paul ("inherit incorruptibility"). The moralism of this text, just as that of similar texts from the *Acts of Paul* and Matthew, demonstrates that Pauline theology remained marginal in many places. Rather, second-century Christianity was, above all, concerned with discipline; the requirements of the Sermon on the Mount won out over the Pauline kerygma. Might this already be true for certain currents of first-century Christianity? Do we really have to postulate that the community of Q was based on the kerygma of cross and ressurection?

The Integrity of the Gospels

If the conditions under which the Synoptic Gospels were circulating before 180 C.E. are comparable to that of the later apocrypha, if Matthew and Luke used the same editorial methods as the authors of the apocrypha, and if the first scribes who copied the Synoptic Gospels at that time exercised the same liberty that we have observed among those who copied apocryphal or hagiographic works, then the question of the integrity of the Synoptic Gospels deserves renewed exploration. This does not imply that we are forced to agree with Celsus or Porphyry, or that we have to accept Marcion's assertion about the deliberate falsification of the gospels. But the orthodox Christian witnesses deserve to be treated with the same degree of credit and with the same amount of suspicion as the writings of their heretical adversaries. Let us not forget that the book of Jeremiah was revised and edited on several occasions until the beginning of the Common Era.[37] We also should not forget the Christian attacks upon the Jews, claiming that they had modified certain messianic sections of their scriptures (Justin, *Dial.* 71–73).[38] Fi-

---

[36] *Acts Phil.* 5.25 (63) according to the Athos, Xenophontos 32, fol. 58[r]. The equivalent, but very different passage in the Vaticanus gr. 824 is edited by Bonnet, "Acta Philippi," 26.

[37] Cf. J.G. Janzen, "Double Readings in the Text of Jeremiah," *HTR* 60 (1967) 433–47; cf. the summary of his dissertation, "Studies in the Text of Jeremiah," *HTR* 59 (1966) 447; and the second part of Christian Wolff's *Jeremia im Frühjudentum und Urchristentum* (TU 118; Berlin: Akademie, 1976).

[38] Cf. Marcel Simon, *Verus Israel. Étude sur les relations entre Chrétiens et Juifs dans l'empire romain (135–425)* (Paris: de Boccard, 1964) 185. Simon stresses Christian interpolations rather than Jewish excisions.

nally, we should remember that the gnostic theologian Ptolemy charged that the law of Moses had later been interpolated.[39]

Concerning the New Testament texts, let us move to Origen's testimony that besides the four inspired Evangelists there were others, already criticized by Luke, who had only "tried" to write gospels.[40] With this statement, Origen furnishes us with a testimony to the variety of gospels in circulation at his time; he provides definitive evidence for the antiquity of these gospels as he admits that they were written prior to the composition of Luke. Another text from Origen is pertinent here.[41] According to Origen, Celsus affirmed that certain Christians, as if drunk with wine, revised the gospels. Celsus claims that these revisions were repeated "three or four or several times over" for apologetic purposes ("to deny difficulties in face of criticism"). Origen responds by admitting that there were revisions, but notes that such modifications were few, affirming that he knew those of Marcion, Valentinus, and Lucian (an independent Marcionite). Thanks to Irenaeus and Clement, we can expand this list.[42] The fact of these modifications cannot be doubted. We have positive knowledge of examples from both the second and first centuries C.E. The question arises: Why are the revisions of the second century less legitimate than those of the first century? Are they not of the same nature? Are not the modifications from the first century as ideological and apologetic as those of the second century? After all, the canonical gospels were written to transmit a message to their time in order to legitimize the community that transmitted them.

One should not forget that the most extensive exegetical efforts of the Fathers were devoted to the solution of discrepancies among the gospels of the New Tes-

---

[39] Cf. Ptolemy, *Letter to Flora* 4.1–2. Cf. Ptolémée, *Lettre à Flora, analyse, texte critique, traduction, commentaire et index grec* (ed. G. Quispel; SC 24 [bis]; Paris: Cerf, 1966) 20–33.

[40] Origen, *Hom. Luke* 1:1–2. Cf. Origène, *Homélies sur S. Luc: Texte latin et fragments grecs: Introduction, traduction et notes* (eds. Henri Crouzel, François Fournier and Pierre Périchon; SC 87; Paris: Cerf, 1962) 99–106; Merkel, *Pluralité des Évangiles*, 7–8.

[41] Origen, *Cels.* 2.27: "After this he says that 'some believers, as though from a drinking bout, go so far as to oppose themselves and alter the original text of the gospel three or four or several times over, and they change its character to enable them to deny difficulties in face of criticism.'" Translation from Henry Chadwick, *Contra Celsum, Origen; Translated with an Introduction and Notes* (3d ed.; Cambridge: Cambridge University Press, 1980) 90.

[42] Irenaeus, *Adv. haer.* 3.11.7. Irenaeus attacks those who concentrate on one gospel alone and understand it badly. But he adds, "So great is the authority attached to these Gospels [the canonical gospels] that the heretics themselves give witness to them and each of them tears away a bit to attempt to strenthen his argument." Cf. *Adv. haer.* 3.2.1. According to the letter of Clement of Alexandria to Theodorus, fol. 1ᵛ lines 2–10, Carpocrates would have falsified the secret gospel written by the evangelist Mark. Cf. Morton Smith, *Clement of Alexandria and a Secret Gospel of Mark* (Cambridge: Harvard University Press, 1973) 446–52. Furthermore, we know that Tatian modified the synoptic sayings in an encratite sense. Cf. Louis Leloir, *Ephrem de Nisibie. Commentaire de l'Évangile concordant ou Diatessaron traduit du syriaque et de l'arménien. Introduction, traduction et notes* (SC 121; Paris: Cerf, 1966) 12. According to Eusebius of Caesarea (*Hist. eccl.* 4.19.6), he would have modified several expressions of the apostle Paul. Tertullian (*Adv. Marc.* 4.5) rebukes Marcion for constantly changing his text of the gospel.

tament, whose texts had become untouchable because they were canonical.[43] Prior to the constitution of the canon, more drastic but simpler solutions were customary.[44] Harmonies were produced in order to overcome the embarrassment of a multiplicity of contradictory texts. As Daniel A. Bertrand has recently shown,[45] the *Gospel of the Ebionites* must have been a harmony of Matthew, Mark, and Luke, produced prior to the *Diatessaron* of Tatian (who also includes John). Other examples of harmonization are evident in the modifications introduced by the gospel writers themselves. Consider Luke 1 and 2. There, Luke modifies a text that located both the annunciation and the birth of Jesus at Nazareth. Luke retains the locale of Nazareth for the annunciation but replaces the story of the birth at Nazareth with an account of the proclamation to the shepherds and the birth at Bethlehem.[46] Luke thus revised the earlier tradition according to his missionary and apologetic concerns. This fact must be faced. Celsus is not entirely wrong: there were indeed believers who corrected the sources of the gospels as well as the gospels themselves (τινὰς τῶν πιστευόντων ... μεταχαράττειν ἐκ τῆς πρώτης γραφῆς τὸ εὐαγγέλιον) [*Cels.* 2.27]).

Another problem is presented by Marcion. According to Tertullian, Marcion reproached the church for possessing only a modified edition of the Gospel of Luke. Tertullian writes, "I say that *my* Gospel is the true one; Marcion that *his* is. I affirm that Marcion's gospel is adulterated; Marcion, that mine is."[47] Since Marcion is considered a heretic, Christian scholars usually side with Tertullian and accuse Marcion of modifying the gospel himself. From a historical perspective we must acknowledge that Marcion has apparently corrected his gospel. But we should also admit, as R. Joseph Hoffmann does,[48] that the ecclesiastical form of this Gospel is possibly not its oldest version.

[43] Cf. Oscar Cullmann, "Die Pluralität der Evangelien als theologisches Problem im Altertum. Eine dogmengeschichtliche Studie," *ThZ* 1 (1945) 23–42, taken up in Cullmann, *Vorträge und Aufsätze 1925–1962* (ed. K. Fröhlich; Tübingen: Mohr Siebeck, 1966) 548–65; Helmut Merkel, *Widersprüche zwischen den Evangelien. Ihre polemische und apologetische Behandlung in der Alten Kirche bis zu Augustinus* (WUNT 13; Tübingen: Mohr Siebeck, 1971).

[44] To mention only three examples, the *Epistle of the Apostles*, the *Apocalypse of Peter*, and the *Protevangelium of James* know several, or all, of our canonical gospels, but they use them so liberally that they must not have yet recognized their canonical normativity. Note also the hesitations of Serapion of Antioch regarding the value and the authority of the *Gospel of Peter*. Cf. Eusebius of Caesarea, *Hist. eccl.* 6.12.2–6.

[45] Cf. Daniel A. Bertrand, "*L'Évangile des Ébionites:* une harmonie évangélique antérieure au *Diatessaron*," *NTS* 26 (1979–80) 548–63.

[46] Concerning the prehistory of Luke 1–2, see François Bovon, *Luke 1,* trans. Christine Thomas (Hermeneia; Minneapolis: Fortess, 2002) 26–115.

[47] Tertullian, *Adv. Marc.* 4.4. I am citing Peter Holmes' translation of *The Five Books of Quintus Sept. Flor. Tertullianus against Marcion* (Ante-Nicene Christian Library 7; Edinburgh: Clark, 1868) 183–84.

[48] R. Joseph Hoffmann, *Marcion: On the Restitution of Christianity: An Essay on the Development of Radical Paulinist Theology in the Second Century"* (AARAS; Chico, Calif.: Scholars Press, 1984) 109–45.

The story of the origin and development of the Gospels of Matthew, Luke, and John proves that Celsus was not wrong when he states that the believers had modified their holy scriptures. Such rewriting was tolerated until the definitive constitution of the canon which then, and only then, outlawed further revisions of the text. The transgression of Marcion, the Ebionites, Valentinus, and Tatian was not that they attempted to modify the gospels, but that they accomplished their attempts too late.

The Justification of the Canon

At the end of the second century it became necessary to legitimate the selection of our four gospels. Justifications for this choice were duly produced. One reason was drawn from biblical exegesis (with reference to the four beasts of Ezek 1:10 and Rev 4:7). Other reasons were provided on the basis of legends of a nature that hardly differs from that of the apocryphal acts. Irenaeus and Epiphanius argue that the personal history of each evangelist enabled him to write a gospel.[49] We are also told how the different testimonies given by each gospel writer strenghten and complement one another. In some cases these legends went so far as to construct an entire history of successive periods of darkness and revelation. Thus the Gospels were written chronologically to dispel another recurring period of darkness and to cast again the light of divine revelation.[50]

Paradoxically, the canonicity of the four Gospels was justified through apocryphal legends. It is my hope that today the study of the apocrypha will enable us to renew the study of the canonical Gospels.[51]

Conclusion

I see two tasks for exegetical scholarship at the beginning of this century. First, a scientific integration of several disciplines is needed. Specialization is already revealing its limitations. Textual critics should reach back into the discipline of codicology and forward into the field of hermeneutics. The history of the canon must

---

[49] Cf. Irenaeus, *Adv. haer.* 3.1.1–2.1 (a short note on the identity of the four evangelists and the circumstances of the redaction of their gospel); 3.11.8–9 (the justification of the four Gospels by the four regions of the world, and placing the four Gospels in relation to the four living beings in Rev 4:7); Epiphanius, *Pan.* 51.6.6–7.8. These texts are cited, translated and commented upon by Merkel, *Pluralité des Évangiles*, 110–15.

[50] This is the case with the testimony of Epiphanius, which is referenced in the preceding note.

[51] W. Schmithals (*Einleitung in die drei ersten Evangelien* [de Gruyter Lehrbuch; Berlin: de Gruyter, 1985]) hardly integrates Christian apocryphal literature into his research concerning the origin of the canonical gospels. But the scholar to whom these pages are dedicated rightly gives these writings great attention. Cf. Helmut Koester, "Apocryphal and Canonical Gospels," *HTR* 73 (1980) 105–30.

be combined with the history of the reception of canonical writings, for the canon is at the same time the consequence and the cause of the existence of the Gospels. As the dividing line between *Urchristentum* and ancient Christianity becomes more and more artificial, New Testament scholarship and the discipline of patristics must join hands. The exegetical comment of a Church Father, insofar as it reflects on an initial problem, may be a better and more pertinent interpretation than a modern scholarly commentary. Palaeography and theology should be intimately related. Through its actual material data a codex may teach us the thought of the first Christians; similarly, a simple textual variant can reveal much concerning the "encratism" of a social group. Much will be gained by perceiving the mundane features of the formation of the gospels.

The second task for exegesis is to move exegetes towards a more critical self-examination – an increased awareness of their own prejudices. Exegetes must impose upon themselves the regimen recommended above: a respect for the historical contingencies of the canonical texts and a corresponding integration of several scholarly disciplines. In so doing, they will adopt an attitude that respects not only the incarnation of the Son but also the incarnation of the documents that bear witness to him.

The Suspension of Time in Chapter 18 of
Protevangelium Jacobi

I.

The vision of Joseph in chapter 18 of the *Protevangelium Jacobi* is situated within the content of the birth of Jesus. In the preceding chapters the author has told the story of Joachim and Anna, the parents of Mary, of the birth and youth of the Virgin, and of her bond with Joseph (chaps. 1–10). Then, concurring with Luke, he tells of the annunciation (chap. 11), the visitation (chap. 12), Mary's pregnancy (chaps. 13–14), an ordeal (chaps. 15–16), and of the edict of Caesar Augustus and the consequent trip from Galilee to Judah. As they approach Bethlehem, Mary, both sad and joyful, feels that her hour is near. Joseph gets her settled in a cave along with his sons and then goes to find a midwife (chaps. 17–18.1). At this point there occurs an evocation of a vision seen by Joseph. (18.2–3), marked by a sudden change in the narration from the third to the first person. Joseph continues speaking in the first person until he has found the midwife and spoken to her.

When the midwife arrives, a cloud that was previously overshadowing the cave dissipates, she sees a bright light and the infant appears to her (chap. 19). She comes out of the cave and meets a certain Salome, whose disbelief is first punished and then pardoned as she is forced to admit the postpartum virginity of Mary (chap. 20). The narrative goes on to tell of the visit of the three wise men (chap. 21), the sheltering of Jesus during the massacre of the innocents, the miracle of the split boulder that protected Elizabeth and her son, John (chap. 22), and the martyrdom of Zacharias, the father of John (chaps. 23–24). In the last chapter (25), the author declares himself to be James, explains certain circumstances of his life, and indicates the title of his work.

Joseph's vision occupies a precise place in the book: Mary, in her cave, is about to give birth to her only son and Joseph has left to fetch a midwife who will not even be needed. He is separated from the event, just as it was necessary that he should be separated from Mary at the time of her conception (9.3). But separation does not necessarily mean indifference; Joseph will have a vision that must coincide, even if the text does not expressly say so, with the birth of Jesus. What he sees gives meaning to what is happening; the cessation of nature and of the activities of beasts and humans underscores the importance of the event. The midwife arrives at the cave too late to assist Mary, but early enough to be a witness. The cloud that overshadowed the cave is symmetrical to Joseph's vision; in the same instant, the last prophet and the first witness meet – both are contemporary with the saving event. Joseph is a prophet – not as a foreteller of events but as an interpreter of the event because he has been given a vision. He is the witness not only of what happens, but of Truth itself.

II.

The following is the Greek text of 18:2–3, according to my translation of Émile de Strycker's edition:

2. Ἐγὼ δὲ Ἰωσὴφ περιεπάτουν καὶ οὐ περιεπάτουν. καὶ ἀνέβλεψα εἰς τὸν πόλον τοῦ οὐρανοῦ καὶ εἶδον αὐτὸν ἑστῶτα, καὶ εἰς τὸν ἀέρα καὶ εἶδον αὐτὸν ἔκθαμβον καὶ τὰ πετεινὰ τοῦ οὐρανοῦ ἠρεμοῦντα. καὶ ἐπέβλεψα ἐπὶ τὴν γῆν καὶ εἶδον σκάφην κειμένην καὶ ἐργάτας ἀνακειμένους, καὶ ἦσαν αἱ χεῖρες αὐτῶν ἐν τῇ σκάφῃ. καὶ οἱ μασώμενοι οὐχ ἐμασῶντο καὶ οἱ αἴροντες οὐκ ἀνέφερον καὶ οἱ προσφέροντες τῷ στόματι αὐτῶν οὐ προσέφερον, ἀλλὰ πάντων ἦν τὰ πρόσωπα ἄνω βλέποντα. 3. καὶ εἶδον ἐλαυνόμενα πρόβατα, καὶ τὰ πρόβατα ἑστήκει· καὶ ἐπῆρεν ὁ ποιμὴν τὴν χεῖρα αὐτοῦ τοῦ πατάξαι αὐτά, καὶ ἡ χεὶρ αὐτοῦ ἔστη ἄνω. καὶ ἐπέβλεψα ἐπὶ τὸν χείμαρρον τοῦ ποταμοῦ καὶ εἶδον ἐρίφους καὶ τὰ στόματα αὐτῶν ἐπικείμενα τῷ ὕδατι καὶ μὴ πίνοντα. καὶ πάντα θήξει ὑπὸ τοῦ δρόμου αὐτῶν ἀπηλαύνετο.

2. But I, Joseph, was walking and yet I was not walking. I lifted my gaze toward the vault of heaven[1] and saw it standing still; then at the air and I saw it seized with dread; and the birds of heaven, motionless. Then I looked upon the earth and saw a cooking-pot placed there and workmen reclining with their hands in the pot. Those who were chewing[2] did not chew; those who were in the midst of serving themselves[3] did not take[4]; and those who were raising food toward their mouths did not raise it. But the faces of all were turned upwards. 3. Then I saw sheep being driven and the sheep were stopped. The shepherd raised his hand to smite them,[5] but his raised hand was immobilized. Then I looked upon the flow of the river[6] and I saw kidgoats with their mouths posed over the water, but they did not drink. Then all things, in one instant, were being on[7] again by their own impetus.[8]

Though brief, this fragment presents several textual problems. Three manuscripts omit the vision – the *Vaticanus graecus* 455,[9] the *Vaticanus graecus* 654,[10] and,

---

[1] On πόλος, see below.

[2] Μασάομαι ("to chew") must not be confused with μάσσω ("to knead"), an error found in the first two Armenian versions.

[3] Literally, "to lift up."

[4] Literally, "to carry."

[5] In πατάσσω ("to beat," "to knock") the sound of the blow is heard; cf. Mark 14:27 (a quote from Zech 13:7).

[6] ὁ χείμαρρος has the meaning of "torrent"; the author clearly wants to emphasize the movement of the river.

[7] Note the imperfect tense ἀπηλαύνετο.

[8] ὁ δρόμος, meaning "course," "race."

[9] F[b] in the edition by Émile de Strycker (*La forme la plus ancienne du Protévangile de Jacques* [Subsidia Hagiographica 33; Brussels: Société des Bollandistes, 1961] 31). Particularly useful for the manuscript tradition is Émile de Strycker, "Die griechischen Handschriften des Protevangeli-

most important, the *Papyrus Bodmer* V (third century).[11] However, the evidence provided by these versions and by other Greek manuscripts, especially the *Turin Papyrus* PSI 6, fourth century),[12] convinces me that the vision did belong to the original text.

The second problem is that the evidence of the manuscripts and the versions vacillates between the first and third person: should the text be read with "I"[13] or "he"?[14] If external criticism hesitates, internal criticism imposes the first person; it comes so much as a surprise, that the reader naturally senses why the text has been modified. The sudden changeover to "I," shocking as it may seem, is not an aberration in an ancient that seeks to substantiate the truth of its message.[15]

In the first sentence, I retain, with the best manuscripts, the words "and yet I was not walking."[16] Joseph himself participates in the suspension of movement and of time that is characteristic of his vision.

In the second sentence of the Greek, I follow de Strycker's reconstruction of the text, based on the very old *Turin Papyrus* (even though the papyrus is fragmentary at this point).

In the last sentence of par. 2, should one read ἄνω βλέποντα ("turned upwards") or κάτω νεύοντα ("bending down one's head")?[17] The latter reading, rarely attested, does not accord with the movement of the text, which orients the gaze of everyone toward the heavens. With de Strycker, therefore, I read the words ἄνω βλέποντα.

---

ums Jacobi (Originalbeitrag 1971/1975)," in *Griechische Kodikologie und Textüberlieferung* (ed. Dieter Harlfinger. Darmstadt: Wissenschaftliche Buchgesellschaft, 1980) 577–612.

[10] G in the edition of de Strycker (*La forme*, 31).

[11] Z in the edition of de Strycker (*La forme*, 34). This manuscript was edited by Michel Testuz, *Papyrus Bodmer V: Nativité de Marie* (Cologny/Geneva: Bibliotheca Bodmeriana, 1958).

[12] Y in the edition of de Strycker (*La forme*, 34). This manuscript was edited by E. Pistelli, *Papiri greci e latini* I (Pubblicazioni della Società italiana per la ricerca dei Papiri greci e latini in Egitto; Florence: Ariani, 1912) 9–15.

[13] The following Greek manuscripts have "I": Y, A, C, D, E, H, and R; and the versions Syr[a], Syr[b], Arm[a], Arm[b], and Georg, as well as the edition of Johann A. Fabricius, *Codex apocryphus Novi Testamenti* I (Hamburg: Schiller, 1703) and that of Konstantin Tischendorf, *Evangelia Apocrypha* (2d ed.; Leipzig: Mendelssohn, 1876; reprint, Hildesheim: Olms, 1987) 34. I follow the abbreviations of de Strycker (*La forme*, 30–49).

[14] The following Greek manuscript have "he": S, B, I, L, M, and N; the versions or adaptions Aeth, Lat[a], Lat[b]; the *Armenian Gospel of the Infancy* (Tay) and the Latin text of Guillaume Postel published by Theodor Bibliander, *Protevangelion s. de natalibus Jesu Christi et ipsius matris virg. Mariae, sermo historicus divi Jacobi minoris, etc.* (Basel: Oporinus, 1552) 43.

[15] See Harm R. Smid, *Protevangelium Jacobi, A Commentary* (Apocrypha Novi Testamenti; Assen: Van Gorcum, 1965) 176–78 (Appendix 3: Transition from the Third to the First Person); de Strycker, *La forme*, 149.

[16] The following Greek manuscripts omit these words: B, D, H, I, L, R, and the Syriac, the Armenian, and the Georgian versions, as well as the Latin edition by Postel and the Greek edition of Fabricius.

[17] Κάτω νεύοντα is attested by the Greek manuscript A and apparently by one Armenian version (Arm[a]).

The last problem is to decide which form, which construction, and which meaning to give to the little word θῆξις. Under the influence of the Syriac and Georgian versions, de Strycker conjectures the dative case without a preposition. All the Greek manuscripts, however, use the preposition ὑπό before θῆξις, rendered with the dative, the genitive, or the accusative. Although it is impossible to reconstruct the text with any certitude, the meaning at least seems sure: "in an instant." One Greek lexicographer defines the rare word θῆξις as "impulse," "prick," "point," or "speed."[18]

III.

Although the *Protevangelium Jacobi* has been known in the West since the voyage of Gulielmus Postel to the orient in the sixteenth century and his subsequent edition of a Latin translation of his discovery in 1552,[19] scientific study of the document, particularly of our passage, dates back only to the nineteenth century. In 1832, Johann C. Thilo presented a good critical edition and a commentary, which are still worth consulting.[20] In 1850, Adolf Hilgenfeld argued that the text as it had thus far been edited could not be the original[21]; our fragment, with its change of grammatical subject, was proof in his view that the document contains interpolations. The introduction by Konstantin Tischendorf to his *Evangelia apocrypha* remains today an important source of information.[22] In 1880, Richard A. Lipsius believed he recognized gnostic characteristics in the chapter under discussion.[23] Adolf Harnack does not hesitate to identify three sources behind the

---

[18] See Hesychius of Alexandria (probably fifth century CE), Συναγωγὴ πασῶν λέξεων κατὰ στοιχεῖον ("Alphabetical Collection of all the words" [= "Lexicon," "Dictionary"]) (ed. Mauricius Schmidt; 2d ed.; Jena: Dufft, 1867) 730. θῆξις is often confused with θίξις. Several Latin glossators quote θίξις and translate it as *tactus* (θίξει, "through touching," *tactu*); see references in the index Georgius Goetz, *Thesaurus Glossarum emendatarum* (Corpus Glossariorum Latinorum 7: Leipzig: Teubner, 1901) 329.

[19] See n. 14. It has been known now for some years that several Latin versions and adaptations of the *Protev. Jacobi* did exist and were circulated in ancient times, and certainly in the Middle Ages. See de Strycker, *La forme*, 39–41 and 363–71; J. A. de Aldama, "Fragmentos de una versión latina del Protoevangelio de Santiago y una nueva adaptación de sus primeros capítulos," *Bib* 43 (1962) 57–74; Émile de Strycker, "Une ancienne version latine du Protévangile de Jacques, avec des extraits de la Vulgate de Matthieu 1–2 et Luc 1–2," *Analecta Bollandiana* 83 (1965) 365–402; and an appendix by J. Gribomont, 402–10: Émile de Strycker, "Une métaphrase inédite du Protévangile de Jacques," *Miscellanea in hon. I. Vergote, OLP* 6/7 (1975/76 174–84; J. Gijsel, "Het Protevangelium Jacobi in het Latijn," *L'Antiquité classique* 50 (1981) 351–66; Henricus Fros, *Bibliotheca Hagiographica Latina Antiquae et Mediae Aetatis, Novum Supplementum* (Subsidia Hagiographica 70; Brussels: Société des Bollandistes, 1986) 137–38.

[20] Johann C. Thilo, *Codex apocryphus Novi Testamenti* (Leipzig: Vogel, 1832).

[21] Adolf Hilgenfeld, *Kritische Untersuchungen über die Evangelien Justins, der clementischen Homilien und Marcion's: Ein Beitrag zur Geschichte der ältesten Evangelien-Literatur* (Halle: Schwetschke, 1850) 153–54.

[22] Tischendorf, *Evangelia Apocrypha*.

Protevangelium Jacobi: a biography of Mary up until the age when the canonical Gospels take charge of her (chaps. 1–17), an *Apocryphum Josephi* (chaps. 18–20), and a legend about Zachariah (chaps. 22–24).[24] He holds the change of subject in 18:2 as a decisive criterion for his hypothesis of an *Apocryphum Josephi*. The reworking of these sources must date from the end of the second or third century.

In 1904, A. Meyer made some important philological observations.[25] He understands πόλος not as the fixed pole but as the celestial vault, grounding his idea in an expression of a certain Alexis: τὸ τοῦ πόλου τοῦ παντὸς ἡμισφαίριον ("the hemisphere of the whole celestial vault").[26] That same year, Gustaaf Adolf van den Bergh van Eysinga was the first to remark that a suspension of time similar to that in *Protevangelium Jacobi* accompanied the birth of the Buddha.[27] He concluded that the vision of Joseph had its origins in India and that we are thus plunged into the marvelous world of oriental tales. In 1909, Walter Bauer summarized well the function of the incident: "Die Natur nimmt Anteil an dem weltgeschichtlichen Ereignis, das sich vorbereitet."[28] He indicates a parallel in the *Sibylline Oracles* 8.474–75 (upon the birth of the infant, the earth stretches out joyfully, the throne of heaven laughs, and the world rejoices).

A year later, Émile Amann added two other parallels to the list (Ignatius of Antioch, *Ephesians* 19.1; Wis 18:14–15) and made the suggestion that if Joseph were able to observe the celestial vault in an arrested state, the cessation of its movement must have happened at sunset.[29] A later Christian tradition connects the midnight prayer with the suspension of time. Nor should one forget that Christians situated the birth of Christ and the Christmas celebration near the time of the winter solstice. Along with polemical factors, they must have had a doctrinal reason for doing so: it is from this day forward that the sun, therefore light and life, waxes in strength. The etymological meaning of "solstice" is that the sun is made to stand still. There is an instant when the pendulum of time, before swing-

---

[23] Richard Adelbert Lipsius, *Die apokryphen Apostelgeschichten und Apostellegenden ...*, I–II und Ergänzungsband (Braunschweig: Schwetschke, 1883–1890; reprint, Amsterdam: Philo Press, 1976).

[24] Adolf Harnack, *Geschichte der altchristlichen Literatur*, Teil II, *Die Chronologie bis Eusebius* (Leipzig: Hinrichs, 1897) 1.600–1.

[25] A. Meyer, "Protevangelium des Jakobus," in *Handbuch zu den Neutestamentlichen Apokryphen* (ed. Edgar Hennecke; Tübingen: Mohr Siebeck, 1904) 125–27.

[26] Quoted by Athenaeus, *The Deipnosophists* (Δειπνοσοφιστῶν), 2.60A; cf. 2.61B; Euripides, *Orestes* 1685.

[27] Gustaaf Adolf van den Bergh van Eysinga, *Indische Einflüsse auf evangelische Erzählungen* (FRLANT 4; Göttingen: Vandenhoeck & Ruprecht, 1904) 65–67.

[28] Walter Bauer, *Das Leben Jesu im Zeitalter der neutestamentlichen Apokryphen* (Tübingen: Mohr Siebeck, 1909; Darmstadt: Wissenschaftliche Buchgesellschaft, 1967) 67.

[29] Émile Amann, *Le Protévangile de Jacques et ses remaniements latins. Introduction, textes, traduction et commentaire* (Les Apocryphes du Nouveau Testament; Paris: Letouzey et Ané, 1910) 248–59. At the same time, two scholars published two important volumes of annotated translations: Charles Michel and Paul Peeters, *Évangiles apocryphes* I–II (Textes et Documents pour l'étude historique du christianisme 18; Paris: Picard, 1914).

ing in the opposite direction, seems to stop. Amman examines in detail the patristic notices and the reception of the *Protevangelium Jacobi* in the east and west.

A quarter of a century later, A. Klawek denied the Buddhist origin of the motif of the suspension of time, rooting it rather in the biblical and extrabiblical Jewish tradition of miraculous signs that usually accompany a theophany.[30] In 1958, Michel Testuz published the Greek text of the *Protevangelium Jacobi* in its abbreviated form (without our chapter) according to the *Papyrus Bodmer* V and picked up again, with some modifications, the literary hypothesis of Harnack.[31] The commentary by Harm Smid has a good presentation of the textual evidence and a list of religious-historical parallels that are useful for our particular study.[32] Smid also makes the following two assertions: (1) What Joseph sees in his ecstasy is not just a dream: in the eyes of the narrator it corresponds to reality. (2) The account in Luke 2:8–14 is not at all used by the narrator, nor does it constitute the literary background of the scene (a point of view I do not share). In an appendix, Smid expounds the literary phenomenon, common in antiquity, of the sudden use of the first person in a text written in the third person (so the sudden switch-over does not necessarily indicate a new source).[33] More recently, Alfonso di Nola has interpreted the vision of Joseph in the light of the biblical notion of the silence of creatures whenever God speaks and manifests Godself.[34] The vision is "un esempio di reazione cosmico-creaturale alla teofania-epifania."[35] Di Nola provides the most complete assessment of Jewish, Greek, and Buddhist parallels.

IV.

The theme of the suspension of time is extremely common.[36] One can find it in the fairy tale of Sleeping Beauty as well as in a recent novel by Milan Kundera.[37] It

---

[30] A. Klawek, "Motyw bezruchu w Protevangelium Jacobi," *ColT* 17 (1936) 327–38. I express my thanks to Prof. Irena Backus who helped me understand the content of this Polish contribution.

[31] Testuz, *Nativité*, 16–18.

[32] Smid, *Commentary*, 127–30.

[33] Ibid.

[34] Alfonso M. di Nola, "Sospensione della vila cosmica," in idem, *Antropoligia religiosa: Introduzione al problema e campioni di ricerca* (Florence: Vallecchi, 1974) 173–99. Cf. idem, *Vangeli apocrifi, Natività e infanzia* (Biblioteca della Fenice; Milan: Guanda, 1977) 26–28.

[35] di Nola, "Sospensione," 173.

[36] A modern example: a journalist, L. Greilsamer, writes that upon the death of Salvador Dali, "... lundi matin, à 10h. 13, les aiguilles de toutes les 'montres molles' du monde se sont arrêtées" (*Le Monde* 25 January 1989) 10. A Greek friend recently explained to me that at sunset there are a few minutes of silence when the passing of time is interrupted: cicadas have become quiet and the chirring of crickets is not yet heard.

[37] Milan Kundera, *La plaisanterie* (Folio; Paris. Gallimard, 1985) 86–87, 113. See also Michel Tournier, *Gaspard, Melchior & Balthazar* (Folio; Paris: Gallimard, 1987) 166: "Le temps s'était effacé dans une éternité sacrée"; G.G.Marquez, *Des feuilles dans la bourrasque* (*La Hojarasca*)

emerges often in ancient texts that tell of the intervention of a god or of the birth or death of a hero. It has not been forgotten in the Latin Christmas liturgy where Wis 18:14–15 is quoted in the Introit of the Mass of the Dawn. Although such far-flung parallels cannot explain the origin of our text, they can throw light on similarities and particularities as well as underline the coherence of the theme (cf. *Lalita Vistara*, 1; Limenios, *Delphic Paean to Apollos*; Homer, *The Odyssey* 6.42–46; *Homeric Hymn to Athena* (no. 28); Euripides, *Bacchae* 1084–87; Sophocles, *Oedipus Coloneus* 1620–30; Plato, *Politicus* 273E-274A; Plutarch, *De defectu oraculorum* 17, quoted by Eusebius, *Praeparatio evangelica* 5, 17, 6–9; *Corpus Hermeticum* 13, 16; Pseudo-Callisthenes, *Historia Alexandri Magni* 1,12; 1 Kgs 19:11–13; Hab 2:20; Zeph 1:7; Zech 2:13; Wis 18:14–15; Pss 65:8, 107:29; Job 4:12, 16; *Sifre* Deut 32:1 piska 306; 4 Ezra 7:39–43; *Sib. Or.* 3.199–201; *Testament of Adam* [Syriac and Greek] 1.7; Josh 10:12–14; Sir 46:4; *Midrash Rabbah* Exod 29:9; *Targum Ps.-Jonathan* Deut 28).

Although the *Protevangelium Jacobi* is one of the few to indicate the suspension of time, other ancient Christian texts do mention miracles of nature in connection with the birth or the crucifixion of Jesus. The Synoptic Gospels indicate three hours of darkness and the tearing of the temple curtain at the time of the crucifixion.[38] One can understand how the Church Fathers exploited as much as they could the text by Phlegon concerning a certain eclipse of the sun.[39] Although for Matthew the standing of the star over the place where Jesus was born had an informative function (Matt 2:9), the same event is given other meanings in the *Syriac History of the Virgin*: miracles were to accompany the miraculous birth and symbolize the bond God was renewing with the earth.[40] The *Protevangelium Jacobi*, the *Gospel of Pseudo-Matthew*, as well as other apocryphal infancy gospels, mention the supernatural light that filled the cave where Mary had taken refuge to give birth to Jesus.[41] Origen also seems to suppose that miracles accompanied the birth of Jesus (*Cels.* 1.34 and 38). Later, one would even tell how miracles occurred in Rome[42]; and the *Golden Legend*[43] would contain attempts to list those supernatural events.[44]

(Paris: Grasset, 1983) 106; Rainer M. Rilke, Acht Sonette aus dem Umkreis der Sonette an Orpheus, 6 ("Welche Stille um einen Gott!" Muzot, 16.-17. Februar 1922), in idem *Werke* II,1 (3d ed.; Frankfurt: Insel, 1984) 250; and, of course, the poem by Alphonse de Lamartine, *Le Lac*, and his famous line "O temps, suspends ton vol ..."

[38] Matt 27:45–51//Mark 15:33–38//Luke 23:44–45. Luke adds the eclipse of the sun.

[39] Pierre de Labriolle, *La Réaction païenne: Étude sur la polémique antichrétienne du Ier au VIe siècle* (Paris: L'artisan du livre, 1948) 204–20.

[40] Suspended over the cave, the star became a column of light, or fire, that reached from the earth to heaven; see Peeters, *Évangiles apocryphes* 2.2–6.

[41] *Protev. Jacobi* 19:2; *Pseudo-Matt.* 13:2; *Arabian Infancy Gospel* 3.

[42] See C. Druthmar, *Expositio in Matthaeum* 3 (PL 106.1287). See Amann, *Protévangile*, 150.

[43] *Legenda aurea* 6, ed. Johann G.T. Graesse, *Jacobi a Voragine Legenda Aurea* ... (3d ed.; Dresden/Leipzig, 1890; Osnabrück: Zeller, 1969) 39–47: concomitant miracles to the nativity: the fall of the temple of peace, the springing up of a fountain of oil that runs into the Tiber, three

V.

In my opinion, the search for the origins of the motif has stood in the way of progress toward an exact defining of its contours. Scholars have preferred to study the origin and growth of the text rather than the coherent meaning of its structural content. The latter is what we now take up here.

The emphatic "I," with which our fragment begins, fulfills a double function: it makes the vision personal in the manner of apocalyptic writing (see Rev 1:9) and it serves to "authenticate" the subject matter. By switching over from "he" to "I," the author forcefully induces the reader to accept the news and marvel at it.[45]

The phrase "But I, Joseph, was walking and yet I was not walking" causes some difficulty. Is it a way of saying that everything is going to happen in a vision, that is, in a fundamentally unreal fashion, or is it, on the contrary, a means of making Joseph participate in a most real way in the cessation of the normal course of things? All the interactions between the visionary and his vision impose the latter view; Joseph is in fact interrupted in the midst of the act of walking.

The attention given by some commentators to the notion of silence is exaggerated, since the register of the vocabulary is more of sight than of sound.[46] The perspective is more apocalyptic than prophetic. Joseph looks up in the manner of visionaries, as, for instance, does the protomartyr Stephen (Acts 7:55–56). He looks at the πόλος of heaven, that is, the "vault" of heaven, and sees it ἑστῶτα ("standing still").[47] As this verb can be an antonym of the verb κινοῦμαι ("to move"),[48] it must mean in the case of Joseph "immobile" or "standing still," and not "straight" or "standing." The word πόλος, which is absent from the Septuagint and rare in Jewish literature, belongs to the cosmological vocabulary of the Greeks.

---

suns, the appearance of a heavenly altar to the Sibyl who was consulted by the emperor Augustus, and so on. Concerning this work, see Alain Boureau, *La Légende dorée: Le système narratif de Jacques de Voragine* († *1298*) (Cerf-Histoire; Paris: Cerf, 1984).

[44] A very important text that contains the motif of the suspension of time linked to the hour and the prayer of midnight is to be found in some versions of the *Apostolic Tradition* 41: "For the elders who handed down the tradition taught us that at this hour all creation rests a moment to praise the Lord: the stars, the trees, the water stop an instant and all the host of angels that serve him praise God at this hour with the souls of the righteous ..."; see Hippolyte de Rome, *La tradition apostolique d'après les anciennes versions: Introduction, traduction et notes*, ed. Bernard Botte (2nd ed.; SC 11bis; Paris: Cerf, 1968) 130–31; H. Chadwick, "Prayer at Midnight," in *Epektasis: Mélanges Patristiques offerts au Cardinal J. Daniélou* (ed. Jacques Fontaine and Charles Kannengiesser; Paris: Beauchesne, 1972) 47–49. The motif reappears in numerous medieval and Byzantine texts.

[45] See the excursus of Smid, *Commentary*, 176–78.

[46] Principally Klawek, "Mot. bez. Prot. Jac."; and di Nola, "Sospensione."

[47] Seeing the heavens opened, Stephen notices Jesus ἑστῶτα ("standing") at the right hand of God.

[48] One finds the contrast between κινοῦμαι and ἵστημι already in Plato, *Rep.* 4.436C; *Theaet.* 181E; *Leg.* 10.893B; *Symp.* 175B; *Soph.* 252A; *Phaedr.* 252E; *Parm.* 165D.

In the second instance, Joseph shifts his gaze slightly downward and steadies it on the air, the space situated between the moon and the earth. The air is also still, frozen from dread and astonishment. The adjective ἔκθαμβος ("seized with dread")[49] demonstrates the religious character of this seizure. The immobility of the air, difficult to represent, is illustrated in a third instance by the tranquillity of the birds. Like ἑστῶτα, the verb ἠρεμῶ ("to be still") is contrasted to movement and suggests the immobility of the birds in mid-flight.

After these three touches, the text lowers the eyes of Joseph – and of the readers – toward the earth. To the verb ἀνέβλεψα ("I lifted my gaze") responds ἐπέβλεψα ("I looked upon"); to εἰς ("toward"), ἐπί ("upon"); after the heavens, comes the earth. Joseph sees more there than in the heavens: first, the deep dish, probably a cooking pot, surrounded by workers who are serving themselves from it (sitting rather than reclining). A general statement says that they are in the midst of serving themselves. Then, with the use of three antithetical clauses, the author describes to us their sudden paralysis: some can no longer chew; the hands of others are stopped as they are being pulled out of the pot; and still others are transfixed with food just raised to their lips.[50] Their various positions, so easily visualized, are indeed different, but one and the same paralysis holds them all, and one movement orients their gaze toward the sky. Note the emphatic position of πάντων ("of all"): everyone's gaze is turned upward. The men, like Joseph himself, are struck by astonishment and locked into a state of inertness. The gaze of Joseph, who looked first to the sky and then to the earth, is once again directed toward heaven by the turning upward of the scrutinizing look of the workers. The reader is made to understand that though something is about to happen down here (concerning Mary in her cave), it is from on high that the meaning will come, the movement, the life, the miracle.

At this moment, Joseph looks away (εἶδον, "I saw," with no indication of high or low) to see the suspension of movement reach the flock of sheep, then their shepherd, whose guiding gesture is interrupted. (For the third time, the verb ἵστημι ["to make to stand"] expresses this interruption.)

Then the eyes of Joseph are again diverted upward (ἐπέβλεψα ἐπὶ ..., "I looked upon") to the last corner of the scene: the flowing river, of which, strangely enough, no indication of its interruption is made, and the thirsty kidgoats, brought to a standstill as they bend over to drink. They are immobilized just like the birds, the workers, the sheep and the shepherd, the heavens and the air. Then, in one sentence, the curtain falls and nature regains in one stroke its normal course. The author expresses this in terms meant to be abstract and learned: πάντα

---

[49] On ἔκθαμβος, see G. Bertram, "θάμβος κτλ.," *TDNT* 3 (1965) 3–7.

[50] A curious parallel exists in the apologue of the body mentioned by Menenius Agrippa in Titus Livius *Ab urbe condita* 2.32: "Hands refused to lift the food to the mouth, the mouth to receive it and the teeth to chew it."

("all things"), θῆξις ("instant"), δρόμος ("course," "race"), ἐλαύνω ("to set in motion").

Studying the whole picture, one realizes that its perspective is cosmic (only fire is missing alongside the elements of air, earth, and water; should one imagine it under the cooking pot?) Yet "cosmic" is a pretentious word for the little scene that is shown us. (Only in the beginning and at the end does the vocabulary in our text take on a philosophical hue.) Furthermore, this country scene near the gate of Bethlehem is dominated by human beings: the animals, such as the birds, are harmless or domesticated, as are the sheep and the kidgoats. As it should be, the larger beasts are absent, since they are rare in Palestine. From this we can infer that the author does not wish to signal the arrest of all creation but rather the destiny – if one dares to say it thus – of a small and local universe. The hour is perhaps the evening, at sunset, when tired humans rest and eat, when flocks are led to sources of water. The more agile kidgoats are there already and the sheep are approaching.

Before saying what the author desires to communicate by this, let us suggest one hypothesis: if we surmise that the workers are agricultural laborers and that a tie binds them to the shepherds, we could have here a narrative based on a verse in Luke's Gospel. Luke begins his story with the angels' appearance to the shepherds who were spending the night out in the open air, watching over their flocks (Luke 2:8). Does not the description of the laborers at table evoke ἀγραυλοῦντες ("dwelling in the field"), and the episode with the shepherd, φυλάσσοντες ("keeping watch") in Luke's story? If this is the case, the author of the *Protevangelium Jacobi* takes his inspiration from a brief piece of information from the Gospel, which he then illustrates and develops.

The mysterious vision given to Joseph corresponds to the appearance of the angels to the shepherds in the Gospel of Luke. What then is the function of this vision, which adds to the canonical narrative the temporary suspension of movement and time? The religious significance of ἔκθαμβος ("seized with dread") gives us a hint: it is the awe felt before the presence of the divine. The created world is immobilized because God is about to act. When God intervenes, one feels it on earth; the author, who must be more Greek than Jewish, is trying to express in his own fashion the eschatological character of the birth of Jesus: he knows that in the end times, there will be no more day or night (see 4 Ezra 7:39–43). This means, within his cultural horizons, that there will be no more movement or time. The birth of Jesus is part of this end of time, but it is only the first phase; that is why the cosmic horizon is limited, just as the divinity of the Son is reduced to incarnation. It is just as important that the eschatological immobility be only temporary, for salvation history is not yet at its completion, several stages must still be crossed before the end. The author of the vision of Joseph, by evoking the universe and nature in Greek fashion, points to a decisive moment in the Jewish history of salvation: the birth of Jesus as the beginning of a new age, the last times.

VI.

A history of the reception of the *Protevangelium Jacobi* has not yet been written.[51] The eastern church seems not to have condemned it, skillfully according it honorary, though not canonical, status. The Byzantines just call it a "story" after one of its titles.[52] The word ἱστορία ("written account," "narrative," "history") could denote either a narrative or a historical document. In any case, the Byzantines generally accorded it their confidence and used it as source material for historical, homiletic, and liturgical works. The western church was more reserved. Jerome condemned it, as did Pope Innocent I and the *Decree* of Pseudo-Gelasius.[53] What is less known is that it was not only adapted but also translated into Latin several times, as recent discoveries have shown.[54] Its destiny in the West was therefore maybe not so grim as has been thought.

The time will come when, with the help of that still unwritten story of its reception, one will be able to follow the theme of the suspension of time, our chapter 18, down through the centuries of the Christian church. What I am able to indicate at present is the translations and recastings of the work that use this theme. Several western adaptions are ignorant of it, such as the *Gospel of Pseudo-Matthew*, the *De nativitate Mariae*, and the *Golden Legend*.[55] The *Story of Joseph the Carpenter* tells of the birth of Jesus but does not mention our vision of Joseph. Nor is it used, apparently, by Roswitha of Gandersheim.[56] However, the survival of the theme was assured in the East: first, by the *Turin Papyrus* and by the Byzantine manuscripts from the tenth to the seventeenth century, which reproduce the vision of Joseph; then by the oriental versions – two in Syriac, two in Armenian, the Georgian translation, the Ethiopic (which contracts our chapter 18 into a thin summary), a fragment of a Slavic-Glagolithic translation; and, finally, by the Armenian *Gospel of the Infancy*.[57]

When Postel published his work in 1552, he believed he was presenting something new to scholars and devotees.[58] This was not incorrect, since the work had been lost to the West. However, in spite of its absence from the most notable texts,

---

[51] See however, chap. 3 ("Histoire du livre") of Amann, *Protévangile*, 61–169.

[52] See for instance, Pseudo-Eustathius, *Commentary on the Hexaemeron* (PG 18.772); see Amann, *Protévangile*, 116–17.

[53] Jerome, *De perpetua virginitate beatae Mariae adversus Helvidium* 8 (PL 23.192); Innocent I, *Letter* 6, to Exuperius of Toulouse 7:13 (PL 20.501); *Decree* of Pseudo-Gelasius, No. 8: Evangelia nomine Jacobi minoris (see Amann, *Protévangile*, 143 and 104).

[54] See the works cited in n. 19.

[55] *Pseudo-Matthew* 13.2 is content to use the miracle of the illuminated cave. Obviously polemical, *De nativitate Mariae* 10.2 asserts that Mary had childbirth "as the Evangelists taught us," understood "not as the Apocryphal texts tell"!

[56] *Story of Joseph the Carpenter* 7; and Roswitha of Gandersheim, *Historia nativitatis laudabilisque conversationis intactae dei genitricis* ... (PL 137.1065–80).

[57] See de Strycker, *La forme*.

[58] Postel, *Protevangelion*, 43–44.

the theme of the suspension of time had not entirely disappeared; the *Liber de infantia salvatoris* neither forgot nor omitted it,[59] and Irish monks possessed this work – and thus the vision of Joseph – as attested by the book called *Leabhar Breac*.[60]

[59] See M.R. James, ed., *Latin Infancy Gospels* (Cambridge University Press, 1927) manuscripts of Arundel *404* and Herford *0.3.9*. The text has been reedited and translated into Spanish by A. de Santos Otero, *Los Evangelios Apócrifos* (BAC 148; Madrid: Editorial Catolica, 1963) 266. New manuscripts have been found: see J. Gijsel, "Les Évangiles latins de l'enfance' de M.R. James," *Analecta Bollandiana* 94 (1976) 289–302.

[60] The *Leabhar Breac* was edited and translated into English by Edmund Hogan, *The Irish Nennius from L. Na Huidre and Homilies and Legends from L. Breac* (Todd Lecture Series 6; Dublin: Academy House, 1895) 38–73. The translation has been reproduced in James, *Latin Infancy Gospels*, 111–19. On our motif in this text, see Martin McNamara, *The Apocrypha in the Irish Church* (Dublin: Dublin Institute for Advanced Studies, 1975) 43. Two more recent publications are Jean-Daniel Kaestli, "Le *Protévangile de Jacques* en latin. État de la question et perspectives nouvelles," *Revue d'histoire des textes* 26 (1996) 41–102; and *Apocrypha Hiberniae,* vol. 1: *Evangelia infantiae* (ed. Martin McNamara et al. 2 vols.; CCSA 13–14; Turnhout: Brepols, 2001). I express my gratitude to my friend Carlo Ossola who put me on the trail of this fascinating theme. I would also like to thank Jane Haapiseva-Hunter, lic. theol., who made this translation with interest and competence.

The Words of Life in the *Acts of the Apostle Andrew**

Christianity always expressed the necessity of the proclamation of the gospel. During the second century, however, the different groups and churches were not able to agree on the nature of this proclamation. For some, the apostolic witness was constituted by a memory of fundamental salvific events, namely, the birth, death, and resurrection of Christ. For others, particularly the author of the *Acts of Andrew*, preaching the gospel meant communicating divine wisdom and proclaiming life-giving words.[1]

Two recent editions by Jean-Marc Prieur and by Dennis Ronald MacDonald help us to recognize this emphasis on the words uttered by the apostle in the *Acts of Andrew*.[2] They have brought to light large new sections of the original text

---

* This paper was presented at the meeting celebrating the hundredth anniversary of the Section des Sciences religieuses at the École Pratique des Hautes Études at Paris in 1986 and was also delivered as a lecture in the same year at the Harvard Divinity School. It is published in French as "Les paroles de vie dans les *Actes de l'apôtre André*," *Apocrypha: Le champ des Apocryphes* 2 (1991) 99–111. I would like to thank Jane Haapiseva-Hunter, David Warren, and Laura Nasrallah who helped me with the translation and the annotations, and the support staff of the New Testament Department for their help with word processing this article.

[1] In the first case – the memory of salvific events – the apostle withdraws behind his message; in the other – the communication of wisdom – he tends to become a mediator of the revelation. See Jean-Marc Prieur, "La figure de l'apôtre dans les *Actes apocryphes d'André*"; and François Bovon, "La vie des apôtres: traditions bibliques et narrations apocryphes," both in François Bovon, ed. *Les Actes apocryphes des apôtres: Christianisme et monde païen* (Geneva: Labor et Fides, 1981) 121–39, 141–59, respectively; and Helmut Koester, "La tradition apostolique et les origines du gnosticisme," *RThPh* 119 (1987) 1–16. Hereafter, the abbreviation *AAgr* will stand for the Greek text of the *Acts of Andrew*.

[2] Jean-Marc Prieur, *Acta Andreae* (2 vols.; CCSA 5–6; Tournhout: Brepols, 1989); Dennis Ronald MacDonald, *The Acts of Andrew and The Acts of Andrew and Matthias in the City of the Cannibals* (SBLTT 33, Christian Apocrypha 1; Atlanta: Scholars Press, 1990). Prior to these, the best edition available was that of Maximilien Bonnet in Richard Adelbert Lipsius and Maximilien Bonnet, *Acta apostolorum apocrypha* (2 vols. in 3; Leipzig: Mendelssohn, 1891–1903; Darmstadt: Wissenschaftliche Buchgesellschaft, 1959) 2. 1.1–64. The text of the *Acts of Andrew* found in mss. *H* (Jerusalem, S. Sabas 103) and *S* (Cod. Sinait. gr. 526), which was discovered by Jean-Marc Prieur, has been published by Théocharis Detorakis, "τὸ ἀνέκδοτο μαρτύριο τοῦ ἀποστόλου Ἀνδρέα," *Peloponnesiaca. Journal of the Society of Peloponnesian Studies*, suppl. 8 (1982) 325–50. Both Prieur and MacDonald have written extensively on the *Acts of Andrew* in the editions just mentioned as well as in other publications: see article cited in n. 1 as well as Jean-Marc Prieur, "Les Actes apocryphes de l'apôtre André. Présentation des diverses traditions apocryphes et état de la question," in *ANRW* 2.25.6 (1988) 4384–414; idem, "Découvertes sur les *Actes d'André à Patras*," *Peloponnesiaca. Journal of the Society of Peloponnesian Studies*, suppl. 8 (1982) 321–24;

even if the first parts of the work remain lost. We can only imagine the context and the sequences of these first parts through the sixth-century life of Andrew, written in Latin by Gregory of Tours.[3] Since Gregory intentionally sacrificed the apostle's speeches, however, preferring instead to summarize the apostle's activities, for our topic we must depend exclusively on what remains from the original Greek *Acts of Andrew*. These *Acts* are nevertheless sufficient to express their author's conviction: the apostle's words were powerful and they were able to bring life to their auditors, connecting them with God's eternal reality.

The following exposition will begin with a summary of the principle passages in the accounts of Andrew's ministry and martyrdom at Patras that are relevant to our subject. This will be followed by an analysis of the text, and then I shall conclude by raising questions concerning the historical origin of soteriology by words.

Principle Passages

First meeting of Andrew and Stratocles at the house of Maximilla (AAgr 6–12)[4]

Arriving at Patras, the apostle heals Alcmanes, the servant of Stratocles, the brother of the governor Aegeates. Maximilla, the wife of the governor, who has already been won to the apostle's cause, invites Andrew into her room. There, Andrew gives a speech directed to Stratocles alone; having provoked many by his miracle, the apostle, like a midwife, hopes for the spiritual birth of this listener. Maximilla, too, wishes the apostle to lead Stratocles to the truth. Initiated[5] in the art of maieutics and divination, Andrew wants to awaken in Stratocles the inner

---

idem, "The Acts of Andrew: Introduction," in *New Testament Apocrypha* (2d ed.; Wilhelm Schneemelcher; trans. from the 6th German ed. by Robert McL. Wilson; 2 vols.; Louisville: Westminster/John Knox, 1991–92) 2.101–18; Dennis Ronald MacDonald, "The *Acts of Andrew and Matthias* and the *Acts of Andrew*," *Semeia* 38 (1986) 7–39 (with a response by Prieur and an answer to Prieur); idem, *Christianizing Homer: The Odyssey, Plato, and the Acts of Andrew* (New York: Oxford University Press, 1994). For more bibliography on the *Acts of Andrew*, see James H. Charlesworth, *The New Testament Apocrypha and Pseudepigrapha: A Guide to Publications, with Excursuses on Apocalypses* (ATLA Bibliography Series 17; Metuchen: Scarecrow, 1987) 159–63. For indications on the different texts related to the apostle Andrew, see Maurice Geerard, *Clavis Apocryphorum Novi Testamenti* (CC; Turnhout: Brepols, 1992) 135–46.

[3] Gregory of Tours, *Liber de miraculis beati Andreae apostoli*, in William Arndt, Maximilien Bonnet, and Bruno Krusch, eds., *Gregorii Turonensis opera* (2 vols.; MGH 1; Hannover: Hahn, 1884–85) 1.821–46; see also Maximilien Bonnet, "Preface," 1.827 in the same book. The Latin text of Gregory is reprinted, along with a French translation, in Prieur, *Acta Andreae*, 2.551–651. It is also in good part reedited and translated into English in MacDonald, *Andrew and Matthias*, 188–99, 202–5, 210–13, 218–41, 256–65, 268–73, 276–317.

[4] Here I follow Prieur's new chapter division and I indicate in brackets those paragraph numbers used in older editions.

[5] *AAgr* 7: οὐκ εἰμὶ ἀμύητος.

man, who first is quiet and then begins to speak to the apostle.[6] Thus Stratocles, the future convert, does not set forth his shameful past and his present awakening, but the apostle guesses it through his prophetic art and brings it to light like a midwife.

The effect of the speech takes place within Stratocles. Convinced of the futility of his past life, he groans like a woman giving birth and declares that he will attach himself to the apostle in order to know himself. After this Stratocles never leaves Andrew and becomes the "true friend of the hearing of salvation."[7] Stratocles' initiation by the word continues. He passes precious moments alone with the apostle, for this is the occasion to ask questions. The apostle then introduces the questions again in the presence of the community, explaining to Stratocles, "It is not right not to expose your birth pangs with those like you."[8] Just as women "participate in the same mysteries"[9] during childbirth, Andrew reveals that at a spiritual birth, "It is also necessary for us to witness publically, your newborn being, my child, Stratocles, and not to be quiet, in order that it be recorded by the largest number of its relatives and openly put forward so as to offer liberally the saving words that I have discovered that you are a part."[10] Stratocles, "henceforth leaning on all the words to which he was related,"[11] possesses a solid soul; in faith and joy, with the title "neophyte"[12] he participates in the life of the nascent community at Patras. Andrew seizes the opportunity for a parenetic discourse concerning the mark of God, which Andrew's disciples must protect.[13] The account of the birth of Stratocles to spiritual life ends with two remarks by the author: Stratocles, the brother of the governor, henceforth bears the name of "neophyte" – we should not forget the etymological sense "newly planted" – and, lifted up to the heights of thought, he abandons all his goods "in order to attach himself to the word alone."[14]

---

[6] Ibid.: ἤδη μοι λαλεῖ ὁ καινός σου ἄνθρωπος.

[7] Ibid., 8: ἀληθῶς φίλος σωτηρίας ἀκροάσεως.

[8] Ibid., 9: οὐ γάρ ἐστι δίκαιον μὴ οὐχὶ καὶ τοῖς ὁμοίοις τὰς σὰς ὠδῖνας ἐκτίθεσθαι.

[9] Ibid.: τῶν αὐτῶν μυστηρίων μετεχούσαις.

[10] Ibid.: οὕτως δὲ καὶ ἡμᾶς, τέκνον μου Στρατοκλῆ, τὰ σὰ κυήματα εἰς μέσον φέρειν δεῖ καὶ μὴ ἠρεμεῖν, ἵνα ὑπὸ πλειόνων τῶν συγγενῶν ἀναγράφηται καὶ προαγάγηται εἰς ἐπίδοσιν τῶν σωτηρίων λόγων ὧν κοινωνόν σε εὗρον.

[11] Ibid., 10: καὶ στηριζομένου λοιπὸν ἐπὶ πάντων τῶν αὐτοῦ συγγενῶν λόγων.

[12] Ibid., 12: νεόφυτος.

[13] To those who have been considered worthy of the seal, Andrew declares: "My small children, if you keep this mark safe from the other seals which stamp the opposite imprint, God will approve you and welcome you amongst his goods" (ibid., 11: ἐὰν τοῦτον τὸν τύπον φυλάξητε, τεκνία μου, ἀνεπίδεκτον ἄλλων σφραγίδων ἐντυπουσῶν τὰς ἐναντίας γλυφάς, θεὸς ὑμᾶς ἐπαινέσεται καὶ εἰς τὰ αὐτοῦ δέξεται).

[14] Ibid., 12: μόνῳ δὲ τῷ λόγῳ προσαρτῆσαι ἑαυτόν.

The meeting of Andrew and Maximilla (AAgr 37–41 [5–9])[15]

The second scene we shall analyze takes place later in the story.[16] Andrew is in prison and, according to their custom, Maximilla and Iphidamia visit the apostle. In ritual fashion,[17] the wife of the governor presents an ethical problem to Andrew: Should she respond to the sexual demands of her husband, Aegeates? Maximilla, in asking this question, expects as an answer the opinion, the γνώμη of the apostle, but Andrew introduces a moral and doctrinal discourse. Andrew encourages Maximilla to refuse the advances of her husband, for by her chaste fidelity she reverses Eve's fault and allows the apostle to reverse Adam's sin. Disobedience and obedience form the backdrop to Andrew's words: "And what she [Eve] did not want to hear, you have heard."[18] The words of the apostle, which until this moment had been moral and doctrinal, become complimentary.

Having said these things as I have just said, I could still say the following: "Bravo, o nature, in the process of being saved, for you did not harden your heart nor hide yourself! Bravo, soul, which shouts what you have suffered and comes back to yourself! Bravo, human being, who knows what is not your own and hurries toward what is yours! Bravo, you who listen to what is said! I know that you are greater than what is thought and said."[19]

Continuing the speech, the apostle justifies the parallel between Eve and Maximilla: "I have said this concerning you, Maximilla, for by their power, these words are applied to you."[20] Andrew then explains that should Maximilla fall, he himself would be chastised.[21] Just as the apostle directed his words to Stratocles, here, he speaks to Maximilla, but in fact the words are offered to any attentive listener who

---

[15] This passage has been known through the cod. Vat. gr. 808 and was edited by Bonnet in *Acta apostolorum apocrypha* (2.1.39–42), where it is numbered 5–9.

[16] Between the two passages summarized here we find in particular the romanesque episode of Maximilla's avoidance of sexual relations with her husband through the substitution of her servant Eucleia. See Jean-Daniel Kaestli, "Fiction littéraire et réalité sociale: que peut-on savoir de la place des femmes dans le milieu de production des *Actes apocryphes des apôtres?" Apocrypha: Le champ des Apocryphes* 1 (1990) 295–98.

[17] She puts the apostle's hands over her eyes, then kisses them (*AAgr* 37 [5]).

[18] Ibid., 37 [5]: καὶ ὃ ἐκείνη παρήκουσεν, σὺ ἤκουσας.

[19] Ibid., 38 [6]: ἐγὼ μὲν οὖν ταῦτα εἰπὼν ὡς εἶπον, εἴποιμι ἂν δὲ καὶ τὰ ἑξῆς· εὖγε ὦ φύσις σῳζομένη μὴ ἰσχύσασα ἑαυτὴν μηδὲ ἀποκρύψασα· εὖγε ψυχὴ βοῶσα ἃ ἔπαθες καὶ ἐπανιοῦσα ἐφ' ἑαυτήν· εὖγε ἄνθρωπε καταμανθάνων τὰ μὴ σὰ καὶ ἐπὶ τὰ σὰ ἐπειγόμενος· εὖγε ὁ ἀκούων τῶν λεγομένων. ὡς μείζονά σε καταμανθάνω νοουμένων ἢ λεγομένων.

[20] Ibid., 39 [7]: ταῦτα εἶπον ἐπὶ σοῦ, Μαξιμίλλα· τῇ γὰρ δυνάμει καὶ εἰς σὲ τείνει τὰ εἰρημένα.

[21] The author later mentions the effect of Andrew's words: "For as she listened to the words which he directed toward her, they affected her in such a way that she became what the words intended. In haste, with resolution and purpose, she went to the praetorium" (ibid., 46 [14]: ἐκείνη γὰρ τοὺς λόγους κατακούσασα οὓς πρὸς αὐτὴν ἀπετείνατο καὶ τρόπον τινὰ διατεθεῖσα ἀπ' αὐτῶν καὶ γενομένη τοῦτο ὅπερ οἱ λόγοι ἐδείκνυον, ἐξορμήσασα οὐκ ἀκρίτως οὐδὲ ἀστοχάστως παρεγένετο εἰς τὸ πραιτώριον).

is willing to apply them to himself or herself: "I have said this speech for you and whoever is listening, if he or she wants to hear."[22]

The second meeting of Andrew and Stratocles (AAgr 42–45 [10–13])

Maximilla departs, and Andrew turns to one of these listeners, Stratocles, addressing him with a long series of questions. Andrew is concerned because Stratocles is crying; doubtless he has become aware of the imminent martyrdom of the apostle. Andrew's questions allow us to understand how the narrator visualizes the incrustation of the words of salvation in the human soul.

Do you understand what has been said and why I pray you, my child, to be favorably disposed? Do you know to whom these words were addressed? Has each one [of these words] reached your thought? Have they touched your thinking part? Do I have you as one who has listened to me and remains [watchful]? Do I find myself in you? Is there someone who lives in you and that I can consider my own? Does he love the one who has spoken in me and does he desire to live in communion with him?[23]

The litany of questions culminates in the answer which the apostle himself gives: "Is it not in vain that I discourse? Is it not in vain that I have spoken? No, says the man in you who has cried again, Stratocles."[24] Andrew begins a new section of this discourse by affirming Stratocles: "Andrew then took the hand of Stratocles[25] and said: 'I have the one for whom I have sought ... For it is not in vain that I addressed these words to you, these words which are my relatives.'"[26]

Stratocles can finally express himself:

Do not think, blessed Andrew, that it is anything other than you which causes me sadness. For the words which you utter are like bolts of fire thrown at me, and each one hits and truly inflames and consumes me with love for you. And the affective part of my soul, which leans to what has been heard, and sequeezed me with sadness, is tormented. For you are leaving, and I know well that it is good this way, but if after this, I seek your solicitude and tenderness, where will I find them, or with whom? I have received the seeds of the saving words and you were the sower for me. Yet for them to germinate and grow, they need you and no other, very blessed Andrew. What else do I have to say to you but this, servant of God? I need great mercy and the help which comes from you to be able to be worthy of the

---

[22] Ibid., 42 [10]: ταῦτα εἶπον πρὸς σὲ καὶ πάντα τὸν ἀκούοντα, εἰ ἄρα ἀκούσῃ.

[23] Ibid.: γνωρίζεις τὰ λεγόμενα, καὶ διὰ τί σε εὔχομαι, τέκνον, ὅπως διατεθῇς; μανθάνεις πρὸς τίνας εἴρηται τὰ εἰρημένα; ἥψατό σου ἕκαστον τῆς διανοίας; ἔθιγέν σου τοῦ διανοητικοῦ μέρους; ἔχω μένοντα τὸν ἀκούσαντά μου; εὑρίσκω ἐν σοὶ ἐμαυτόν; ἔστιν τις ἐν σοὶ ὁμιλήσας ὃν ἐγὼ ὁρῶ ἴδιόν μου; ἀγαπᾷ τὸν ἐν ἐμοὶ λαλήσαντα, καὶ βούλεται αὐτῷ κοινωνῆσαι;

[24] Ibid.: μὴ μάτην λαλῶ; μὴ μάτην εἶπον; οὔ φησιν ὁ ἐν σοί, Στρατοκλῆ, πάλιν δακρύσας ἄνθρωπος. To say that Stratocles "has cried again" probably means that he has been able to cry again for the right reasons, motivated by repentance and truth.

[25] Again we should be attentive to this gesture, as we already have noticed above Maximilla's attitude (n. 47).

[26] AAgr 43 [11]: καὶ λαβόμενος ὁ Ἀνδρέας τῆς χειρὸς τοῦ Στρατοκλέους εἶπεν· ἔχω ὃν ἐζήτουν ... ὅτι οὐ μάτην πεποίημαι πρὸς σὲ τοὺς συγγενεῖς μου λόγους.

seeds which come from you. For they will not grow unharmed and we will not see them grow if you do not want them to and do not pray for them and for all of me.[27]

Andrew can then only rejoice in the attitude by his disciple: "This is what I also saw in you, my child, and I glorify my Lord that my thought concerning you was not useless but knew what it was saying."[28] With this, he goes toward his martyrdom.

Andrew and the gathered community (AAgr 47–50 [15–18])

As is typical in this genre, in a first farewell speech addressed to the disciples, Andrew looks retrospectively at his activities:

As for me, brothers, the Lord sent me as an apostle to the regions of which my Lord judged me worthy, not to teach anyone but to remind everyone related to these words that they are living in temporary evils ... I deem as blessed those who have become obedient to the words preached and who through them see as in a mirror the mysteries of their own nature, for whose sake all things were built."[29]

Then he announces his martyrdom and the last interventions of the Evil One, who is angry since "the light of the word has been shown."[30] The discourse ends with an exhortation which contains an enigmatic phrase that is important for our discussion, given the key function attributed to the word λόγος throughout the text: "But may we all, lifted up by the whole word, welcome joyfully the end."[31]

---

[27] Ibid., 44 [12]: μὴ νόμιζε, μακαριώτατε Ἀνδρέα, ὅτι ἕτερόν τί ἐστι τὸ ἀνιῶν με ἀλλ᾽ ἢ σύ. οἱ γὰρ διὰ σοῦ ἐξιόντες λόγοι πυρὶ ἀκοντιζόμενοι εἰς ἐμὲ ἐοίκασιν, καὶ ἐμοῦ ἕκαστος αὐτῶν καθικνεῖται ὡς ἀληθῶς ἐκκαίων με καὶ καταφλέγων πρὸς τὴν σὴν στοργήν· καὶ τὸ παθητικὸν μέρος τῆς ψυχῆς μου, τὸ πρὸς τοῖς ἠκουσμένοις ὄν, τὸ μετὰ τοῦ ἀνιᾶν μαντευόμενον, κολάζεται. ἀπαλλάσσῃ γὰρ αὐτός, καὶ εὖ οἶδα ὅτι καλῶς. τὴν δὲ μετὰ ταῦτά σου ἐπιμέλειαν καὶ στοργὴν ζητῶν ποῦ εὕρω ἢ ἐν τίνι; τὰ μὲν σπέρματα τῶν σωτηρίων λόγων δέδεγμαι, σοῦ ὄντος μοι τοῦ σπορέως. τὸ δὲ ἀναβλαστῆσαι ταῦτα καὶ ἐκφῦναι οὐχ ἑτέρου ἀλλ᾽ ἢ σοῦ δεῖται, Ἀνδρέα μακαριώτατε. καὶ τί γὰρ ἔχω σοι εἰπεῖν, δοῦλε τοῦ θεοῦ, ἀλλ᾽ ἢ τοῦτο; πολλοῦ ἐλέου δέομαι καὶ βοηθείας τῆς παρὰ σοῦ, ὅπως δυναίμην ἄξιος γενέσθαι ὧν ἔχω σου σπερμάτων· ἃ οὐκ ἄλλως ἐπιδώσει ἄπληκτα καὶ εἰς τὸ φανερὸν ἀνίσχοντα, μὴ οὐχί σου βουληθέντος καὶ εὐξαμένου ὑπὲρ αὐτῶν καὶ ἐμοῦ ὅλου.

[28] Ibid., 45 [13]: ταῦτα ἦν, τέκνον, ἃ καὶ αὐτὸς ἑώρων ἐν σοί. καί μου τὸν κύριον δοξάζω ὅτι μου ἡ περὶ σὲ ἔννοια οὐκ ἐκενεμβάτησεν, ἀλλ᾽ οἶδεν ὃ εἶπεν.

[29] Ibid., 47 [15]: ἐγώ, ἀδελφοί, ἐξεπέμφθην ὑπὸ τοῦ κυρίου ἀπόστολος εἰς τὰ κλίματα ταῦτα ὧν με κατηξίωσεν ὁ κύριός μου, διδάξαι μὲν οὐδένα, ὑπομνῆσαι δὲ πάντα τὸν συγγενῆ τῶν λόγων ἄνθρωπον ὅτι ἐν κακοῖς τοῖς προσκαίροις διάγουσιν. ... μακαρίους οὖν ἐκείνους τίθεμαι τοὺς κατηκόους τῶν κεκηρυγμένων λόγων γεγονότας καὶ δι᾽ αὐτῶν μυστήρια ὀπτριζομένους περὶ τὴν ἰδίαν φύσιν, ἧς ἕνεκεν τὰ πάντα ᾠκοδόμηται.

[30] Ibid., 50 [18]: καὶ τὸ τοῦ λόγου φῶς ἐδείχθη.

[31] Ibid.: ἀλλ᾽ ὅλοι ἐν ὅλῳ τῷ λόγῳ ἐπαιωρούμενοι τὸ τέλος πάντες ἀσμένως προσδεξώμεθα. The Armenian reads: "But raise all of you your spirit toward all these words [that I am telling you]"; Louis Leloir *Écrits apocryphes sur les apôtres. Traduction de l'édition arménienne de Venise* (CCSA 3; Turnhout: Brepols, 1986) 236.

Andrew and Aegeates (AAgr 51–55 [1–5])[32]

The arrest of Andrew places the future martyr in the presence of his judge, the governor Aegeates.[33] With literary skill, the author shows that Aegeates cannot achieve a real dialogue with Andrew. Andrew makes no reply to Aegeates' attack,[34] and when the apostle speaks to the governor, he does not address the latter directly but instead, referring to Aegeates in the third person, exhorts Stratocles regarding the evil nature of men like Aegeates, who are outside and foreign.[35] Between Andrew's discourse at the cross and his last sermon, pronounced while being crucified,[36] Andrew again refers to Aegeates: when Stratocles asks Andrew why he is smiling, he replies that he smiles at the vain wiles of Aegeates, "He cannot even hear, since if he could, he would have heard that the person who belongs to Jesus, having been known then by him, cannot be punished."[37]

Andrew and the crowd (AAgr 56–64 [6–10])

In his second farewell speech, called a κοινὸς λόγος ("common speech"),[38] Andrew addresses the crowd from the cross. He invites his hearers to leave behind what is corporeal and exterior and join the soul of the apostle, which is rushing toward "what is above the word."[39] He hopes that "you may now see, you too, with the eyes of the soul, those things which I tell you … Clean your ears to hear what I say,"[40] and he continues by saying, "But now I know well that you are not deaf to

---

[32]   In the narrative of the martyrdom, which begins here, I am again following the critical text established by Prieur in his *Acta Andreae*. It is a composite text established mainly from mss. *H* (Jerusalem, S. Sabas 103), *S* (Sinait. gr. 526), *C* (Ann Arbor 36), the two forms of the *Martyrium secundum*, and the Armenian version; see Prieur, "Découvertes sur les *Actes d'André à Patras*, 321–24.

[33]   I shall cite all references to the Armenian version of Andrew's martyrdom from the French edition – the only one in a modern language. This translation is the work of the late Father Louis Leloir (*Écrits apocryphes sur les apôtres*, 232–57). On the great value of this Armenian version and the Greek text it presupposes, see idem, "La version arménienne de la Passion d'André," *Handes Amsorya* 90 (1976) 471–74; see also Valentina Calzolari Bouvier ("La versione armena del *Martirio di Andrea*: alcune osservazioni in relazione all' originale greco," *Studi e Ricerche sull' Oriente Cristiano* 16 (1993) 3–33.

[34]   *AAgr* 51 [1]: Leloir, *Écrits apocryphes sur les apôtres*, 236–37.

[35]   Ibid., 53 [3]: Leloir, *Écrits apocryphes sur les apôtres*, 239 n. 6.

[36]   For the discourse at the cross, see *AAgr* 54; and Leloir, *Écrits apocryphes sur les apôtres*, 242–45; for Andrew's last sermon, see *AAgr* 56–58 [6]; and Leloir, *Écrits apocryphes sur les apôtres*, 245–50.

[37]   *AAgr* 55 [5]: οὐκ ἔχει τὸ ἀκούειν· ἐπεὶ εἰ εἶχεν, ἀκηκόη ἂν ὅτι ὁ Ἰησοῦ ἄνθρωπος ἀτιμώρητός ἐστιν λοιπὸν αὐτῷ γνωρισθείς. Leloir, *Écrits apocryphes sur les apôtres*, 245.

[38]   *AAgr* 56 [6]: Leloir, *Écrits apocryphes sur les apôtres*, 245–47.

[39]   *AAgr* 57: εἰς τὰ ὑπὲρ λόγον. This probably refers to the human word; see also Leloir, *Écrits apocryphes sur les apôtres*, 245.

[40]   *AAgr* 57: εἴθε δὲ ἑωρᾶτε νῦν καὶ αὐτοὶ περὶ ὧν λέγω τοῖς τῆς ψυχῆς ὀφθαλμοῖς. … καὶ διασμήξατε ὑμῶν τὰς ἀκοὰς ἀκοῦσαι ἃ λέγω. Leloir, *Écrits apocryphes sur les apôtres*, 248.

my words. This is why men have peaceful confidence in the knowledge of our God."[41] The crowd reacts positively: "Having heard what Andrew had said and, so to speak, held by him, the crowd did not leave the spot. And the blessed one continued to tell them even more than what he had said, so that it was fixed in the mind of those who where listening. Three days and three nights he spoke to them, and no one grew tired nor left him."[42]

Because of popular pressure, Aegeates comes to the cross to deliver the apostle, but Andrew condemns the crowd for trying to prevent his martyrdom. For the first time, Andrew attacks the governor directly, but not without hesitation: "But now that Aegeates comes near to me, I will be silent and hold my children together. What I have to tell him before departing, I will tell him. Why do you return to us, Aegeates?"[43]

The author of the Acts of Andrew (AAgr 65 [11])

After having told the last adventures of the martyrdom, the author surreptitiously introduces himself into the account by using "we," thus giving a feeling of immediacy and truthfulness.[44] He then summarizes Maximilla's attitude and Stratocles' decision, concluding his story with a shift to the first person singular:

I am ending here my blessed accounts of the acts and mysteries which are difficult, if not impossible to express; may this stroke mark the end [of this book]. I will pray first for myself: that I may have heard what was truly said, and this in a clear manner, also what was not apparent, but could be caught by the thought; I will then pray for all those who were established by what has been said: may they be in communion together, God opening the ears of his hearers so that they may receive all his gifts in Jesus Christ our Lord, with whom is glory, honor and power to the Father, as well as with the very holy, good and quickening Spirit, now, always and forever and ever, amen.[45]

---

[41] *AAgr* 58: ἀλλὰ καὶ νῦν εὖ οἶδα οὐκ ἀνηκόους ὑμᾶς τῶν ἐμῶν λόγων ὄντας· ἠρέμα τοιγαροῦν ἄνδες θαρροῦσιν ἐπὶ τὴν τοῦ θεοῦ ἡμῶν γνῶσιν. Leloir, *Écrits apocryphes sur les apôtres*, 248.

[42] *AAgr* 59: καὶ οἱ ὄχλοι ἀκούσαντες τῶν εἰρημένων ὑπὸ τοῦ Ἀνδρέα καὶ τρόπον τινὰ ἠρημένοι ὑπ' αὐτοῦ οὐκ ἀφίσταντο τοῦ τόπου. καὶ ὁ μακαριώτατος μᾶλλον προήγετο λέγειν πρὸς αὐτοὺς πλείονα ὧν εἰρήκει, καὶ τοσαῦτα ἦν ὡς ἔστιν τεκμαίρεσθαι τοὺς ἀκούοντας. τριῶν νυχθημέρων αὐτοῖς προσωμίλει, καὶ οὐδεὶς καμὼν ὅλως ἐχωρίζετο αὐτοῦ. Leloir, *Écrits apocryphes sur les apôtres*, 250.

[43] *AAgr* 62: ἀλλ' ἐπεὶ πρόσεισί μοι νῦν ὁ Αἰγεάτης, σιγῶν τὰ ἐμὰ τέκνα συνέχω. ἃ δεῖ με πρὸς αὐτὸν εἰπόντα ἀναλῦσαι ταῦτα ἐρῶ. τίνος χάριν πάλιν πρὸς ἡμᾶς, Αἰγεάτα; Leloir, *Écrits apocryphes sur les apôtres*, 253.

[44] *AAgr* 64 [10]: Leloir, *Écrits apocryphes sur les apôtres*, 256. In the Armenian version, the "we" does not appear.

[45] *AAgr* 65 [11]: ἐνταῦθά που τὸ τέλος τῶν μακαρίων μου διηγημάτων ποιήσαιμι καὶ πράξεων καὶ μυστηρίων δυσφράστων ὄντων, ἵνα μὴ καὶ ἀφράστων εἴπω, ἡ κορωνὶς τελευτάτω. καὶ ἐπεύξομαι πρῶτον μὲν ἐμαυτῷ ἀκοῦσαι τῶν εἰρημένων ὡς εἴρηται καὶ τούτων εἰς τὸ συμφανές, εἶτα καὶ τῶν ἀφανῶν, διανοίᾳ δὲ ληπτῶν, ἔπειτα καὶ πᾶσι τοῖς διατιθεμένοις ὑπὸ τῶν εἰρημένων, κοινωνίαν ἔχειν ἐπίπαν θεοῦ δὲ ἀνοίγοντος τὰς ἀκοὰς τῶν ἐντυγχανόντων, ὅπως ᾖ ληπτὰ ἅπαντα αὐτοῦ τὰ χαρίσματα ἐν Χριστῷ Ἰησοῦ τῷ κυρίῳ ἡμῶν μεθ' οὗ τῷ πατρὶ δόξα τιμὴ καὶ κράτος σὺν τῷ παναγίῳ καὶ ἀγαθῷ καὶ ζωοποιῷ πνεύματι νῦν καὶ ἀεὶ καὶ εἰς τοὺς αἰῶνας τῶν αἰώνων. ἀμήν. This is the text and translation of a Greek text constructed from mss. *H, S* and *C* (see n. 32 above). The critical appa-

Analysis of the *Acts of Andrew*

Because of the relation of Andrew's inner nature with the divinity, the apostle is an indispensible intermediary. His person as well as his authority, mission, and name require that all respect him.[46] Far from hiding behind the message he proclaims, he represents it. The bonds that link him to the divine words enable his unswerving mediation of these words. The necessity of speaking weighs upon him: "I transmitted words to you which I pray are received by you in the way these words themselves require,"[47] Andrew explains, and he describes his words as "what I above all had to say to you."[48] God entrusted Andrew with a mission not to teach everybody in general – perhaps an attack on the great church and its universalist mission – but to remind those who are related to these words that they are living among foreign evils (*AAgr* 47 [15]). Indicating the divine origin of the message, the author specifies that Andrew filled others without having eaten anything.[49]

With regard to the communication of the words of life, certain details in the text may reflect the cultic practices of the author's community. Maximilla takes the apostle and the future neophyte, Stratocles, by the hand and leads them into her room. The other brothers then arrive. All of them sit down and look at the apostle in the expectation of his sermon (*AAgr* 6). A privileged hearer seizes the hands of the preacher, lifts them to her own eyes and then to her lips before explaining her problem (*AAgr* 37 [5]).[50] Finally, the master in turn seizes the hand of the neophyte to whom his message is addressed (*AAgr* 43 [11]).[51]

Different types of communication and different genres of speech, moreover, are important in what we may call a rite of initiation in the *Acts of Andrew*. The seeker gains a private nocturnal meeting with the apostle; in this vein, the first meeting of Andrew and Stratocles (*AAgr* 8–9) is similar to the meetings of Jesus and Nicodemus (John 3:1–20) or of Jesus and the young man (*Secret Gospel of Mark* 3.4–5).[52] The initiatory meeting between Andrew and Stratocles is charac-

---

ratus in Prieur's edition (*Acta Andreae*, 2. 549) provides readings – which differ greatly from each other – that are found in the other manuscripts. In the Armenian version (see Leloir, *Écrits apocryphes sur les apôtres*, 257), these last lines are put on the lips of Stratocles in a similar, yet more condensed, form.

[46] See n. 1.

[47] *AAgr* 48 [16]; λόγους ὑμῖν παρέδωκα οὓς εὔχομαι οὕτως καταδέχεσθαι ὑφ᾽ ὑμῶν ὡς αὐτοὶ οἱ λόγοι θέλουσιν.

[48] Ibid., 37 [5]; ὃ γὰρ μάλιστα ἐχρῆν με εἰπεῖν πρὸς σέ.

[49] Ibid., 59; Leloir, *Écrits apocryphes sur les apôtres*, 251.

[50] See n. 17.

[51] On such a gesture, see *Acts of John* 62 in Éric Junod and Jean-Daniel Kaestli, *Acta Iohannis* (CCSA 1–2; Turnhout: Brepols, 1983) 1. 250–51 (text); 2. 436–38 (commentary).

[52] See Morton Smith, *Clement of Alexandria and a Secret Gospel of Mark* (Cambridge, Mass.: Harvard University Press, 1973) 99–120.

terized by the questions of the future initiate and the answers of the mystagogic apostle.

This private teaching, however, must be repeated in front of the gathered community. Thus the apostle avoids discrimination, and the repetition of the apostle's answers allows the disciple effectively to engrave the master's message in his or her mind. This initiation, or birth of the spiritual man or woman, is then similar to a childbirth where many are present (*AAgr* 8–9).

The second meeting of Andrew and Stratocles (*AAgr* 42–45 [10–13]) directs us toward another ecclesiastical practice, namely, the edification of a member of the community who is distressed and in a state of crisis because the imminent martyrdom of the leader disturbs him or her. The parenetical intervention of the apostle can be subdivided. First, a litany of rhetorical questions (*AAgr* 42 [10]) allows the apostle to test the fidelity of the believer. Second, without waiting for the responses of the believer, the preacher presents a series of affirmations (*AAgr* 43 [11]) that express his confidence in the positive attitude the faithful listener has made, or is in the process of making. Only then can the faithful one – in this case, Stratocles – express himself (*AAgr* 44 [12]). Stratocles celebrates both the adequacy of the words of the apostle as they relate to his own commitment to Andrew and the affective union that the words have provoked. This intervention by the master of the salvific words was doubly necessary for Stratocles. First, this speech caused the words of the apostle to be sown – this is the act of initiation, the spiritual procreation and birth. Second, the apostle's intervention caused the germination of the words – this is the moment of trial and edification. The moral aspect of the second step appears clearly in the following exclamation of Stratocles: "I need great mercy and the help which comes from you to be able to become worthy of the seeds I have from you."[53]

In *AAgr* 56, we find an ecclesiastical emphasis on missionizing. The author of the *Acts of Andrew* notes a shift in the audience. Having formerly conversed with Stratocles privately, the apostle now addresses everyone, telling the entire public – a public made up of believers and unbelievers – to come and witness his martyrdom. Referring to Andrew's speech, the author uses the expression κοινὸς λόγος.[54] This is a significant indication for us, since with this term, the author designates the speech as a missionary sermon. From the example that we find in the *Acts of Andrew*, such an oratorical piece has its own structure, tonality, and themes. Andrew first unsettles his listeners with a series of hypothetical propositions that force each one to situate himself or herself personally; for example, Andrew insists, "If you think that death is the end of the passing life, then leave this

---

[53] *AAgr* 44 [12]: πολλοῦ ἐλέου δέομαι καὶ βοηθείας τῆς παρὰ σοῦ, ὅπως δυναίμην ἄξιος γενέσθαι ὧν ἔχω σου σπερμάτων.

[54] Ibid., 56 [6]: Leloir, *Écrits apocryphes sur les apôtres*, 245. See also p. 244.

spot immediately."[55] The discourse continues this destabilizing of the public with a brief series of questions concerning the vanity of a life that focuses on the visible and the material; Andrew states, for example, "What is the good of possessing what is exterior, and not possessing yourselves?"[56] Then Andrew invites each listener to change his or her life.[57] For the author, this change requires the act of fleeing the world and binding one's interior being to the soul of the apostle which, thanks to his impending martyrdom, is beginning to let loose of earthly things.[58] Christology is strangely absent here; the apostle alone offers a soteriological bridge. By contemplating what is taking place, the hearers attach themselves to the apostle and receive his intelligence. Thus "another communion"[59] is established, a communion that is, without doubt, different from human sharing. The discourse ends with a promise that is Johannine in tone – "I am going to prepare the paths over there for those who gave me their accord,"[60] namely, those who accepted Andrew and his message – and with a final appeal which ends with this statement: "O men, choose what you prefer, for the choice depends on you."[61]

Stratocles, who listens, and Aegeates, who refuses the message, represent for the author the two types of hearers who seem, paradoxically, both to determine their lives freely and to be predestined to their fate, according to their relation or lack of relation to the words of life. Aegeates, the governor, is not even able to listen (*AAgr* 55 [5]), he is an enemy of the word, a μισολόγος (*AAgr* 42 [10]). His brother, Stratocles, on the contrary, depends upon all the related words (*AAgr* 10) and has a part in these words of salvation (*AAgr* 9).

The faithful in general are also characterized by their relationship to the words of salvation. They must clean their ears (*AAgr* 57);[62] they know how not to be deaf (*AAgr* 58);[63] they are related to the words (*AAgr* 47 [15]); they are attached to the word alone (*AAgr* 12) and are lifted up by it (*AAgr* 50 [18]); they are seized by the apostle (*AAgr* 59).[64] The word must be affirmed in the disciples (*AAgr* 16), who are congratulated for their attention (*AAgr* 38 [6]). The simple circuit of communication is explained in the following manner: "The word given to me is ad-

---

[55] *AAgr* 56 [6]: εἰ τοῦτο ἡγεῖσθε τὸ τέλος τῆς ζωῆς τῆς προσκαίρου τὸ τεθνάναι, ἤδη ἀπαλλάσσεσθε τοῦ τόπου τούτου. Leloir, *Écrits apocryphes sur les apôtres*, 246.

[56] *AAgr* 57: τί γὰρ ὄφελος ὑμῖν ἐστιν τὰ ἐκτὸς κεκτημένοις, ἑαυτοὺς δὲ μή; Leloir, *Écrits apocryphes sur les apôtres*, 247.

[57] *AAgr* 57: ἀλλὰ μετάθετε, παρακαλῶ πάντας ὑμᾶς, τὸν ἐπίπονον βίον. Leloir, *Écrits apocryphes sur les apôtres*, 247.

[58] *AAgr* 57; Leloir, *Écrits apocryphes sur les apôtres*, 248.

[59] *AAgr* 57: ἑτέραν ... κοινωνίαν. Leloir, *Écrits apocryphes sur les apôtres*, 248.

[60] *AAgr* 58: ἄπειμι προετοιμάσαι τὰς ἐκεῖ ὁδοὺς τοῖς μὲν συνθεμένοις μοι. Leloir, *Écrits apocryphes sur les apôtres*, 249.

[61] *AAgr* 58: ἕλεσθε τοιγαροῦν, ἄνδρες, ὁπότερα βούλεσθε, ἐφ᾿ ὑμῖν γὰρ τέθειται τὸ τοιοῦτον. Leloir, *Écrits apocryphes sur les apôtres*, 250.

[62] Leloir, *Écrits apocryphes sur les apôtres*, 248.

[63] Ibid.

[64] Ibid., 250. Here the Armenian version seems to weaken the text.

dressed to you again, Maximilla."[65] If the author places before the hearers a real choice (*AAgr* 58),[66] he also seems to accept the dysphoric possibility of falling away: "Oh! the great lazines of those I have instructed! Oh! the sudden fog that has enveloped us after so many mysteries! Oh! the many discourses we have spoken until now, without being able to convince our own people!"[67]

The conclusion of the work is of great importance, for, like the Gospel of John (John 20:30–31 and 21:24–25), the book claims to transmit in writing the mysteries and words that the apostle communicated orally. The author, remaining anonymous, nevertheless dares to use the first person singular and states that the work is a revelation, initiation, and unveiling of the mysteries, the author's own "blessed accounts of the acts and mysteries which are difficult, if not impossible, to express."[68] The author announces a double prayer: first, that the text correspond to what was said and heard; and, second, that the readers might receive the gifts of the God in Christ and live in communion together after having been transformed by these words (*AAgr* 65 [11]).[69]

With regard to these words of life, the author sometimes uses "word" in the singular (*AAgr* 12; *AAgr* 50 [18]: λόγος), but generally prefers "words" (*AAgr* 48 [16]; λόγοι), that is, maxims and discourses which confer life. The author hardly distinguishes the nature of God from the nature of the inner man and thus does not separate the word of God from the apostolic speeches which convey it. The unity of the apostle with God confers upon the apostle's words a divine effectiveness, as is seen, for example, in the divine power of Andrew's speech over Maximilla (*AAgr* 39 [7]). Not only the effectiveness of the words is significant, but also the truth of these λόγοι (*AAgr* 29) and the salvation that they confer (*AAgr* 8, 9, 44 [12]).

In his Latin summary of the *Acts of Andrew*, Gregory of Tours places on the lips of an admirer these words: "And now, that makes two days that I have heard your sermons full of words of life."[70] If the apostle is the herald of these words, Jesus Christ himself is the master of them, as Andrew exclaims: "Glory to you, Jesus Christ, master of true words and promises."[71] Thanks to the words that are proclaimed, the inner man can awaken and come to life. The words reach a privileged part of the thought (διάνοια): "they touched your thinking part."[72] Further-

---

[65] *AAgr* 40 [8]: πρὸς σὲ δέ μοι πάλιν ὁ λόγος, Μαξιμίλλα.

[66] Leloir, *Écrits apocryphes sur les apôtres*, 250.

[67] *AAgr* 61: ὦ ἡ πολλὴ τῶν ὑπ᾽ ἐμοῦ μαθητευθέντων νωθρία· ὦ ἡ ἐπικαλυφθεῖσα ἡμῖν μετὰ πολλὰ μυστήρια ταχινὴ ὁμίχλη· ὦ πόσα εἰρηκότες ἕως τοῦ νῦν οὐκ ἐπείσαμεν τοὺς ἰδίους. Leloir, *Écrits aporcryphes sur les apôtres*, 251–52.

[68] *AAgr* 65 [11]; see n. 45 above and n. 79 below. Leloir, *Écrits apocryphes sur les apôtres*, 257.

[69] Leloir, *Écrits apocryphes sur les apôtres*, 257.

[70] Praedicationes tuas, quae sunt plenae verbis vitalibus (Gregory of Tours, *Liber de miraculis beati Andreae apostoli* 28).

[71] *AAgr* 29: δόξα σοι Ἰησοῦ Χριστέ, ἀληθῶν λόγων καὶ ὑποσχέσεων πρύτανις.

[72] *AAgr* 42 [10]: ἔθιγέν σου τοῦ διανοητικοῦ μέρους.

more, a part of the soul – "the affective part of my soul," as Stratocles says[73] – leans toward what has been heard. The divine words thus reach the cognitive and affective centers of the inner man. Just as declarations of human love provoke a good feeling of understanding and of being understood, of loving and of being loved, the saving words of the apostle arouse knowledge and love in the neophytes. The images used, such as those of embracing flames (*AAgr* 44 [12]) or growing seeds (*AAgr* 44 [12]), confirm this interpretation.[74]

Historical Origins of the *Acts of Andrew*

Having described the events of the acts and having presented an analysis, I may now turn to the question of the origin of this theology of the "words," I propose three answers, none of which excludes the other.

First, in the Jewish and Christian tradition, wisdom literature – from the Proverbs (called λόγοι in the Septuagint) to the Wisdom of Solomon, in which chapters 6–9 sing the merits and benefits of Wisdom, or σοφία – offers the reader a path toward life by means of the knowledge of and meditation on certain salvific phrases. Indeed, it seems that the author of the Gospel of John was inspired by this very idea: Peter's messianic confession of faith is transformed into an adherence to the vivifying words of Jesus: "Lord, Simon Peter answers, to whom will we go? You have the words (ῥήματα) of eternal life, and we believe and we know now that you are the holy one of God" (John 6:68–69; see also John 8:51).[75] Luke, too, may lean on this theology of the words when he proposes to Theophilus "the assurance concerning the words (λόγων) that you have learned" (Luke 1:4). Is the author of the *Acts of Andrew* also inspired by this conception? The text's silence with regard to Christology and the dualistic content of its moral teachings prevent us from immediately answering the question in the affirmative.

Second, I propose that the *Acts of Andrew* might have found its origin in the gnostic tradition. Like the author of the Gospel of John, the authors of gnostic literature also believe that they possess words of salvation. For example, in the beginning of the *Gospel of Thomas*, we find the following statement: "Here are the secret words which Jesus the Living One said and which Didymus Jude Thomas wrote. And he said: He who will find the interpretation of these words will not

---

[73] Ibid., 44 [12]: τὸ παθητικὸν μέρος τῆς ψυχῆς μου. The first three words of this quotation, as well as some others prior to them, are omitted by the cod. Vat. gr. 808.

[74] On the image of the seed in Jewish and Greek traditions, see Hans-Josef Klauck, *Allegorie and Allegorese in synoptischen Gleichnistexten* (NTA n.s. 13; Münster: Aschendorff, 1978) 189–200, 213–18, 221–27.

[75] James Robinson, "Λόγοι σοφῶν: On the Gattung of Q," in James M. Robinson and Helmut Koester, *Trajectories through Early Christianity* (Philadelphia: Fortress, 1971) 71–113; Koester, "La tradition apostolique et les origines du gnosticisme," 1–16.

taste death."[76] Unlike many gnostic texts, the *Acts of Andrew* do not affirm the secret character of the sayings and the privilege of an esoteric doctrine. Like the
Gospel of Thomas, however, the *Acts of Andrew* particularly emphasizes the mysterious, saving, and vivifying nature of the words: "I deem as blessed those who
have become obedient to the words preached and who through them see as in a
mirror the mysteries of their own nature for whose sake all things were built"
(*AAgr* 47 [15]);[77] Andrew also cries, "Oh! the sudden fog which has enveloped us
after so many mysteries!" (*AAgr* 61).[78] We also recall the author's comment regarding the "blessed accounts of the acts and mysteries which are difficult, if not
impossible to express" (*AAgr* 65 [11]).[79]

Finally, the *Acts of Andrew* often echos Plato's thought. The spiritual maieutics,
the invitation addressed to the soul to flee the sensual, or the correspondence of
the divine truth with the human being, the emphasis on precise parts of the
thought or soul[80] – all these suggest that the *Acts of Andrew* finds its origins in the
milieu of middle Platonism.[81] Does this mean that the idea of the words of life
found in the *Acts of Andrew* can be explained by this source alone? This merits

---

[76] *Gos, Thom.* prologue, 1. Henri-Charles Puech commented at length concerning this prologue and logion 1 in his course, "Explication de l'Évangile selon Thomas et recherches sur les paroles de Jesus qui y sont réunies," at the Collège de France in 1957–58. The summary of this course appeared in Henri-Charles Puech, *En quête de la Gnose, II. Sur l'Évangile selon Thomas. Esquisse d'une interprétation systématique* (Bibliothèque des sciences humaines; Paris: Gallimard,
1978) 74–76. This study notes several parallels to the prologue of the *Gospel of Thomas* in the *Acts
of Thomas* 10, 39, 47, and 78. See Bentley Layton, ed., *Nag Hammadi Codex II, 2–7: Together
with XIII. 2*, Brit. Lib. Or. 4962(1) and P. Oxy. 1, 654, 655* (NHS 20; Leiden: Brill, 1989).

[77] What does the expression περὶ τὴν ἰδίαν φύσιν mean? It probably signifies the nature of the
divinity, at the origin of all things.

[78] These last words, "after so many mysteries," mean, according to the context, "after the unveiling of so many mysteries"; see Leloir, *Écrits apocryphes sur les apôtres*, 251–52 (the Armenian
text is rather different here); see also *AAgr* 9, where by childbirth the women participate in the
same mysteries.

[79] See Leloir, *Écrits apocryphes sur les apôtres*, 257. Richard A. Lipsius (*Die apokryphen Apostelgeschichten und Apostellegenden* [2 vols.; Braunschweig: Schwetschke, 1883; Amsterdam:
APA-Philo, 1976] 1.543–662) believed that the primitive *Acts of Andrew* was a gnostic text.

[80] Plato *Tim.* 89A (διανοητικός); Pseudo-Plato *Tim. Locr.* (περὶ ψυχᾶς κόσμω καὶ φύσιος) 102E
(παθητικός); Albinus, *Didaskalikos* 32; see also several scholia of Plato: William Chase Greene,
Scholia Platonica (Haverford, Pa.: American Philological Society, 1938) s. v. διανοητικός, μέρος,
παθητικός. Jean-Marc Prieur called to my attention Evagrius Ponticus, *Tractatus practicus* 78:
πρακτική ἐστι μέθοδος πνευματικὴ τὸ παθητικὸν μέρος τῆς ψυχῆς ἐκκαθαίρουσα ("The spiritual
method is practical, because it purifies the affective part of the soul"). See Manfred Hornschuh,
"Acts of Andrew," in *New Testament Apocrypha* (ed. Edgar Hennecke and Wilhelm Schneemelcher; 2 vols.; Philadelphia: Westminster, 1964) 2. 393.

[81] Joseph Flamion (*Les Actes apocryphes de l'apôtre André. Les Actes d'André et de Mathias,
de Pierre et d'André et les textes apparentés* [Louvain: Université de Louvain, 1911] 157–67) believed that the *Acts of Andrew*, in a form inspired by the Greek novel, communicates a Christian
message sharply influenced by neoplatonism and the neopythagoreanism. Manfred Hornschuh
("Acts of Andrew," 394) prefers to speak of middle platonism and quotes several platonic parallels to the *Acts of Andrew*.

discussion, and it is precisely to provoke this discussion that I have presented these texts and synthesized this information, leaving to others more competent than myself the task of locating the *Acts of Andrew* within the religious and philosophical trends of late antiquity.

Miracles, Magic, and Healing in the Apocryphal Acts of the Apostles*

For over thirty years now, scholars have rightly demanded a particularized investigation into each of the apocryphal acts of the apostles.[1] Aware as I am of having infringed upon this rule by the global approach that characterizes this study, I implore the readers' indulgence by invoking the same *episteme*, in the sense that Michel Foucault has given to this word,[2] that conditions these texts and by assuming an identical conception of eternal life that goes beyond doctrinal and ethical divergences.

In the following pages, I will seek to determine the place occupied by the miracle narratives in the apocryphal acts of the apostles. I will defend the thesis that the interaction of other elements, such as the discourse of the apostles, the sacraments, and martyrdom, alone yields a correct definition of the function of miracles in these texts. These four poles – miracle, proclamation, sacrament, and martyrdom – form a system, and they must not be isolated one from another. What all of them express is the conviction that behind our world there lies a divine world, which is the only one that matters.[3] Our texts are invitations, addressed to readers for the purpose of earnestly accessing this spiritual realm. In light of this unique, truly real and decisive realm the miracle fulfills a limited function, namely, to be a sign; likewise the apostolic discourse fulfills a hermeneutic, kerygmatic, and liturgical function; and accordingly, the sacraments and martyrdom fulfill an initiative and mysterious function, and a convincing – perhaps glorifying – function respectively.

I. The Miracles of the Apostles

The victory over evil

The apocryphal acts of the apostles communicate in a narrative way the conviction that this world must be abandoned because it has been left at the mercy of de-

---

* This article was translated by Helene Perdicoyanni Paleologou, to whom I express my gratitude.
[1] See François Bovon and Éric Junod, "Reading the Apocryphal Acts of the Apostles," *Semeia* 38 (1986) 165.
[2] Michel Foucault, *Les mots et les choses. Une archéologie des sciences humaines* (Bibliothèque des sciences humaines; Paris: Gallimard, 1966).
[3] See Bovon and Junod, "Reading the Apocryphal Acts," 167–69.

monic forces. Thus many exorcisms are recounted as tests and signs; the fifth act of *Thomas*, for instance, relates the misfortunes of a very beautiful woman who is attacked by a lustful demon.[4] After she is liberated, she recovers her original nature and receives grace and peace.

The apostle makes willing use of prayer in order to attest that it is only God, the source of all power, who allows the miracle worker to expel the demon and render the divine world accessible to the one who was formerly possessed. Thus, in the *Acts of John* the beloved disciple heals old, sick women from Ephesus, while distancing himself from all kinds of magical works. The apostle is also concerned to instruct the people of Ephesus to care about their souls rather than being content with admiring the miracle.[5]

In the *Acts of Philip*, the apostolic procession confronts dragons, both male and female, that cross its path. Accomplished victories tell readers that God's realm does not belong to this world and that pain and violence still afflict humanity. The reconciliation of animals that Philip performs in the course of the same travels,[6] as well as their progressive humanization, attest to and anticipate in their own way the nature of God's reign.[7] This forthcoming world will overcome the forces of evil and human vices. The apocryphal literature does not share the same reservation as the New Testament with regard to miracles of punishment; these are frequent in the apocryphal writings. Thus in the *Infancy Gospel of Thomas* the child Jesus acts ruthlessly and punishes with all his strength.[8] The apostles will imitate him; this is especially true of Paul, who sentences an adulterous woman to paralysis at the beginning of the *Acts of Peter*.[9]

Because of this ability and willingness to punish wrongdoers, it does not make sense to contradict the apostles, God's lieutenants on earth. Simon the magician becomes keenly aware of this as he loses his combat against the prince of the apostles and his attempt ends shamefully on the ground of the Via Sacra in Rome, with his leg broken at three points.[10]

---

[4] *Acts Thom.* 42–50.

[5] *Acts John* 30–36.

[6] We find this motif in the *Infancy Gospel of Pseudo-Matthew* 19.

[7] See *Acts Phil.* 8.1–5, 15–21 (94–101) and 12.1–8. I am using here the new critical edition and the new division into acts and paragraphs; see François Bovon, Bertrand Bouvier, and Frédéric Amsler, eds., *Acta Philippi: Textus* (CCSA 11; Turnhout: Brepols, 1999). See also the important commentary by Frédéric Amsler. *Acta Philippi: Commentarius* (CCSA 12; Turnhout: Brepols, 1999).

[8] *Inf. Gos. Thom.* 3–5, 8, 14–15. See Sever J. Voicu, "Verso il testo primitivo dei Παιδικὰ τοῦ κυρίου Ἰησοῦ, 'Racconti dell' infanzia del Signore Gesù," *Apocrypha* 9 (1998) 7–95.

[9] *Acts Pet.* 2.

[10] Ibid., 32.

The variety of miracles

There are all sorts of miracles and fantastic occurrences in the apocryphal works. I have already indicated some of these, such as exorcisms, healings, and punishments. Some of these miracles express the honor that is due to God, to his Son, or to his representatives on earth; thus during the escape to Egypt, dragons and other monsters, followed by lions, wolves, and other wildcats, bow and adore the infant Son of God.[11] The three hundred sixty-five idols of the city, standing where the procession arrives, crush themselves, an event that provokes the adoration of Aphrodise, the governor.[12] And in the *Acts of Thomas*, wild asses are enlisted in the service of the apostle to pull his cart.[13]

Others miracles underscore the authority and legitimate the power of the apostle: these include, for example, divine messages that attribute[14] to him premonitory miracles,[15] exercises of prescience,[16] appearances of Christ,[17] or even, in the case of Philip, the apostle's transfiguration.[18] Trivial and apparently useless, and even fantastic, marvels in the *Acts of Peter* are used to attest to the superhuman power of the apostle and to accelerate the process of conversion: thus the speaking dog[19] and the broken statue that is rehabilitated in the end.[20]

Others miracles serve as reminders of the protection with which the Lord surrounds his favorites. Hence we see that storms are appeased and shipwrecks have favorable outcomes,[21] and through repeated interventions poor Thecla is rescued; in the arena, a lioness protects her from a savage bear, then from a furious lion. Thecla's prayer sends away many wildcats and draws her toward baptism; the seals of the basin where the saint baptizes herself are prevented from devouring her by the perfume of the women spectators and a flash of lightning; and a cloud of fire discreetly veils the nudity of the young girl before frenzied bulls, crazed by bonds and burns, are let loose upon her. The bulls are thus prevented from unleashing their fury on the young girl.[22] It is often the case that when martyrdom threatens, divine pressure intensifies: the resurrection and, especially, the conver-

---

[11] *Infancy Gospel of Pseudo-Matthew* 18–19.

[12] Ibid., 22–24.

[13] *Acts Thom.* 69–70.

[14] *Acts Pet.* 1; *Acts Paul Mart.* 1.

[15] *Acts John* 48.

[16] *Acts Andr.* 49 (new numeration; 17 according to the ancient); *Acts Phil.* 5.8 (49); 5.12 (54); 5.16 (58).

[17] *Acts Pet.* 1, 5; *Acts Andr.* 40 (8); *Acts Phil.* 13.

[18] *Acts Phil.* 5.22–23 (60–61).

[19] *Acts Pet.* 9.

[20] Ibid., 11.

[21] *Acts Phil.* 3.10–14 (33–34); *Acts of John by Pseudo-Prochorus* (see Theodor Zahn, *Acta Joannis* [1880; Hildeshem: Gerstenberg, 1975] 7–10); *Acts of Timothy*, see Hermann Usener, *Acta S. Timothei* (Bonn: Karl Georg Universität, 1877) 9 (allusion to John's shipwreck).

[22] *Acts of Paul and Thecla* 33–39.

sion of Patroclus arouse Nero's ire against the apostle Paul. When the apostle's executioner completes his task it is milk, not blood, that gushes forth.[23] The divine power conferred on the apostle lasts beyond death: thus, in order to prove to the emperor that he did not himself have the last word and that physical death is but a phase, Paul makes an appearance to Nero following his martyrdom,[24] then to two of his disciples, and to two new converts as well.[25] This divine power of the apostle can take yet another form: a dust, having become famous because it lay on the tomb of the apostle John in Ephesus, manifests the rhythm of the apostle's breathing, since he is supposed to have slept and not to have died (one knows this legend especially from the *Acts of John* by Pseudo-Prochorus and from Augustine).[26] From the tomb of the apostle Thomas, in the absence of relics, a similar dust heals one of king Misdeus' sons, finally converting him.[27]

The varied significance of narratives

Often, particularly in the *Acts of Peter*, miracles arouse and strengthen the faith of beneficiaries and spectators.[28] Thus we read in the *Acts of Philip* that three thousand people believed following a miraculous resurrection that took place within the context of a dispute, an ἀγών, between the apostle and Aristarchus, his adversary.[29]

As in the canonical Gospels, many miracles are visible signs of a higher recovery. When burnt or paralyzed hands recover their health,[30] when families are brought together again by resurrections[31] or reunions,[32] the function is clear: the miracle signals that the God of Christians has an agenda of communion and life. God has carried through this great work of redemption through Christ, then through the apostles.

The narrative proof that best demonstrates this will toward salvation is obviously the miracle of resurrection.[33] This event, difficult as it was for a Greek to

---

[23] *Acts Paul Mart.* 5. See *Acts Phil. Mart.* 41 (147) (recension Θ): a μύρον ("perfume" or "ointment") flows from the apostle's head after his martyrdom.

[24] *Acts Paul Mart.* 4, 6.

[25] Ibid., 5, 7.

[26] *Acts John by Pseudo-Prochorus*; for the Latin text according to certain manuscripts, see Zahn, *Acta Ioannis*, 252; Augustine, *Tractatus in Ioannem* 124. 2. See François-Marie Braun, *Jean le Théologien et son Évangile dans l'Église ancienne* (3 vols.; EBib; Paris: Gabalda, 1959) 1: 365.

[27] *Acts Thom.* 170.

[28] *Acts Pet.* 10–13, 17, 26–27; *Acts Andr.* 48 (16); *Acts John* 42; *Acts of Paul and Thecla* 38; *Acts Paul Mart.* 5, 7; *Acts Thom.* 59.

[29] *Acts Phil.* 6.15–2? (80–86).

[30] *Acts Thom.* 52; *Prot. Jas.* 19–20.

[31] *Acts Phil.* 1.1–4, 18 (1–5).

[32] Pseudo-Clement, *Recognitiones* 7.

[33] We have also to note the prison releases: *Acts of Paul*, Papyrus of Hambourg, pp. 3–4; *Acts Thom.* 106–07, 118–22, 154, 162. See Gérard Poupon, "L'accusation de magie dans les Actes

believe in (see the philosophers of Athens in Acts 17:32) and even for a Hebrew (see King David at the death of his son in 2 Sam 12:22–23), is the most decisive example found in the apocryphal literature. The abundance is eloquent here.[34] The God proclaimed seeks life, restores it, and orients it toward the eternal and supernatural life; the corporal resurrection and ascetic life constitute its anticipation and preparation.[35] In order to convey this message, the *Acts of Thomas* and the *Acts of Philip* relate how human souls can glimpse both the delicious residences of Paradise and the horrible tortures of Hell.[36]

As if to reinforce God's project and further persuade the reader, the God of the apocryphal narratives comes willingly out of silence and steps forward from retreat. The celestial voices are innumerable.[37] Appearances are countless.[38] Christ appears in various forms as the apostle who is his representative on earth[39] (the apostle can appear himself after his martyrdom),[40] as a beautiful child,[41] even as an eagle[42] or a luminous cross.[43] Again, the purpose is always to orient consciences towards the only real world, the divine and celestial space.

Scholars[44] have repeatedly stressed that the narration of a miracle had to lead to faith, but in the case of the apocryphal acts this was a weak faith, prompted only by visible proofs. It is true that the *Acts of Thomas* and the *Acts of Peter* speak explicitly of the link between miracles and conversion.[45] In my opinion, however, the concern is not so much with earning a conviction as with guiding the believer's look in the right direction, that of the spiritual world of God: "Is it any great mat-

---

apocryphes," in *Les Actes apocryphes des apôtres: Christianisme et monde païen* (ed. François Bovon; Publications de la Faculté de théologie de l'Université de Genève 4; Geneva: Labor et Fides, 1981) 71–93.

[34] See *Acts John* 19–25, 46–47, 51, 75, 80, 82–83; *Acts Pet.* 26–27; *Acts of Paul*, Papyrus of Heidelberg, pp. 41–42; *Acts Thom.* 33, 53–54, 80–81; *Acts Phil.* 1.1–4, 18 (1–5), 6.15–22 (80–86); *Epistle of Pseudo-Titus* (narrative on the resurrection of a farmer's only daughter that was performed by Peter), see Wilhelm Schneemelcher ed., *Neutestamentliche Apokryphen in deutscher Übersetzung* (5. Auflage der von E. Hennecke begründeten Sammlung; 2 vols.; Tübingen: Mohr Siebeck, 1983–89) 2.54–55.

[35] See *Acts John* 47.

[36] See *Acts Thom.* 21–25, 55–58; *Acts Phil.* 1.1–16.

[37] See for instance, *Acts Thom.* 121, 158.

[38] See for instance, *Acts John* 97; *Acts Phil. Mart.* 29 (135).

[39] See *Acts Thom.* 11; *Acts of Paul and Thecla* 21.

[40] See *Acts Pet.* 40 (11); *Acts Paul Mart.* 6–7.

[41] See *Acts Phil.* 4.2 (38); François Bovon, "Les Actes de Philippe," in *ANRW* 2.25.6 (ed. Wolfgang Haase and Hildegard Temporini; Berlin/New York: de Gruyter, 1988) 4483.

[42] *Acts Phil.* 3.5–6.

[43] See *Acts John* 98 (The divine Christ shows a luminous cross and appears himself, above this cross, in the form of a voice); Éric Junod and John-Daniel Kaestli, *Acta Iohanni* (CCSA 1–2; 2 vols.; Turnhout: Brepols, 1983) 2.656–61.

[44] See Léon Vouaux, *Les Actes of Pierre: Introduction, textes, traduction et commentaire* (Les Apocryphes du Nouveau Testament; Paris: Letouzey et Ané, 1922) 85–86.

[45] See above, p. 256 n. 28.

ter if bodily sicknesses are cured?"[46] asks the apostle John. The miracle has to lead to belief in the other world as well as to ascetic behavior in this world.

Varied images of the apostle

Following Jesus, who in the apocryphal literature affirms God's message from his childhood and repeats it beyond his death, the apostles hammer out the message of the celestial kingdom. The most diverse models then enter into the service of this cause. It does not suffice to say that the apostle heals, resurrects, or even – and this is an amplification compared to the New Testament[47] – allows others to perform resurrections in order to win affection. It is appropriate to add that while doing all these things, the apostle also assumes various conventional roles.

He acts, for example, as a physician of souls or as the celestial physician's nurse. At the beginning of the *Acts of Peter*, the Lord appears to the apostle Paul while he is staying in Rome and commands him, saying: "Paul, get up, and be, by your corporal presence, the physician of those of Spain."[48] In the *Acts of Philip*, the apostle settles into an abandoned clinic (ἰατρεῖον) without so much as a wink from the author.[49] He carries a physician's instrument case (ὁ νάρθηξ) that Christ has given him in Galilee.[50] In Azot, Charitine, the daughter of the wealthy Nikokleides, was privileged to be cared for by the best physicians, all in vain. But then the young girl indicates to her despairing father the unexpected godsend of the foreign physician's arrival in the city.[51] The father concedes to making a final attempt and, when he meets Philip, bestows on him the title of physician. The apostle refuses the homage, which in his opinion is unmerited, and attributes the honor to his master, Christ, "the healer of the hidden and the visible"[52]; the young girl is, however, sensitive to nuances and offers her homage "to the physician who is in you."[53] The terminology of medicine and the image of the physician are not unique to the *Acts of Philip*. We find these elsewhere, especially in one of the endings to the *Acts of Paul and Thecla*.[54] The apostle is a healer, but it is only souls that he intends to take care of and save.

---

[46] *Acts John* 47.

[47] Ibid., 24 (Cleopatra is invited by the apostle to resurrect her husband Lycomedes).

[48] *Acts Pet.* 1.

[49] *Acts Phil.* 13.4.

[50] Ibid.

[51] *Acts Phil.* 4.4 (40).

[52] Ibid., 4.4 (41).

[53] Ibid., 4.4 (42).

[54] *Acts of Paul and Thecla* (according to the manuscripts G and M); see Léon Vouaux, *Les Actes de Paul et ses lettres apocryphes* (Les Apocryphes du Nouveau Testament; Paris: Letouzey et Ané, 1913) 232–38; *Acts John* 22, 56, 108; *Acts Thom.* 10, 37, 95, 143, 156.

Elsewhere, the image of war comes to mind. Just as a general besieges a city, the apostle cuts off the first demonic entrenchment.[55] Then, if we take the example of Philip, he reduces to silence the enemy's sentries, the vipers in charge of controlling the foreign visitor's honesty.[56] Finally, the apostle exterminates the enemy himself, the viper whose cult is in the heart of the city.[57]

In others texts the apostle resembles an orator, a philosopher, or a lawyer. The force of his word is then impressive. Signs and prodigies – ἀρεταί, δυνάμεις, and τέρατα – accompany his triumph. In *Acts of Philip* 2, which draws on Acts 17 (Paul at the Areopagus), the apostle opposes three hundred Athenians philosophers whom the great Jewish priest from Jerusalem comes to sustain, all to no avail. The apostle's garment plays a role here. This is not an orator or a philosopher's toga, but – quite the contrary – the shirt (λέντιον) and the garment (ἐπενδύτης) of an ascetic, which Christ, as the text specifies, gave to his apostles.[58]

The conflict between the apostle and his adversaries sometimes takes the form of an athletic race (the Greek term ἀγών appears here).[59] In the course of a real duel that spectators who have paid for their seats[60] attentively and impatiently watch, Peter triumphs over Simon the magician.[61] The match unfolds through several rounds. The verbal contest in which the adversaries engage through biblical verses is followed by the decisive challenge of a resurrection to be accomplished. And this is where the adversary gives in, then finally cracks. The confrontation ends dramatically on the Via Sacra, where Simon, who had attempted to fly, suffers a fatal crash.[62]

The apostle is also the divine man who delivers those who have been ensnared in Satan's net. Exorcism scenes demonstrate this role. The numerous liberations from prison (inspired by the dionysiac tradition, of which Euripides' *Bacchai* is the best known)[63] occur most often for the benefit of the apostles.[64] These nar-

---

[55] See *Acts Phil.* 9.1–5 (102–06) and 11.1–10; see Bovon, "Les Actes de Philippe," 4500–03. In the *Acts of Paul, Martyrdom* 2–4, the apostle appears as a soldier in the service of Christ, his emperor. He enrolls recruits from everywhere.

[56] *Acts Phil.* 13.1–5; see Bovon, "Les Actes de Philippe," 4504–7.

[57] This narrative should appear in the lost part of the *Acts of Philip*. We read references in the Byzantine texts, see Bovon, "Les Actes de Philippe," 4445, 4449, 4500, 4555.

[58] *Acts Phil.* 2.1 (6).

[59] *Acts Pet.* 12, 16; *Acts Phil.* 5.6–8 (48–50), 6.16 (80). See the Nag Hammadi texts.

[60] *Acts Pet.* 23; see Poupon, "L'accusation de magie," 79 n. 50.

[61] *Acts Pet.* 23–28. *Acts Phil.* 6.1–22 (64–86) relates a parallel story, inspired without any doubt by that of the *Acts of Peter*; see Bovon, "Les Actes de Philippe," 4487–89.

[62] *Acts Pet.* 32 (3).

[63] See O. Weinreich, "Gebet und Wunder," in *Religionsgeschichtliche Studien* (1929; Darmstadt: Wissenschaftliche Buchgesellschaft, 1968) 39–298; Joachim Jeremias, Art. "θύρα," *TDNT* 3 (1965) 175–76; Hans Conzelmann, *Die Apostelgeschichte erklärt* (HNT 7; Tübingen: Mohr Siebeck, 1963) 71; Poupon, "L'accusation de magie," 71–93.

[64] See n. 33.

ratives indicate to the reader that the disciple of Christ, a liberator of souls, is himself a former prisoner who was liberated by his master.

There is a criterion that is becoming established here. Time and again the apostle risks being thought of as a magician, a sorcerer, or a charlatan. Thomas is continually accused of being a magician.[65] John enters the theater of Ephesus naked in order to prove that he uses neither philters nor potions, nor magical sticks.[66] Paul and Philip are also accused of witchcraft.[67] The authors of the apocryphal acts are convinced that, by contrast, it is the adversaries of the Christians who are overcome by witchcraft or black magic. They express themselves via Peter's voice and address Simon, the person whom, in what follows, they continue to refer to as the Magician.[68]

To undercut this accusation of magic, the apocryphal acts refer to the divinity. Despite all the thaumaturgic power that is invested in him, the apostle always depends on his Master, who – in the final analysis – is the real author of the miracle. And the miracle does not contradict the laws of creation; on the contrary, according to these authors, it is Creation's proper copy in a world tainted by vice and death. Thus the apostle is established as a true disciple and an authentic servant of God. The contrast between the true and the false prophet, which is rooted in the Scriptures[69] but also present in pseudepigraphic[70] and patristic[71] literature, permits us to underscore the faithfulness of the messenger to his God and the pertinence of its evidence. As his power does not come from himself, the apostle offers the healing without pay.

---

[65] *Acts Thom.* 16, 20, 89, 96, 98–102, 104, 106, 114, 116–17, 123, 130, 134, 138–39, 162–63.

[66] *Acts John* 31. According to the *Acts Phil. Mart.* 19 (125), the apostles are undressed and searched by the authorities, who think they are going to find magicians' instruments on them.

[67] *Acts of Paul and Thecla* 20; *Acts Pet.* 4 (as far as we know, the *Acts of Peter* begins with an interest in the apostle Paul's fate); *Acts Phil.* 4.1 (37) and *Acts Phil. Mart.* 19 (125).

[68] *Acts Pet.* 28, 31 (2).

[69] See Jer 28.

[70] See *Ascension of Isaiah* 2–5.

[71] See Hermas, *The Shepherd* 43 (= Mand., 11). Enrico Norelli directs me to Pseudo-Clement, *Recognitiones* 3.57–61, where the problem of miracles is approached explicitly. It is the apostle Peter who is supposed to give the explanation. According to the theory of the syzygies, miracles arrive by pairs (we count ten from Cain and Abel to the expected Antichrist and Christ, passing through the magicians of Egypt and Moses, Simon, and Peter). Various arguments are advanced to account for the faith that both simple folk and informed people can attribute to miracles. The orator underscores the uselessness of miracles, such as those performed by Simon, and the profit that one can receive from the true miracles, such as those performed by the Lord. In the end times, some miracles will seduce even the elect of God.

II. The Word, the Sacraments, and Martyrdom

The word

Like the Johannine Christ, who utters discourses following the "signs" he dispenses, or like the apostles Peter and Paul in the canonical Acts, the heroes of the apocryphal legends always join the word to an act;[72] the miracle would be equivocal if it remained isolated from preaching. The apostolic proclamation first eliminates the suspicion of magic that can be attached to memory. Then, as there is a risk of material value being attributed to the miracle, the voice of the disciple of Christ gives a transcendent meaning to the concrete event.

In the canonical scriptures, biblical anthropology and eschatological expectation more often include the totality of the real in a holistic perspective. A healing or a resurrection attest to the conformity of the original creation to the reign of God and underscore the corporal status of the final resurrection in a legitimate manner – by anticipation. In the apocryphal literature, the material miracle assumes a paradoxical status from the moment that eschatology appears as the hope of an exclusive membership in the spiritual world and from the moment that ethics are reduced to an escape from the world. The word of the apostle becomes here a corrective and a vector of sense. It underlines the figurative character of the thaumaturgic gesture and gives meaning to the miraculous event; in other words, there is something beyond the tangible gesture. Consequently, it would be a mistake to return to the terrestrial, to a creation that is basically irreparable and deprived of value. An expression found in the *Acts of John* illustrates this bond between miracle and preaching; after having resurrected the patricide's father, the apostle John indicates to the beneficiary of the miracle: "If you are resurrected in order to encounter the same realities, it would be better for you to be dead. But it is for better realities that you have to be resurrected!"[73] Thus the hermeneutics of the miracle can take, as in this case, an exhortative tone.

Elsewhere, the hermeneutics have a doctrinal connotation. Sometimes this is transmitted to the reader by means of a prayer that the apostle addresses to his Lord. This petition, which reminds one of the healer's human nature,[74] asserts especially the divine origin of the thaumartugic force. This certainty then leads the one who has been miraculously cured to opt for a spiritual existence detached from corporal seductions. Thomas, for example, prays on behalf of a mother and her daughter who are possessed by demons: "You who blow to us your force and give us courage and provide your servants with liberty of words in love, I pray to

---

[72] See Jean-Marc Prieur, "La figure de l'apôtre dans les Actes apocryphes d'André," in *Les Actes apocryphes des apôtres*, 121–39; François Bovon, "Les paroles de vie dans les *Actes de l'apôtre André*," *Apocrypha* 2 (1991) 99–117. English translation above, pp. 238–52.

[73] *Acts John* 52.

[74] See *Acts Thom.* 66.

you, may these souls be healed and resurrected and become as they were before they were struck by demons."[75]

The dialogue form that the kerygmatic discourse of the apostle[76] sometimes assumes facilitates our next step. The misery that prompts the beneficial intervention of the divine message is linked to a fault: corporal malaise is the consequence of a carnal, delinquent existence and submission to demonic forces. The widow in *Acts of Philip* 1, for instance, lost her son because she adored idols, consulted soothsayers, and despised Christians. The retrieval of her happiness, due to her child's resurrection, will not restore her to family comfort but it will grant her an existence henceforth determined by purity and continence.

The sacraments

Several narratives from among the apocryphal acts of the apostles combine miracles with conversion tales. These often end with adherence to an ascetic form of Christianity, marked by the seal of the baptism.[77] This ending deserves reflection that goes beyond superficial observation, according to which the miracle has lifted reticence and favored the birth of faith. Some texts, if not all, entail a deeper idea: the miracle removes the scar imprinted by the endemic evil and directs the spirit to the divine reality. From then on, the male or female beneficiary of apostolic considerations rushes toward the purity that sees God[78] and, through asceticism, toward the celestial world. Here is the point where the sacrament intervenes in a more real manner than the miracle.

The miracle is a figure, the sacrament is an efficient sign. The former draws attention, the latter retains it. By means of the rites of initiation, unction, baptism and communion, the newly converted is brought into contact with, and benefits from, the celestial world. He or she understands that the logic of the miracle leads him to the sacrament. The same thing occurs with the young, resurrected man and his mother in *Acts of Philip* 1.

There is a logical consistency in this: it is not only from the miracles that we pass on to the sacrament, but from preaching as well. In fact, these two poles, constituted by the gesture of the miracle and the proclamation of the gospel, are the prolegomena to the sacramental initiation and the forerunners of faith and a life of renunciation. In the *Acts of Thomas*, Mygdonia has grasped the apostle's message: "I have truly received, my Lord, the seed of your words, and I will give birth to fruits that are similar to this seed."[79] Therefore this woman became aware of two

---

[75] Ibid., 81.

[76] See *Acts Phil.* 1.1–4 (1–4).

[77] See Han J. W. Drijvers, "Thomasakten," in Schneemelcher, *Neutestamentliche Apokryphen*, 2. 298–99.

[78] See *Acts Phil.* 1.3 (3); 4.1 (37); 5.5 (46); Bovon, "Les Actes de Philippe," 4483–84, 4486.

[79] *Acts Thom.* 94.

distinct realities, the terrestrial and the celestial: "He whom I love," she says to her husband Charisios, "is better than you and all your relatives. For what you possess, made of the earth, returns to the earth; but the one that I love is from heaven and he will take me to heaven …"[80] Mygdonia then wishes to receive the complete initiation: "Give me, she says to the apostle, Jesus Christ's seal and I will receive the gift from your hands before you depart from life."[81] Then she tries to carry along her nurse: "Share with me the eternal life, in order that I receive from you the perfect food. After you take bread, bring me wine mixed with water and see to my liberty."[82] Mygdonia is first going to be anointed with oil. To this end, Thomas pronounces a prayer over the oil, which underscores the importance of the rite: "Holy oil that was given us for our sanctification, hidden mystery in which the cross has been shown us, you are the rectifier of curved members … may your power come, may this power be established in your servant Mygdonia, and heal her with your liberty."[83]

The narrative continues: "There was a fountain. The apostle climbed onto the fountain and baptized Mygdonia in the name of the Father, the Son and the Holy Spirit. When she had been baptized and had dressed, he broke the bread, and, having taken the cup of water, he made her to participate in the body of Christ and in the cup of the Son of God and said: 'You have received the seal, gain eternal life.' And immediately a voice was heard from above, saying: 'Yes, amen.'"[84]

When her husband Charisios returns to his wife's house at dawn he finds her praying, giving thanks to God for the celestial glory she obtained through the intercessions of the apostle. Charisios then says to his wife that Thomas is only a sorcerer, incapable of accomplishing what he promises, and he invites his wife to return to "the good old times" when she loved him. But she hurls at him a bitter reply that confirms the primary hypothesis of this article: "This past time was the time of the beginning, and this present time is that of the end. This past time was the time of the pleasure which passes, and this present time is that of permanent pleasure."[85]

Martyrdom

The apostle's martyrdom occupies the longest and most solemn place.[86] According to the apocryphal acts, the intimate disciples of Jesus accept that they must

---

[80] Ibid., 117.

[81] Ibid., 120.

[82] Ibid. On the sacraments and their encratite character in the *Acts of Thomas*, especially on the cup of water rather than of wine, see Drijvers, "Thomasakten," 229.

[83] *Acts Thom.* 121.

[84] Ibid.

[85] Ibid., 124.

[86] In the case of the apostle John, who does not perish as a martyr, the author sketches a death scene that is fully acceptable; see *Acts John* 106–15.

give their lives for the cause of the gospel. Yet in spite of its greatness, martyrdom is also a failure and raises a problem: what has become of the force from which so many people benefited during their lives?[87] Does it suddenly abandon them?[88] How can the theology of power inherent in the miracle narratives be harmonized with the theology of weakness that is implied in martyrdom?

Apocryphal authors are not insensitive to this tension. They treat this tendency with the proliferation of miracles that accompany the hero's death. Exceptionally, miracles go so far as to spare the protagonist agony or suffering. Thus we have seen[89] various prodigies, divinely programmed, disarm the Roman authorities and hostile crowds who harbored murderous intent toward saint Thecla.[90] In the martyrdom of Philip, it is the apostle who defends himself and invokes the example of the vindictive Elias. He employs his coercive power in order to push his enemies – above all the governor whose terrifying name is Tyrannognophos – down into a dramatically progressive abyss. An ultimate reprimand of Christ reminds the apostle that we must not render evil for evil. The luminous cross of the Savior brings back to earth the good population of Orphioryme by pulling it back from the infernal Hades. As the only truly culpable one, the governor is not entitled to receive this gesture of clemency.

This negative usage of the thaumaturgic force helps us to understand better its righteousness; it does not contradict martyrdom. If one admits that between body and soul it is the soul with which martyrdom is concerned, if one does not expect happiness to be a matter of worldly pleasures, if one trusts the divine word that liberates and enrolls one in the beyond, if one admits – finally – the auxiliary role of the miracle, which from this world visited by God points towards the world where God resides in plenitude, then martyrdom ceases to be a denial of divine power and offers access to the beyond. From death comes a birth; from departure, an arrival; from imprisonment, a deliverance.

Perhaps we should distinguish the function of martyrdom in the acts from its function in the books of revelation, both canonical and apocryphal. In the acts, God's presence is often linked to miracles and the narrative supports a theology of glory. In the apocalypses, such as those of John and Peter, martyrdom represents the eschatological imminence of divine intervention. The acts do not, however, ignore a theology of the cross since they integrate persecutions and deaths; nor do the apocalypses forget the victories of Christ and his apostles. The difference, therefore, is more one of emphasis than an absolute theological opposition. If in the acts the miracle allows one to temporarily escape the world dominated by evil,

---

[87] The theme is already present in the canonical Gospels. See Mark 15:29–32 par.

[88] See *Gos. Pet.* 19: "My power, [my] power, you have forsaken me." Such is, in this apocryphal writing, the version of "My God, my God, why have you forsaken me?" of the canonical Gospel (Mark 15:34 par).

[89] See above, p. 255.

[90] Sometimes, the martyr expresses his superiority by a smile; see *Acts Andr.* 55 (5).

then martyrdom signifies in the final analysis here, as it does in the apocalypses, the most definitive victory.

If the articulation of the word and the miraculous sign is everywhere evident, it may not be the same for martyrdom as it relates to the other poles. A few of the apocryphal acts, among them the most ancient ones, indeed present a martyrdom at the end of the book without having truly introduced it. In other, later acts, however, all of the action converges at this point of hagiographic climax. Unable as I am to analyze each narrative singularly, I will nonetheless put forward one final opinion: what counts here and there is the meaning attributed to the hero's death. In some cases, this corresponds to the agony of the suffering just; martyrdom then legitimates the testimony previously given. In other cases, where death is not painful, it represents a supreme combat, a last miracle, and an ultimate victory for the apostle. But whether undergoing martyrdom or even orchestrating his own death, the hero of the apocryphal acts triumphs finally over a perverted and impotent world. Whether this truth is explicitly stated or remains implicit, it is, it seems to me, certain at the doctrinal level. Martyrdom is therefore everywhere articulated in the global ministry of the apostle. The error of the faithful, who attend their master's death, would be precisely to spare him this glorious exit.

In the apocryphal narration, everything – miracle, word, sacrament, martyrdom – is combined and enlisted in the service of a single cause. The miracle underscores the power of the proclaimed divinity, a power which, flowing through the apostolic medium, invites the reader to leave appearances for the sake of earning invisible goods. The word, which assumes the form of proclamation, prayer or dialogue, evokes explicitly this other world. Does it not help to invoke the Lord's name and thereby sow eternal life in souls?[91] Sacraments, whatever their number, name, rite, or nature might be, all have a mysterious value. They truly introduce into the sphere of salvation men and women who renounce themselves in the purity of their hearts. Martyrdom, finally, confirms the decisive importance of spiritual life in God. All miracles, even if they are a resurrection, remain fleeting and pale before the divine life.

Conclusion

The system I have been concerned with here does not seem to me to be the exclusive privilege of apocryphal literature. Patristic theology, when it seeks to be apologetic or missionary, sets up an analogous theological organization. This world pales before the glorious light of the expected celestial world. The Church, through the proclamation of the word, the administration of sacraments, the prestige of martyrs, and (why not?) the beneficial function of miracles intends to attract pagans to a faith that communicates with the celestial God, to a practice that

---

[91] See Bovon, "Les paroles de vie," 99–117 (English translation above, pp. 238–52).

ignores mundane seductions and aspires to the best of goods, integrating suffering with occasional eruptions of transcendence. What renders the apocryphal acts of the apostles suspicious in the eyes of the Church Fathers are a number of other items: an exaggerated asceticism, a deficient Christology, an excessive valorization of the apostle, and – above all – a doubtful reception by heretical sects.

A New Citation of the *Acts of Paul* in Origen

Though less tolerant than Clement of Alexandria, Origen still adopts an attitude toward the apocryphal writings that is not as exclusive as that of Eusebius of Caesarea.[1] Origen is careful to make a distinction between the apocryphal writings he regards as compatible with the church's faith and those that must be vigorously rejected.[2] He is aware of the contours of holy scripture, yet whenever scripture remains silent or is elliptical, he ventures to use noncanonical texts that are less suspect in order to undergird his theological position.[3] One such work is the *Acts of Paul*, which he specifically cites on one or two occasions, and from which he sometimes draws inspiration elsewhere.[4]

This article was translated by David Warren, whom I thank for his work

[1] On Origen's attitude toward the Christian apocryphal writings, see Ferdinand Piontek, *Die katholische Kirche und die häretischen Apostelgeschichten bis zum Ausgange des 6. Jahrhunderts. Ein Beitrag zur Literaturgeschichte* (Breslau: Nischkowsky, 1907); Adolf von Harnack, *Der kirchengeschichtliche Ertrag der exegetischen Arbeiten des Origenes* (2 vols.; TU 42.3, 42.4; Leipzig: Hinrichs, 1918–1919) 1.7–38, 2.34–54; Gustave Bardy, "Les traditions juives dans l'œuvre d'Origène," *RB* 34 (1925) 217–52; Jean Ruwet, "Les 'antilegomena' dans les œuvres d'Origène," *Bib* 23 (1942) 18–42, 24 (1943) 18–58; idem, "Les apocryphes dans les œuvres d'Origène," *Bib* 25 (1944) 143–66, 311–334; Éric Junod and Jean-Daniel Kaestli, *L'histoire des Actes apocryphes des apôtres du IIIe au IXe siècle. Le cas des Actes de Jean* (Cahiers de la Revue de théologie et de philosophie 7; Geneva/Lausanne: Revue de théologie et de philosophie, 1982); Concetta Aloe Spada, "Origene e gli Apocrifi del Nuovo Testamento," in *Origeniana Quarta. Die Referate des 4. Internationalen Origeneskongresses (Innsbruck, 2.–6. September 1985)* (ed. Lothar Lies; Innsbrucker theologische Studien 19; Innsbruck/Vienna: Tyrolia-Verlag, 1987) 44–53; Ernst Bammel, "Die Zitate aus den Apokryphen bei Origenes," in *Origeniana Quinta. Historica, Text and Method, Biblica, Philosophica, Theologica, Origenism and Later Developments.* Papers of the 5th International Origen Congress, Boston College, 14–18 August 1989 (ed. Robert J. Daly; Louvain: University Press/Peeters, 1992) 131–36; Annewies van den Hoek, "Clement and Origen as Sources on 'Noncanonical' Scriptural Traditions during the Late Second and Earlier Third Centuries," in *Origeniana Sexta. Origène et la Bible/Origen and the Bible: Actes du Colloquium Origenianum Sextum, Chantilly, 30 août-3 septembre 1993* (ed. Gilles Dorival, Alain Le Boulluec, Monique Alexandre et al.; BETL 118; Louvain: Leuven University Press/Peeters, 1995) 93–113.

[2] See Origen, *Hom. Luc.*, prologue; Antonio V. Nazzaro, "Il prologo del vangelo di Luca nell'interpretazione di Origene," in *Origeniana Secunda. Second colloque international des études origéniennes (Bari, 20–23 septembre 1977)* (ed. Henri Crouzel and Antonio Quacquarelli; Quaderni di "Vetera Christianorum" 15; Rome: Edizioni dell'Ateneo, 1980) 231–44.

[3] Cf. Spada, "Origene e gli Apocrifi," 50.

[4] The two specific citations from the *Acts of Paul* are *Princ.* 1.2.3 and *Comm. Jo.* 20.12. Other apparent references would include *Hom. Jer.* 20.1 and the mention preserved in Eusebius, *Hist.*

Although he does not mention it explicitly in his treatise *On the Passover* (*De pascha*), which was discovered in Tura in 1941 and edited in 1979,[5] Origen certainly makes use of the *Acts of Paul* one time in this treatise. And yet this citation, which thus should be added to the others, appears to have escaped the notice of editors and translators until the present moment.

In his comments on Exodus 12, the Alexandrian master gives a traditional interpretation of the "girded loins": the divine command demands that we keep the flesh on a leash and that we master our passions. But then Origen goes beyond this exegesis, which is also found in Pseudo-Hippolytus,[6] and he tries to make the words sound ascetic: if the biblical text specifies that the believers must eat the Passover "with girded loins" and "by families," this means that "the command is given for us to abstain from carnal defilement whenever we eat the Passover." Without being truly encratic, this reading of the biblical text casts sexuality in a negative light and prohibits, it would appear, all conjugal relations before participation in the Eucharist.[7] (And if "to eat the Passover" has a greater meaning, such as "to benefit from the word of God," then the asceticism can be even more rigorous.)[8] At this point Origen brings in two witnesses in support of such rigorous practice: John the Baptist, whose leather belt about the loins symbolized mortifi-

---

eccl. 3.1.1–3. For further discussion, see Harnack, *Kirchengeschichtliche Ertrag*, 2.38–39; Léon Vouaux, *Les Actes de Paul et ses lettres apocryphes. Introduction, textes, traduction et commentaires* (Les Apocryphes du Nouveau Testament. Documents pour servir à l'étude des origines chrétiennes; Paris: Letouzey et Ané, 1913) 27–29; Ruwet, "Antilegomena," 39–40; Éric Junod, "Origène, Eusèbe et la tradition sur la répartition des champs de mission des apôtre (Eusèbe, *HE* III, 1,1–3)," in *Les Actes apocryphes des apôtre. Christianisme et monde païen* (Publications de la Faculté de théologie de l'Université de Genève 4; Geneva: Labor et Fides, 1981) 233–48; Wilhelm Schneemelcher, "Acts of Paul," in *New Testament Apocrypha: Revised Edition of the Collection Initiated by Edgar Hennecke* (ed. Wilhelm Schneemelcher; 2 vols.; Cambridge, Eng.: James Clarke, 1991–1992) 2.215; and Hoek, "Clement and Origen," 108 n. 96.

[5] Octave Guéraud and Pierre Nautin, *Origène. "Sur la Pâque." Traité inédit publié d'après un papyrus de Toura* (Christianisme antique 2; Paris: Beauchesne, 1979); cf. the long review of Adele Monaci Castagno in *Rivista di Storia e Letteratura Religiosa* 17 (1981) 87–92; Stuart G. Hall, "Textual Notes on Origen *Peri Pascha* 40," in *Origeniana Tertia. The Third International Colloquium for Origen Studies (University of Manchester September 7th-11th, 1981): Papers* (ed. Richard Hanson and Henri Crouzel; Rome: Edizioni dell'Ateneo, 1985) 119–20; Giuseppe Sgherri, *Origene. Sulla Pasqua. Il papiro di Tura. Introduzione, traduzione e note* (Letture cristiane del primo millennio 6; Milan: Edizioni Paoline, 1989); Robert J. Daly, *Origen. Treatise on the Passover and Dialogue of Origen with Heraclides and His Fellow Bishops on the Father, the Son, and the Soul* (ACW 54; New York: Paulist, 1992).

[6] Cf. Pierre Nautin, *Homélies pascales*, vol. 1: *Une homélie inspirée du traité sur la Pâque d'Hippolyte* (SC 27; Paris: Cerf, 1950).

[7] For a comparison with the Eucharist, see Ezekiel Fragment 7.22 (PG 13.793) and 1 Corinthians Fragment 34.2–15; see further Claude Jenkins, "Origen on 1 Corinthians, III," *JTS* 9 (1907–1908) 501–02; and Henri Crouzel, *Virginité et mariage selon Origène* (Museum Lessianum, section théologique 58; Paris: Desclée, 1963) 53–65.

[8] On the ambiguity of the expression "to eat the Passover," see Sgherri, *Origene. Sulla Pasqua*, 108; and Daly, *Origen. Treatise on the Passover*, 100. On Origen's austerity, his distrust of sexuality, and his view of women, see Harnack, *Kirchengeschichtliche Ertrag*, 2.60–65.

cation,[9] and the apostle Paul. Concerning Paul he writes: "The married man who eats the Passover 'shall gird' also his 'loins' because the Apostle has said, 'Blessed are those who have wives [if they live] as those who have none.'"[10]

From Octave Guéraud and Pierre Nautin to Robert J. Daly, and including Giuseppe Sgherri, all editors and translators, without any hesitation, have regarded this statement as a reference to the First Letter of Paul to the Corinthians (1 Cor 7:29).[11] But, on the contrary, in my opinion the Alexandrian is citing one of the beatitudes found in the *Acts of Paul*.[12]

In order to facilitate one's judgment about this matter, the pertinent texts are displayed below:

On the Passover 36.6

μακάριοι γὰρ οἱ ἔχοντες γυναῖκας ὡς οἱ μὴ ἔχοντες.

Acts of Paul 5

μακάριοι   οἱ ἔχοντες γυναῖκας ὡς   μὴ ἔχοντες.

1 Corinthians 7:29

ἵνα καὶ   οἱ ἔχοντες γυναῖκας ὡς   μὴ ἔχοντες ὦσιν.

Expressions of the type "as the Apostle said" are frequent in this treatise and serve to introduce or accompany citations.[13] In this capacity, the one that concerns us here would not be suitable in the narrative parts of the *Acts of Paul*. It is, on the other hand, perfectly suited to a discourse such as the sermon the Apostle supposedly delivered on this occasion. According to Origen, it is Paul who formulates this beatitude, and it is the *Acts of Paul* that transmits this saying.[14] The Alexandrian doctor, therefore, hears the voice of the same person who stated this same truth when writing First Corinthians (1 Cor 7:29).

It needs to be stated that the Greek text of this beatitude in Origen's treatise *On the Passover* has puzzled editors. It contains, indeed, a cumbersome reduplication of the definite article: μακάριοι γὰρ οἱ ἔχοντες γυναῖκας ὡς οἱ μὴ ἔχοντες. Translated literally, the beatitude reads "For blessed are those who have wives as those

---

[9] Origen, *Pasch.* 36.23–33.

[10] Ibid., 36.33–37.2. On the textual problem, see further below.

[11] Guéraud and Nautin, *Origène. "Sur la Pâque,"* 226, 246; Sgherri, *Origene. Sulla Pasqua,* 108; Daly, *Origen. Treatise on the Passover,* 47.

[12] *Acts of Paul* (= *Acts of Paul and Thecla*) 5. While awaiting the critical edition of Willy Rordorf, see "Acta Pauli et Theclae" in *Acta apostolorum apocrypha* (ed. Richard Adelbert Lipsius and Maximilien Bonnet; 2 vols. in 3; Leipzig: Hermann Mendelssohn, 1891–1903; Darmstadt: Wissenschaftliche Buchgesellschaft, 1959) 1.238–39.

[13] Under one form or another (ὁ ἀπόστολος εἴρηκεν, ὁ ἀπόστολος ... λέγει, διδάσκει λέγων, ὡς ὁ ἀπόστολος μαρτυρεῖ λέγων), cf. *Pasch.* 3.12–13; 6.17; 12.17, 30; 26.-13, -9; 33.16, 32; 34.12, 18–19; 35.5; 37.2 (our passage); 37.26; 38.27.

[14] The scene transpires in the house of Onesiphorus, where Paul has just crossed the threshold. The setting is a worship service: during the breaking of the bread, the apostle preaches "the word of God about abstinence and the resurrection." He begins his discourse with a series of beatitudes that have an encratic character and take their inspiration from the Gospels and the Pauline Epistles.

who have none." The repetition of the οἱ certainly cannot mean "some and others" but rather "some after the manner of others." According to the ethical logic of *On the Passover*, which is as rigorous as that found in the *Acts of Paul*, it means: "For blessed are those who have wives [if they live] as that those who have none." Such an interpretation is unavoidable unless one wishes to correct the text. If, on the other hand, one dares to amend the text and eliminate the second οἱ as a scribal error, as Octave Guéraud and Pierre Nautin propose, assuming that "the copyist responsible for the mistake has allowed himself to be influenced by the οἱ ἔχοντες of the preceding line," then one must translate the words as follows: "For blessed are those who have wives as if they had none."[15]

Personally, I am reluctant to correct this text since it bears a satisfactory sense as it stands. Moreover, the repeating of the article is also attested in the manuscript tradition of the *Acts of Paul* with the exception of an inversion: *Parisinus graecus* 769 reads μακάριοι οἱ μὴ ἔχοντες ὡς οἱ ἔχοντες.[16] To this may be added the presence of ὧσιν ("that they may be") in 1 Cor 7:29, from which the author of the *Acts of Paul*, whom Origen cites, evidently drew his own inspiration. The phrase from the Epistle "that they may be as those not having any" could well have given birth to the reading in our citation, "as those who do not have any." Therefore, one does not have to amend Origen's text.[17] In any case, the beatitude that Origen's treatise attributes to the Apostle appears to betray, as far as the difficulty of its textual form is concerned, a consanguinity with the *Acts of Paul* and not with the First Letter to the Corinthians, since such hesitations do not crowd the critical apparatus of the canonical text.[18]

In conclusion, I believe that Origen is referring here to one of the beatitudes found in the *Acts of Paul*. In so doing, he demonstrates a respect for this noncanonical work, a respect that other citations have already shown.[19] For the Alexandrian, it is the same person who expresses himself on both occasions: in one place (*Acts of Paul*), the words are spoken; in the other (1 Cor 7:29), they are written.

---

[15] See Octave Guéraud and Pierre Nautin, *Origène. "Sur la Pâque,"* 46 n. 5, 225–27. It is necessary to point out that the editors are depending on the absence of the second οἱ in 1 Cor 7:29 in order to support their conjecture.

[16] See the note in the apparatus pertaining to line 16 in Lipsius and Bonnet, *Acta apostolorum apocrypha,* 238.

[17] The ethics of the Pauline ὡς μὴ and of 1 Cor 7:29 have been the object of numerous studies; see in particular Gottfried Hierzenberger, *Weltbewertung bei Paulus nach 1 Kor. 7,29–31. Eine exegetisch-kerygmatische Studie* (KBANT; Düsseldorf: Patmos-Verlag, 1967); and Christophe Senft, *La première épître de saint Paul aux Corinthiens* (CNT 2, 7; Geneva: Labor et Fides, 1992) 101–3.

[18] There is no variant indicated at this point in the editio octava critica maior of Konstantin von Tischendorf, *Novum Testamentum Graece* (2 vols.; Leipzig: Giesecke & Devrient, 1869–1872) 2.495, nor in the twenty-seventh edition of Nestle-Aland, *Novum Testamentum Graece* (Stuttgart: Deutsche Bibelgesellschaft, 1993) 452.

[19] See further n. 4 above.

Eusebius of Caesarea's *Ecclesiastical History* and the History of Salvation[1]

In his remarkable dissertation, Jean Sirinelli questions whether the author of the *Historia ecclesiastica* merits the title "theologian of history."[2] His cautious conclusions tend toward the negative. In contrast, Marguerite Harl's long review devoted to this work, which was published in the *Revue des Études Grecques*,[3] discovers in Eusebius an authentic Christian vision of history. In these pages I will take up this question again and attempt to demonstrate that Eusebius, under the influence of the Bible, defends a history of salvation that emphasizes various periods. If the connections between this history of salvation and secular history are not studied here, it is because I have dedicated myself instead only to critiquing this very idea of the history of salvation. While I can support Eusebius's theologically positive valuation of the first generation of Christianity within the history of salvation, I must critique his triumphalist understanding of his own time, and especially his equation of Constantine's empire with the kingdom of God.

Creation and the History of Salvation

The history of salvation[4] Eusebius defends is clearly christocentric.[5] It portrays the history of relations between the Logos and humans.[6] Eusebius begins his *Historia ecclesiastica* with a résumé of the history of the elect people from creation up

---

[1] I wish to express my gratitude to Laura Nasrallah for the translation of this paper into English. For introductory questions regarding Eusebius's *Historia ecclesiastica*, see the third volume of Eduard Schwartz, ed., *Eusebius Werke II. Die Kirchengeschichte* (GCS 9.1, 2, 3; Leipzig: Hinrichs, 1903–1909) and idem, "Eusebios von Caesarea" (PW 6.1; Munich: Druckenmüller) 1395–407; David S. Wallace-Hadrill, *Eusebius of Caesarea* (London: Mowbray, 1960) 39–43, 158–65; and Jean Sirinelli, *Les vues historiques d'Eusèbe de Césarée durant la période prénicéenne* (Ph.D. diss., University of Paris, 1961) 23–24 (published at the same time in Université de Dakar. Faculté des lettres et sciences humaines. Publications de la Section de langues et littératures 10 [1961]).

[2] Sirinelli, *Les vues historiques d'Eusèbe*, 109, 132–33, 490–95.

[3] Marguerite Harl, "L'histoire de l'humanité racontée par un écrivain chrétien au début du IVe siècle," *REG* 75 (1962) 524–25.

[4] On the notion of ἱστορία, see Eduard Schwartz, "Über Kirchengeschichte," in *Nachrichten von der K. Gesellschaft der Wissenschaften zu Göttingen. Geschäftliche Mitteilungen* (1908) 113–17. This work later appeared in Schwartz's *Gesammelte Schriften*, vol. 1: *Vergangene Gegenwärtigkeiten* (Berlin: de Gruyer, 1938) 110–30. It is this later version that I cite in this paper. See also K. Heussi, "Zum Geschichtsverständnis des Eusebius von Cäsarea," *Wissenschaftliche Zeit-*

to the incarnation; this is characteristic of his salvation-historical concept but it is also evident that this construction of history serves to prove the great antiquity of both Christianity and the Logos,[7] its founder. Since the Logos is the Creator, creation itself demonstrates the anteriority of the Logos and his intervention in history.[8] By this first act of creation, a cosmic dimension is thus conferred upon Christ: he is frequently given the title δημιουργός[9] – a term the New Testament avoids[10] – and Eusebius understands Christ to be the master of the universe. The Father, in turn, is frequently called "Father of all things."[11] It does not seem to me (and here I differ with Sirinelli[12]) that this cosmic function diminishes the power of the Logos, and thus the power of God, in history. To be sure, the mode of directing history that God chose up until the time of Christ appears to be indirect and limited: after the creation, God's plan is accomplished first through theophanies of the Logos.[13] These divine manifestations are limited to certain people and reveal a person more than imposing a will; they are, however, part of a universal economy. Although Eusebius does not explain these ideas sufficiently (and he is guilty of imprecision regarding the notion of election), he is concerned with ideas such as a chosen minority, the patriarchs, and Israel for example, in view of the larger issue of the salvation of the majority.[14] He is most interested in this partial

---

schrift der Friedrich-Schiller-Universität Jena. Gesellschafts- und Sprachwissenschaftliche Reihe 7 (1957/58) 89. After analyzing the literary form of the *Historia ecclesiastica*, these two scholars conclude that in this work Eusebius did not intend to recount the historical destiny of the church, but to reunite materials that dealt with the history of the church. I willingly acknowledge that Eusebius did not wish to narrate, in the style of the great historiographies of antiquity, the history and evolution of the church. He did, however, intend to compose a continuous account of history. Does he not announce in the first lines of his prologue (*Hist. eccl.* 1.1.1) his plan for recounting "the number and character of the transactions recorded in the history of the Church"? (ET: Kirsopp Lake; 2 vols.; LCL; Cambridge: Harvard University Press, 1926; 1992) 1.7.

[5] See Guiseppe del Ton, "Contenuto, struttura, scopi della Storia Ecclestiastica di Eusebio di Cesarea," *Divinitas* 6 (1962) 323.

[6] See Sirinelli, *Les vues historiques d'Eusèbe*, 255–300.

[7] The question of whether the prologue is limited only to chapters 1–4 of book 1 or to book 1 in its entirety has been debated. Our inquiry is not unduly influenced by scholarly responses to this question. See Joachín Salaverri, "El origen de la revelación y los garantes de su conservación en Iglesia según Eusebio de Cesarea," *Gregorianum* 16 (1935) 351 n. 8; and Franz Overbeck, *Über die Anfänge der Kirchengeschichtsschreibung* (Basel: Reinhardt, 1892) 58ff.

[8] See the unfortunate subtitle "Dieu absent de l'Histoire" in Sirinelli, *Les vues historiques d'Eusèbe*, 253.

[9] See *Hist. eccl.* 1.2.3. Other references can be found in the index of Greek words compiled by Pierre Périchon in *Eusèbe de Césarée. Histoire ecclésiastique* (text and trans. Gustave Bardy; SC 31, 41, 55, 73; Paris: Cerf, 1952–60) 73.301.

[10] See W. Foerster, "κτίζω" *TDNT* 3 (1965) 1022–25, 1027. The term appears only one time, in Heb 11:10.

[11] *Hist. eccl.* 1.2.3. Eusebius uses the words τὰ ὅλα in place of the New Testament expression τὰ πάντα.

[12] Sirinelli, *Les vues historiques d'Eusèbe*, 284–86.

[13] See *Hist. eccl.* 1.2.6–13.

[14] See below n. 17.

realization of the will of God because he is a theologian of salvation history, rather than of history as such.[15] Moreover, Eusebius does not pass over the necessity of this special revelation in silence. The fall of humanity provoked this divine economy, although it is true that Eusebius depicts this fall in terms borrowed more from pagan poets than from the Bible:[16] "Then indeed, when the great torpor of evil [after the fall of the first humans] had come nigh overwhelming all ... the preexistent Logos himself, in his exceeding *love for humans appeared* to his subjects, at one time by a vision of angels, at another personally to one or two of the those men of old who loved God."[17] It was out of love for humanity that God decided to reveal Godself to certain people: this is, according to Eusebius, divine diplomacy.

From Adam to Christ

This preparatory history, like the rest of the history of salvation, unfolds itself according to God's plan, which resembles a scholarly program. Since the model is that of pedagogy,[18] the free participation of humans is important and necessary. Here again we find one of Eusebius's weaknesses: he does not note the effect of the fall upon human free will.[19] This plan is realized in stages marked by famous persons[20]: Noah, Abraham, and Moses.[21] The *Chronikon* of Eusebius, written a little before the *Historia ecclesiastica*, begins with the time of Abraham. The theological importance of this fact has not been adequately noted.[22] By beginning at this point, Eusebius causes his reader to feel that the centuries before Abraham, while they are part of history, differ from the following epochs.[23] The time that followed was marked by the diversifying of nations (hence he develops syn-

---

[15] I believe that some of the misunderstandings in Sirinelli's book derive from the fact that the author does not attend to this theological problem.

[16] *Hist. eccl.* 1.2.18–20. See Bardy's note in *Eusèbe de Césarée* (SC 31:10 n. 29); and Sirinelli, *Les vues historiques d'Eusèbe*, 210–13.

[17] *Hist. eccl.* 1.2.21 (ET: 1. 23, 25 [trans. slightly modified]).

[18] See Harl, "L'histoire de l'humanité," 524–25.

[19] On free will, see Sirinelli, *Les vues historiques d'Eusèbe*, 358–60.

[20] On the fall, the first religion of humans, Adam, and the historical sequence of these first events, see Harl ("L'histoire de l'humanité," 525–30), who has dealt with all the essential points and corrected Sirinelli's reconstruction.

[21] These periods are better marked than Sirinelli (*Les vues historiques d'Eusèbe*, 100–9) judges in his evaluation of the *Chronikon*.

[22] In his introduction to the *Historia ecclesiastica*, Bardy speaks of Eusebius's modesty (*Eusèbe de Césarée*, SC 73: 27), but it is not clear what he means by this. Schwartz ("Eusebios von Caesarea," 1379) thinks that Eusebius begins with Abraham due to the fact that the earlier dates are less certain. Sirinelli (*Les vues historiques d'Eusèbe*, 49–52, 101, 491) gives many explanations without sufficiently emphasizing the theological reasons for such a choice.

[23] A similar opinion is expressed by Oscar Cullmann, *Heil als Geschichte. Heilsgeschichtliche Existenz im Neuen Testament* (Tübingen: Mohr Siebeck, 1965) 118ff.

chronic lists, which delineate contemporaneous kingdoms, nations, and even episcopacies) and by the setting aside of one people in particular. With Abraham, the election of Israel commences. It is worth noting that in the _Historia ecclesiastica_ Eusebius follows the example of the apostle Paul in Romans 4, bringing together Abraham's epoch and the Christian period, the faith of the patriarch and the belief of Christians.

The differences between the comparisons made by Paul and Eusebius are also instructive: for Paul, the common denominator for Abraham and Christians is the certitude that there is a God who resurrects the dead, the eschatological faith in a God of the future (Rom 4:17). According to Eusebius, it is faith in a unique God, who is Creator and Lord, God of both the past and the present, that links the patriarch Abraham to Christian believers.[24] Eusebius adds a non-legalistic morality to this common monotheism. He even goes so far as to identify wrongly the religion of the patriarch and the Christian faithful, and to describe Abraham and his offspring as Christians.[25] The error here resides not in a lack of historical perspective[26] but in the a priori assumption that Christianity is a natural religion: the Christian faith is nothing but the return to reason; revelation and reason become identified with one another.[27]

Does Eusebius disparage Moses, his law, and his time by elevating the importance of Abraham and his times? Although this is Sirinelli's assertion,[28] I do not think this is the case. Moses, "the great Moses,"[29] had the distinction of having written the Pentateuch.[30] Following after Abraham, Moses distinguished himself "by justice and the virtue of religion."[31] Like the patriarch, he was privileged with a theophany of the Logos.[32] He "was inspired very clearly to foresee the title 'Jesus.'"[33] He in effect chose Joshua the son of Nun for a successor, knowing that

---

[24] _Hist. eccl._ 1.4.7. I shall return later to Eusebius's disinterest in the final times.

[25] Ibid., 4.6. Concerning this identification, see Wallace-Hadrill, _Eusebius of Caesarea_, 169–71, and Sirinelli, _Les vues historiques d'Eusèbe_, 142–47. Harl ("L'histoire de l'humanité," 528) rightly corrects the meaning Sirinelli gives to the word "Hebrews" in the work of Eusebius.

[26] It suffices to compare what Eusebius says here to the interpretation of the patriarchs given by Philo in his _De Abrahamo_.

[27] See Henrikus Berkhof, _Die Theologie des Eusebius von Caesarea_ (Ph.D. diss., University of Amsterdam, 1939) 139; and H.G. Opitz, "Euseb von Caesarea als Theologe. Ein Vortrag," _ZNW_ 34 (1935) 3–4.

[28] See Sirinelli, _Les vues historiques d'Eusèbe_, 147–63. It is true that Sirinelli sees a double movement in Eusebius's thought: Eusebius traces both progress and decline in the history of Israel. Wallace-Hadrill (_Eusebius of Caesarea_, 169–71) also believes that the time of Moses represents a period of decline for Eusebius.

[29] _Hist. eccl._ 1.2.4.

[30] Ibid.

[31] Ibid., 1.2.6.

[32] Ibid., 1.2.6, 13. In the _Eclogae_, however, Eusebius does not think that Moses saw the Logos. See Sirinelli, _Les vues historiques d'Eusèbe_, 265, 280.

[33] _Hist. eccl._ 1.3.3 (ET: 1.29).

by this he announced the true Jesus "according to type and symbol."[34] Moreover, he predicted the coming of Christ in giving the name Christ (the Anointed) to the high priesthood.[35] The time of Moses is thus a period ponderous with images, albeit an ambivalent time. It is negative because God embarks upon a partial rescue of humanity adrift. Not able to expose humans to a reality they cannot bear, God confronts them with mere images of this reality. This negative assessment, however, is also positive: any image, although only an image, is full of the reality it signifies. The law, which is characteristic of the time of Moses, is only symbolic, but its symbols definitely point to reality. The prophets and their oracles prove this.[36]

The examination of this theory of images reveals to us two schemata that intersect in the *Historia Ecclesiastica* and render Eusebius's conception of history quite surprising. The bishop of Caesarea juxtaposes, and sometimes also interweaves, a spatial and a temporal scheme. On one hand, the earthly is a symbol of the heavenly: "Moses gave figures, symbols, and mysterious images of *heavenly realities.*"[37] Is it surprising that Eusebius next cites the only verse in the Old Testament where this scheme appears (Exod 25:40)? On the other hand, the present is a type of the future: the anointed priest is the image of Christ, just as Joshua prefigured Jesus.[38] The very existence of these types, like the existence of the prophets, also reveals to us another aspect of the history of salvation that Eusebius, here faithful to scripture, observes: discontinuity in continuity, meaningful epochs followed by slack times, and memorable events linked over deserted years or centuries.[39]

Eusebius neither condemns nor especially glorifies the time of the law. Instead, he sees it in the double perspective of an increase in the intervention of God (see the image of the seed in *Hist. eccl.* 1.2.22) and the intensification of human evil.

---

[34] Ibid.

[35] Ibid., 1.3.2.

[36] Concerning prophecies, see Sirinelli, *Les vues historiques d'Eusèbe*, 367ff.; H. Eger ("Kaisar und Kirche in der Geschichtstheologie Eusebs von Cäsarea," *ZNW* 38 [1939] 101) and Harl ("L'histoire de l'humanité," 529–30) have both noted the positive aspects of the time of Moses and the law.

[37] *Hist. eccl.* 1.3.2 (ET: 1.29 [trans. slightly modified]).

[38] Ibid., 1.3.1–5.

[39] See Cullmann, *Heil als Geschichte*, 108–16.

Jesus Christ and the Apostles

For Eusebius,[40] to speak of the church is to speak of Jesus Christ[41]; to narrate the history of the church, one must first of all establish the origin of the Son of God. This origin, as we have seen, precedes the creation of the world, since the Logos collaborated in creation. The "economy" of Christ thus does not begin only with the incarnation nor is it limited to the appearance of Jesus on earth.[42] As the plan of book 1 demonstrates,[43] this economy has its point of departure in creation, it proceeds into the theophanies, and it continues with the gift of the law and the incarnation.

The incarnation and life of Jesus Christ fulfill the prophecies. The coming of Jesus constitutes something new, certainly, but this novelty has been prepared for[44]; it is a new stage in the divine pedagogy. The life of Christ[45] was double, like his nature: it was marked by sufferings, but also by acts of power.[46] During his lifetime and because of his agency, the era of universalism begins.[47] Several of Eusebius's phrases reveal that, in his view, eschatology was already partially realized. Eusebius thus calls the coming of Christ the "*final* reign of Christ."[48] While the New Testament applies the celebrated prophecies of Daniel 7 to the Son of Man who is to come, Eusebius seems to attribute them to Christ who has already come. In the same way, while most earlier Christian writers awaited the realization of the prediction of seventy weeks (Daniel 9) in the future, Eusebius indicates that this has already found its fulfillment in Christ.[49] Until the time of Christ, one only lived in images and prophecies; but from the time of Christ forward, the re-

---

[40] Concerning Eusebius's christology, see D.S. Balanos, "Zum Charakterbild des Kirchenhistorikers Eusebius," *TQ* 116 (1935) 309–22; and Gustave Bardy, "La théologie d'Eusèbe de Césarée d'après *l'Histoire Ecclésiastique*," *RHE* 50 (1955) 5–20.

[41] Eusebius writes in his prologue: "My starting point is therefore no other than the first dispensation of God touching our Saviour and Lord, Jesus the Christ" (*Hist. eccl.* 1.1.2; ET, 1: 9).

[42] Concerning the word "economy," see Bardy, *Eusèbe de Césarée* (SC 31. 3 n. 4), and Sirinelli, *Les vues historiques d'Eusèbe*, 259 n. 1. Like Sirinelli, I opt for a broad definition of the term.

[43] Concerning book 1, see Sirinelli, *Les vues historiques d'Eusèbe*, 275–80; and Overbeck, *Anfänge*, 58–63.

[44] Sirinelli sometimes contradicts himself in his analyses: here he affirms (*Les vues historiques d'Eusèbe*, 223, 226, 242) that the incarnation brought about an absolute renewal; elsewhere he states that the incarnation reveals a "manifestation plus décidée et plus considérable d'une puissance qui s'est déjà exprimée" (p. 258).

[45] Ibid., 233–59; Eusebius is reserved regarding the earthly existence of Jesus.

[46] *Hist. eccl.* 1.2.23.

[47] Ibid.

[48] Ibid., 1.2.24. I think that Sirinelli is probably wrong, when, contrary to Bardy, *Eusèbe de Césarée* (SC 31: 12), he argues that Eusebius speaks here of Christ's reign to come (*Les vues historiques d'Eusèbe*, 479 n. 2). The prophecies of Daniel 7 are already realized (see below n. 49). That which Sirinelli (p. 479) considers a contradiction in Eusebius' mind seems to me to be a faithful interpretation of the New Testament idea of "already and not yet."

[49] *Hist. eccl.* 1.2.24–25, regarding Daniel 7; and *Hist. eccl.* 1.6.11, on the subject of Daniel 9. Regarding this last prophecy, see Sirinelli, *Les vues historiques d'Eusèbe*, 459–65, esp. 465 n. 3.

ality is already here, and so is the realization: the δύναμις of Christ is manifested; Ps 110:1 has seen its fulfillment.[50] The demons and their leader have been vanquished by the preaching of Jesus and his cross, as we learn elsewhere in Eusebius's work.[51] In one sense, the kingdom is already realized as early as the incarnation and the passion.

Nevertheless, the coming of the Messiah is, at the same time, the next stage of salvation history; this stage is marked by the ascension of Christ, which acts as the hinge between book 1, with its prologue and retrospective of history, and book 2, which opens with a chapter on what the apostles did after the ascension of Christ.[52] The apostles provide the link between these first two books, joining the age of Christ to the years that follow. Eusebius takes pains to introduce the apostles in book 1 by specifying that they are not limited only to the Twelve[53] (a datum important to remember with regard to the problem of apostolic succession). He then inserts them at the beginning of book 2 and keeps them in the foreground until chapter 31 of book 3. Here, the recital of the apostolic age ends in a clear-cut fashion.[54] Franz Overbeck has already demonstrated the particular importance Eusebius accords to the time of Christ and the apostles.[55] If, contrary to Salaverri's contention,[56] Eusebius indeed places a caesura at the end of the apostolic time, then from that time forward there is no important break in his *Historia* up to his own time.[57] Since the end of the apostolic age, we have lived in the time of the church, a time marked by the tradition and the conservation of the "deposit" handed down to us by the apostles. According to Eusebius, the period of Christ and the apostles had a normative value that the time of the church no longer possesses. It seems to me that the interest Eusebius brings to the problem of the canon confirms this: the question of canon receives an inordinate amount of attention in the *Historia ecclesiastica*. Scholars have often failed to explain the theological reason behind this focus on canonical developments in a historical

---

[50] *Hist. eccl.* 1.3.9–11, 16.

[51] On the defeat of the demons, see Sirinelli, *Les vues historiques d'Eusèbe*, 201–204, 323–26.

[52] *Hist. eccl.* 2.1.

[53] Ibid., 1.12.

[54] Ibid., 3.31.6; see Franz Overbeck, *Die Bischofslisten und die apostolische Nachfolge in der Kirchengeschichte des Eusebius* (Basel: Fr. Reinhardt, 1898) 31; and Schwartz, "Über Kirchengeschichte," (GCS 9.3, 21), and idem, "Eusebios von Caesarea," 1397.

[55] Overbeck, *Die Bischofslisten*, 31–32.

[56] See Joachín Salaverri, "La idea de Tradición en la Historia Eclesiástica de Eusebio Cesariense," *Gregorianum* 13 (1932) 221–37. Salaverri is, I think, wrong in believing that each book of the *Historia ecclesiastica* describes a clearly delimited period in the history of the church (book 1, that of Christ; book 2, that of the apostles; book 3, the "subapostolic age"; book 4, the first apostolic succession; etc.).

[57] See Overbeck, *Die Bischoftslisten*, 31; and more recently, del Ton, "Contenuto, struttura, scopi," 323–35.

work, instead paying attention only to the content of the proposed canon.[58] According to Eusebius, the correct transmission of the true gospel is not possible if the canon of scriptures is not made clear. Moreover, the normative writings that constitute the canon cannot come from any period except the privileged time of the apostles, who were eyewitnesses.[59] The ideal image Eusebius gives to the church of the apostolic time also testifies to the unique position this epoch occupies in salvation history.[60] The concept of the διαδοχαὶ τῶν ἀποστόλων, which has provoked so much discussion,[61] supports this idea even more: the fact that it is a question of the line of apostolic successors and not directly of Christ proves that the apostles are situated with Christ at the source; they are not included in the company of their successors – bishops, doctors, etc.[62] Eusebius, it seems to me, has resolved the relationship between the apostolic and postapostolic times in a satisfying fashion, and, in his understanding of the history of salvation he has cleared the way for an admissible solution to the problem of scripture and tradition.

The Church

Let us now consider the form the kingdom of God takes at the time of the persecuted church.[63] Here, two schemata of which I have already spoken intersect: the royalty of Christ *in the heavens* is established, and it seems that one need not await the ascension for this.[64] In contrast, the kingdom *on earth* commences only with Christ, as we have seen, and even then only partially. The powers are already vanquished, certainly, but they still act.[65] These demons have enough forces at their disposal to provoke persecutions[66] and allow heresies to be born.[67] The "al-

---

[58] It is true that Salaverri ("El origen de la revelación," 355–61) is interested in this question, but he comes to the opposite conclusion. According to him, Eusebius's idea of the canon of the New Testament proves the importance Eusebius accords to the tradition. Wallace-Hadrill's interpretation (*Eusebius of Caesarea*, 68–69) seems to me to be closer to the truth.

[59] Eusebius's position is close to that of Cullmann, *Heil als Geschichte*, 270–73.

[60] *Hist. eccl.* 2.14.3. I was unable to locate the work of G. Heinrici, *Das Urchristentum in der Kirchengeschichte des Eusebius* (Leipzig: Edelman, 1894).

[61] See Overbeck, *Die Bischofslisten*, which was corrected and completed by Schwartz, *Über Kirchengeschichte*, 119–20; and idem, "Eusebios von Caesarea," 1395ff.

[62] Concerning the guarantors of the succession, see the polemic of Overbeck against Adolf von Harnack (in Overbeck, *Die Bischoftslisten*, 13ff.).

[63] Regarding the idea of the church, see Heussi, "Zum Geschichtsverständnis des Eusebius von Cäsarea," 89–90.

[64] See *Hist. eccl.* 8.13.2 regarding Lucian of Antioch, who "preached the heavenly kingdom of Christ."

[65] See Sirinelli, *Les vues historiques d'Eusèbe*, 337–38.

[66] See the references contained in the "Index rerum et doctrinarum," s.v. "Démon," in Bardy, *Eusèbe de Césarée* (SC 73: 241–42).

[67] Ibid., 73: 242. Eusebius seems to resolve quantitatively the "already and not yet": some de-

ready and not yet" of the New Testament thus finds itself again in Eusebius. Certain exegeses elsewhere in his work allow one to surmise that Eusebius brings together the two senses of scripture interpretation that constitute part of this eschatological tension: in a spiritual sense, for believers and their faith, Christ is already the enthroned Lord even now; in a literal sense, for the world and what can now be seen, the royalty of Christ appears only intermittently. The flashes of lightning cut across the sky at night, but the light is not yet complete. Eusebius seems to characterize hymns, spiritual gifts, and miracles among these flashes of light. The eschatological character of the hymns is evident: speaking of the martyrs of the Thebaid, Eusebius asserts that "the divine presence" becomes visible by their courage and by the fact "that they sang and sent up hymns and thanksgivings to the God of the universe even to the very last breath."[68] Here Eusebius's interest in charismatic gifts, which are nothing less than present manifestations of the Spirit, the first-fruit of the kingdom,[69] differs from that of other third-century authors. The attention Eusebius pays to Montanism, among the other heresies, is an indication of his preoccupation with charismatic gifts, and with prophecy in particular. He takes pains to recopy a passage from Miltiades, which states: "For the Apostle considered that the charism of prophecy must exist in all the Church until the final parousia."[70] Despite his caution as a historian, Eusebius frequently points to miracles as signs of the partial presence of the kingdom here below.[71]

We can thus situate this "already and not yet" within the context of a *theologia crucis* and a *theologia gloriae*. Eusebius, faithful to the Christian tradition as he is, defends a theology of the cross: the Christian faith is spiritual, the kingdom is not of this world and it is normal that the Church experiences tribulation. The martyrs of Tyre, whom Eusebius has seen with his own eyes, must suffer and die.[72] But the theology of glory also dawns very often in Eusebius's work: the Christian faith is in the process of visibly conquering the world; already the kingdom is partly manifest in plain sight. Eusebius thus recounts how these same martyrs, by the power of the Lord, terrified lions and made them recoil many times (and the Bible and other literature of antiquity attach great symbolic and eschatological

---

mons are already vanquished and cast into Tartarus; the rest still live and fight in the air. See Sirinelli, *Les vues historiques d'Eusèbe*, 316–17.

[68] *Hist. eccl.* 8.9.5 (ET: 2. 277). See again the "Index rerum et doctrinarum" (s.v. "Hymnes") in Bardy, *Eusèbe de Césarée* (SC 73. 249).

[69] Concerning Eusebius's views on gifts of the Holy Spirit in souls, see *Hist. eccl.* 10.4.66.

[70] Ibid., 5.17.4. Cf. again the references in the "Index rerum et doctrinarum" (s.v. "Charisme") in Bardy, *Eusèbe de Césarée* (SC 73. 238). On this point, see also Walther Voelker, "Von welchen Tendenzen ließ sich Eusebius bei der Abfassung seiner Kirchengeschichte leiten?" *VC* 4 (1950) 169–72.

[71] See the numerous references in the "Index rerum et doctrinarum" (s.v. "Miracles") in Bardy, *Eusèbe de Césarée* (SC 73. 255–56) and Sirinelli, *Les vues historiques d'Eusèbe*, 373–87.

[72] *Hist. eccl.* 8.7.1 and 6.

value to combat against wild beasts).[73] The stories of the martyrs are weapons in Eusebius' arsenal that demonstrate the accuracy of his doctrine and strengthen the apology that underpins the entire work. A series of apologetic arguments[74] – arguments concerning the contemporaneous rise of the *pax Romana*, the coming of Christ, and the prosperity of the empire when persecutions ceased – provide evidence of this theology of glory. The fame of certain bishops and Christian writers who made ecclesiastical history provides another example.

This theology of glory is associated with a realized eschatology in the *Historia*, as we see, for example, from the importance of two terms: the "justice" of God (Eusebius uses δίκη, and not δικαιοσύνη) and "providence" (πρόνοια). Like Lactantius, Eusebius occasionally develops a theory regarding the death of the persecutors:[75] such is the realization of justice here on earth. Even now the arm of God falls upon tyrants and heretics, who will be subjected to the vindicating justice of God again at a later time. As for providence, it is not mentioned often, except when there is a question of some material benefit to believers, such as the peace of the church, the relaxation of persecutions.

The Contemporary Epoch

Franz Overbeck has already noted the division between books 7 and 8 in the *Historia*.[76] With book 8, Eusebius commences his account of his own times. This epoch interests Eusebius not only because it is his own, but also because – and in my opinion this is both Eusebius's originality and his error – it marks anew a sort of realization of eschatology after a final test, indeed the most terrible test, similar to the coming of the Antichrist.

In speaking of his own time, Eusebius first of all secularizes the vocabulary of the New Testament: in *Historia Ecclesiastica* 8.1.1, the Christian παρρησία signifies visible religious liberty, and in 9.1.8 the light after the night has nothing to do with "light" in its Johannine (John 8:12) or Pauline (1 Thess 5) sense. In *Historia* 9.7.15, ἐλπίς has lost its religious meaning: the term has come to define the human hopes of Christians. The same is true for εἰρήνη (10.1.1), ἡμέρα (10.1.8), and χαρά (10.2.1). These New Testament terms have not lost their eschatological force, but they are transposed from the realm of faith to that of the visible world. Eschatology is newly realized, but this time it is realized in Constantine's empire,

---

[73] Ibid., 8.7.2–5. It is significant that John 18:36 ("my kingdom is not of this world") is only cited – and then rarely – in Eusebius's earlier works. See Wallace-Hadrill, *Eusebius of Caesarea*, 177.

[74] See Sirinelli, *Les vues historiques d'Eusèbe*, 388–411.

[75] See *Hist. eccl.* 2.7 and 10.8. See the appendix in Bardy, *Eusèbe de Césarée* (SC 55: 41–42). See also Voelker, "Von welchen Tendenzen," 167–68.

[76] Overbeck, *Anfänge*, 48ff.

in the era that is still wrongly called "the peace of the Church." Salvation history risks becoming an ideology, however, when such secularization takes over – when, like Christ, Constantine becomes the λυτρωτής, the σωτήρ, the εὐεργέτης.[77]

A series of biblical citations applied to Constantine and his time confirms that we can certainly speak of Eusebius's idea of a newly realized eschatology. Sirinelli has already directed attention to the parallel construction of Constantine's victory over Maxentius with the miraculous crossing of the Red Sea.[78] In addition to the citations of Pss 33:16–19 (LXX 32)[79] and 146:3–4 (LXX 145),[80] we can mention Ps 46:9–10 (LXX 45), the prophecy of God's final victory, which leads to definitive peace; Eusebius uses these passages to characterize his own historical situation.[81] Eusebius's citation of Ps 98:1–2 (LXX 97) has the same implications: it invites one to sing the new song for, according to Eusebius, the Lord has already manifested his salvation[82] (note that the author of Revelation reserves this "new song" for the end times[83]). In order to show that eschatology is realized in the victories of Constantine, Eusebius applies to his own time a saying of Jesus that refers, in turn, to those whose lives are recorded in the Hebrew scriptures: "Let us now cry aloud the new song, since, after those terrible and gloomy spectacles and narratives, we were accounted worthy now to behold and to celebrate in panegyric such things as of a truth many righteous men and martyrs of God before us desired to see upon earth and saw them not, and to hear, and heard them not [Matt 13:17]."[84] One phrase Eusebius uses demonstrates explicitly that this is a question of eschatology newly realized: "With our very eyes do we behold that those things committed to memory long ago are faithful and true; and so we can sing a second hymn of victory."[85]

Following these last remarks, we are not surprised to find that the parousia is far from being imminent for Eusebius. He does not doubt its reality, but he awaits it without impatience. His indifference toward a future-oriented eschatology

---

[77] *Hist. eccl.* 9.9.9. On the origin of the doctrine of "mimesis," which Eusebius applies to Constantine and his empire later in his work, see N. H. Baynes, "Eusebius and the Christian Empire," *Annuaire de l'Institut de philologie et d'histoire orientales* 2 (1934) 13–18. On the role of Constantine in salvation history, see Wallace-Hadrill, *Eusebius of Caesarea*, 180.

[78] Sirinelli, *Les vues historiques d'Eusèbe*, 375–76.

[79] *Hist. eccl.* 9.10.5.

[80] Ibid., 9.11.8.

[81] Ibid., 10.1.6.

[82] Ibid., 10.1.3.

[83] Rev 14:3.

[84] *Hist. eccl.* 10.1.4 (ET: 2.391, 392). Wallace-Hadrill has shown (*Eusebius of Caesarea*, 172–73, 176) that for Eusebius, Constantine and his reign constitute the realization of the promises made to Abraham. History thus culminates in Constantine (p. 187).

[85] *Hist. eccl.* 10.4.6 (ET: 2. 401). Although he does not speak of a renewal of a partially realized eschatology, Wallace-Hadrill (*Eusebius of Caesarea*, 188–89) also think that Eusebius believes that the time of Constantine is the fulfillment of history. See Opitz, "Euseb von Caesarea," 13–15.

draws attention to the small role the second coming plays in his thought,[86] to his negative disposition toward the book of Revelation, and to his hatred of millenarianism.[87] All this is well known in scholarship, and cannot detain us here.

Conclusion

Eusebius thus thinks in terms of the history of salvation. He even strives, through his *Chronikon* and his synchronic lists of contemporaneous kingdoms, nations, and episcopal rules,[88] to define the relationship between history and the history of salvation. In the *Historia ecclesiastica*, he obviously focuses on the time of the church, emphasizing its unfolding by providing lists of bishops. He does not forget the role of Jerusalem in the history of salvation; indeed, the apostolic succession of Jerusalem is the most important from Eusebius's standpoint – even more important than that of Rome (contrary to Gustave Bardy's view).[89] It is for theological reasons that he notes the succession in this holy city since, in his time, the Jerusalem see did not play a very large political role. He takes care to recount at length the fall of Jerusalem, for the church must not be confused with Judaism, and he enumerates the bishops of this city, for he knows that the church marches on towards the celestial Jerusalem.

Eusebius, who gave such satisfying answers regarding the apostolic period and the question of the canon, has his weaknesses, however. Sirinelli has pointed out his imprecision regarding the issue of original sin; Berkhof his erroneous identification of revelation and reason. I add to this list his abuse of the *theologia gloriae*, which causes him to accord too great a place to what he believes concerning visible images of invisible realities and to defend a false eschatology. There was a change of spirit at the beginning of the fourth century; nothing depicts this better than the comparison of two dreams, one dating to the third century and the other to the fourth. The *Martyrdom of Perpetua and Felicitas* recounts how, during a night in prison, Perpetua sees in a dream, or a night vision, a ladder that leads up to heaven and is surrounded by instruments of torture. Under the ladder, a dragon

---

[86] See Sirinelli, *Les vues historiques d'Eusèbe*, 470–86.

[87] See Voelker, "Von welchen Tendenzen," 178; and Sirinelli, *Les vues historiques d'Eusèbe*, 455–59.

[88] See Eusebius's synchronism of the birth of Christ and contemporary political events (*Hist. eccl.* 1.5.2–6), which is even more emphatic than Luke's. Consider also the fact that the Roman emperors – and not bishops – serve to define the chronological framework of the *Historia*. Most scholars have observed this, most recently del Ton, "Contenuto, struttura, scopi," 327; but, in contrast, see Salaverri, "La idea de Tradición" and idem, "La sucesión apostólica en la Historia Eclesiástica de Eusebio Cesariense," *Gregorianum* 14 (1933) 219–47. Eger ("Kaisar und Kirche," 100) also believes that Eusebius thinks in terms of the history of salvation.

[89] In Bardy, *Eusèbe de Césarée* (SC 73. 91); see also Salaverri, "La sucesión apostólica," 226–38.

waits to terrify those who climb it. Perpetua then sees herself climbing the ladder and glimpsing a garden above and, in the midst of this garden, a shepherd who tends his grazing flock and offers her delicious food.[90] In contrast to this eschatological perspective of the kingdom that awaits the martyr, Eusebius's *Life of Constantine* presents an eschatology that is quite different: the bishop of Caesarea speaks of the council of Nicea, the glory of the ceremonies, and the banquet offered by the emperor on the occasion of twenty years of his reign. Remembering the bishops who surrounded the emperor and feasted with him, Eusebius exclaimed, "One might have thought that a picture of Christ's kingdom was thus shadowed forth, and a dream rather than reality."[91]

---

[90] *Martyrium der Perpetua und Felicitas* 4, in Rudolf Knopf, *Ausgewählte Märtyrerakten* (2d ed.; Tübingen: Mohr Siebeck, 1913) 44–45.

[91] *Vita Constantini* 3.15 in *Eusebius Werke*, vol. 1: *Über das Leben Constantins; Constantins Rede an die heilige Versammlung; Tricennatsrede an Constantin* (ed. I.A. Heikel; GCS; Leipzig: Hinrichs, 1902); ET: *Life of Constantine* 3.15 (ed. Philip Schaff and Henry Wace; NPNF 2/1; Peabody, Mass.: Hendrickson, 1994).

From St. Luke to St. Thomas by Way of St. Cyril[*]

The ties between Greece and the West have always been at the heart of Bertrand Bouvier's life.[1] It is one of the little known aspects of such connections that the following pages attempt to bring to light, namely the knowledge that the medieval Latin exegetes had of Greek patristic exegesis, and in particular their awareness of the *Commentary on the Gospel of Luke* by Cyril of Alexandria; this work came to them through the *Catena aurea* of Thomas Aquinas.[2] From my brief inquiry I learned that, by placing a priority on the meaning of holy scripture over doctrinal purity, Western theologians did not hesitate to cross confessional and linguistic boundaries in order to reap a benefit from the harvest of Eastern exegesis.[3] Thanks to selected translations, medieval readers thus profited from the contributions of Greek patristic commentators. Let us not forget that Aquinas (as his name suggests, "from Aquino") was from southern Italy, a region where Greek was still a living language. Let us also remember that under the impetus of the Germanic emperor Frederick II there had been a renewed interest in Greek culture in Sicily. Finally, let us recall that several translations of Greek philosophical texts, and of Aristotle in particular, were undertaken in the thirteenth century.

I.

Compared with Aquinas's justly famous *Summa theologica*, the *Catena aurea* is a poor relation. Edited by Stanislas Édouard Fretté at Paris, it appeared among the complete works of Aquinas in 1876 and then reappeared in the new Turin edition in 1953.[4] It was also translated into Italian, French and English.[5] Although only a

---

[*] I wish to express my gratitude to David Warren for the translation of this paper into English.

[1] It is a long and beautiful friendship which ties me to him. For a number of years we have been preparing together the critical edition of the *Acts of the Apostle Philip*. I express to him my warm wishes on the occasion of his birthday and the official end of his university teaching career.

[2] On the Bible in the Middle Ages, see Ceslas Spicq, *Esquisse d'une histoire de l'exégèse latine au Moyen Age* (Bibliothèque thomiste 26; Paris: Vrin, 1944); Beryl Smalley, *The Study of the Bible in the Middle Ages* (3d ed.; Oxford: Blackwell, 1983); and Pierre Riché and Guy Lobrichon, eds., *Le Moyen Age et la Bible* (Bible de tous les temps 4; Paris: Beauchesne, 1984).

[3] In his *Catena aurea*, Thomas Aquinas did not hesitate to cite fragments of Origen or of any other authors suspected of heresy.

few studies have been devoted to it,[6] this much seems certain: the *Catena* is an authentic work of Thomas Aquinas. Aquinas was, however, assisted by others, especially in translating the Greek into Latin.[7]

As its name indicates, the *Catena aurea* is a "chain," or collection, of exegetical fragments. These quotations, whose length rarely exceeds fifteen lines per column, are explicitly attributed to various authors. Aquinas supplies the precise reference, however, only in those cases where the quotation does not come from a commentary on a specific biblical book.

One peculiarity of the section devoted to the Gospel of Luke in the *Catena aurea* is the strong presence of Greek authors[8]; an examination of the 192 quotations that interpret Luke 11 reveals that excerpts from Greek writers in this section are more numerous than those from Latin writers.[9] Among Western authors, Augustine (even though he does not write a commentary on Luke), Ambrose, and the venerable Bede receive the lion's share. Among the Greeks, Cyril, Chrysos-

---

[4] Thomas Aquinas, *Catena aurea in Matthaei euangelium – in Marci euangelium* (ed. Stanislas-Édouard Fretté; Opera omnia 16; Paris: Louis Vivès, 1876); and idem, *Catena aurea in Lucae euangelium – in Joannis euangelium* (ed. Stanislas-Édouard Fretté; Opera omnia 17; Paris: Louis Vivès, 1876). In the following notes, references to the *Catena aurea* refer to the volume of this work devoted to the Gospels of Luke and John (= vol. 17 of the complete works). Both volumes were later reprinted as *Catena aurea in quatuor euangelia. Noua editio Taurinensis* 2 (ed. Angelico Guarienti; 2 vols.; Taurini: Marietti, 1953).

[5] The *Catena aurea* was translated into Italian by Edamo Logi (3 vols.; I classici cristiani, 1. serie Antichi medievali moderni 29.4, 32.1, 35.1; Siena: Edizioni Cantagalli, 1954–1960). I do not know whether or not the whole work has been translated into Italian. I have access only to these three volumes, which offer the translation of the commentary only on the Gospel of Matthew. Émile Ferdinand Xavier Castan translated the catena into French in *Exposition suivie des quatre Évangiles par saint Thomas d'Aquin ... appelée à juste titre La chaîne d'or* (8 vols.; Paris: Louis Vivès, 1854–1855), but this work too has remained inaccessible to me. Mark Pattison, John Dobrée Dalgairns, Thomas Dudley Ryder [and Charles Brook Bridges] translated the catena into English as *Catena aurea: Commentary on the Four Gospels Collected Out of the Works of the Fathers by S. Thomas Aquinas* (ed. John Henry Newman; 4 vols.; Oxford: John Henry Parker; London: Rivington, 1841–1845). This translation has been reprinted recently under the same title with a new introduction by Aidan Nichols (Southampton, N.Y.: Saint Austin Press, 1997).

[6] A lot of good information is provided by Thomas Dudley Ryder, the translator of the volume on Luke, in the preface (signed with the initials J.H.N. = John Henry Newman) to vol. 3 of the English translation by Pattison et al., *Catena aurea*, 3. vii-xv. This information was considerably updated in the introduction to the 1997 reprinting by Aidan Nichols, who provides a valuable bibliography in his notes (esp. 1.V-IX). See also Jean-Pierre Torrell, *Saint Thomas Aquinas*, vol. 1: *The Person and his Work* (Washington, D.C.: Catholic University of America Press, 1996) 136–41.

[7] Aquinas refers to others helping him in his dedicatory epistle to Pope Urban IV, which opens the commentary on the Gospel of Matthew, and in his dedicatory epistle to Cardinal Annibaldi della Molara, which is placed before the commentary on the Gospels of Mark, Luke and John; see Aquinas, *Catena aurea in Matthaei euangelium* (ed. Fretté) 2, 499.

[8] Already noted in *Catena aurea* (trans. Pattison et al.) 3. vii.

[9] If the single reference to a certain Maximus (*Catena aurea*, 190) refers to Maximus the Confessor and not to Maximus of Turin, then one arrives at the following result: one hundred and eleven quotations from Greek writers and eighty-one from Latin writers.

tom and Theophylact stand out. But above them all, it is Cyril of Alexandria who is quoted most often: thirty-seven times, compared with twenty-eight times for Bede, twenty-seven times for Augustine, twenty-two times for Ambrose, twenty-one times for Chrysostom, and fifteen times for Theophylact. Greek patristic exegesis is thus represented, and represented well, in medieval times.

"CYRIL": it is the repetition of this name of Greek origin in a Latin work that is so surprising. Its presence is all the more intriguing since no particular work of the Alexandrian patriarch is indicated. This observation leads to the following conclusion: the excerpts derive from Cyril's commentary devoted to the Gospel of Luke.

II.

With the exception of three homilies, Cyril of Alexandria's voluminous commentary (156 sermons altogether) on the Gospel of Luke has not been handed down to us by direct tradition. Fortunately, it survived in a Syriac version, which was edited and translated into English in the nineteenth century, and then partially re-edited (with additions) and translated into Latin in the twentieth century.[10] It is thanks to the existence of this version that the numerous fragments contained in the Greek catena can be authenticated and attributed to Cyril's commentary on the Gospel of Luke.

The works of Joseph Sickenberger, Adolf Rücker, Max Rauer, Robert Devreesse, Christos Krikones, Joseph Reuss, J. Harold Greenlee, Gilles Dorival, and Michel Aubineau have all distinguished several Greek exegetical catenae relating to Luke's Gospel.[11] What is so surprising among the results of this research is that

---

[10] In the last century, Robert Payne Smith prepared a critical edition, entitled *S. Cyrilli Alexandriae archiepiscopi commentarii in Lucae evangelium, quae supersunt syriace e manuscriptis apud Museum Britannicum* (ed. Robert Payne Smith; Oxford: Oxford University Press, 1858) as well as an English translation: *A Commentary upon the Gospel according to S. Luke by S. Cyril, Patriarch of Alexandria, Now First Translated into English from an Ancient Syriac Version* (trans. Robert Payne Smith; 2 vols.; Oxford: Oxford University Press, 1859). William Wright (*Fragments of the Homilies of Cyril of Alexandria on the Gospel of S. Luke, Edited from a Nitrian Ms.* [London: Gilbert and Rivington, 1874]) identified some additional fragments of homilies 113, 114, 115, and 116. Today the standard critical edition is that of Jean-Baptiste Chabot, see *S. Cyrilli Alexandrini Comentarii in Lucam I* (ed. Jean-Baptiste Chabot; CSCO 70, Scriptores syri 4.1 = 27; Paris: E Typographeo Reipublicae, 1912), which has also been translated into Latin by Raymond Tonneau; see *S. Cyrilli Alexandrini Commentarii in Lucam I* (ed. and trans. Raymond Tonneau; CSCO 140, Scriptores syri 70; Louvain: Imprimerie Orientaliste L. Durbecq, 1953). See further Joseph-Marie Sauget, "Nouvelles homélies du *Commentaire sur l'Évangile de S. Luc* de Cyrille d'Alexandrie dans leur tradition syriaque," in *Symposium syriacum 1972, célébré dans les jours 26–31 octobre 1972 à l'Institut Pontifical Oriental de Rome. Rapports et communications* (OrChrAn 197; Rome: Pontifical Institute of Oriental Studies, 1974) 439–56.

[11] Joseph Sickenberger, *Titus von Bostra. Studien zu dessen Lukas-Homilien* (TU 21.1 = n. F. 6.1; Leipzig: Hinrichs, 1901); idem, *Die Lukaskatene des Nicetas von Heracleia* (TU 22 = n. F. 7.4; Leipzig: Hinrichs, 1902); idem, *Fragmente der Homilien des Cyrill von Alexandrien zum*

the work of Cyril dominates each of these collections.[12] At the end of a long endeavor, Reuss succeeded in restoring whole sections of Cyril's commentary on Luke and in furnishing a critical edition of all the excerpts. Indeed it was Reuss's critical edition of the Greek fragments and Jean-Baptiste Chabot's edition of the Syriac version of Cyril's commentary that made it possible for me to test some of the quotations in Aquinas's *Catena aurea*.

III.

Whereas the modern Turin edition of the *Catena aurea*, curiously, does not indicate the source of the excerpts made by Aquinas, Fretté's edition and the English translation do attempt to locate these. The English translation of the *Catena aurea* preceded the edition of the Syriac version of Cyril, however, and in his edition Fretté was content simply to refer to the Greek exegetical catenae as a whole. Thus, the present situation is a more favorable one than that of the past.

The results of my investigation are as follows: with the logical exception of two passages that come from Cyril's other works, all the fragments attributed to Cyril

---

Lukasevangelium (TU 34.1 = n. F. 3.4; Leipzig: Hinrichs, 1909); Adolf Rücker, *Die Lukas-Homilien des hl. Cyrill von Alexandrien* (Breslau: Goerlich & Coch, 1911); Max Rauer, *Der dem Petrus von Laodicea zugeschriebene Lukas-Kommentar* (NTAbh 8.2; Münster: Aschendorff, 1920); idem, *Die Homilien zu Lukas in der Übersetzung des Hieronymus und die Griechischen Reste der Homilien und des Lukas-Kommentars* (2d ed.; Origenes Werke 9 = GCS 35; Berlin: Akademie-Verlag, 1959); Robert Devreesse, "Chaînes exégétiques grecques," in *DBSup* 1 (ed. Louis Pirot and A. Robert; Paris: Letouzey et Ané, 1928) 1084–1233, esp. 1084–99 and 1181–94; Christos. Th. Krikones, Συναγωγὴ Πατέρων εἰς τὸ κατὰ Λουκᾶν Εὐαγγέλιον ὑπὸ Νικήτα Ἡρα-κλείας (Βυζαντινὰ κείμενα καὶ μελέται 9; Thessaloniki: Kentron Byzantinon Ereunon, 1973) (see the review by Michel Aubineau in *ByzZ* 70 [1977] 118–21); Joseph Reuss, "Bemerkungen zu den Lukashomilien des Titus von Bostra," *Bib* 57 (1976) 538–41; idem, *Lukas-Kommentare aus der griechischen Kirche. Aus Katenenhandschriften gesammelt und herausgegeben* (TU 130; Berlin: Akademie-Verlag, 1984); J. Harold Greenlee, "The Catena of Codex Zacynthius," *Bib* 40 (1959) 992–1001; Gilles Dorival, "Des commentaires de l'Écriture aux chaînes," in *Le monde grec ancien et la Bible* (ed. Claude Mondésert; Bible de tous les temps 1; Paris: Beauchesne, 1984) 361–83; Gilles Dorival, "Chaînes," *Dictionnaire encyclopédique de la Bible* (ed. Pierre-Maurice Bogaert et al.; Turnhout: Brepols, 1987) 255–56; and Michel Aubineau, "Les 'catenae in Lucam' de J. Reuss et Cyrille d'Alexandrie," *ByzZ* 80 (1987) 29–47.

John Anthony Cramer furnished a useful edition of the Greek catenae in his *Catenae graecorum patrum in novum testamentum* (Oxford: Oxford University Press, 1844). Both Reuss (*Lukas-Kommentare*, x) and Devreesse ("Chaînes exégétiques grecques," 1181–84) provide good lists of the previous editions and translations of these catenae. See also Maurice Geerard, *Clavis patrum graecorum* (5 vols.; CC; Turnhout: Brepols, 1974–1987) 3. 5–7 (no. 5207). Scholars have identified either five or six different forms and their subgroups; see esp. Reuss, *Lukas-Kommentare*, x-xvii, and Aubineau, "J. Reuss," 29–32.

[12] Reuss, *Lukas-Kommentare*, xi-xvii. Cardinal Angelo Mai culled Cyril's quotations from the catenae and published them as Cyril's commentary on Luke in vol. 2 of his *Novae patrum bibliothecae* (Rome: Typis sacris consilii propagando christiano nomini, 1844) 109–444, which was republished by Migne in PG 72.476–950.

by Aquinas in the pages devoted to Luke 11 are also found in the Syriac version, such that these can be considered authentic. Whereas modern scholars have sometimes distrusted the value of the catenae, my own research, on the contrary, offers the reader some assurance.[13]

Moreover, the fragments relative to Luke 11 are also found in the Greek catenae. It is likely, then, that Aquinas and his collaborators made use of one, or several, Greek exegetical catenae, and that they did not have direct access to Cyril's complete commentary in Greek. At any rate, in this section of the *Catena aurea*, there is never any agreement between the Latin (*Catena aurea*) and the Syriac (commentary) in the absence of the Greek (catenae).

There is, moreover, other evidence that confirms this conclusion. First, both Aquinas and the Greek catenae sometimes contain an identical text that is more compact than that of the complete commentary as represented in the Syriac. Second, Aquinas's style is reminiscent of the style of the authors of the catenae, from whom he seems to draw inspiration: the theologian strives for brevity and so omits here and there an opening line or a quotation of scripture. Third, on two occasions Aquinas attributes a fragment to Cyril without indicating where it came from, believing – along with his source! – that he is quoting from the commentary. Actually, in these two instances he is recopying a passage taken from another work by Cyril.[14]

IV.

To illustrate my conclusion, below are a series of five quotations from Cyril that are taken from the pages Thomas Aquinas devotes to the Lord's Prayer in its Lukan version (Luke 11:1–4).[15] The first column corresponds to Fretté's edition

---

[13] On page 195 (left col.) of his edition of the *Catena aurea*, Fretté points out that some manuscripts attribute a certain fragment to Chrysostom while other manuscripts attribute it to Cyril. Actually, this particular excerpt goes back to Cyril (see Reuss, *Lukas-Kommentare*, 125, frg. 138). In this same regard, it is also necessary to correct the English translation of the *Catena aurea* (trans. Pattison et al.) 3.402, second quotation attributed to Chrysostom. In addition, on pages 195–96 of the *Catena aurea*, another of Cyril's fragments is attributed to the *Thesaurus de sancta consubstantiali trinitate* 13.2, which I did not find in PG 75.217–44. Actually, once again this is an excerpt from Cyril's commentary (= frg. 141 in Reuss, *Lukas-Kommentare*, 126).

[14] See *Catena aurea*, 204 (left col., first fragment attributed to Cyril). According to the English translation (Pattison et al., 3.421), it concerns an excerpt from book 10 of Cyril's treatise against Julian the Apostate. See also *Catena aurea*, 205 (left col.). This quotation is a fragment I found in Reuss (*Lukas-Kommentare*, 290), in a group of excerpts from Cyril that actually comes from some of his other works. In this particular instance, the excerpt comes from his commentary on Matthew. See Joseph Reuss, *Matthäus-Kommentare aus der Griechischen Kirche aus Katenenhandschriften gesammelt und herausgegeben* (TU 61 = n. F. 5.6; Berlin: Akademie-Verlag, 1957) 242 (frag. 262, lines 7–10), which corresponds to PG 72.721A.

[15] On Aquinas's own understanding of the Lord's Prayer, see Marc Aillet, *Lire la Bible avec s. Thomas. Le passage de la littera à la res dans la Somme théologique* (Studia Friburgensia n. s. 80; Fribourg: Éditions universitaires, 1993) 221–35, who analyzes Aquinas' comments in *Summa theologiae* 2.2.Q83.A9 and shows that Aquinas understood the words to have both a literal and a deeper, theological sense.

of the *Catena aurea*, the second column to Reuss's edition of the exegetical catenae, and the third column to the Syriac version of Cyril's commentary (Chabot's edition):

1. Since Jesus possesses all good things, why does he need to pray (Luke 11:1)? It is because of the salvific nature of his incarnation. Obliged to eat and drink, he has taken up the habit of praying. For this reason, he can teach us to pray on our own.

Catena aurea	Greek Exegetical Catenae	Syriac Version
p. 187 (left col.)	Frg. 125, lines 7–12 (p. 118)	p. 279

2. With regard to "Hallowed be your name" (Luke 11:2): as long as faith has not affected them, unbelievers will hold the name of God in contempt. But as soon as the light of truth appears, they confess God as the Most Holy One.

Catena aurea	Greek Exegetical Catenae	Syriac Version
p. 188 (left col.)	Frg. 127, lines 17–21 (p. 119)	p. 289

3. With regard to "Your kingdom come" (Luke 11:2): those who express this request aspire to the glorious return of Christ. Jesus informs them that this shall be a terrible time for which they must prepare by living a worthy life.

Catena aurea	Greek Exegetical Catenae	Syriac Version
p. 188 (right col.)[16]	Frg. 128, lines 2–3, 9–12 (p. 120)	pp. 292–93

4. With regard to "Give us each day our daily bread" (Luke 11:3): even though the saints seek spiritual blessings, it is not improper for them to ask God for material blessings. The spiritual meaning of "bread" that Cyril is aware of is not the one he retains here. According to Cyril, Jesus was referring to the material bread, or indispensable nourishment, the saints need for their practice of poverty as a virtue.

Catena aurea	Greek Exegetical Catenae	Syriac Version
p. 189 (left col.)[17]	Frg. 130, lines 1–2, 5–8, 11–12 (p. 121)	p. 300

---

[16] Although Aquinas condenses the reference to judgment, he underscores that it is equivalent in meaning with "Your will be done," a request found in Matt 6:10 but absent in Luke 11:2.

[17] Aquinas simplifies the beginning without garbling Cyril's reasoning.

5. With regard to "Forgive us our sins as we forgive ..." (Luke 11:4, translation mine): God is invited, so to speak, to imitate our own forbearance and generosity.

Catena aurea	Greek Exegetical Catenae	Syriac Version
p. 189 (right col.)	Frg. 131, lines 5–8 (p. 122)	p. 305

What the reader realizes in regard to the exegesis of the Lord's Prayer (Luke 11:1–4) is fully verified in the explanation of the rest of Luke 11. Following the Greek catenists, Aquinas respected the order of the catena with its excerpts from Cyril's commentary.[18] The catenae, and the *Catena aurea* in particular, are not an unordered collection of quotations, but an abridgment of an exegetical sequence. Contrary to the Greek catenists who were faithful to the original, however, Aquinas did not hesitate to condense Cyril's long sentences and reassemble their argumentation. It was as if the obligation to translate also gave him permission to modify the text at the same time – not of course to change its meaning but to abbreviate its expression.

It is probable that Aquinas used the most recent of the Greek exegetical catenae, which would have been that of Nicetas of Heraclea (last third of the eleventh century, ca. 1080).[19] The nine fragments of Cyril relative to Jesus' teaching on prayer[20] in Luke 11:1–13 offer another means of testing and can all be found in four of the five witnesses to type C of Reuss, that is to say, in the catena of Nicetas.[21] Of course, verification would have to be made on a larger scale, but everything thus far seems to support the conclusion that Aquinas used a copy of the Greek exegetical catena of Nicetas of Heraclea.

---

[18] The equivalents of the next four citations from Cyril, which concern the parable of the importunate friend at midnight (Luke 11:5–8) and conclude with Jesus' teaching on prayer (Luke 11:9–13), are as follows:
Catena aurea, p. 190 (right col.) = frg. 133, lines 1–8 (p. 123) = Syriac version, pp. 315–16;
Catena aurea, p. 192 (left col.) = frg. 134, lines 1–3 (p. 123) = Syriac version, p. 317;
Catena aurea, p. 193 (both cols.) = frg. 135, lines 1, 4–15 (p. 124) = Syriac version, pp. 320–21;
Catena aurea, pp. 193 (right col.) –94 (left col.) = frg. 135, lines 9–10, 16–17 (p. 124) = Syriac version, p. 322.

[19] Actually, there are three groups of manuscripts for this catena. Devreesse ("Chaînes exégétiques grecques," 1184) regards the third group, which is an abridgment of the previous two, as the source Aquinas used for his *Catena aurea*.

[20] I remind the reader here that this section concerns those citations in the *Catena aurea* (pp. 187–94) that correspond to fragments 125, 127, 128, 130, 131, 133, 134, and 135 (twice) in the edition of Reuss, *Lukas-Kommentare*, 117–24.

[21] Of the nine fragments, eight also appear in one of the two manuscripts that represent the earliest text of Type B, and two appear in a popular edition of the very same Type B, that is, in the catena attributed to Peter of Laodicea. Only three appear in Type E, Cod. *Zacynthius* (Ξ) of the New Testament, and only one in Type D. None are attested in Type A, the catena wrongly attributed to Titus of Bostra (i.e., Pseudo-Titus of Bostra).

V.

At the end of this excursion into the domain of the history of exegesis, I want to compare a quotation from Cyril, according to Aquinas, with a Greek fragment from Cyril's commentary as it has been transmitted in the Greek exegetical catenae, and also with its counterpart in the Syriac version.[22] With regard to the request for forgiveness in the Lord's Prayer (Luke 11:4), Aquinas quotes Cyril as follows:

CYRILLUS, *ubi sup.* Vult enim, ut ita loquar, patientiae quam homines colunt, imitatorem fieri Deum, ut qualem ipsi exhibuerunt conservis bonitatem, talem pari lance recipere petant a Deo, qui juste recompensat, et novit omnium misereri.
(CYRIL, [in the same place] as above: For he desires, if I may so speak, that God become the imitator, of the forbearance which humans practice, so that the same kindness which they themselves exhibit to their fellow servants they may ask to receive in an equal measure from God, who recompenses justly and who knows how to have mercy on all.)

Fragment 131 begins with a general statement: Jesus is concerned that his disciples be generous and without malice so that they can make the following request without reproach. Then Cyril, quoting the first half of Rom 11:33, admires the depth of the riches, wisdom, and knowledge of God before paraphrasing the request thus: the Christ, he says in substance, first directs his disciples to ask forgiveness for their own shortcomings and then affirms that they in turn will have to forgive others.

This the text quoted in the *Catena aurea* then continues in the Greek catena as follows:

καὶ ἵνα οὕτως εἴπω, τῆς ἐνούσης αὐτοῖς ἀνεξικακίας μιμητὴν ἐθέλουσι γενέσθαι τὸν θεὸν καὶ ἣν ἂν αὐτοὶ παράσχωνται τοῖς ὁμοδούλοις χρηστότητα, ταύτην ἐν ἴσῳ μέτρῳ ζητοῦσι λαβεῖν παρὰ τοῦ τὰ δίκαια νέμοντος καὶ κατοικτείρειν ἅπαντας εἰδότος[23] θεοῦ.
(And, if I may so speak, they desire that God become the imitator of the forbearance which is in them, and whatever kindness they themselves exhibit to their fellow servants, this in equal measure they seek to receive from God, who dispenses what is righteous and who knows how to have mercy on all.)

The Greek fragment then continues for seven lines more, in which Cyril explains that when we ask God for forgiveness it is just and indispensable to take it upon ourselves to live in a holy manner and to offer first our own forgiveness to those who have offended us.

---

[22] I am referring here to the fragment cited by Thomas Aquinas in *Catena aurea*, 189 (right col.), which corresponds to fragment 131 in Reuss, *Lukas-Kommentare*, 122, and to homily 76 in Cyril's *Commentary on Luke* as translated into Syriac (ed. Chabot, 304).

[23] I correct here the edition of Reuss (*Lukas-Kommentare*, 122), which reads εἰδότας.

Finally, the Syriac version reads as follows:

ܘܗܟܢܐ ܐܡ̇ܪ: ܕܢܬܚܪܘܬ ܢܘܚܐ ܕܒܗܘܢ̇ ܒܥܝܢ ܠܗ ܠܐܠܗܐ ܕܢܗܘܐ
ܡܕܡܝܢܐ. ܘܗ̇ܝ ܒܝܬ ܒܣܝܡܘܬܐ ܕܝܗܒܝܢ ܗܢܘܢ ܠܟܐܢܘܬܗܘܢ. ܗܕܐ
ܒܡܫܘܚܬܐ ܫܘܝܬܐ ܒܥܝܢ ܕܢܣܒܘܢ ܡܢ ܐܠܗܐ ܗܘ ܕܟܐܢܘܬܐ ܝܗ̇ܒ. ܘܝܕܥ
ܕܢܚܘܢ ܠܟܠ ܐܢܫ.

(And so I would say: they ask God that he become the imitator of the forbearance that is in them, and whatever in the setting forth that they themselves give for their righteousness, this in equal measure they ask that they receive from God, who gives what is righteous and who knows how to have mercy on all humans.)

A comparison of these three quotations shows that Aquinas omits both the beginning and end of the fragment and that, in order to make the sentence intelligible, he modifies it by writing a new beginning. In the place of the Greek "he [i.e., Jesus] affirms ... that they desire," Thomas writes "he [i.e., Jesus] desires ... that they ask." Aside from this necessary adjustment, the Western theologian respects Cyril's statement and so shares in his risky interpretation that God is ready to conform himself to human beings.

Conclusion

Perhaps a complete Latin version of the *Commentary of Luke* by Cyril of Alexandria has never existed. Western scholars, however, were not unaware of the exegesis of the Patriarch of Alexandria. Thanks to Greek exegetical catenae, and especially to the borrowings that Thomas Aquinas made from them in his *Catena aurea,* they were able to draw spiritual profit from Greek patristic wisdom. While political and linguistic realities, dogmatic and canonical problems, episcopal ambitions and rivalries, were dividing Byzantine and medieval Christians, exegesis remained common ground where the East and West could meet. The best influences – Greek and Latin, orthodox and heterodox – could exist fraternally side by side and so mutually enrich one another in a biblical ecumenism.

The Apocryphal Reception of Luke's Gospel
and the Orthodox Reading
of the Apocryphal Acts of the Apostles[*]

Just as the term "apocryphal" was used in several ways in the late antiquity, the relationships established between the apocryphal Christian writings and the canonical books during this same period were also varied. According to certain authors, in the same way that a door stood either open or closed, a text was either canonical or apocryphal. Yet for other writers, such as Origen, followed by Eusebius and even Athanasius, a third category existed between biblical works and illegitimate texts: these were books that were beneficial for private meditation, but not known well enough to be brought into public usage, that is, into the liturgies of the church. In some circles a scale of value was imposed: the canonical writings represented the elementary stage of piety, and the esoteric or "apocryphal" – in the positive sense of the term – writings corresponded to the advanced state of knowledge. Still other Christians thought that the biblical texts had been corrupted and needed to be revised. This revision could be done thanks to the oral traditions and to the "apocryphal" texts, here again used in a positive sense. But the inverse was equally possible: if the New Testament was without fault, it was nonetheless open to complementary texts. These "hypertexts," to borrow a term from Gérard Genette, had to be refined. To express this in relational terms, the biblical and the apocryphal writings have been in turn both antagonists and companions. In the pages that follow, I will reflect on two contrary situations and their theological implications: the apocryphal reception of the canonical text and the orthodox re-reading of apocryphal traditions. An oil painting by Aert of Gelder, entitled *Rest on the Flight into Egypt*, will give us not only entrance into this set of problems, but a meditative framework within which to reflect on them.[1]

---

[*] This paper was translated by Laura Beth Bugg, whom I thank warmly.
[1] Aert de Gelder, Dutch, 1645–1727. *Rest on the Flight into Egypt*, about 1690. Oil on canvas, 109.9 x 118.8 cm (43¼ x 46¾ in.). Museum of Fine Arts, Boston, M. Theresa B. Hopkins Fund, 57.182.

Aert of Gelder (1645–1727) was one of the last of Rembrandt's students. In this oil painting (110 x 118.8 cm), which is housed at the Museum of Fine Arts in Boston, the artist invites us to join the holy family on the road into exile in Egypt. This journey, which is mentioned in the Gospel of Matthew (Matt 2:13–25), was expanded by the development of the apocryphal legends. From the *Gospel of Pseudo-Matthew* and its various later rewritings during the Middle Ages, we learn the details of the stops as well as the trials and triumphs along the way. The scene depicted here is an apocryphal episode that is not treated by the canonical Gospels: the holy family's evening sojourn for rest. The incident, however, is not unaligned with New Testament thought; the journey is mentioned in the Gospel of Matthew, and indeed, Joseph's surprising posture is orthodox, as he comtemplates the Son incarnate and, at the same time, places his finger on the scriptures, undoubtedly on the prophecies of the Hebrew Bible. In my view, this one painting – solely and in totality – captures on canvas the complexity of the relationship between holy scripture and the apocryphal writings.

I.

A brief inquiry into the mysterious fate of the Gospel of Luke in the second century permits the observation that historical events have a theological impact. Luke, the historian and theologian, encountered curious circumstances in Christian antiquity. For a long period of time he appears to have been unknown to theologians and scholars. The so-called "Apostolic Fathers" and later, with the exception of Justin Martyr, the apologists who followed Paul and the author of the Epistle to the Hebrews, were certainly familiar with traditions related to Jesus and probably with the Gospel of Matthew, but they were unaware of the Gospel of Luke. In contrast, the authors of apocryphal writings knew Luke well and used his gospel. The author of the *Protevangelium of James*, for example, incorporates entire scenes from the canonical Gospel of Luke. The final redactor of Mark (Mark 16:12–18) mentions two Lucan scenes of the resurrection (in the same order, the appearance to the disciples on the road to Emmaeus and the appearance to the eleven). The *Gospel of Thomas* transmits seven logia whose only other occurrence is in Luke (*Gos. Thom.* 3//Luke 17:21; 10//12:49; 39//11:52; 63//12:16–21; 79//23:29 and 11:27–28; 95//6:35; 113//17:20–21). The *Gospel of Peter* shares with Luke the knowledge of a dialogue between Jesus and the robbers (*Gos. Pet.* 4.13//Luke 23:39–43). An apocryphal opinion, mentioned by Clement of Alexandria and most likely embedded in the *Traditions of Matthias*, considers that the dialogue between Jesus and Zacchaeus (Luke 19:8–10) actually took place between Jesus and Matthias;[2] the *Pseudo-Clementine Homilies* preserve the memory of the same Zacchaeus (Luke 19:2).[3] The *Gospel of the Ebionites*, a Gospel harmony that is earlier than Tatian's *Diatessaron*, attests to knowledge of Luke's gospel when it refers to the priestly lineage of John the Baptist and names Zechariah and Elizabeth as his parents.[4] The *Epistle of the Apostles* furnishes a list of Jesus' miracles from an orthodox point of view and indicates a saying of the Master that is found elsewhere only in Luke. Here, after the miracle of the woman with the flow of blood, the Master exclaims: "I noticed that a power went out from me" (Luke 8:46). The *Epistle of the Apostles* is also familiar with the infancy

---

[2] Clement of Alexandria, *Stromata* 4, 6.35.2. The *Traditions of Matthias* is mentioned in *Stromata* 2, 9.45.4; *7*, 13.82.1, and perhaps *3*, 4.26.3.

[3] Pseudo-Clement, *Homilies* 2.1.2; 2.21.1; 2.35.1, 5; 3.29.1; 3.63.1–2; 3.71.1; 3.72.1; 13.8.3; 17.1.1, 3; 17.6.2. Zacchaeus is also present in Pseudo-Clement, *Recognitiones;* cf. Georg Strecker, *Die Pseudoklementinen III: Konkordanz zu den Pseudoklementinen* (2 vols.; GCS; Berlin: Akademie Verlag, 1989) 2.486.

[4] This passage is preserved in the work of Epiphanius of Salamis, *Panarion*, 30.13.6; cf. Philipp Vielhauer and Georg Strecker, "Judenchristliche Evangelien," in *Neutestamentliche Apokryphen in deutscher Übersetzung* (ed. Wilhelm Schneemelcher; 5. Auflage der von Edgar Hennecke begründeten Sammlung; 2 vols.; Tübingen: Mohr Siebeck) 1. 140–41. Compare D.A. Bertrand, "L'Évangile des Ebionites: une harmonie évangélique antérieure au Diatessaron," *NTS* 26 (1980) 548–63, esp. 555–56.

narratives, and with the parable of Lazarus and the rich man (Luke 16:23).[5] As Enrico Norelli has noted,[6] the *Ascension of Isaiah* shares an impressive eschatological hope with Luke 12:37: Christ in glory, when he welcomes the elect during the Messianic banquet, will begin to serve them at table.[7] The *Questions of Bartholomew*, recently translated and critically reviewed by Jean-Daniel Kaestli,[8] provides a narrative reinterpretation of the Lukan narrative of the annunciation (Luke 1:26–39).[9] And in certain manuscripts, such as the *Infancy Gospel of Thomas*, the Lukan episode of Jesus in the temple at the age of twelve is not only known, but borrowed.[10] If we add to the preceding examples the *Apocalypse of Peter*, which uses the Lucan parable of the fig tree (Luke 13:6–9),[11] the *Acts of Thomas*, which adapts Luke 11:23–26 (the return of the unclean spirits, also known from Matt 12:43–45),[12] the *Diatessaron*, whose only fragment (preserved in Greek and found at Dura Europos) attests to knowledge of Luke 23:49 and 56,[13] and the *Sibylline Oracles*, which summarize in three verses the birth of Jesus as told in Luke

---

[5] *Epistle of the Apostles* 5 (16); 3 (14); 14 (25) and 27 (38) (the Coptic text); cf. C.D.G. Müller, "Epistula apostolorum," in *Neutestamentliche Apokryphen*, 1.208, 212–13 and 220; Jean-Noël Pérès, *L'Épître the des apôtres, accompagnée du Testament de notre Seigneur et notre Sauveur Jésus-Christ. Présentation et traduction de l'éthiopien* (Apocryphes 5; Turnhout: Brepols, 1994) 31–33, 65–66, 71, 91, 94.

[6] Enrico Norelli, "AI 4,16 e la parabola del ritorno del padrone (Lc 12. 36–38)," in idem, *L'Ascensione di Isaia. Studi su un apocrifo al crocevia dei cristianesimi* (Origini n.s. 1; Bologna: EDB, 1994) 213–19.

[7] *Ascension of Isaiah* 4.16; cf. C.D.G. Müller, "Die Himmelfahrt des Jesaia," in *Neutestamentliche Apokryphen*, 2. 553; Enrico Norelli, *Ascension du prophète Isaïe* (Apocryphes 2; Turnhout: Brepols, 1993) 117.

[8] Cf. Jean-Daniel Kaestli, *L'Évangile de Barthélemy d'après deux écrits apocryphes* (Apocryphes 1; Turnhout: Brepols, 1993).

[9] *Questions of Bartholomew* 2.14–22; cf. Felix Scheidweiler and Wilhelm Schneemelcher, "Bartholomäus-Evangelium," in *Neutestamentliche Apokryphen*, 1.430–31; Kaestli, *L'Évangile de Barthélemy*, 47–48, 68–80, 110–13.

[10] *Infancy Gospel of Thomas* 19; cf. Oscar Cullmann, "Kindheitsevangelien," in *Neutestamentliche Apokryphen*, 1.359; cf. Charles Michel, "Évangile de Thomas," in *Évangiles apocryphes* (ed. Charles Michel and P. Peeters; 2 vols.; Textes et documents pour l'étude historique du christianisme 13, 18; Paris: Picard, 1911) 1.187–89 and XXIII-XXVIII.

[11] *Apocalypse of Peter* 2; cf. C.D.G. Müller, "Offenbarung des Petrus," in *Neutestamentliche Apokryphen*, 2.567; Richard Bauckham, "The *Apocalypse of Peter*: A Jewish Christian Apocalypse from the time of Bar Kokhba," *Apocrypha* 5 (1994) 7–111; Richard Bauckham, "The Two Fig Tree Parables in the *Apocalypse of Peter*," *JBL* 104 (1985) 269–87.

[12] *Acts of Thomas* 46; cf. Han J.W. Drijvers, "Thomasakten," in *Neutestamentliche Apokryphen*, 2.322; André-Jean Festugière, *Les Actes apocryphes de Jean et de Thomas. Traduction française et notes critiques* (Cahiers d'Orientalisme 6; Geneva: Cramer, 1983) 68.

[13] Cf. Bruce Metzger, *The Text of the New Testament: Its Transmission, Corruption and Restoration* (New York: Oxford University Press, 1981) 89–91; a photograph of this fragment is found in Kurt Aland and Barbara Aland, *Der Text des Neuen Testaments. Einführung in die wissenschaftlichen Ausgaben sowie in Theorie und Praxis der modernen Textkritik* (Stuttgart: Deutsche Bibelgesellschaft, 1982) 66; cf. William Lawrence Petersen, *Tatian's Diatessaron: Its Creation, Dissemination, Significance, and History in Scholarship* (VCSup 25; Leiden: Brill, 1994) 453–54.

2:7–10,[14] then we become even more aware of the considerable impact that Luke's gospel had on authors of Christian apocryphal literature.

There is, however, another way to observe the effect of Luke's gospel on non-canonical Christian literature, and that is to follow the first exegesis of the Gospel of Luke, which no longer observes a narrative path of exegesis but a reflexive one. Yet again, these first commentaries on Luke do not appear primarily in literature that came to be considered orthodox, but in texts that came to be labeled as "gnostic" and "heretical." As we know, Marcion was not the only person who appropriated the Gospel of Luke, whether in a form we are familiar with or in an earlier form, but the Ophites read Luke's gospel as well. According to Irenaeus (*Haer.* 1.30.11), these earliest exegetes saw in Elizabeth and Mary two kinds of procreation. The Valentinians speculated about the daughter of Jairus as an image of Achamoth and interpreted the three calls to follow Jesus (Luke 9:57–62) as illustrations of the three types of human beings: the hylic or material, the psychic or natural, and the pneumatic or spiritual (Irenaeus, *Haer.* 1.8.3). The Valentinians also meditated on the number 12, saying that Jesus at the age of 12 represented the sending forth of the twelve aeons (Irenaeus, *Haer.* 1.3.2) and on the number 30 because Jesus, according to Ptolemy, was 30 when he began his ministry (Irenaeus, *Haer.* 1.1.3; 1.3.1; cf. 1.16.1). Mark the magician interpreted the scene with the boy Jesus in the temple, and particularly Jesus' declaration that he is occupied with his father's business (Luke 2:49), as scriptural proof for the unknown gospel (Irenaeus, *Adv. haer.* 1.20.2). The story of the centurion from Capernaum (Luke 7//Matt 8) as an image of the demiurge, and the parable of the reconciliation before the judge (Luke 12:58–59; Matt 5:25–26) also received attention from various gnostic exegetes (Irenaeus, *Haer.* 1.7.4; 4.6.1; 1.25.4).

Though these gnostic authors admired the Gospels, considering them worthy of interest and faith, they did not accord them unquestioning devotion. Feeling unconstrained by the presence of these predecessors, they dared to carry out in narrative form the theology of Mark, Matthew, and Luke. The *Acts of Peter* bears eloquent witness to apocryphal allegiance to the canonical text. In fact, it offers us one of the first attestations of a liturgical reading of a New Testament text, the account of the transfiguration.[15]

Orthodox authors who came after these gnostic writers were forced to defend themselves. Julian the African, for example, attempted to reconcile the divergences in the genealogies of Jesus,[16] and Origen mentions a presbyter who, it

---

[14] *Sibylline Oracles* 8.477–79; see Johannes Geffcken, *Die Oracula Sibyllina* (GCS 8; Leipzig: Hinrichs, 1902; 1927) 172; Ursula Treu, "Christliche Sibyllinen," in *Neutestamentliche Apokryphen* 2.616 (The sequence of the verses in this text is not certain).

[15] *Acts Pet.* 20; cf. Léon Vouaux, *Les Actes de Pierre, introduction, textes, traduction et commentaires* (Les Apocryphes du Nouveau Testament; Paris: Letouzey et Ané, 1922) 338–49; Wilhelm Schneemelcher, "Petrusakten," in *Neutestamentliche Apokryphen*, 2.274–76.

[16] The witness of Julian the African is preserved by Eusebius of Cesaraea, *Hist. eccl.* 1.7.1–16;

seems, was the first in the orthodox church to give an allegorical and christological meaning to the parable of the good Samaritan.[17]

II.

We now turn to the opposite situation, that of the reverence that orthodox
authors showed for marginal and apocryphal traditions. Though this reverence
was not accorded without hesitation, nor without ulterior motives and mental
reservations, we may describe it as reverence nonetheless.

During the patristic era, and then during the Byzantine period, the churches
that triumphed over countless adversaries both from within and without were insistent nevertheless that the cloth of apocryphal narrative not come unraveled.
This considerable effort to maintain the apocryphal narratives intact was evident
everywhere: in the Latin churches, where we have the example of Gregory of
Tours[18] saving the *Acts of Andrew* from oblivion, as well as in the Greek churches,
where we encounter Simeon the Methaphraste,[19] who, though severe towards the
deviant tendencies that preceded him, preserved numerous apocryphal legends in
his lives of the saints.

Among the orthodox rereadings of apocryphal texts, there is one that is associated with the transmission of the canonical gospels, which is of considerable
charm and interest. The orthodox churches attempted to justify the canonical
choice of Matthew, Mark, Luke and John – these four alone and standing together
– and in order to justify this choice they did not hesitate to draw on legendary and
apocryphal sources. This was an ancient practice that dates as far back as the second century. Indeed, Papias[20] and Clement[21] make use of legendary stories to justify the existence and choice of the canonical gospels. And the Muratorian Canon[22] follows suit when it appeals to apocryphal legends in order to justify the

---

cf. François Bovon, *L'Évangile selon saint Luc (1, 1–9, 50)* (CNT 3a; Geneva: Labor et Fides,
1991) 183.

[17] Origen, *Hom. Luc.* 34, 3. Curiously, the presbyter is not mentioned in Greek Fragment 71,
which has been preserved: cf. Henri Crouzel, François Fournier, Pierre Périchon, *Origène,
Homélies sur S. Luc. Texte latin et fragments grecs, introduction, traduction et notes* (SC 87; Paris:
Cerf, 1962) 402–05, 520–21.

[18] Gregory of Tours, *Life of Andrew*; the text of Bonnet's edition (1885), along with a French
translation of this work, appear thanks to the attention of Jean-Marc Prieur, *Acta Andreae*, vol. 2:
Textus (CCSA 6; Turnhout: Brepols, 1989) 551–651.

[19] Symeon Metaphrastes, *Vitae sanctorum* (PG 114–16).

[20] The witness of Papias is preserved by Eusebius, *Hist. eccl.* 3.39.15–16; cf. Helmut Merkel,
La pluralité des Évangiles comme problème théologique et exégétique dans l'Église ancienne
(trans. J.-L. Maier; Traditio Christiana 3; Bern: Lang, 1978) 2–3.

[21] The witness of Clement, which comes from his lost *Hypotyposes*, is found in Eusebius, *Hist.
eccl.* 6.14.5–7; cf. 2.15.2; Merkel, *La pluralité des Évangiles*, 16–17.

[22] The Latin text and the French translation of the Muratorian Canon are found in the work of

choice of the Gospels. This attitude is particularly evident in the case of the Gospel of John, where the Muratorian Canon imagines an entire scene that explains the origin of the fourth Gospel: "The Fourth of the Gospels is that of John, one of the disciples. As his fellow disciples and bishops were urging him, he said to them: 'Fast with me for three days from today and what will have been revealed to each one of us, we shall tell it to each other.' That same night, it was revealed to Andrew, one of the apostles, that John was to write everything in his name with the approval of all."

In the fourth century, Epiphanius expressed a similar attitude regarding the relationship between canonical and apocryphal texts.[23] While the plurality of gospels could be troublesome, it could also be reassuring and even beneficial. The bishop of Salamis recounts the story of the last episodes in the history of salvation, whose high and low points we know begin with Adam and Noah. The plurality of the gospels relates to human sinfulness, and their redaction in successive order corresponds to the demands of a church more in decline than in triumph. Each gospel marked a period of awakening and light, but unfortunately darkness followed these bright periods of light, and then in each new period of darkness the brightness of a new gospel shone forth. This edifying apocryphal legend not only legitimizes the presence of a canon but the coherence of the established canon with its four Gospels.

There is a literary genre that allows us to visualize this importation of apocryphal texts into the canonical realm: this is the genre of the gospel prologues, which inform the reader of the circumstances for the composition of a biblical text. But while these prologues to the Gospels and Epistles certainly serve the interests of the canon, they also had recourse to legendary information. Attesting to the impact of the apocryphal word on orthodox consciences, they demonstrate that the defenders of the canon acknowledged their debt, perhaps in spite of themselves, to the crafters of apocryphal texts.

A text that Yuko Taniguchi, Athanasios Antonopoulous, and I recently edited allows us to illustrate this orthodox usage of apocryphal information. The text, two leaves of a Greek manuscript that have been identified as belonging to a twelfth-century tetraevangelion (a codex with four gospels), contains a prologue, or ὑπόμνημα, with one of these legends welcomed for its explanation of the origin of the Gospels.[24] The first part of the prologue provides biographical information

Marie-Joseph Lagrange, *Introduction à l'étude du Nouveau Testament*, vol. 1: *Histoire ancienne du Canon du Nouveau Testament* (Études bibliques; Paris: Gabalda, 1933) 68–74. The section pertaining to the Gospels may also be read in the collection of Merkel, *La pluralité des Évangiles*, 10–13.

[23] Epiphanius of Salamis, *Panarion* 51.4.5–12.6; cf. Merkel, *La pluralité des Évangiles*, 104–15, which supplies the main part of the Greek text and a French translation.

[24] See Yuko Taniguchi, François Bovon, and Athanasius Antonopoulos, "The *Memorial of Saint John the Theologian* (BHG 919fb)," in *The Apocryphal Acts of the Apostles: Harvard Divinity School Studies* (ed. François Bovon, Ann Graham Brock, and Christopher R. Matthews;

about John that is taken from the New Testament itself and from the tradition; it contains nothing unexpected. But when we read what follows John's arrival in exile on Patmos, we find that he receives a letter from Denys the Areopagite, who is writing to him from Athens at almost one hundred years of age.[25] After the conventional greetings, Denys reminds the apostle that what is happening to him is not at all surprising, because the Lord warned his disciples about persecutions and tribulations. The author comes to the essential part of his letter: an oracle of salvation, which decrees that John will be freed from prison and will regain Ephesus. The account continues with the story of John's liberation and the description of an episode of a familiar type: at the moment of John's departure to regain Ephesus, the Christians of Patmos request compensation from the apostle for his impending leave. He has been busy preaching on the island, and the residents ask for a written gift to compensate for his future bodily absence.

This exchange of a written text for a bodily presence is striking and deserves our attention. John agrees to the proposal, while at the same time imposing a period of fasting for himself and for the community. He then climbs a mountain with Prochorus and, in the manner of Moses and the tablets of the law, John receives from God the text of his gospel in the midst of a resounding and brilliant theophany. The methods of divine dictation, apostolic mediation, and human writing through Prochorus are suggested before the citation of the prologue's first words occur. The text ends with these words: "[A]nd he leaves for Ephesus even though the islanders are unwilling. And the Gospel has been dispersed to all those who believe, for our benefit and to the glory of Christ our God."[26]

Conclusion

There remains scholarly research to be done and discoveries to be made concerning the attitudes and convictions held by first-millennium Christians. To uncover the variety of these attitudes and to reconstruct the history of the canonical and non-canonical texts is exciting work, and theological reflection on the subject should also remain vibrant as a new century dawns. This reflection, which is also a process of construction, urges us to re-evaluate the bonds between canonical writings and apocryphal texts in the same manner in which Orthodox and Cath-

---

Harvard University: Center for the Study of World Religions; Cambridge: Harvard University Press, 1999) 333–53.

[25] This letter is known elsewhere and is part of a collection of letters attributed to Pseudo Denys the Areopagite. It is taken from his Epistle No. 10; see Günter Heil and Adolf Martin Ritter, eds., *Pseudo-Dionysius Areopagita, De coelesti hierarchia. De ecclesiastica hierarchial. De mystica theologia. Epistulae* (Corpus Dionysiacum 2; PTS 36; Berlin: de Gruyter, 1991) 208–10. I sincerely thank my friend Enrico Norelli for providing me with this information.

[26] Taniguchi, Bovon, and Antonopoulos, "Memorial of Saint John," 352–53.

olic theologians have linked scripture and tradition. Scripture is placed within the church, and the community of believers nourishes itself not only on canonical texts but also on traditional stories – legendary, and even distorted, tales about the apostles and saints. Certainly a normative rule, kerygma more so than canon law, rules out the inclusion of the most outlandish texts, such as the most docetic and fantastic ones, but the coexistence of the canonical and the apocryphal has become possible again. Scholarly investigation reveals that the two have been side by side since the very beginnings of Christianity: the apocryphal authors showed respect for canonical writings and then, respectively, the readers of canonical writings venerated the apocryphal legends.

Publication Credits

1. The Apostolic Memories in Ancient Christianity
   Published here for the first time.

2. Studies in Luke-Acts: Retrospect and Prospect
   (*Harvard Theological Review* 88 [1995] 175–96).

3. Wetterkundliches bei den Synoptikern (Lk 12,54–56)
   (*Berliner Theologische Zeitschrift* 10 [1993] 175–86).

4. Apocalyptic Traditions in the Lukan Special Material: Reading Luke 18:1–8
   (*Harvard Theological Review* 90 [1997] 383–91).

5. The Law in Luke-Acts
   (*La Loi dans l'un et l'autre Testament*, edited by Camille Focant [Lectio Divina 168; Paris: Cerf, 1997] 206–25). English translation by Laura Beth Bugg.

6. The Lukan Story of the Passion of Jesus (Luke 22–23)
   (*The Synoptic Gospels: Source Criticism and the New Testament*, edited by Camille Focant [BETL 110; Leuven: Leuven University Press and Peeters, 1993] 393–423). English translation by Charles Frederic Stone.

7. The Role of the Scriptures in the Composition of the Gospel Accounts: The Temptations of Jesus (Luke 4:1–13 par.) and the Multiplication of the Loaves (Luke 9:10–17 par.)
   (*Luke and Acts*, edited by Gerald O'Collins and Gilberto Marconi [New York/Mahwah, N.J.: Paulist Press, 1993] 26–31, 215–16).

8. "'Schön hat der heilige Geist durch den Propheten Jesaja zu eueren Vätern gesprochen' (Act 28, 25)"
   (*Zeitschrift für die neutestamentliche Wissenschaft* 75 [1984] 226–32).

9. Parabel des Evangeliums–Parabel des Gottesreiches
   (*Die Sprache der Bilder. Gleichnis und Metapher in Literatur und Theologie*, edited by Hans Weder and Gerd Mohn [Gütersloh: Gütersloher Verlagshaus, 1989] 11–21).

10. The Church in the New Testament, Servant and Victorious.
    (*Ex auditu* 10 [1994] 45–54).

11. These Christians Who Dream: The Authority of Dreams in the First Centuries of Christianity

(Geschichte–Tradition–Reflexion. Festschrift Martin Hengel, vol. 3: *Frühes Christentum*, edited by Hermann Lichtenberger [Tübingen: Mohr (Siebeck), 1996] 631–53). English translation by Laura Nasrallah.

12. The Canonical Structure of Gospel and Apostle

(Cristianesimo nella Storia 15 [1994] 559–76). English translation by Laura Beth Bugg.

13. Israel in the Theology of the Apostle Paul

(Le christianisme vis-à-vis des religions, edited by Joseph Doré [Namur: Artel, 1997] 153–68). English translation by David Warren.

14. Jesus' Missionary Speech as Interpreted in the Patristic Commentaries and the Apocryphal Narratives

(Texts and Contexts: Biblical Texts in Their Textual and Situational Contexts: Essays in Honor of Lars Hartmann, edited by T. Fornberg and David [Hellholm Oslo/Copenhagen/ Stockholm/Boston: Scandinavia University Press, 1995] 871–86). English translation by Jane Haapiseva-Hunter.

15. The Synoptic Gospels and the Non-canonical Acts of the Apostles

(Harvard Theological Review 81 [1988] 19–36). English translation by Ken McKinney.

16. The Suspension of Time in Chapter 18 of the *Protevangelium Jacobi*

(The Future of Early Christianity: Studies in Honor of Helmut Koester, edited by Birger A. Pearson [Minneapolis: Fortress Press, 1991] 393–412). English translation by Jane Haapiseva-Hunter.

17. The Words of Life in the *Acts of the Apostle Andrew*

(Harvard Theological Review 87 [1994] 139–54). English translation by Jane Haapiseva-Hunter, David Warren, and Laura Nasrallah.

18. Miracles, Magic, and Healing in the Apocryphal Acts of the Apostles

(Journal of Early Christian Studies 3 [1995] 245–59). English translation by Helene Perdicoyanni Paleologou.

19. A New Citation of the Acts of Paul in Origen

(Apocrypha 5 [1994] 113–17). English translation by David Warren.

20. Eusebius of Caesarea's *Ecclesiastical History* and the History of Salvation

(Heilsgeschichte als Thema der Theologie. Festschrift Oscar Cullmann, edited by Felix Christ [Hamburg: H. Reich, 1967] 129–39). English translation by Laura Nasrallah.

21. From St. Luke to St. Thomas by Way of St. Cyril

(ΒΟΥΚΟΛΕΙΑ. *Mélanges Bertrand Bouvier*, edited by Anastasia Danaé Lazaridis, Vincent Barral, and Terpsichore Birchler [Geneva: Belles lettres, 1995] 93–102. English translation by David Warren.

22. The Apocryphal Reception of Luke's Gospel and the Orthodox Reading of the Apocryphal Acts of the Apostles

(*Apocrypha* 8 [1997] 137–46). English translation by Laura Beth Bugg.

Index of Ancient Authors

1. Manuscripts

2. Greek, Latin, and Other Ancient Literature

3. Hebrew Bible

4. Deuterocanonical and Pseudepigraphical Literature

5. Qumran Literature

6. Rabbinic Literature

7. New Testament

8. Christian Apocrypha (including Nag Hammadi Literature)

9. Patristic, Byzantine, and Medieval Literature

Index of Modern Authors

Index of Subjects